Confronting the Human Rights Act

This book critically examines the Human Rights Act 1998 (HRA) and evaluates its impact from a multi-disciplinary perspective. The book includes both a domestic and an international analysis of the effectiveness of the HRA, and also considers possible future developments in policy and practice as well as contemplating the potential for a British Bill of Rights. The editors have collected pieces from contributors drawn from diverse spheres, all of whom are internationally recognised for their impact in the field of human rights law. Contributors include members of the bench in the United Kingdom and Australia, academics, researchers, members of NGOs and campaigners, alongside people's testimony of lived experiences in relation to the Human Rights Act. Valuable contributions from the likes of Keith Ewing, Helen Fenwick, Lady Hale, Irene Khan, Michael Kirby, Francesca Klug, Peter Tatchell and others have resulted in a book which draws out the connections between legal framework, theory, and the actual experience of the protection afforded to groups and individuals by the HRA.

Confronting the Human Rights Act will be of particular interest to scholars and students of Law, International Studies and Political Science.

Nicolas Kang-Riou is a lecturer at the University of Salford and is currently researching the concepts of truth and virtue in relation to human rights law and international law.

Jo Milner is a lecturer in Sociology at the University of Salford whose research interests focus on the areas of public law, identity politics, social exclusion, discrimination and human rights.

Suryia Nayak is senior lecturer in Social Work at the University of Salford, with a particular interest in psychoanalysis, feminism, post-colonialism and deconstructivism.

Confronting the Human Rights Act

Contemporary themes and perspectives

Edited by Nicolas Kang-Riou,
Jo Milner and Suryia Nayak

Routledge
Taylor & Francis Group

LONDON AND NEW YORK

First published 2012
by Routledge
2 Park Square, Milton Park, Abingdon, Oxon OX14 4RN

Simultaneously published in the USA and Canada
by Routledge
711 Third Avenue, New York, NY 10017

Routledge is an imprint of the Taylor & Francis Group, an informa business

British Library Cataloguing in Publication Data
A catalogue record for this book is available from the British Library

Library of Congress Cataloging in Publication Data
Confronting the Human Rights Act : contemporary themes
and perspectives / edited by Nicolas Kang-Riou, Jo Milner, and
Suryia Nayak.
     p. cm.
ISBN 978-0-415-67470-6 (hardback)—ISBN 978-0-203-12279-2
(e-book) 1. Great Britain. Human Rights Act 1998.   2. Civil
rights—Great Britain.   3. Human rights—Great Britain.
I. Kang-Riou, Nicolas.   II. Milner, Jo.   III. Nayak, Suryia.
KD4080.C59 2012
342.4108'5—dc23   2011041148

ISBN: 978–0–415–67470–6 (hbk)
ISBN: 978–0–203–12279–2 (ebk)

Typeset in Garamond
by RefineCatch Limited, Bungay, Suffolk

Printed and bound in Great Britain by
CPI Antony Rowe, Chippenham, Wiltshire

Contents

Contributors

Lisbeth Bourne is a lecturer in Adult Nursing and Health Care Law and Ethics. Her research interests include the legal and ethical issues associated with self-injury, how equality law impacts on people's experiences and consent issues.

Kate Cook is a feminist activist, academic and researcher. She teaches criminal law and criminology and is always concerned with issues pertaining to violence against women and girls. Kate is active within a number of women's groups, including Trafford Rape Crisis.

Alice Donald is senior research fellow in the Human Rights and Social Justice Research Institute at London Metropolitan University. Her research focuses on human rights implementation in public services and in relation to socio-economic rights in the UK and internationally. She previously spent 15 years as a journalist in the BBC World Service.

Keith Ewing has been professor of Public Law at King's College London since 1989. His publications include *The Bonfire of the Liberties: New Labour, Human Rights, and the Rule of Law* (Oxford University Press, 2010).

Helen Fenwick is professor of Law at the University of Durham and Director of the Human Rights Centre. Among other publications, she is the author of *Civil Liberties and Human Rights* (Routledge-Cavendish, 2007) and *Media Freedom under the Human Rights Act* (Oxford University Press, 2006), with Gavin Phillipson.

Brenda Hale, The Right Hon the Baroness Hale of Richmond, became the United Kingdom's first woman Lord of Appeal in Ordinary in January 2004, after a varied career as an academic lawyer, law reformer and judge. She is now the first woman Justice of The Supreme Court.

Nicolas Kang-Riou is a law lecturer at the University of Salford. His research interests lie especially in human rights law. He is currently looking at the concepts of truth and virtue in relation to human rights law and international law.

Irene Khan is chancellor of Salford University and an international thought leader on human rights. She was Secretary General of Amnesty International from 2001 to 2009. She is the author of *The Unheard Truth: Poverty and Human Rights* (W. W. Norton & Co, 2009).

Michael Kirby, The Hon Michael Kirby AC CMG, was, from February 1996 until February 2009, one of the seven Justices of Australia's highest constitutional and appellate court, the High Court of Australia. He is currently a member of the Eminent Persons Group investigating the future of the Commonwealth of Nations; and has been appointed to the UNDP Global Commission of HIV and the Law.

Francesca Klug is a professorial research fellow at the LSE and director of the Human Rights Futures Project. She assisted the government in devising the model for incorporating the European Convention on Human Rights into UK law reflected in the Human Rights Act. Her publications include *Values for a Godless Age: The Story of the UK Bill of Rights* (Penguin, 2000).

Catherine Little is principal lecturer in Criminology and Socio-legal Studies in the School of Law at Manchester Metropolitan University. Her teaching and research interests are in gendered violence. She is an active member of Trafford Rape Crisis and Campaign to End Rape.

Jo Milner is an applied sociologist based within Sociology at Salford University. Her research interests derive from an inter-disciplinary socio-legal background, and centre on the area of public law, identity politics, social exclusion, discrimination and human rights.

Derek McGhee is professor of Sociology in Sociology and Social Policy at the University of Southampton. He is the author of four books including *Security, Citizenship and Human Rights: Shared values in Uncertain Times* (Palgrave, 2010); and *The End of Multiculturalism? Terrorism, Integration and Human Rights* (Open University Press, 2008).

Ronagh McQuigg is a lecturer in the School of Law, Queen's University Belfast. Her research interests are in the area of international human rights law, particularly in relation to how human rights law can be used as regards violence against women. Her recent book is entitled *International Human Rights Law and Domestic Violence* (Routledge, 2011).

Elizabeth Mottershaw is an independent human rights consultant. She works with NGOs, universities and think tanks, carrying out research and providing policy and legal advice. Her work focuses on poverty, conflict and human rights, covering Africa and the UK. From 1998 to 2008 she worked at Amnesty International.

Suryia Nayak is a senior lecturer in Social Work at the University of Salford, with a particular interest in psychoanalysis, feminism, post-colonialism and deconstructivism as tools for understanding and creating social transformation. She is involved in anti-racist, feminist activism.

Revive and The Salford Forum for Refugees and People Seeking Asylum United for Change Campaign is an organisation supporting refugees and people seeking asylum. The Forum is made up of representatives from Salford-based community groups that provide help and support to refugees and people seeking asylum.

Diane Sisely is the director of the Australian Centre for Human Rights Education (ACHRE) at RMIT University (Australia). Dr Sisely led the Victorian Equal Opportunity Commission from 1994 to 2004. Her research interests centre on developing knowledge and understanding of the application of human rights in everyday life.

Dave Smith now teaches education courses on behalf of the TUC. He was a UCATT safety representative. He has been systematically blacklisted by the construction industry for doing his job – as a trade union safety representative. He is currently involved in a landmark case against the construction multinational Carillion.

Peter Tatchell has been campaigning for human rights, democracy, global justice and LGBT liberation for over 40 years. He is director of the human rights lobby, the Peter Tatchell Foundation, and is the Green Party's human rights spokesperson.

Helen Wildbore is research officer for the Human Rights Futures project at the LSE. She has a degree in Law from UCL and a Masters in Human Rights Law from the University of Nottingham. Her research interests include the impact of the Human Rights Act inside and outside the courts.

Introduction

*Nicolas Kang-Riou, Jo Milner and
Suryia Nayak*

Editors' note

This book was initiated through a conference which took place at the University of Salford in June 2010, to mark ten years of implementation of the Human Rights Act (HRA) 1998, as the HRA only entered into force in 2000. We are very grateful to the University of Salford, particularly Vice-Chancellor Martin Hall for his generous financial and personal backing. We also extend further gratitude to Professor Alistair Alcock, then Head of Salford University Law School, for supporting and furthering the project from the very outset. This conference was not alone in doing so. The Human Rights Act has been widely discussed within the legal/socio-legal community and has been the focus of many scholarly activities (e.g. as the featured topic of the Socio-Legal Studies Association and the Society of Legal Scholars conferences in 2010, and human rights organizations' conferences, such as the Human Rights Lawyers Association (HRLA) and British Institute of Human Rights (BIHR) with conferences in 2010 and 2011[1]). Clearly there is no denying that the HRA has had a significant impact on the UK socio-legal landscape.

The chapters come from a selection of the papers presented at the University of Salford conference. We are really grateful to all the authors who have contributed to this project. They represent a wide array of interests and backgrounds, and all have distinctive voices, including some leading voices in the field. And although we were unable to include all the papers presented, we very much appreciate their high quality, which served to contribute to a very successful conference.

They may not share all of our views; some of them explicitly do not. But we believe they all are committed to the discourse of human rights, at least from a purely pragmatic standpoint. This book comprises the following, firstly, it is pluri-disciplinary with law at the centre, secondly, it aims to avoid two main pitfalls in analysing the current situation of human rights in the UK; an

---

1 For more information on these conferences, see <http://www.slsa.ac.uk>, <http://www.legalscholars.ac.uk/southampton/>, <http://www.hrla.org.uk/Events/Programme%20Oct%20event%20Final.pdf>, <http://www.bihr.org.uk/annualconference2011programme> (all accessed 16 June 2011).

apology on the one hand, and cynicism on the other.[2] It is not about defending the HRA as a generally progressive tool, no matter what, nor is it about implying that the HRA is a mere façade.

Our views, as the book editors, are grounded, first, in a multi-perspective approach, as could be expected of a group where Jo Milner has a background in sociology/politics, Suryia Nayak in social work and Nicolas Kang-Riou in law. More importantly, it reflects our shared understanding of the necessity of seeing the law operating in a wider context than the mere issue of interpretation and application of rules. Although we agree on the importance of human rights law in the institutional/political sphere, we also feel the need to question the blind spots of the legal discourse over human rights issues. So, in a sense, we 'believe in human rights'[3] as a tool for advancing some progressive arguments. But we also understand that there are important structural issues with the way human rights law behaves and is implemented; there is a clear gap between the imagined world represented by the HRA and the world experienced by many. The choices made within the human rights legal field have clear political consequences.

Structure of the book

This section will briefly outline the book's chapters, and will thread the sometimes very different topics and themes of the chapters into a common narrative. Although these chapters are written by authors from various backgrounds and interests, they can all be brought together because they represent crucial features of the human rights legal discourse, highlighting its achievements and its limits.

The multi-perspective outlook is evidenced by the different backgrounds of the authors. Lawyers comprise the biggest contingent, but activists are included, as are sociological, political and critical perspectives. We hope that it not only reflects the need to understand how the law is playing its part, but also why other approaches are necessary to make the human rights discourse more than just a tool in the hands of a few.

Chapter 1 by Nicolas Kang-Riou contextualizes the role of the HRA. It covers a range of key issues connected with the legalization of the human rights discourse. Structurally, the legal system produces exclusions, which, by definition, go against the aim of universality of human rights. In analysing this tension between exclusion through legalization and universality, the chapter expands on the reasons for confronting the HRA from multiple perspectives.

---

2 Slavoj Žižek has formulated it in these words: 'the appearance of *égaliberté* is a symbolic fiction which, as such, possesses actual efficiency of its own; the properly cynical temptation of reducing it to a mere illusion that conceals a different actuality should be resisted', S. Žižek, 'Against Human Rights', *New Left Review* 34, 2005, p. 130.
3 See M.-B. Dembour, *Who Believes in Human Rights? Reflections on the European Convention*, Cambridge: Cambridge University Press, 2006.

Part I: Confronting the HRA as a legal tool

This is a traditional confrontation, a gentle and amicable one, from authors who share the dominant institutional ethos and perspective.[4] This says that human rights law is a good thing per se, only implementation can be tricky at times. It is presumed overall that, with goodwill and skills, human rights law brings progress. Section 1 stays within the traditional bounds of the legal discourse.

Drawing upon history, in Chapter 2, Professor Francesca Klug takes us further back than the usual history of the HRA, and also highlights the role of the Conservatives in the process, as well as the role of the 1997 Labour manifesto. She shows that the lines between Tories and Labour are less clear than one might presume, and more importantly that the contradictions existing, as with any piece of human rights legislation, were also clearly (but involuntarily) expressed by politicians; with the vision that the HRA was only the logical (and not so important) consequence of ratifying the ECHR on the one hand, but, on the other hand, that it heralded a major constitutional reform by placing much more power for activism in the judiciary's hands. This mirrors the criticisms of the lack of change (as opposed to the promise of change) and of power being devolved to judges and to Europe (as opposed to a cosmetic transformation). It also highlights the consensual nature of the reference to human rights.

In Chapter 3, Lady Hale, using her rich experience as a Supreme Court Justice, and, before that, in the House of Lords,[5] reviews the (internal) politics[6] of the legal implementation, which brought with it the decision to increase the creative powers of judges, without exceeding what the Strasbourg court might do. Lord Bingham famously stated that British judges should do 'no more, but certainly no less' than what the European Court of Human Rights would.[7] Lady Hale's chapter also carries a unique twist, as she has decentred the analysis in taking a traditional theme, the highs and lows, but from the angle of family issues. She subtly questions what highs and lows actually can be. She hints at the problem of the foundations of human rights, and the lack of agreements on their aims. The main point of reference is the Strasbourg

---

4 One could put them in the dominant 'natural school' of human rights, as described by Dembour, in M.-B. Dembour, 'What Are Human Rights? Four Schools of Thought', *Human Rights Quarterly* 32, 2010, pp. 1–20.

5 The Appellate Committee of the House of Lords was replaced in October 2009 by the Supreme Court, in application of the Constitutional Reform Act 2005.

6 The insertion of the word politics is mine only; Lady Hale does not use it in her chapter. By legal politics, I am not suggesting that judges are not independent from political parties. I believe they are. But as Duncan Kennedy has brilliantly showed, judgments have an intrinsic political dimension, as judges often use arguments referring to competing visions of the political good in order to decide legal cases. See Duncan Kennedy, *A Critique of Adjudication {fin de siècle}*, Cambridge, MA: Harvard University Press, 1997.

7 *R (Ullah) v Special Adjudicator* [2004] UKHL 26, para 20.

Court, even though she accepts that it can sometimes get it wrong. But establishing how and when it gets it wrong is a problem that persists.

Section 2 draws upon the Australian experience, and compares the impact of human rights interpretation in the context of the refusal of incorporation at the federal level, to the similar path to the HRA taken by the Australian State of Victoria.

In Chapter 4, Michael Kirby, a retired justice of the Australian High Court[8] with a strong human rights reputation,[9] first develops an overview on how the Commonwealth countries have responded to the human rights legal challenge. He then moves on to evaluate how Australia has coped without a Charter. His conclusion is that a Charter is not necessary for human rights considerations to be taken into account in order to transform the application of ordinary legislation, through the normal interpretative role of judges. This is in line with the way British judges used to take into account the Strasbourg case law prior to the incorporation of the ECHR within the HRA. A really important point is made when he underlines the role of the ethos of judges in the integration of human rights into legislation. The personality of judges is crucial, but at the same time, even 'human rights-minded' judges cannot change the law in some situations.

If Australia has resisted the call for a HRA at the federal level, Diane Sisely's Chapter 5 analyses the Human Rights Charter implemented in the Australian State of Victoria. By stressing the level of public engagement towards the Charter, it highlights, by contrast, the lack thereof concerning the HRA. But, more importantly, she raises the issue of the transformation of the culture in order to see rights implemented, the necessity of having individuals being able to connect with what (legal) human rights are, and how they can be relevant in our developed societies.

The two Australian chapters, notwithstanding that they focus on only one part of the Commonwealth, are quite representative of the worldwide pervasiveness of the human rights legal culture, even if one is opposed to it. The legal language has won the battle over significance and meaning, however, this is only part of the story.

Part II: Topical confrontations of the HRA

Part II is less favourable to the HRA, as it focuses on situations where the HRA's capacity to resist is questioned. The contributors to this section insist, even if it is not formulated as such, on the connections between human rights legal interpretations and the general political context. It is not sufficient for

---

8 The High Court is Australia's highest Court.
9 See his personal website for an overview of his activities, <www.michaelkirby.com.au> (accessed 16 June 2011).

judges, lawyers, and academics to argue that human rights should better be left to experts who would discover the true meaning of the founding triptych of the contemporary state: human rights, democracy and the rule of law. This lies at the core of Section 1. Human rights law and politics cannot be disconnected. There is no technical way to implement human rights without a more general political understanding of what the rules are for.

In Chapter 6, Irene Khan, as a former Secretary General of Amnesty International, is very well placed to witness how the political perceptions of the time come to bear on the implementation and understanding of human rights law. She focuses on how politicians in the UK have used the 9/11 terrorist attacks to reformulate the debate from absolute rights, to rights which have to be balanced with security. This approach has led to an 'erosion' of the rights and has started a dangerous trend which needs to be resisted.

In Chapter 7, Keith Ewing makes an even more critical charge against believing in the HRA. Unlike Irene Khan, he does not see British judges as having been really effective against the pressures imposed by the political system. For him, the gap between what is being depicted in the media as happening to individuals, and the few and far between court victories, is sufficient to deny value to the HRA and to any solutions coming from more legal argumentations. He suggests that the only current legal hope emanates from Strasbourg, even if, there also, one needs to stay vigilant.

In Section 2, the lacunae in the connection of the rights enshrined in the HRA and the socio-economic dimensions are assessed. First, in Chapter 8, Alice Donald and Elizabeth Mottershaw draw a rather grey picture when evaluating the impact the HRA has had on poverty-related rights. They can see some elements of response from public authorities to legal findings of violation of the HRA, due to an underlying issue connected to poverty. However, in most cases, there is a failure to engage because of 'rationing of resources'. Even when the fight against poverty was an official political priority, it was not connected to human rights.

In Chapter 9, Jo Milner and Lisbeth Bourne are critical of the way the cuts to health and social care budgets have a direct and unseen connection with the push towards the legalization of assisted suicide. Their analysis reveals a gap in this debate, which is mainly framed for the affluent, those who can afford to have a choice. But for the rest, a growing number, it could be seen to have very dire consequences. Resource-wise, death is a far cheaper solution than long-term care.

Part III: Activist confrontations

In this part, activists' voices are heard. The idea is to challenge the boundaries of the human rights legal discourse, which often falls short of the people it tries to represent.

In Section 1, the HRA is seen from the point of view of feminist activists. In Chapter 10, Ronagh McQuigg focuses on the protection of women against domestic violence under the ECHR/HRA. Her aim is to evaluate what the law under the HRA/ECHR can offer for victims of domestic violence. If it took until 2007 for the Strasbourg court to finally recognize domestic violence as a violation of the Convention, there remain many issues left unturned. The main one rests on the justiciability of issues having a strong resource allocation dimension. It is not sufficient to find a State guilty of not establishing a sufficiently protective legal and administrative framework. There is also a need for the protection to be effective, to provide for social support measures.

In Chapter 11, Catherine Little and Kate Cook take a different approach, and do not engage from within the bounds of the human rights legal discourse, as they challenge its capacity to deal with the ongoing and widespread issue of rape. The HRA, even if it can be brought to bear on some aspects of rape, fails to capture many of its dimensions as experienced by women. Instead, the authors have switched their position in order to focus their intervention on the basis of what the women directly express. They believe in the need for 'some more radical departure' in order to effect change.

Section 2 also reintegrates the voices of those who are claiming rights. These chapters show that victims and activists can both be faces of the same coin. Firstly, asylum seekers' voices need to be reintegrated into society, as their authenticity is doubted, challenged by the very nature of the legal system. In Chapter 12, Suryia Nayak, along with her co-authors, remind us of how much the system operates on doubt, on the disavowal of the 'constitutive outside' and the anxiety of maintaining 'mastery' over national, ideological and political borders. She deconstructs particular conceptual foundations at the heart of human rights discourse and practice to expose key tensions within the concepts of hospitality, tolerance and testimony.

In Chapter 13, Peter Tatchell's approach is that of the consummate campaigner, the activist. If he cares about the means, the end matters most. He shares how he has come to use human rights law in his long career as a human rights campaigner, especially in the defence of the rights of homosexuals. However, some of the greater gains, such as the end of prosecution of homosexual public kissing, have been obtained through a direct confrontation with the police rather than through dialogue or legal avenues. Human rights law has also been used strategically; it is not an end in itself, contrary to what many lawyers do.

In Chapter 14, Dave Smith and Keith Ewing use the experience of blacklisted trade unionists to expose the limits of the HRA and also to demonstrate that it is not only about being victims. They show that, even if human rights have been declared violated, the legal remedies fall far short of being effective. Once blacklisted, these workers continue to fail to find work, even after blacklisting has been held to be illegal. But this does not mean that it is the end of the road, and it does not deny their capacity to be actors of change, as exemplified by Dave Smith.

Part IV: The future? Confronting the Bill of Rights

In this final part, more dangers than promise are unveiled, as the proposals for a British Bill of Rights (BoR) are discussed.

In Chapter 15, Derek McGhee unravels the tensions at play between a British Bill of Rights and Responsibilities and the universal and outward-looking ideals behind the HRA/ECHR, in the last years of the Labour administration. But these tensions are also voiced by the Tory/LibDem coalition. The Tories also want a Bill of Rights to curb the unwanted limits set by the judges on policing the State. The Bill of Rights highlights the dimension of the rights of the citizens at the expense of the universality of the rights.

In Chapter 16, Helen Fenwick discusses the fundamental challenge behind the proposed Bill of Rights, which is to reconcile Parliamentary sovereignty with rights protection. The question is who should make decisions about the exceptions to the rights: the legislator or the judge? She retraces the history of the application of the ECHR through the HRA and notes that under Labour there was no open defiance, but rather indirect confrontation through restrictive legislative measures taken in the name of the fight against terrorism. She further questions the capacity of the Bill of Rights Commission to make any meaningful changes, but sees a possibility for the Conservatives to radically reconsider relations with the Strasbourg court and the pre-eminence of its case law if they win the next general election.

1 Confronting the legalization of human rights

A counterpoint

Nicolas Kang-Riou

Introduction

> Only when the last prisoner of conscience has been freed, when the last
> torture chamber has been closed, when the United Nations Universal
> Declaration of Human Rights is a reality for the world's people, will our
> work be done.
>
> Peter Benenson, Founder of Amnesty International[1]

Human rights are historically new, emerging within the Enlightenment, but
at the same time we cannot seem to be able to do away with them. They are
now claimed and deemed to be universally applicable, East and West, North
and South, even though they depend on the culture where they are implemented. If the debate of universality is still alive, the question of the importance of implementing human rights law is no longer disputed in Europe, at
least in the mainstream political arena.[2] All 47 members of the Council of
Europe[3] had to ratify the European Convention on Human Rights (ECHR)[4]
and accept the European Court of Human Rights (ECtHR) as its supervisory
body with the individual right of petition.[5] Furthermore, the ECHR has
now been legally implemented into the normative framework of all Member
States, the Human Rights Act (HRA) marking the end of the UK exception.
Thus, there is now no dispute over the applicability of human rights law in
Europe.

---

1 See Amnesty International website, <http://www.amnesty.org.uk/content.asp?Category
  ID=10087> (accessed 16 June 2011).
2 In that regard, the ambiguous position of the Conservative Party, as highlighted in their
  proposal for a British Bill of Rights, is exceptional in Europe.
3 See 'Council of Europe in brief', <http://www.coe.int/aboutCoe/index.asp?page=47
  pays1europe&l=en> (accessed 16 June 2011).
4 As a consequence of the interpretation of Art. 3, Statute of the Council of Europe, ETS 1.
5 The European Court of Human Rights is located in Strasbourg (France), home of the
  Council of Europe. Hence, it is also sometimes referred to as the Strasbourg Court.

However, the discourse comprises many contradictions. A short step back into the history of human rights law reveals a foundational one.[6] The Preamble of the ECHR declares the signatory States to 'have a profound belief' in 'fundamental freedoms which are the foundation of justice and peace in the world', in 'political democracy', and in 'the rule of law'. Clearly, these three elements are mentioned in order to describe an idea of freedom as resistance to oppressive regimes, such as the ones which emerged in the first half of the twentieth century in Europe.[7] There is a paradox here. If human rights embody an idea of empowerment and resistance to oppression, they also state an aim to attain a utopia[8] where human rights would be respected along with peace and justice. It is thus 'non-law', as it is a name used for mounting challenges to legal and political exclusions. However, these utopian ideas have been legalized. So now, simultaneously, human rights are part of (positive) law, in the way they are used within the legal system to decide claims, but are still the vernacular used to argue that the (positive) system is deficient, as it still does not (and cannot) fully protect human rights. This ambivalence makes the discourse really politically appealing.[9]

The quotation from Peter Benenson, at the beginning of this chapter, is a clear expression of the contradiction that is still at the heart of today's discourse about human rights protection. The first two elements can be decided by courts: communicating the illegality of an arrest or the illegality of the use of torture. The consequences should be to free the prisoner and close the torture chamber, which has more or less been done, in Europe at least. The last part is the (truly) utopian part. So, at the heart of human rights lies this tension between the world of freedom, equality and dignity established through law, and the world in which we live and which we would like to change. In order to explore this original contradiction, we need to look first at some of the structural effects that the legalization is having on rights.

6 A long step back to the origins of the discourse would have revealed the same tension. See C. Douzinas, *The End of Human Rights*, Oxford: Hart, 2000.
7 See *Collected edition of the 'Travaux préparatoires' of the European Convention on Human Rights*, vol. V, 1976, The Hague: Martinus Nijhoff, p. 285, and S. Marks, 'The European Convention on Human Rights and its "democratic society" ', *British Yearbook of International Law*, 66, 1995, pp. 209–38.
8 Utopian in the literal sense: as the place which does not exist and maybe cannot.
9 The term 'political' is used here in the sense of the participant in the *polis*, the one who is recognized as being a legitimate voice in the city. Anyone who is denied this, in any particular environment, can be said to be denied a particular form of citizenship and denied human rights.

A confrontation and a counterpoint

A confrontation can be defined as a 'focused comparison',[10] an attempt to bring several elements face to face,[11] but also as an attempt 'to present a bold front, to stand against, oppose'.[12] Two main dimensions are thus established: to compare and contrast, and to oppose what keeps situations in the dark, thus revealing what is left unwanted or excluded.

The first strand is quite traditional. This can also be done in order to evaluate any piece of legislation. It is always useful to contrast the aims and purpose of the legislation with the way it has been implemented. In this approach, negative and positive elements can emerge. With the HRA, we can look at its implementation and decide which changes can be seen as positive or negative. The commitment here is to an insider view, to the traditional way to represent legal change and especially human rights law, as part of 'bringing progress through reason'[13] or, at least, an attempt to bring progress. It is a firm but gentle confrontation.

The second is much more critical. Through the multi-disciplinary approach, law is reintegrated in its social context, and human rights become human again. Issues of legal interpretation and application are questioned, such as the lack of convincing explanations as to the foundations of the choices made, the politics of the law, and also through the structural issues of the elements taken out of the law. This position mainly comes from experiencing the gap between the proclamation of rights and their daily experience, and trying to see what role the law is playing in creating or maintaining the gap.

In music, a counterpoint is the 'melody added as accompaniment to a given melody'.[14] But to see the counterpoint, the main melody has to be set. Thus, a contrapuntal approach brings the main and additional melodies side by side, hoping to create something new through the combination, something other than the simple juxtaposition of the two. By bringing together the internal dimension of the law (the 'standard', 'positivist' view of the (human rights) law) with the external (the socio-legal and critical), there comes a counterpoint.

The Human Rights Act 1998 is the main legal tool for arguing a violation of human rights within the UK legal system. There are good reasons to celebrate over ten years of implementation, as it has fostered decisive changes in many individual situations, as many of the contributors to this book argue.[15]

---

10 'Confrontation', n., *American Heritage Dictionary of the English Language*, 4th edn, 2002, Houghton Mifflin.
11 'Confront', v., *Oxford English Dictionary*, 2nd edn, 1989.
12 Ibid.
13 Douzinas, *The End of Human Rights*, op. cit, n. 6, p. 5.
14 'Counterpoint', n., *Oxford English Dictionary*, 2nd edn, 1989.
15 See, for instance, the first part of this book and the chapters by Francesca Klug and Brenda Hale.

Nevertheless, it is impossible to simply draw a rosy picture due to structural issues undermining the protection of human rights through the legal framework highlighted by many of the authors in this book.

This chapter will try to explain why although the tensions of the human rights discourse cannot be removed, the usefulness of the discourse can be kept, if the exclusions from the discourse are continuously challenged and the discourse rewritten.

The legalization of human rights

> (L)egal reasoning . . . is now virtually the only possible way of working within the conceptual field of human rights.[16]

It is clear from the history of the implementation of the ECHR, and from the other international treaties, that as soon as they came to be supervised by treaty bodies, the controlling language became the language of lawyers. The first reason is simple: arguing rights violations, the legality or illegality of actions, is what lawyers do. The language of law is based upon this binary distinction, this code of legality and illegality. The second is a consequence of the first. Lawyers came to populate such bodies[17] as a requirement of treaty interpretation, again formulated and thought of as an issue of the definition of legal rights. The legal doctrine became the prominent voice in order to analyse what the former were doing.

It is quite easy to find evidence of the domination of lawyers in the human rights field, and not only within legal presentations. There is numerous external anecdotal evidence of this. For instance, such domination is completely embedded in how publishers present human rights research. Human rights are largely found under their own heading within the law subdivision.[18] This evidence is from the perspective of the market: publishers ought to know who is going to buy, and where from. This does not mean that non-lawyers cannot publish academic books on human rights; they just won't own a human rights category. For instance, the recently published *Sociology and Human Rights: New Engagements*[19]

---

16 A. Woodiwiss, 'The law cannot be enough: human rights and the limits of legalism', in S. Meckled-García and, B. Çali (eds), *The Legalization of Human Rights: Multidisciplinary Approaches*, London: Routledge, 2006, p. 32.

17 See for instance, Art. 21(2) ECHR: 'The judges shall be of high moral character and must either possess the qualifications required for appointment to high judicial office or be jurisconsults of recognised competence.'

18 See for instance, the websites of OUP, CUP, Routledge, Taylor and Francis, Hart, etc. (all accessed 16 June 2011).

19 P. Hynes et al. (eds), *Sociology and Human Rights: New Engagements*, London: Routledge, 2011.

finds itself in the 'Sociology and Social Policy' subject area, not in 'Human Rights Law and Civil Liberties'.[20]

Another sign comes from the NGOs. The most visible human rights NGOs in the UK (Liberty, Amnesty International, Justice, the British Institute of Human Rights, Interights, etc.) are led by individuals with a legal background,[21] with the notable exception of Amnesty International.[22] One could also point out that masters programmes in human rights are, in the main, led by lawyers and taught within law schools.[23]

As mentioned above, the legalization is more structural. The choice of legal institutionalization was made first at the UN with the Universal Declaration on Human Rights (UDHR), then in the Council of Europe, following the hints given by the UDHR. And as soon as rights were to be adjudicated upon, lawyers were bound to get the upper hand. In Europe, it is clearly the Strasbourg judges, along with the highest national courts, who are setting the tone of what constitutes a human rights violation. As a consequence, the dominant vernacular of human rights is the legal discourse. The alternative ways to see the problems, the administrative/political and the sociological, are not construed as being necessarily relevant to the issues at stake. Non-legal arguments can influence or be part of the legal justification, but ultimately the judge decides exclusively on what s/he perceives the legal arguments to be.

The domination of the legal discourse on human rights has been enshrined in the UK through the Human Rights Act 1998. It has, in the same way, redefined the balance between politics and law as to how best to protect and guarantee human rights, with a further push towards law. It is this domination that will be confronted with a contrapuntal approach, as this domination leads to many exclusions. The limits of human rights law have been tackled by numerous authors in some challenging and groundbreaking pieces.[24] Here, I would like to focus on some elements.

Human rights and system theory

The domination of human rights by the legal profession has given rise to some very particular effects. Luhmann's description of law in terms of the social

20 See Routledge website, <http://www.routledge.com> (accessed 16 June 2011).
21 See the respective websites of these NGOs for a CV of their directors (accessed 15 May 2011).
22 AI, however, also used to be led by a lawyer (Irene Khan) and their director of policy is legally trained. See also Irene Khan, Chapter 6 in this volume.
23 Of course there are many exceptions, including the one being run at the University of Salford.
24 For a more complete systematic analysis of the problems with rights, see M. Koskenniemi, 'The Effect of Rights on Political Culture', in Philip Alston et al. (eds), *The EU and Human Rights*, Oxford: Oxford University Press, 1999, pp. 99–116, and David Kennedy, 'The International Human Rights Movement: Part of the Problem?', *Harvard Human Rights Journal* 15, 2001, p. 99.

system theory is a powerful means of understanding the role of human rights within it.[25] Law, as with any social system, distinguishes itself from other social systems, like politics or media, through its own vocabulary, and the way the system looks at itself.[26] The vocabulary of the law, its system, is based upon the production of decisions centring on its binary code: legal/illegal. The purpose of the law is to stabilize expectations by declaring a situation legal or illegal.[27] By incorporating them into the legal system, human rights must function in this binary way, but are now also decided by the agents of the legal system who control the operation of the binary code. In essence, this means that the law is what the lawyers[28] say it is, and as law has taken over human rights, human rights are also what lawyers say they are.

But what, then, is the role of human rights within the legal system? In practice, human rights law works as an ultimate test of legality, of what can be included within the legal system. Human rights claims act at the border of the system, as the claims should normally be dealt with under ordinary legislation. A norm becomes acceptable only in so far as it is compatible with human rights. In this sense, it is constitutional, the constitution thus defining what the law is.

At the primary level, a judge's task is to check the application of the common legislation; at the secondary, level of self-observation,[29] the judge needs to verify if this interpretation is compatible with human rights as enshrined in the HRA. This constitutional foundation has not been fully accepted in the HRA, as directly incompatible statutes cannot be set aside or annulled by judges.[30] Nevertheless, judges do their utmost to interpret the law in a compatible fashion,[31] with the assumption that any other interpretation would be illegal, because it would be in violation of human rights.[32] Potentially, it transforms any interpretation of the law into a delimitation of what law is, through the application of the HRA. One simple example is where police officers kill someone through the use of their weapons. Under primary legislation, they only have to behave according to their statutory obligations for their actions to be legal. Under the HRA, they also have to preserve the right to life, which means that if statutory obligations are insufficient, then they can be complemented through interpretation, where even additional obligations can be read into the statute.[33]

---

25 N. Luhmann, *Law as a Social System*, trans. K. Zieger, Oxford: Oxford University Press, 2008.
26 Ibid., pp. 86–7.
27 Ibid., chapter 3.
28 The courts, of course, but not only. It also includes the doctrine, or anyone who argues according to the legal vocabulary and techniques; ibid., chapter 11.
29 Ibid., pp. 103–4.
30 Section 3 Human Rights Act 1998.
31 See B. Hale, Chapter 3 in this volume.
32 See s 4 Human Rights Act 1998.
33 See, for instance, *McCann and others v UK* (1996) 21 EHRR 97.

So human rights law is also law. The interpretation of the ECHR/HRA now forms a particular set of rules, which have achieved a certain level of consistency and, as such, have been the subject of legal textbooks.[34] As Luhmann wrote, jurists construct the legal system in a manner which is dependent upon principles connecting the various decisions in a coherent way.[35] This stabilization, or structuring of the legal system, occurs essentially through self-observation, and continuity in the ways courts understand their case law as jurisprudence. In practice, each time the ECtHR makes a decision, it looks at it in such a way as to reproduce its own specificity to form a consistent discourse. A previous decision explicating the obligations under the right to life must be followed.[36]

At the most fundamental level, all the decisions are taken principally on the ECHR, and on the ECHR alone; any other elements are only elements to be taken into account. At the same time the HRA should also provide a way to test the boundaries of the system; whilst the test itself becomes less and less about an ad hoc verification of the (in)justice of the situation. Rather, it is about seeing if the situation can be re-described in terms which are consistent with the description of previous decisions. Thus, the stabilization of the legal system requires the human rights discourse to lose its capacity to change previous situations. Necessarily, the legalization dulls the edges of the human rights discourse.

Institutionalization and judges

If we agree that the human rights legal system risks becoming more conservative, it is crucial to check what types of values the system will tend to preserve. According to legal reasoning, the first operation of adjudication of human rights claims should be to define what human rights violations are. The second is to check the facts. The last is to see whether the facts constitute a violation. This presupposes that judges have a way of knowing what human rights violations are. Problematically, they do not, or not in a way uncontestable. Rights

---

34 See for instance, C. Ovey and R.A. White, *Jacobs, White & Ovey The European Convention on Human Rights*, 5th edn, Oxford: Oxford University Press, 2010; D. Harris et al., *Harris, O'Boyle & Warbrick: Law of the European Convention on Human Rights*, 2nd edn, Oxford: Oxford University Press, 2009; D. Hoffman and J. Rowe, *Human Rights in the UK*, 3rd edn, London: Longman, 2010; P. Van Dijk et al., *Theory and Practice of the European Convention on Human Rights*, 4th edn, Leiden: Intersentia, 2006.
35 Luhmann, op. cit., note 25, p. 103.
36 See the explanations given by the Grand Chamber of the Court to explain a reason behind a change of jurisprudence as an exceptional situation. See, A. Mowbray, 'An Examination of the European Court of Human Rights' Approach to Overruling its Previous Case Law', *Human Rights Law Review*, 9(2), 2009, pp. 179–201.

can be given different meanings and, more importantly, rights are seldom absolute.[37]

If there are some situations which were clearly targeted by the drafters of the ECHR as being illegal, such as arbitrary detention without any legal basis or banning all press media, plenty of them fall into areas which have had to be adjudicated in order to know their outcome. The clear violation of the Convention could only arise if it was at odds with the minimum level of the mainstream dominant vision. However, this is not mainly what the legal interpretation of human rights treaties is about. It is not enough for a right to be granted to a person, where the situation falls within the ambit of the right, for a violation to have occurred. For instance, it is not enough to know that a journalist was condemned for publishing an article, for a violation of the freedom of expression to occur. There are legitimate reasons that can allow for a restriction of the right: for instance, the article in question could be defamatory. This opens up the opportunities for legally legitimate contradictory arguments. A right can be limited for a legitimate purpose. Then the issue of violation becomes an issue of defining the proportionality of the restriction or the balance between the different interests in question. This is no longer about injustice; it is about rights allocation – politics in short.[38]

The first stark debates between highly experienced and prominent lawyers took place right at the start of the operation of the Strasbourg court, which hinged on how the interpretation should take place, with some deciding that rights should be read with a view to limiting their reach, and limiting as little as possible the freedom of States.[39]

It is not enough to feel that an injustice has been committed to prove that human rights laws have been was violated. Such law has many problems when assessing the legality of certain practices, and even more so in terms of human

---

37 Only the prohibition of torture, prohibition of indefinite detention without trial and of slavery can really be proved to be absolute in the Strasbourg case law. Even within Article 3 ECHR, the 'inhuman and degrading' dimensions can be said to be relative. See, for instance, M.K. Addo and N. Grief, 'Does Article 3 of the European Convention on Human Rights enshrine absolute rights?', *European Journal of International Law*, 9(3), 1998, pp. 510–24.

38 See, for instance, G. Beck, 'Human rights adjudication under the ECHR between value pluralism and essential contestability', *European Human Rights Law Review*, 2008, pp. 214–44; O. De Schutter, 'L'Interprétation de la Convention Européenne des Droits de l'Homme: Un Essai en Démolition', *Revue de Droit International, de Sciences Diplomatiques et Politiques*, 2, 1998, pp. 83–128; N. Valticos, 'Interprétation juridique et idéologies in Protection des droits de l'homme: la perspective européenne', in P. Mahoney et al. (eds), *Mélanges à la mémoire de Rolv Ryssdal*, Köln: Carl Heymanns Verlag, 2000, pp. 1471–82.

39 See for instance Sir Gerald Fitzmaurice, the 'Great Dissenter' and defender of the intention of the Contracting States in the early Court; G. Merrils, 'Sir Gerald Fitzmaurice's Contribution to the Jurisprudence of the European Court of Human Rights', 1982, 53, *British Yearbook of International Law*, pp. 115–62.

rights. A legal body having to settle legal disputes about rights has to take a decision, knowing full well that there are usually at least two reasonable (legal) ways to argue a case.[40] As a consequence, the premise for entrusting judges with declaring what human rights are must change. There are two main (rational, explicit) reasons as to why we should entrust judges with such legal decisions. First, we trust the judges because of who they are. Second, we trust the judges because of their technical skills. The latter, since abandoning wisdom as the leading legal virtue, is the current preferred but problematic version. If so, judges should only be the 'mouth of the law':[41] judgment should not be about wisdom but about knowledge. However, adjudicating on human rights is not, decisively, about technique, but about being able to convince the majority of the judges constituting a particular court that one's position is the right one. Of course, British judges will tend to follow the Strasbourg court, so at the national level it might be said to be more about skills. However, even if this is true,[42] this just displaces the issue. It is no longer only about convincing a court, but convincing the court which has the upper hand.

In the end, it is the dominant view in the legal system as to what a human rights violation is that makes a human rights violation. In human rights law it mostly depends on judges,[43] on their vision about what (human rights) law is, or means. It is therefore not surprising that many discussions will turn upon the judges' values. Justice Kirby's chapter in this volume is very enlightening in this context, as he clearly highlights that a court relies upon its judges as being able to recognize the exclusions of the world, and, having experienced it themselves, they would then be more able to recognize it elsewhere.[44] If we want justice coming from judges, then we need judges to possess compelling wisdom, and not only to be technically skilled.[45] What is being institutionalized in the name of the ECHR is then the dominant view of the most persuasive judges of the court (including previous judges).[46] It is thus also not surprising that a court which had been seen as protecting human

---

40 See the seminal demonstration made by Duncan Kennedy in: D. Kennedy, *A Critique of Adjudication*, Cambridge, MA: Harvard University Press, 1997.

41 Montesquieu, *De l'Esprit des Lois*, Paris: Firmin-Didot, 1862, p. 130.

42 Even there, this position is questionable, as national judges can decide to prioritize national legislation over the Strasbourg interpretation. See Hale, Chapter 3 in this volume.

43 There is very little legislative intervention in the matter of European human rights law. Concerning the ECHR, it has only happened through additional rights and never through a rewriting of the original rights. It could also be said to happen through more specialized conventions, but that again is quite exceptional.

44 See M. Kirby, Chapter 4 in this volume.

45 And also to be recruited as such. However, this criterion does not appear in art. 21 ECHR, see supra note 17.

46 There is still a need to know the technical arguments, for judges to be listened to by their colleagues in the first place. It is the price of entry into the legal arena. But it should not be the end quality required.

rights, such as the European Court of Justice, can seem to make a U-turn.[47] Caution towards judges is therefore suggested; we have been lucky, so far, to get sufficiently justice-minded judges at the Strasbourg court.

The limits of relying on judgments

The fact that the personality of judges is of utmost importance as to where the law is heading is not the only problem with the law. First, obviously but decisively, the law applies only if the law is applied. If one does not follow the legal procedures, one will not get a legal decision. Then, all those who do not know how, or cannot afford, to access to the legal system cannot trigger the protection of human rights law. Problematically, then, the destitute are less likely to be able to access the legal system (for lack of knowledge and/or money) but quite likely to be in need of human rights protection. And in another tragic consequence, if one is in an illegal situation then the law fails one, not once, but twice: once for declaring the first situation illegal; twice for refusing the protection of the law from then on. Recently, a rape victim was allowed to be deported before the trial, because of her illegal migrant status. She was thus not protected by the law: she was a failed asylum seeker, but also incapable of truly exercising her rights to access human rights protection.[48]

Then, even if access to the law is granted, judgments can do only so much. Lawyers principally seek the legal declaration that a particular situation involves a violation of legally protected human rights, such as the rights guaranteed under the HRA. Then what about the victim? The victim might really appreciate the decision, at least in parts. It can provide some moral satisfaction for the victim, and maybe some financial compensation. It will tell administrations that some actions are prohibited and should not be repeated. It is possible for a foreigner not to be deported to a country where that person could be tortured,[49] or for individuals suspected of being a terrorist to actually have someone to review their situation.[50]

But the problem with litigation is the general lack of perspective about the overall cause and sources of human rights violations and the particular situation that the victim is faced with. Litigation will never undo torture, or any abuse,[51] nor will it improve the situation for the future (not directly at least).

47 See K. Ewing on the European Court of Justice, Chapter 7 in this volume.
48 'Asylum seeker faces deportation despite police investigation into rape', *The Guardian*, 21 June 2011.
49 See *Chahall v UK*, (1996) 23 *EHRR* 413.
50 See the high points discussed by Baroness Hale in Chapter 3 in this volume.
51 See the issues discussed surrounding violence against women in the Feminist section of Part III of this volume.

For instance, as discussed by Little and Cook,[52] a finding of a violation of Article 3 or Article 8 in case of the rape of a woman will not change the overall situation of women, for instance, if the problem lies in the way the testimony of women is mishandled by the police. The only way to make a further impact is for the law to add what have been called positive or imperfect obligations:

> Imperfect obligations are general duties of anyone in a position to help to consider what he or she can reasonably do in the matter involved.[53]

However, these imperfect obligations to fulfil the rights of others need something more than just the law to be defined, as they depend on the individual capacity and will of the individual who is in a position to help, or act. In her chapter about the issue of the exclusion of failed asylum seekers, Nayak adopts the parable of the Good Samaritan as an example of how to redraw the boundaries of hospitality and define the fulfilment of the imperfect obligation to help the stranger in need.[54]

But first, the obligations will directly only be imposed on the State apparatus, not on individuals in general. Human rights law shifts the issue onto the State and only the individuals attached to the State become obliged to act.[55] Then, the State will be forced to act, only if resources allow.[56] The Good Samaritan therefore is not, and cannot, be created by human rights law.

The addition of all the issues of the human rights legal system makes it possible for the existence of structural exclusions of groups of people from human rights protection. There are situations where the gap between the promised rights and rights as experienced cannot seem to be bridged by human rights law.

Some structural exclusions: economic and social rights, asylum seekers and foreigners

Previously in this chapter, I have tried to establish that the legalization of human rights necessarily entails exclusions, for law to keep its operating capacities, and that furthermore these exclusions were not necessarily connected to any substantial debate about justice, and that something more than State intervention is needed. I would like to discuss two of these major exclusions, the exclusion of socio-economic dimensions and of asylum seekers, as they are also the focus of several chapters within this book.

---

52 C. Little and K. Cook, Chapter 11, in this volume.
53 Amartya Sen, 'Human Rights and Limits of Law', *Cardozo Law Review* 27(6), 2006, p. 2922.
54 S. Nayak, Chapter 12 in this volume.
55 Section 6, Human Rights Act 1998.
56 See below, and also A. Donald and E. Mottershaw, Chapter 8 in this volume.

These two exclusions are grounded in the contradictory approach of human rights to the cost–benefit analysis. The philosophical foundations behind human rights exclude a cost calculation, as a way to establish right from wrong.[57] Human rights are conceived as trump cards[58] and, as such, reject utilitarian arguments. However, if, at the foundational level, human rights are deemed to flow from human nature and, consequently, cannot be excluded from anyone considered a human being, there are very few truly absolute rights[59] which cannot be balanced against competing interests.[60] And as soon as a balancing act takes place, as the proportionality test unfolds, the utilitarian arguments reappear.[61]

Two major topics, including cost–benefit analyses, have figured highly in recent years and have been a reason for diminishing or excluding human rights claims. The first is the continued tightening of the possibility to claim asylum in the UK,[62] and the second one deals with the consequences of the marginalization of economic and social rights through the concept of non-justiciability. Asylum seekers have been excluded from the main operation of the ECHR through the accepted principle in international law that States have the rights to control their borders and decide who can enter. The reason for the control of asylum seekers is quite obvious. States do not want to allow 'poor' aliens access for economic reasons under the 'pretence' of being persecuted; there is clearly a balancing act which lies at the heart of granting asylum. The second type of issue is very straightforward. These rights are costly to implement, thus they have to fall under the discretion of the government to decide the best possible allocation of scarce resources.

Even if, like the ECHR, the UK Human Rights Act bears a name which suggests that it deals with all human rights, in fact, as is quite clear from the list of the rights enshrined, it concentrates on civil and political rights, thus implicitly not only excluding economic and social rights but also the economic and social rights dimensions of the civil and political rights. Of course, this view is problematic. Economic conditions bear, to a large extent, on the possibility of human rights implementation.[63] The have-nots, in our economically

---

57 Even if the foundations are hotly debated and there is no agreement as to what they could be, there is consensus around the natural quality of the attributes. See Douzinas, *The End of Human Rights*, op. cit., note 6.

58 R. Dworkin, *Taking Rights Seriously*, Cambridge, MA: Harvard University Press, 1977.

59 See supra, note 37.

60 On conflicts between rights, see, P. Ducoulombier, *Les conflits de droits fondamentaux devant la Cour européenne des droits de l'homme*, Bruxelles: Bruylant, 2011.

61 See G. Beck, 'The Mythology of Human Rights', *Ratio Juris*, 21(3), 2008, pp. 312–47.

62 See, for instance, S. Chakrabarti, 'Rights and Rhetoric: The Politics of Asylum and Human Rights Culture in the United Kingdom', *Journal of Law and Society*, 32, 2005, pp. 131–47.

63 See M. Koskenniemi, 'The Effect of Rights', op. cit., n. 24.

liberal and developed societies, will also be socially marginalized.[64] However, it is usually reconciled within the discourse of human rights, with economic and civil rights being an indivisible component of human rights, as something that was there at the beginning of contemporary human rights protection.[65]

Yet in practice, the ECHR is the only European legal landmark regarding the meaning of human rights protection, as unfortunately its counterpart for economic, social and cultural rights, the European Social Charter (ESC), may never become as important for individuals living in Europe as the ECHR is. It is clearly not by accident that the ESC has taken a different path from the ECHR, as the monitoring mechanism and the resources attached to it are far weaker.[66] The issue of the treatment of the ESC is crucial, as it was never able to play the role assigned to it under the theory of the indivisibility of human rights, but it materially covers many of the important issues of the day, especially where individuals may feel hard done by in their dignity and human rights. Nevertheless, even with the intention to exclude these types of issues, they could not be completely removed from the ECHR picture, for the main reason that all rights bear a cost, as they need the existence of the liberal institutional framework. For instance, the right to a fair trial cannot exist if there are no judges or tribunals, and the right to life cannot exist without a police force, but such institutions are costly to run.[67]

There are multiple contradictions here. Of course, utilitarian arguments are used by the courts to assess the proportionality of interference to qualified rights, including economic and social policies. This is, by definition, the only way to conduct a proportionality assessment, as the benefit for the collective has to be sufficient as to justify the restriction.[68] Human rights are a demand on the community and, as with any demands, realizing them can be costly in a number of ways. But because they are not meant to be interpreted as dependent upon economic situations, they are then thought as being

---

64 For a philosophic and economic take on human rights, see A. Sen, *Development as Freedom*, Oxford: Oxford University Press, 1999.

65 See for instance, Roosevelt's four freedoms discourse (available at <http://www.fdrlibrary. marist.edu/fourfreedoms>, accessed 16 June 2011) and the inclusion of socio-economic rights in the Universal Declaration on Human Rights (1948).

66 There is no court, but a monitoring body making non-binding recommendations; no individual remedy but a little-known and generally not ratified protocol allowing for collective complaints; and very little funding. See D.J. Harris, 'A Fresh Impetus for the European Social Charter', *International and Comparative Law Quarterly*, 41, 1992, pp. 659–76.

67 See also the fact that they have been cut by the Coalition Government in response to the UK's rising debt.

68 See for instance, M.-A. Eissen, 'The Principle of Proportionality in the Case-Law of the European Court of Human Rights', in R. St. J. Macdonald et al. (eds), *The European System for the Protection of Human Rights*, Dordrecht: Nijhoff, 1993, pp. 125–37.

cost-free, at least in the sense that cost is excluded. Of course, the rest of society and politics in general work on resource allocation. And in times of financial squeeze, they will, of course, bear on rights, whatever their type. Thus, the confrontation with utilitarianism is always an ambivalent and contradictory one. Human rights lawyers do not want to be embroiled in costing rights, because it opens to the door to utilitarianism, which was excluded at the start. But by ignoring this argument, the economic issues can easily be swept under the carpet, and not be confronted for what they are, with the consequences they have for the enjoyment of rights.

Aliens are seen less as human beings (and all they can carry and be as such) and more as potential charges, economic demands on the system. On that premise, they are excluded from common humanity and only granted a residual humanity; the one afforded if all the legal hurdles are jumped to be granted asylum. The question of who and what asylum seekers are is not really an issue: as such they are seen as suspicious; they could be lying and trying to exploit the system. The whole system is now tilted towards disproving that they are lying. And they should be happy if the system recognizes some truth in their testimony.[69] The consequence is their exclusion from society. Even if they are here, they are not seen. When they are seen, they are not treated as human, once their claim has been rejected.[70]

The counterpoint: including the excluded through personal testimonies

From the point of view of the legal system, once situations are excluded they cannot be included, unless the system so decides through its own internal code. In practice, it means that either the courts change their interpretation of the law, or that statutes are created to tell judges that these particular situations have to be reintegrated. However, both these interruptions/transformations of the law do not easily occur, otherwise the legal structure itself would be in danger of losing consistency. One way to radically interrupt non-representation is to create a space for personal testimonies to be heard, testimonies which would not be regulated by the legal discourse but could be an expression of the human behind the rights.[71]

---

69 See S. Nayak et al., Chapter 12 in this volume.
70 Ibid.
71 On testimony, see among others: J. Lackey and E. Sosa (eds), *The Epistemology of Testimony*, Oxford: Oxford University Press, 2006; G. Yudice, 'Testimonio and Postmodernism', *Latin American Perspectives*, 1991, 18(3), 'Voices of the Voiceless in Testimonial Literature', Part I, Summer, pp. 15–31; N. Strejilevich, 'Testimony: Beyond the Language of Truth', *Human Rights Quarterly* 28(3), 2006, pp. 701–13.

Personal testimonies as a breakthrough

Personal testimonies are a way to reconnect with the unity of the human experience and to restate what human rights are about, from the point of view of the individual story. They can be said to bring a glimpse of the truth, the story of those who would like to be counted in the situation. 'Truth is summoned in the cause of denouncing a present situation or exploitation and oppression or in exorcising and setting aright official history.'[72] The beauty, and the problem, of the human rights discourse is its capacity to talk to everyone at once, as each individual can recognize themselves as having rights. It means that, to be part of a community, each individual should recognize these rights as applicable to themselves as to others. This is the basis of the human rights discourse, the fact that anyone can claim to be among the same community, the community of human beings, by the mere fact of being born human.

Personal testimonies are a way to reconnect all the different dimensions: the dimensions of the victim, as user of the law, and as political agent. Of course there is a perspective through which, in the human rights discourse, there needs to be a victim, the victim of human rights violation. The problem, which has been underlined by many,[73] is that when the human rights discourse is focused only upon the victim, the conditions through which the victim became one in the first place is overshadowed, and the focus is on the redeemer, the saviour, symbolized by the white man, the Western army coming to the save the day.[74] Enabling the many dimensions of personal testimonies changes the victim into an actor, a human, from a person under the authority of someone else to an agent of change. As soon as the victim tells their story as a political act, a way to mobilize action, then the position is changed.[75]

Personal testimonies bring forth the empathy element, the idea that we can share, at least in essence, some of what has happened by seeing the way someone was negated as a full human being, which is in practice what a human rights violation means. If Alain Badiou, the French radical philosopher, is ferocious against the human rights discourse when focusing on the victim,[76] he also accepts that, exceptionally, it can be reconnected to truth procedures, the elements which break through the normal fabric of the existent, the connection to the real, the disruption of the contingent.[77] This is what happens

---

72 G. Yudice, op. cit., note 71, p. 17.
73 See among others, H. Charlesworth and C. Chinkin, *The Boundaries of International Law: A Feminist Analysis*, Manchester: Manchester University Press, 2000; and A. Badiou, *Ethics: An Essay on the Understanding of Evil*, trans. P. Hallward, London: Verso, 2001.
74 A. Orford, *Reading Humanitarian Intervention: Human Rights and the Use of Force in International Law*, Cambridge: Cambridge University Press, 2004.
75 See Part III of this volume: Activist confrontations.
76 A. Badiou, *Ethics*, op. cit., n. 23, pp. 9–10.
77 Ibid.

when a powerful story is being told. One just needs to look at the expressions and the feeling in a room with a very varied audience, when something of a breakthrough happens, when people connect to a personal story, faces change, and the modesty of a doctrinal position resurfaces in front of a shared moment.[78]

Finally, one is never very far from a personal testimony when engaged in the human rights field. There has to be a good autobiographical reason for someone to engage in this field, as money cannot be the main motivator.[79] But what is supremely important is to see how, from the victim's perspective, a person has moved from engagement with one story to a point where they try to instil change.

Testimonies are only of partial value when used in legal processes, as they are only used as a matter of evidence. There are many problems with such testimonies, and how a system will enable the factual truth to emerge, if these are contested. Based on the principle of the equal value of single testimonies, the individuals caught up in administrative practices need additional sources of evidence. 'Society wants to use witnesses' accounts as evidence, and testimonies are condemned in case they do not match evidence collected by other means.'[80]

Blacklisting in the construction industry demonstrates how important it is for other types of evidence to confirm the existence of such practices. Trade unionists had suspected for a long time the existence of blacklisting. But it was only through gaining knowledge of written listings that the judiciary finally accepted the situation and declared it illegal.[81] The same happened with the Mau Mau claims over the British administration in Kenya's atrocities and numerous human rights abuses in the 1950s and 1960s. They have only gained access to the legal system in 2011 as internal governmental memos have been released.[82]

Personal testimonies, activism and truth

Human rights can be used as tools for truth procedures, as understood by Badiou.[83] What are human rights? A counterpoint, underlining the necessary exclusion created by the law. Human rights are empty as such. They don't exist concretely but only as an absence.[84] But they are the name which can be

78 This is, for instance, what happened during the 2010 Salford Human Rights Conference, when Angela Nhongo brought her personal testimony.
79 See, for instance, how Peter Tatchell has put his body in danger through campaigning: Chapter 13 in this volume.
80 N. Strejilevich, op. cit., note 71, p. 703.
81 See D. Smith and K. Ewing, Chapter 14 in this volume.
82 BBC News, 6 April 2011, 'Kenyan Mau Mau uprising documents released', available at <http://www.bbc.co.uk/news/uk-12983289> (accessed 15 May 2011).
83 A. Badiou, *Being and Event*, trans. O. Feltham, London: Verso, 2006, chapter 7.
84 Badiou, *Ethics*, op. cit., n. 23, p. 11.

put on the political and legal absence. Then, the HRA could be said to be a tool which can bring forth the absence/exclusion of the law. It is the outer limit of the law. But it is an ever-continued reconstitution of its boundaries as seen from the inside.

In contrast to the standard legal discourse, human rights law recognizes the validity of the political elements coming from outside the traditional legal discourse. By calling attention to a human rights violation, some parts which were not treated as legal, which were not counted as being part of the system, such as failed asylum seekers, can be reintegrated within the legal system without destabilizing the law altogether (for instance through the necessity to protect private and family life). The question of morality and politics at the heart of human rights law perpetually unfolds in an everlasting process.

Thus, by holding on to testimony as an important element in a truth-situation, the recognition of exclusion from the existing state of affairs,[85] it is possible to argue for a use of human rights law which can still provide some elements of the radicalism which was present at the birth of the movement. It then becomes an issue about recognizing the truth-situation, the place where individuals are not represented within particular situations in society, and the use of testimonies as a basis for political claims and actions.

Conclusion

The Human Rights Act is part of a larger European project, where the institutionalization of the rights has and is taking place, the Council of Europe and the Strasbourg court are the main agents. Problematically, the question of the content of the rights is left to (legal) experts.[86] It is no longer a general question of politics to be decided in the normal way politics work. Human rights law sits both inside and outside politics: outside, through the technical independence of the judges; but inside, as they tend to reify the perceived dominant values of the time, thus limiting the way the rights themselves could be rewritten or rethought.

The domination of lawyers and the legal framework over the human rights discourse must be confronted. The legal system, fulfilling its functions, is all too good at limiting the type of information, such as testimony, that can be included. The lack of challenge can only lead to what Martti Koskenniemi states is 'a political culture that officially insists that rights are foundational ("inalienable", "basic"), but in practice constantly finds that they are not,

---

85 Like the suspected terrorist or the failed asylum seekers.
86 M. Koskenniemi, 'Human Rights Mainstreaming as a Strategy for Institutional Power', *Humanity: An International Journal of Human Rights, Humanitarianism, and Development* 1(1), 2010, pp. 47–58.

becomes a culture of bad faith'.[87] At best, this will feed scepticism, at worst cynicism, the postmodern trap.[88]

Human rights law needs to be re-opened with a counterpoint: a focus on the omissions, the untold and the forgotten. The whole process, through which I see human rights being useful in a truthful manner, is first to expose the exclusion. Then, ask for the law to contemplate it. Finally, force through the legal fabric at the point of the void,[89] the void covered by human rights law, thereby creating the possibility for a re-inclusion. Voices outside the legal system need to be heard; names, faces have to be seen in order for lawyers to be able to make sense of the violence exercised upon those who are excluded. By actively exposing the exclusion, using human rights law as the terminology for representing the exclusion through a legitimate discourse, the dominant views can be changed, the acceptable becoming non-acceptable, and human rights law once, for a brief instant, can be re-opened to question the justice of the legal system.

If Carl Schmitt is nowadays frequently evoked each time the exceptional is being underlined,[90] then it is good to remember how he used that exception. There, the exception is built upon a radical difference, an incommensurability of the 'others'. On the contrary, an exceptional use of human rights should mean using human rights law to create holes in the traditional legal fabric, where unheard voices could reappear in the existing context or situation. It has to be the art of the counterpoint, filled with love. (St) Paul clearly understood that the law cannot bring openness to others, but that the law brings the knowledge of the violation.[91] Only love can bring justice. Only love can make people realize the 'imperfect' obligations. The Good Samaritan's attitude, the will to do the right thing for the unknown 'neighbour', can only come from love, not from a sense of obligation or duty.[92] Only with love can the true re-inclusion of the excluded happen.

---

87 M. Koskenniemi, 'The Effect of Rights', op. cit., n. 24, p. 100.
88 P. Sloterdijk, *Critique of Cynical Reason*, Minneapolis: University Of Minnesota Press, 1988.
89 For a philosophical explanation of the void as a possibility for the re-inclusion, see A. Badiou, *Being and Event*, op. cit, n. 83.
90 See for instance, D. Chandler, 'The Revival of Carl Schmitt in International Relations: The Last Refuge of Critical Theorists?', *Journal of International Studies*, 37(1), 2008, pp. 27–48.
91 See A. Badiou, *Saint Paul: The Foundation of Universalism*, trans. R. Brassier, Stanford: Stanford University Press, 2003.
92 The parable of the Good Samaritan comes after the following question: 'What must I do to inherit eternal life?', to which the answer is: 'Love the Lord your God with all your heart and with all your soul and with all your strength and with all your mind' and 'Love your neighbour as yourself', Luke 10: 25–6, NIV, Grand Rapids: Zondervan.

Part I

Confronting the Human Rights Act as a legal tool

Section 1

Confronting the Human Rights Act as legislation

2   The Human Rights Act

Origins and intentions

Francesca Klug

Former US President Ronald Reagan once said: 'In America, our origins matter less than our destination'.[1] The point about the Human Rights Act (HRA) is that it is not possible to understand its destination without *some* knowledge of its origins, which, contrary to tabloid legend, was neither an edict from Brussels nor an ultimatum from Strasbourg.

Beginnings

Like the origin of the species, the HRA's precise evolutionary history is open to some debate. Its gestation can be traced to 1968, a time when the sometimes authoritarian chickens of the British Parliament came home to roost. The 1968 Commonwealth Immigrants Act was passed with all-party support by a panicky Parliament, led by a Labour Government, in three days. Its sole purpose was to deny British Asians expelled from East Africa entry to the UK, at the precise moment when they sought to rely on their UK citizen status to protect them.[2]

A slumbering consciousness began to stir. The renowned lawyers Anthony Lester and John MacDonald produced pamphlets calling for a bill of rights to establish some bottom-line principles and standards which would frame UK law.[3] Commentators and academics began to debate in earnest whether the famed UK doctrine of parliamentary sovereignty could ever adequately protect minorities whose voting power would forever be minimal; in so far as it existed at all. Under this doctrine, Acts of Parliament not only trumped the common law, but were largely safe from judicial review.[4]

In 1974, this nascent debate took a further leap when Sir Leslie Scarman, the esteemed judge and subsequent law lord, chose to devote the first of his

---

1 Address to the Republican National Convention, Houston, 17 August 1992.
2 See David Steel MP, *No Entry: the background and implications of the Commonwealth Immigrants Act 1968*, London: Hurst, 1969.
3 A. Lester, *Democracy and Individual Rights*, Fabian Society, 1968; John MacDonald, *Bill of Rights*, Liberal Party, 1969.
4 Outside the context of EU law.

Hamlyn Lectures to the question of a bill of rights. In a famous passage harking back to the 1968 Immigrants Act he said:

> When times are normal and fear is not stalking the land, English law sturdily protects the freedom of the individual . . . but when times are abnormally alive with fear *and* prejudice, the common law is at a disadvantage; it cannot resist the will . . . of parliament.[5]

Surprisingly to modern audiences (in the light of the Tory Party's 2010 manifesto pledge to scrap the HRA), it was the Society of *Conservative* Lawyers (SCL) who were among the first to link this call for a bill of rights with incorporation of the 1950 European Convention on Human Rights (ECHR) into UK law. The SCL recommended in their 1976 report *Another Bill of Rights?* that 'the ECHR should be given statutory force as an over-riding domestic law'.[6]

Although it had been inspired by the Universal Declaration of Human Rights, promoted by Winston Churchill and largely drafted by UK lawyers, Britain was one of the few countries in Europe that had not incorporated the ECHR into domestic law – only the government was bound by its terms following ratification in 1951.[7] Parliament, the courts and other public authorities were not. Most people in the UK were barely aware of the rights they were entitled to under the ECHR, except when the government lost a case at Strasbourg and the tabloids invariably protested at what they would characterise as ruling by foreign judges.

Two years after the SCL report, the Conservative Lord Chancellor, Lord Hailsham, pronounced that 'in this armoury of weapons against elective dictatorship' – which is how he famously described the then Labour Government – 'a bill of rights, embodying and entrenching the European Convention, might well have a valuable . . . part to play'.[8]

Seeds of change

In the 1980s, the next push came from the perceived failure of Parliament to brook virtually any successful challenges to a now Conservative Government which, on the basis of three elections on a minority vote, could bring in almost any measure it wished. A legislature thoroughly dominated by the executive offered very little protection against a government determined to push

---

5 Sir Leslie Scarman, *English Law – The New Dimension*, Hamlyn Lectures, 1974.
6 Scarman, *English Law – The New Dimension*.
7 The ratification took effect from 1953 and in 1966 individuals were given the right to take cases to the European Court of Human Rights (EctHR). See Jesse Norman and Peter Oborne, 'Churchill's Legacy: The Conservative Case for the Human Rights Act', Liberty, 2009 and Francesca Klug et al., 'Common Sense: Reflections on the Human Rights Act', Liberty, 2010, chapter 2.
8 Quintin Hogg, Baron Hailsham of St Marylebone, *The Dilemma of Democracy*, London: Collins, 1978.

through unpopular laws like the Poll Tax, or – less unpopular, but in the view of civil libertarians just as troubling – measures like the Public Order Act 1986, the Official Secrets Act 1989, successive Prevention of Terrorism Acts[9] and the removal of the ancient right to silence.[10]

Although they sometimes strained to apply human rights principles like proportionality and necessity,[11] judges faced considerable restrictions when seeking to hold the executive to account, compared to many of their European counterparts and jurisdictions with constitutional bills of rights. The decisions or actions of the government or other public bodies could only be overturned if illegal or beyond the range of responses open to a so-called 'reasonable decision maker'.[12] Demonstrating that an interference with a fundamental human right is 'proportionate' and 'necessary' – the post-HRA test – requires a *much* higher level of justification than whether an interference is merely 'reasonable'. Sometimes it seemed as if public officials had to be so 'irrational' as to be virtually certifiable before their *decisions* would be quashed. Pre-HRA, the courts were effectively barred from reviewing primary *legislation* altogether.

The frustration of the judiciary came to a head in the case of *Smith* in 1996 over the ban on gay men and women serving in the military. Sir Thomas Bingham, then Master of the Rolls, strongly signalled his regret that he could not ask whether this measure was 'proportionate' or 'necessary'; only whether it was 'reasonable'.[13]

To the further embarrassment of our courts, the European Court of Human Rights (ECtHR), which subsequently overturned the ban when our courts could not, subtly damned the British constitutional system for effectively excluding any consideration of the human rights of the sacked personnel.[14]

The formation of Charter 88 in 1988 had placed support for a bill of rights firmly on the political agenda. This elite, but growing, campaign provided the impetus for the HRA. In those days, the marriage between calls for a bill of rights and incorporation of the ECHR into UK law seemed as self-evident as that of David Cameron and Nick Clegg today.

Whilst some pressure groups and think tanks – including Liberty and the Institute for Public Policy Research[15] – produced model bills of rights that

---

9 1984; 1989.

10 In the Criminal Justice and Public Order Act 1994.

11 These principles set the parameters within which most rights can be legitimately limited under the ECHR. *Handyside v UK* (1976) 1 EHRR 737. A restriction will be 'proportionate' only if the objective behind the restriction justifies interference with a Convention right, there is a rational connection between the objective and the restriction in question and the means employed are not more than is necessary to achieve the objective. See Francesca Klug and Keir Starmer, 'Incorporation through the back door?' *Public Law*, Summer, 1997.

12 Under the so-called doctrine of Wednesbury unreasonableness.

13 *R v Ministry of Defence ex p. Smith* [1996] 1 All ER 257.

14 *Smith v Grady v UK* (1999).

15 See *A British Bill of Rights*, The Institute for Public Policy Research,1990; *A People's Charter*, Liberty, 1991.

went further than the ECHR, incorporation of a human rights treaty that the UK government was already bound by was generally agreed to be the simplest and most logical way to introduce a bill of rights in the modern world. Canada – and subsequently New Zealand – did something broadly similar in basing their bills of rights on the International Covenant on Civil and Political Rights.[16]

After Labour lost a fourth election in a row in 1992 the new leader, John Smith, a Scottish lawyer who had a long-term personal interest in devolution and constitutional reform, committed his Party to support a British Bill of Rights as part of a package of proposals for democratic renewal. Echoing the former Tory Lord Chancellor, Lord Hailsham, he maintained that 'what we have in this country at the moment is not real democracy; it is elective dictatorship'.[17] In a watershed speech to Charter 88, Smith affirmed, like others before him, that 'the quickest and simplest way' of introducing 'a substantial package of human rights' would be to pass a Human Rights Act 'incorporating into British law the European Convention on Human Rights'.[18]

The 1993 Labour Party conference adopted a National Executive Committee statement, introduced by Home Affairs spokesperson Tony Blair, supporting an all-party commission to 'draft our own bill of rights' which would go further than the ECHR and was presumed to include social and economic rights.[19] In contemporary jargon, this second stage was to be unambiguously 'HRA plus'.

Support for a bill of rights was not uniform on the left – far from it. There was considerable opposition within the Labour Party and among some radical lawyers.[20] The first Labour Party document to propose the incorporation of the ECHR into UK law, *A Charter of Human Rights*, was published in 1976. The National Executive Committee would not allow the paper to be presented as official policy but only as an issue for debate. This bill of rights scepticism was more political than constitutional, revolving round the feared impact on a democratically elected, centre-left government of public-school, Oxbridge-educated judges overturning laws they disagreed with, under the guise of a bill of rights.[21]

New Labour triangulation

New Labour's scepticism about the HRA, which developed over time, was of a different kind. When Tony Blair stood as leader of the Labour Party after

16 Canadian Charter of Rights and Freedoms 1982 and New Zealand Bill of Rights 1990, respectively.
17 'A New Way Forward', speech by John Smith, Leader of the Labour Party, Bournemouth, 7 February 1993.
18 *A Citizen's Democracy*, Charter 88, March 1993.
19 See F. Klug, 'A bill of rights – what for?' *Towards a New Constitutional Settlement*, Smith Institute, 2007, pp. 130–45.
20 See K.D. Ewing and C.A. Gearty, *Democracy or a Bill of Rights*, Society of Labour Lawyers, 1991.
21 See J. Griffiths, *Politics of the Judiciary*, London: Fontana, 1977.

John Smith's untimely death in May 1994, he signalled continuity with his predecessor's agenda by including support for a bill of rights in a candidate statement not overburdened with policies. This was important for Blair politically as in most other ways the birth of New Labour represented discontinuity with even the immediate past.

Only two years later, as the general election was approaching, this pledge for a bill of rights was trimmed to a more technical-sounding commitment to incorporate the ECHR into UK law. It was no longer presented as a bill of rights *based* on the European Convention but as simply the logical next stage for complying with an international treaty which the government was *already* bound by.

Yet at the same time, constitutional reform as a *package* had become one of the badges of New Labour; a set of measures to signal that it still had a distinct radical programme whilst it was fast distancing itself from its socialist past. But there was little attempt to link different aspects of this programme into a coherent whole, let alone tie it into the party's traditional agenda for social justice.

This triangulated message – in which the HRA was simultaneously presented as both a radical departure on the one hand and a technical, tidying up exercise on the other, depending on the audience and the minister – seeped into the parliamentary debate and extra-parliamentary lectures and interviews which greeted the introduction of the HRA.

From this time onwards, ministers presented contrasting purposes for the Act.

On the one hand, it was introduced to 'bring rights home' – in the well-worn phrase and the title of the White Paper which ushered it in – so that individuals could claim the ECHR rights they were entitled to in the domestic courts.[22] The purpose was to 'enable people to enforce their human rights in the courts of the United Kingdom rather than having to take their case to Strasbourg . . . [to provide] better and easier access to rights which already exist'.[23]

On the other hand, the intentions behind the Act were apparently far more ambitious and fundamental. Ministers declared that the HRA was designed as a constitutional measure[24] to modernise and democratise the political system[25]

---

22 'Our aim is a straightforward one. It is to make more directly accessible the rights which the British people already enjoy under the Convention.' *Rights Brought Home, White Paper*, para 1.19, October 1997.

23 Lord Chancellor, Lord Irvine, Hansard, HL vol. 585, col. 755 (5 February 1998).

24 See F. Klug, 'The Human Rights Act 1998, *Pepper v. Hart* and All That', *Public Law*, 1999, p. 246.

25 Jack Straw, then Home Secretary, said on introducing the Human Rights Bill: 'The Bill falls squarely within [our] constitutional programme. It is a key component of our drive to modernise our society and refresh our democracy . . . to bring about a better balance between rights and responsibilities, between the powers of the state and the freedom of the individual.' Hansard, HC vol. 306, col. 782–3 (16 February 1998).

and lead to cultural change beyond the courts.[26] The late Lord Williams, speaking as a Home Office Minister in the House of Lords debate on the HRA, specifically *contradicted* the 'bringing rights home' mantra when he said:

> [this] is not, as the Lord Chancellor pointed out, simply 'you will be able to get your rights enforced quickly and cheaply because you will not have to make the journey to Strasbourg'. *It is much more important than that.* Every public authority will know that its behaviour, its structure, its conclusions and its executive actions will be subject to this culture.[27]

The then Home Secretary, Jack Straw, described the HRA as 'the first major bill on human rights for more than 300 years'[28] and 'the first bill of rights this country has seen for three centuries'.[29] This was then a fairly standard description of the HRA, including the eminent judge Lord Steyn,[30] the *New York Times*[31] and legal academics.[32] But if the *political* rhetoric as to the HRA's purpose was deliberately ambiguous – the better to court different audiences – the *legal* scheme adopted was much clearer as to the *intentions* behind the Act.

The British model

Sometimes referred to by Jack Straw as 'the British model', it is possible to summarise – in very broad terms – the legal and constitutional intentions of the HRA as follows:

1   The primary purpose was *not* the technical incorporation of a human rights treaty, but the adoption of the rights in the ECHR as the basis for a specifically *UK* bill of rights, in response to years of lobbying for such a measure (*HRA s 2*).
2   Almost without precedence in UK domestic law, the HRA would be a *higher law* whose broad principles would set the parameters of all other legislation and policy – past, present and future – except where

---

26 Lord Irvine made many statements to the effect that 'Our courts will develop human rights throughout society. A culture of awareness of human rights will develop.' Hansard, HL vol. 582, col. 1228 (3 November 1997).
27 582 HL AT 1308. My emphasis.
28 Above, n. 25 at col.769.
29 Speech, Institute for Public Policy Research, 13 January 2000.
30 '. . . the Human Rights Act 1998 which is our Bill of Rights'. 'Democracy, the Rule of Law and the Role of Judges', [2006] *EHRLR* 243 at p. 246.
31 'Britain Quietly Says It's Time To Adopt a Bill of Rights', *New York Times*, 3 October 1999.
32 K. Ewing, 'The Human Rights Act and Parliamentary Democracy', *Modern Law Review* 62, 1999, p. 79.

Parliament explicitly, or by strong implication, had contrary intentions (*HRA s 3*).

3   With no judicial strike-down power, the model would not fundamentally disturb the doctrine of parliamentary sovereignty, which there was no general appetite, let alone consensus, to overturn. Parliament would be given an explicit role in overseeing the operation of the HRA (through the establishment of the proposed Joint Committee on Human Rights).[33] Should the courts issue a Declaration that an Act of Parliament was incompatible with the fundamental rights in the HRA there would be no legal obligation on the executive or legislature to change the law in question, or even necessarily to respond to it. Nevertheless, the courts were empowered to hold the executive to account where they were impeded before (*HRA ss 4, 6 and 19*).

Despite contemporary political and media commentary that the HRA was designed not just to incorporate most of the rights in the ECHR but the *totality* of its case law, there was no original intention to require UK judges to slavishly follow Strasbourg jurisprudence. Quite the contrary.[34] The parliamentary debate reveals that the language of the relevant section (2) was purposefully drafted to prevent the domestic courts from being bound by Strasbourg jurisprudence, while still requiring them to 'take [it] into account'. The 'distinctly British contribution'[35] our courts would make to developing European human rights jurisprudence was emphasised in the parliamentary debates on the Human Rights Bill and the accompanying White Paper:

> The Convention is often described as a 'living instrument' . . . In future our judges will be able to contribute to this dynamic and evolving interpretation of the Convention.[36]

33 See F. Klug, 'The Klug Report: Report on the Working Practices of the JCHR', published in 'The Committee's Future Working Practices', Twenty-third Report of Session 2005–06.

34 See F. Klug and H. Wildbore, 'Follow or lead? The Human Rights Act and the European Court of Human Rights', *European Human Rights Law Review* 6, 2010, p. 621.

35 *Rights Brought Home*, para 1.14. The consultation document which preceded the White Paper made no reference to domestic courts having to take into account Strasbourg jurisprudence. It said that the failure to incorporate the ECHR meant that 'British judges are denied the opportunity of building a body of case law on the Convention which is properly sensitive to British legal and constitutional traditions' and that the European Court 'has not been able to benefit from the experience of the UK legal system or to develop an appreciation of British legal principles and traditions.' See Jack Straw and Paul Boateng, *Bringing Rights Home: Labour's plans to incorporate the European Convention on Human Rights into UK law*, Labour Party, December 1996.

36 *Rights Brought Home*, para 2.5.

Jack Straw explained when piloting the Bill through the House of Commons:

> Through incorporation we are giving a profound margin of appreciation to British courts to interpret the Convention in accordance with British jurisprudence as well as European jurisprudence.[37]

Interestingly, given the vocal concerns of the current Prime Minister about the impact of European Court of Human Rights jurisprudence on British law,[38] the then Labour Government rejected an amendment by the Shadow Lord Chancellor, Lord Kingsland, to make our courts 'bound by' Strasbourg jurisprudence.[39] The Lord Chancellor, Lord Irvine, said it would be 'strange' to require our courts to be bound by all European Court decisions when the UK is not bound in international law to follow that Court's judgments in non-UK cases. The Bill would 'of course' permit domestic courts to depart from Strasbourg decisions and 'upon occasion it might be appropriate to do so'. The Tory amendment, he said, would risk 'putting the courts in some kind of straitjacket where flexibility is what is required . . . our courts must be free to try to give a lead to Europe as well as to be led'.[40]

Lord Irvine addressed the question which has subsequently occupied the domestic courts; the extent to which they should *mirror* Strasbourg:[41]

> Should a United Kingdom court ever have a case before it which is a precise mirror of one that has been previously considered by the European Court of Human Rights, which I doubt, it may be appropriate for it to apply the European court's findings directly to that case; but in real life cases are rarely as neat and tidy . . . The courts will often be faced with cases that involve factors perhaps specific to the United Kingdom . . . it is important that our courts have the scope to apply that discretion so as to aid in the development of human rights law.[42]

Differing in his approach to interpreting the HRA (s 2) from a number of his fellow judges, Justice Laws, who determined that 'the English court is not a

---

37 Hansard, HC vol. 313, col. 424 (3 June 1998).
38 David Cameron said: 'It makes me physically ill even to contemplate having to give the vote to anyone who is in prison,' House of Commons, Hansard, 3 November 2010. This was in response to the ECtHR judgment that the blanket ban on prisoners' voting breached Protocol 1 Article 3 ECHR in *Hirst v UK* (2005).
39 Hansard, HL vol. 583, col. 511 (18 November 1997).
40 Ibid. at col. 514–15.
41 The eminent former Law Lord and Lord Chief Justice Lord Bingham controversially affirmed that 'The duty of national courts is to keep pace with the Strasbourg jurisprudence as it evolves over time: no more, but certainly no less.' *R (Ullah) v Secretary of State for the Home Department* [2004] UKHL 26, para 20.
42 Hansard, HL vol. 584, col. 1270–1 (18 January 1998).

Strasbourg surrogate', summed up the original intentions behind the HRA fairly when he said in 2002:

> . . . the court's task under the HRA . . . is not simply to add on the Strasbourg learning to the corpus of English law, as if it were a compulsory adjunct taken from an alien source, but to develop a *municipal law of human rights* . . . case by case, *taking account* of the Strasbourg jurisprudence as s 2 [of the] HRA enjoins us to do.[43]

Lord Scott developed this 'municipal approach' in a more recent House of Lords case, maintaining:

> . . . [under s 2] the judgments of the European Court . . . constitute material, very important material, that must be taken into account, but domestic courts are nonetheless not bound by the European Court's interpretation of an incorporated article.[44]

He also said that the 'possibility of a divergence' between the opinion of the European Court as to the application of a right and the opinion of the House of Lords is 'contemplated, implicitly at least, by the [HRA]'.[45]

Commenting on the relationship between domestic and European human rights law under the HRA, the legal scholar, Andrew Clapham, has suggested that the 'challenge' for 'national courts' is to 'treat international human rights as part of the national heritage' whilst interpreting such rights 'in the national context to give them the appropriate maximum protection at the national level'.[46]

Conclusion

Since the HRA came into force it has had some significant impacts both inside and outside the courts (see the appendix to this chapter). While the profound cultural change among public authorities that some had predicted in the HRA's early days has not materialised, an Equality and Human Rights Commission Inquiry report documented policies and practices that were a

---

43 *Runa Begum v Tower Hamlets* [2002] 2 All ER 668 para 17 (my emphasis). Justice Laws also determined that 'our duty is to develop, by the common law's incremental method, a coherent and principled *domestic* law of human rights,' *R (Pro-life Alliance) v BBC* [2002] 2 All ER 668.

44 *R (Animal Defenders International) v Secretary of State for Culture, Media and Sport* [2008] UKHL 15, para 44.

45 Ibid.

46 A. Clapham, 'The ECHR in the British Courts: problems associated with the Incorporation of International Human Rights, in *Promoting Human Rights through Bills of Rights*, Oxford: Oxford University Press, 1999, pp. 134–5.

direct consequence of the Act.[47] For some commentators the legal and extra-legal effects of the HRA have been much too extensive; for others they have not gone far enough. Depending who you believe, the HRA is either a wolf masquerading as a sheep, or a sheep masquerading as a wolf.

Following the atrocities of 9/11 and 7/7[48] there were, of course, well-documented erosions of rights and freedoms here and elsewhere. But this also occurred in the USA, with its famed bill of rights and powerful judicial strike-down powers, as much as in the UK. The Patriot Act, the Military Commissions Acts, the Real ID Act and the Detainee Treatment Act were all passed by the US Congress after 2001. Lord MacDonald, the former Director of Public Prosecutions, has estimated that, in his words, the HRA 'has stood up to the buffeting' more effectively than the US Bill of Rights, in the post-9/11 era.[49] The reality is that, with very few exceptions,[50] bills of rights *only* allow the courts to review laws once they have been passed, not to stop their introduction.

Now, just over a decade since the HRA came into force, the Coalition Government is establishing a Commission to consider replacing the HRA with a British Bill of Rights.[51] It is, of course, possible to draft a bill that builds on the HRA and is stronger in enforcement powers and broader in scope. There are many good examples to draw from.[52] But, unusually in the history of bills of rights worldwide, most of the pressure for a 'British Bill of Rights' comes from those who wish to *reduce* the scope of the judiciary because, in the words of the Prime Minister, David Cameron, 'it is about time we ensured that decisions are made in this Parliament rather than in the courts'.[53] This is despite the fact that the HRA already leaves *the last word* with parliament and does not require the legislature to change the law, even when judges declare that statutes breach fundamental human rights. The Director of Liberty, Shami Chakrabarti, has asked, 'Are [the government] not prepared to accept even this gentle model of constitutional protection for the people against our rulers?'[54]

---

47 *'Human Rights Inquiry'*, Report of the Equality and Human Rights Commission, 2009.
48 The terrorist atrocities in New York on 9 September 2001 and in London on 7 July 2005.
49 Liberty 75th Anniversary Conference, June 2009.
50 The French constitutional council provides pre-enactment judicial review.
51 The Coalition Programme for Government in May 2010 stated: 'We will establish a Commission to investigate the creation of a British Bill of Rights that incorporates and builds on all our obligations under the European Convention on Human Rights, ensures that these rights continue to be enshrined in British law, and protects and extends British liberties.'
52 See 'A Bill of Rights for the UK?', Joint Committee on Human Rights, 29th Report of Session 2007–08; Richard Gordon QC, *Repairing British Politics: A Blueprint for Constitutional Change*, Oxford: Hart, 2010; 'A Bill of Rights for Northern Ireland', Northern Ireland Human Rights Commission, 2008.
53 Prime Minister's Questions, HC, 16 February 2011.
54 Shami Chakrabarti, 'Warning: anti-justice stomach bug spreading', *The Times*, 21 February 2011.

There are, additionally, growing demands to decouple the HRA, or any subsequent bill of rights, from Strasbourg jurisprudence entirely.[55] Some of the same sources have welcomed high-profile examples where the European Court of Human Rights has come to a different conclusion from the domestic courts, for example on the retention of the DNA of innocent suspects[56] or the use of anti-terrorism legislation to search peaceful protesters.[57] Both of these judgments will lead to changes in the law flagged for inclusion in the Coalition Government's Protection of Freedoms Bill.[58] In the meantime UK judges, whilst not bound by such decisions,[59] are now required to '*take into account*' this case law in subsequent similar fact cases, which they either could not, or would not, do prior to the HRA. It is difficult to see how rights will be enhanced by watering down or removing this link with Strasbourg jurisprudence, even if it were *possible* to ordain to judges – who already frequently cite the common law in interpreting the HRA – which sources of authority they should consult in a subsequent British Bill of Rights.

The eminent QC Rabinder Singh, who has frequently acted on behalf of governments, has described the HRA as 'a success story from a legal perspective. It has not been a damp squib. Nor has it overwhelmed the legal system.'[60] Although most of the cases where the HRA has been cited would have been taken anyway, many of them would not have achieved the same results. The Prime Minister maintains that he is committed to 'proper rights', but that 'they should be written down here in this country', signalling that for the first time since the Second World War a mature democracy may seek to introduce a bill of rights in order to distance its legal system from international human rights law.[61] This could mark a new departure in the history of bills of rights and lead in a direction that the prominent Conservatives who once called for a UK Bill of Rights, based on the European Convention on Human Rights, could scarcely have contemplated.

---

55 Attorney General Dominic Grieve said at a Politeia event on 14 February 2011: 'The [ECtHR] doesn't have the last word. It only has the last word so far as parliament has decided that it should. We could, if we wanted to, undo that . . .', quoted in guardian. co.uk, 14 February 2011.

56 *Marper v UK*, ECtHR Grand Chamber, 4 December 2008.

57 *Gillan and Quinton v UK*, ECtHR 12 January 2010.

58 The Bill proposes the removal of DNA from the database of those arrested or charged but not convicted of minor offences, but the retention of DNA for three years for those arrested but not convicted of a serious or sexual offence. For stop and search, the Bill proposes to narrow searches in place and time and to be linked to a 'reasonably suspected' act of terrorism.

59 Only the government is bound to follow European Court of Human Rights judgments, even when they involve the UK.

60 F. Klug and J. Gordon (eds), 'The HRA and the Courts: a practitioner's perspective,' *European Human Rights Law Review, Special Issue on 10th Anniversary of the HRA*, Issue 6, 2010.

61 Prime Minister's Questions, HC, 1 December 2010.

Appendix[62]

The protection of rights and freedoms under the Human Rights Act: some illustrations[63]

Helen Wildbore

Protest

Preventing demonstrators reaching a protest is unjustified intrusion into right to freedom of assembly

It was a breach of the rights of freedom of speech (Art. 10) and freedom of peaceful assembly (Art. 11) for the police to stop demonstrators reaching a protest. The court said that the police must take no more intrusive action than appeared necessary to prevent a breach of the peace and commented that, post-HRA, it is no longer necessary to debate whether we have a right to freedom of assembly.[64]

Privacy

Damages awarded for unjustified intrusion into private life

Where an invasion of private life is a matter of legitimate public interest because a public figure had previously lied about the matter, there will be a strong argument in favour of freedom of expression that will often defeat a claim of privacy (Art. 8). But publication of additional information, beyond setting the record straight, was an unjustified intrusion into private life and damages were awarded for the breach.[65]

---

62 A similar appendix was published in 'Common Sense: Reflections on the Human Rights Act' by Francesca Klug and others, Liberty, June 2010.

63 Some ECtHR decisions have also been included as illustrations of the development of human rights law which, as a result of the HRA (s2), the domestic courts are bound to 'take into account'. Prior to the HRA, ECtHR decisions were not part of the domestic legal framework.

64 *R (Laporte) v Chief Constable of Gloucestershire* [2006] UKHL 55.

65 *Campbell v Mirror Group Newspapers* [2004] UKHL 22.

Freedom of expression

Responsibly written articles on matters of public interest are protected

The common law defence of qualified privilege in libel cases can protect media articles which are of public importance.[66] Post-HRA the defence has been strengthened[67] and as a result, the media have much more freedom when reporting matters of public interest, where it may not be possible to subsequently prove the truth of the allegations, provided that they act responsibly and in the public interest.

Freedom of expression includes the right to receive information

The right to freedom of expression includes not only the freedom to impart information and ideas but also to receive. The media have been granted access to a hearing in the Court of Protection, when such hearings had previously been closed.[68]

Protecting right to life

Right to life can include positive obligation to protect life

The right to life (Art. 2) not only prevents the State from intentionally taking life, it also requires States to take appropriate steps to safeguard life.[69] As a result, the majority of the 43 police forces in England and Wales now have specific policies on handling immediate and foreseeable risks or threats to life.[70]

Soldiers on military bases in Iraq fall under the jurisdiction of a the HRA

A British soldier serving in Iraq who died from hyperthermia in a UK military base after complaining that he couldn't cope with the heat was subject to the jurisdiction of the HRA. An inquest was necessary to establish by what means and in what circumstances he met his death due to concerns over possible failures by the army to provide adequate systems to protect his life.[71]

---

66 *Reynolds v Times Newspapers* [1999] UKHL 45. The court referred to the need for the common law to be developed and applied in a manner consistent with Art. 10.
67 *Jameel v Wall Street Journal Europe* [2006] UKHL 44.
68 *A v Independent News and Media and others* [2010] EWCA Civ 343.
69 *Osman v UK*, ECtHR, 28 October 1998.
70 See 'Human Rights Inquiry: Report of the Equality and Human Rights Commission', June 2009.
71 *R (Smith) v Oxfordshire Assistant Deputy Coroner and Secretary of State for Defence* [2010] UKSC 29.

Right to liberty

Detention of suspected international terrorists without trial is a breach of HRA

The detention without charge or trial of a group of foreign nationals suspected of terrorism was declared incompatible with the right to liberty (Art. 5) and the prohibition of discrimination (Art. 14).[72] The provisions were repealed by the Prevention of Terrorism Act 2005, which put in place a new regime of control orders.

Control order restrictions violate right to liberty

The non-derogating control orders imposed on a group of asylum seekers under the Prevention of Terrorism Act 2005, which, among other things, imposed an 18-hour curfew and restricted contact only to people authorised by the Home Office, amounted to a violation of Art. 5.[73] The government responded by issuing new orders, with less restrictive conditions.

Right to fair trial

Secret evidence in control order hearings violates right to fair trial

The right to fair hearing (Art. 6) means that a defendant must be given sufficient information about the allegations against him to enable him to give effective instructions to the special advocate representing him.[74]

No torture

Evidence procured by torture must not be admitted in court

The Special Immigration Appeals Commission (Procedure) Rules 2003 determined that the Commission could receive evidence that would not be admissible in a court of law, but this did not extend to statements procured by torture, giving effect to the absolute prohibition of torture in Art. 3.[75]

---

72 *A and others v Secretary of State for the Home Department* [2004] UKHL 56. The claimants received (modest) damages for the violation of their right to liberty at the ECtHR (*A and others v UK*, Grand Chamber, 19 February 2009).
73 *Secretary of State for the Home Department v JJ and others* [2007] UKHL 45.
74 *Secretary of State for the Home Department v AF and others* [2009] UKHL 28.
75 *A and others v Secretary of State for the Home Department* [2005] UKHL 71.

Deportation where there is a real risk of torture would violate the absolute prohibition on torture

Deporting individuals where there is a real risk of their being subjected to torture or to inhuman or degrading treatment or punishment would breach ECHR Art. 3, irrespective of their conduct.[76]

No slavery

HRA protects against modern-day slavery

The Metropolitan Police accepted that their failure to investigate a victim's report of threats and violence by her employer, who withheld her passport and wages, breached the prohibition of slavery and forced labour (Art. 4). The police reopened the investigation and the employer was found guilty of assault.[77]

Investigations into deaths

Duty to investigate death in custody

Where a death has occurred in custody the State is under a duty to publicly investigate before an independent judicial tribunal, with an opportunity for relatives of the deceased to participate.[78]

Article 2 secures inquest into murder

Right to life arguments secured the reopening of the inquest into the death of Naomi Bryant, who was killed in 2005 by convicted sex offender Anthony Rice.[79]

---

76 *Saadi v Italy*, ECtHR Grand Chamber, 28 February 2008; *Chahal v UK*, ECtHR, 15 November 1996.
77 See <http://www.liberty-human-rights.org.uk/human-rights/victims/forced-labour/index. php> (accessed 14 November 2011).
78 *R (Amin) v Secretary of State for the Home Department* [2003] UKHL 51.
79 See <http://www.liberty-human-rights.org.uk/media/press/2011/inquest-secured-by-human-rights-act-finds-institutional-.php> (accessed 14 November 2011).

Destitution of asylum seekers

Duty under HRA to avoid asylum seekers living in conditions amounting to inhuman or degrading treatment

Where asylum seekers were excluded from support for accommodation and essential living needs under asylum legislation,[80] the court ruled that as soon as an asylum seeker makes it clear that there is an imminent prospect of his treatment reaching inhuman and degrading levels, the Secretary of State has a power under asylum legislation and a *duty* under the HRA to avoid it.[81] The Immigration and Nationality Directorate adopted a new approach to comply with the judgment.[82]

Disability

Duty to take positive action to secure dignity of disabled tenant in local authority housing

Where a local authority knew that a disabled tenant's housing was inappropriate but did not move her to suitably adapted accommodation, they failed in their duty to take positive steps to enable her and her family to lead as normal a family life as possible and secure her physical integrity and dignity, for which damages were due.[83]

Policies on lifting must consider competing rights

A lifting policy should balance the disabled person's right to dignity and participation in community life and the care workers' right to physical and psychological integrity and dignity.[84] East Sussex local authority amended its Safety Code of Practice on Manual Handling accordingly. Other authorities were also encouraged to comply.

---

80 They were excluded from support under the Immigration and Asylum Act 1999 Part VI by the Nationality, Immigration and Asylum Act 2002, s 55(1), because the Secretary of State decided they had not made their asylum claims as soon as reasonably practicable.

81 *R (Limbuela and others) v Secretary of State for the Home Department* [2005] UKHL 66.

82 'No claimant who does not have alternative sources of support, including adequate food and basic amenities, such as washing facilities and night shelter, is refused support,' Home Office, 'Asylum Statistics: 4th quarter 2005 UK', 2005.

83 *R (Bernard) v Enfield* [2002] EWHC 2282 Admin.

84 *R (A and B) v East Sussex County Council* [2003] EWHC 167 (Admin).

Mental health

Onus of proof in mental health cases reversed to protect patients

The Mental Health Act 1983 was successfully challenged under the HRA, leading to an amendment to put the burden of proving that continued detention for treatment for mental illness is justified under Art. 5 on the detaining authority, and not the patient.[85]

Children

Unnecessary physical restraint of young people in custody is a breach of HRA

The Secure Training Centre (Amendment) Rules 2007, which allowed officers to physically restrain and seclude young offenders, were quashed. The Secretary of State could not establish that the system was necessary for ensuring 'good order and discipline' and the Rules breached Art. 3.[86]

Sexual orientation

Same-sex partner given 'nearest relative' status

The same-sex partner of a detained mental health patient, whom the local council had refused to afford the status of 'nearest relative', successfully challenged this decision under Art. 8, arguing that private life includes issues of sexuality, personal choice and identity.[87]

HRA provides protection against discrimination on grounds of sexual orientation

The courts have used their powers under the HRA to eliminate the discriminatory effect of the Rent Act 1977 which meant that the survivor of a homosexual couple could not become a statutory tenant by succession while the survivor of a heterosexual couple could.[88]

---

85 *R (H) v Mental Health Review Tribunal* [2002] QBD 1.
86 *R (C) v Secretary of State for Justice* [2008] EWCA 882.
87 *R (SG) v Liverpool City Council* October 2002.
88 *Ghaidan v Mendoza* [2004] UKHL 30.

Race

Changes made to cell-sharing policies following racist murder of prisoner

Following the murder of a prisoner by his racist cell-mate and a successful challenge under the HRA for a public inquiry, the Prison Service introduced changes to its policy and procedures relating to cell-sharing risks, allowing information-sharing to identify high risk factors.[89]

Gender

Gender re-assignment requires legal recognition

A successful challenge was made against the different treatment for post-operative transsexuals in obtaining marriage certificates. The government altered the law and the Gender Recognition Act 2004 now entitles a trans-sexual person to be treated in their acquired gender for all purposes, including marriage.[90]

Separation of mother and baby in prison requires flexibility

The blanket Prison Services rule, requiring compulsory removal of all babies from imprisoned mothers at 18 months, was successfully challenged. Greater flexibility was required to consider the individual circumstances. The Prison Service Order on the management of mother and baby units was amended to comply with the judgment.[91]

---

89 *R (Amin) v Secretary of State for the Home Department* [2003] UKHL 51.
90 *Bellinger v Bellinger* [2003] UKHL 21.
91 *R (P and Q) v Secretary of State for the Home Department* [2001] EWCA Civ 1151.

3 High points and low points in the first ten years
A view from the Bench[1]

Brenda Hale

It is a somewhat weird experience to be speaking in a building which bears my name – most buildings are named after dead people and I do not think that I am quite dead yet! But of course it is a great pleasure to be here with you.

It was a privilege to be among the High Court judges sitting on the woolsack to hear the Queen's Speech at the opening of the new Parliament in 1997. There was great excitement at the announced plan to make the European Convention on Human Rights part of United Kingdom law. It was also a privilege to be among the Supreme Court Justices sitting behind the woolsack to hear the Queen's Speech at the opening of the new Parliament on 25 May 2010. There was some relief to hear that it is not instantly planned to repeal the Human Rights Act.

This is not to suggest that making life more interesting for the judges is an end in itself, although the Human Rights Act has certainly done that. But it has enabled a type of legal debate, both in and out of court, which could not have taken place before it was passed. It has enabled some very good things to be done, both in and out of court. But this conference is an opportunity to reflect upon some of the less good things which may also have resulted from the Act. It has undoubtedly enjoyed a very poor press. We, in the courts, have to ask ourselves whether this is simply because of (innocent or deliberate) misunderstanding or whether we are indeed getting some important things wrong.

There is undoubtedly room for more views than one about what has been good and what has been less good about the Act over the past ten years. So I asked the extremely bright young judicial assistants in the Supreme Court for their views on the high points and the low points. This was an instructive exercise. They were all human rights enthusiasts but they did not always agree on what was high and what was low: some thought, for example, that the Law Lords' decision in the *Marper* case,[2] about the retention of fingerprints and DNA samples and profiles, was a low point – presumably because the United

---

1 This chapter is based on the paper presented at the June 2010 Human Rights conference held in the Lady Hale Building at the University of Salford.
2 *R (S) v Chief Constable of South Yorkshire* [2004] UKHL 39, [2004] 1 WLR 2196.

Kingdom lost in Strasbourg;[3] but one thought that it was a high point – presumably because he thought that the United Kingdom had got this one right and Strasbourg had got it wrong. Rape victims and people wrongly suspected of rape would surely prefer our approach, although real rapists would surely prefer the approach in Strasbourg.

It is not only that one can have two views on a particular case. More fundamentally, it is that we are still working through many of the questions of constitutional principle which have emerged since the Act came into force. These have to do with the relations between the courts and the other branches of government and between the United Kingdom and Strasbourg. So I have picked out a few themes to illustrate these. Because this session is headed 'personal biography' I have concentrated not only on cases with which I have personally been involved, but also on cases with a 'family' theme. It is remarkable how many of these we have had.

For example, 2008 saw a whole series of House of Lords cases about migration and family rights. *Baiai*[4] was about the immigration-control-motivated restrictions on the right to marry which is protected by Art. 12; the House of Lords found them to be discriminatory and disproportionate. *Beoku-Betts*[5] and *Chikwamba*[6] were about the impact of immigration decisions on the right to respect for family life which is protected by Art. 8 – should the impact on other family members be taken into account when considering the impact upon the particular claimant? The House of Lords held that it should. Families are greater than the sum of their constituent parts. These can be seen as very positive developments in immigration law, but they have undoubtedly made the task of immigration control even more complicated.

But it is also remarkable that some of the most important constitutional issues raised by the Human Rights Act have been explored in the context of family and migration cases rather than in the politically more visible context of terrorism.

The role of the courts

When the Human Rights Act was passed, public lawyers assumed that it would be their playground. They were mainly correct, although criminal and family lawyers have also been heavily involved. But they also assumed that the usual remedy would be judicial review. So what was the role of the court? Was

---

3 *S v United Kingdom* (2009) 48 EHRR 50.
4 *R (Baiai) v Secretary of State for the Home Department* [2008] UKHL 53, [2009] 1 AC 287.
5 *Beoku-Betts v Secretary of State for the Home Department* [2008] UKHL 39, [2009] 1 AC 115.
6 *Chikwamba v Secretary of State for the Home Department* [2008] UKHL 40, [2008] 1 WLR 1420.

it simply to review for legality and rationality – albeit with 'heightened scrutiny' in a human rights context[7] – what the administrative decision-makers had done? Or was it to decide whether – as a matter of fact and substance – what they had done was incompatible with the individual's Convention rights?

In *Mahmood*,[8] the Court of Appeal held that it was the first of these. Heightened scrutiny *Wednesbury* would 'in broad terms and in most instances suffice'. Further, the 'Human Rights Act does not authorise the judges to stand in the shoes of Parliament's delegates, who are decision-makers given their responsibilities by the democratic arm of the state.'[9] There was some support for this approach in the speech of Lord Steyn in *Daly*.[10] *Daly* is rightly regarded by the Supreme Court judicial assistants as one of the high spots, because it emphasised the differences between 'heightened scrutiny *Wednesbury*' and proportionality in human rights adjudication. But Lord Steyn went on to say that it was still not a review of the merits of an administrative action or decision.

This begs the whole question. What does it mean for s 6(1) of the Human Rights Act to say that it is unlawful for public authority to act in a way which is incompatible with a Convention right? Does it mean that they must not do it? And who decides whether or not they have done it? The idea that this is not for the courts to decide is questionable enough where the primary decision-maker is a public authority – if a policeman acts incompatibly with a Convention right, we do not say that he is the person charged by Parliament with arresting people so the courts cannot decide whether he has acted unlawfully. But the idea that it is not for the courts to decide is obviously wrong, when the primary decision-maker is a court or tribunal – as it quite clearly is under the immigration appellate structure. The tribunal is expressly charged with deciding whether the decision is compatible with the Convention rights.

It was finally established in *Huang and Kashmiri*[11] that it is for tribunals and courts to make their own judgment – not simply to review the judgment made by the executive. It was also held that there is no presumption that the immigration rules strike the right balance between family life and immigration control, so that any case falling outside the rules had to be exceptional for breach of Convention rights to be established.

I am not sure *Huang and Kashmiri* is the end of the story – we may still get cases where the courts are reluctant to decide whether there was in fact a breach of the Convention if statute provides that the primary decision-

---

7 *R v Ministry of Defence, ex parte Smith* [1996] QB 517.
8 *R (Mahmood) v Secretary of State for the Home Department* [2001] 1 WLR 840.
9 Ibid., paras 30 and 33 respectively.
10 *R (Daly) v Secretary of State for the Home Department* [2001] UKHL 26, [2001] 2 AC 532.
11 *Huang v Secretary of State for the Home Department; Kashmiri v Same* [2007] UKHL 11, [2007] 2 AC 167.

maker is an executive agency. Not everyone may agree with my observations, in the entertaining *Miss Behavin'* case,[12] that it is always for the court to decide whether or not a person's Convention rights have been infringed. It may be instructive that *Huang and Kashmiri* did not feature in the Judicial Assistants' list at all. Does that mean that to them it is not as significant as I think it is?

'No more and no less'

Immigration was also the context for Lord Bingham's famous observation in *Ullah*,[13] that 'the duty of national courts is to keep pace with the Strasbourg jurisprudence as it evolves over time: no more, but certainly no less'. Lord Brown later said in *Al-Skeini*[14] that this could just as well have been 'no less, but certainly no more'. I have associated myself with them both, not only at the time but also in later cases.

But this is a problem. There are several well-known arguments against such caution –

(i) Human Rights Act rights are rights existing in United Kingdom law and protected by United Kingdom courts,[15] not rights existing in European Law and protected by the European Court of Human Rights.

(ii) Section 2 of the Act only requires us to 'have regard' to the European case law, not slavishly to follow it.

(iii) There are indications in the Parliamentary history that Parliament did not intend us to hold back just because Strasbourg had not yet arrived. Ironically, this includes Lord Bingham, as Lord Chief Justice, quoting Milton's *Areopagitica* to the House of Lords: 'Let not England forget her precedence of teaching nations how to live.'[16]

(iv) The stated reason for restraint[17] does not make much sense – that the interpretation of the Convention should be uniform throughout the Member States. We cannot commit other Member States or the European Court of Human Rights to our interpretation of the rights – so why should they mind what we do, as long as we do at least keep pace with the rights as they develop over time?

---

12 *Belfast City Council v Miss Behavin' Ltd.* [2007] UKHL 19, [2007] 1 WLR 1420, para 31; see also *R (SB) v Governors of Denbigh High School* [2007] UKHL 15, [2007] 1 AC 100.
13 *R (Ullah) v Special Adjudicator* [2004] UKHL 26, [2004] 2 AC 323, para 20.
14 *R (Al-Skeini) v Ministry of Defence* [2007] UKHL 26, [2008] 1 AC 153, para 106.
15 *Re McKerr* [2004] UKHL 12, [2002] 1 WLR 807.
16 *Hansard (HL Debates)*, 3 November 1997, col. 1245.
17 In *Ullah, loc. cit.*, but also in *Brown v Stott* [2003] 1 AC 681.

But in fact the question is more complicated than that. Willingness to leap depends upon the type of question being asked. There are at least three cases in which the Law Lords have consciously leapt ahead of Strasbourg. All three were regarded as high points by the Supreme Court judicial assistants. What can we learn from them?

First was *Limbuela.*[18] Deliberately reducing certain asylum seekers to destitution was held to be inhuman and degrading treatment contrary to Art. 3. They could not get any support from the State, nor could they work to support themselves, so if they could not find support from family or charity, they would be forced to live and beg on the streets, which is also unlawful. This has been seen as implying some minimum socio-economic rights into Art. 3. I am not sure that it is, because the breach might have been cured by allowing the asylum seekers to work to support themselves. But it is interesting that a senior Strasbourg judge who has so described it was quite relaxed about our leaping ahead of them.

Second was the adoption case of *Re G*,[19] again regarded as a high point by our judicial assistants. The Law Lords struck down a provision of the Northern Ireland Adoption Order, which counts as secondary, not primary, legislation for the purpose of the Human Rights Act. This discriminated against unmarried couples by not allowing them to adopt jointly, even if this would be in the best interests of the child involved, and even though one of them could adopt alone. As Lord Hoffmann put it, this blanket ban was based on the fallacy that 'a reasonable generalisation can be turned into an irrebuttable presumption for individual cases'.[20] Strasbourg has not yet decided that married and unmarried couples can be equated for this purpose. Three of the Law Lords thought that it would soon do so – although this was based on cases about sole adoption by gay or lesbian applicants, so two of us were not so sure that it would. But the facts were clearly 'within the ambit of Article 8', thus engaging the Art. 14 right not to be discriminated against in the enjoyment of those rights; not being married was a status within the meaning of Art. 14; so the issue was whether the discrimination could be justified. If Strasbourg would not find against the United Kingdom, it would be because this was regarded as being within our margin of appreciation. *Ullah* was not concerned with something within the margin of appreciation. If something is within the margin, it is for the national authorities to decide what suits us best. So we were not (quite) leaping ahead of Strasbourg in deciding that an apparent breach of Convention rights could not be justified.

But in this instance, was it for the court to decide this or should we leave it to Parliament (in this case the Northern Ireland Assembly)? Strasbourg is

18 *R (Limbuela) v Secretary of State for the Home Department* [2005] UKHL 66, [2006] 1 AC 396.
19 *Re G (Adoption: Unmarried Couple)* [2008] UKHL 38, [2009] 1 AC 173.
20 Paragraph 20.

supremely indifferent to this internal question. It is concerned only with whether the United Kingdom as a State has violated a person's Convention rights. Four out of five of us thought that the courts had a particular responsibility to guard against unjustified discrimination: protecting minorities, even unpopular minorities, against the prejudices of the majority is what human rights are all about. The legislature was free to decide upon issues of social policy but not to discriminate on irrational grounds.

Third was *EM (Lebanon)*,[21] also on the judicial assistants' list. This was definitely in the same territory as *Ullah*. The question was whether it would be a breach by the United Kingdom government to expel a mother and child to another country, where their Art. 8 rights would inevitably be breached. Strasbourg has long been firm that Member States must not expel a person to a place where there is a real risk of torture, however good the reasons for wanting to expel him.[22] Strasbourg has acknowledged that the same could apply to the flagrant denial of fair trial rights in a foreign country.[23] It has declined to rule out the possibility for flagrant denial of other rights, including qualified rights such as freedom of religion and belief, protected by Art. 9 (with which *Ullah* was concerned), or the right to respect for private and family life, protected by Art. 8 (with which *EM (Lebanon)* was concerned), but it has never actually so held.[24] One difficulty is that the courts in the expelling country cannot assess the strength and proportionality of the justification in the receiving country. So it has to be clear that the feared interference could never be justified. Here the Law Lords thought that the automatic separation of mother and child could never be justified – the male Law Lords being more concerned with the mother's rights and the female being more concerned with the child's.

The case is as interesting for what was not said, as it is for what was. The reason why mother and child would automatically be separated on return was substantive sex discrimination, but the Law Lords did not want to base their decision on this as opposed to the extreme facts of the case. The father and mother had separated before the child's birth because of the father's serious violence. The child had never seen his father and had lived with his mother all his life. Theirs was the only family life he had ever known. But under Lebanese Muslim law his father or his father's family would have the absolute right to bring up the child and the mother might be reduced to short supervised visits.

Is there a pattern to these examples? If it is likely that the claimant will win in Strasbourg, the courts are more likely to anticipate the predicted outcome even though it has not yet happened. If it is clear that the claimant will lose,

---

21 *EM (Lebanon) v Secretary of State for the Home Department* [2008] UKHL 64, [2009] 1 AC 1198.
22 *Chahal v United Kingdom* (1996) 23 EHRR 413.
23 *Mamatkulov and Askarov v Turkey* (2005) 41 EHRR 494, GC.
24 *Bensaid v United Kingdom* (2001) 33 EHRR 205.

the courts are unlikely to leap ahead. But if the decision is within the State's margin of appreciation the question becomes, not our relations with Strasbourg, but our relations with Parliament.

We are likely to give great weight to a recent Parliamentary verdict on how to strike the balance between competing Convention rights or on the justification for interference with qualified rights – restrictions on political advertising[25] and the ban on hunting with dogs[26] being the two most prominent examples. But it may be different if the legislation was some time ago and passed without reference to the Convention rights – as in *Re G*. Even if it was some time ago, the legislation may have been going with the grain of human rights developments rather than against it – banning corporal punishment in all schools being good example.[27]

I was initially attracted by the idea that there was a distinction between developing the common law and challenging the will of Parliament – that the courts could get ahead of Strasbourg in developing the common law but should not tell Parliament that it was wrong unless it was clear that Strasbourg would require us to do so.[28] That is still attractive constitutionally. But in the Human Rights Act 'the Convention rights' cannot mean different things depending upon whether we are developing the common law, controlling the executive or interpreting the will of Parliament. So I think that we shall continue to strive to reconcile respect for human rights with respect for Parliament.

Interpreting legislation

Respect for Parliament brings me to the power and the duty, in s 3(1) of the Act, to interpret and apply legislation compatibly with the Convention rights if we can. Here again there are some highs and some lows. The high point – although surprisingly not on the judicial assistants' list at all – was *Ghaidan v Godin-Mendoza*,[29] where the House of Lords held that Parliament had intended interpretation under s 3(1) to be the primary cure for incompatible legislation and a declaration of incompatibility under s 4 a last resort. The Court of Appeal anticipated that Strasbourg would hold it unjustifiable to discriminate between opposite and same-sex unmarried

25 *R (Animal Defenders International) v Secretary of State for Culture, Media and Sport* [2008] UKHL 15, [2008] 1 AC 1312. As far as I know, this case has not been taken to Strasbourg.
26 *R (Countryside Alliance) v Attorney General* [2007] UKHL 52, [2008] 1 AC 719. The decision was upheld in Strasbourg: *Friend v United Kingdom* (2010) 50 EHRR SE6.
27 *R (Williamson) v Secretary of State for Education and Employment* [2005] UKHL 10, [2005] 2 AC 246.
28 *DS v HM Advocate* [2007] UKPC D1, 2007 SC (PC) 1, para 92.
29 [2004] UKHL 30, [2004] 2 AC 557.

couples in the right to succeed to a rented family home. In between the Court of Appeal and House of Lords' decisions, the European Court of Human Rights decided *Karner v Austria*[30] just as the Court of Appeal had predicted. The House of Lords had no difficulty in agreeing with the Court of Appeal on the substantive issue. Most of the Law Lords also had no difficulty in interpreting 'living with each other as husband and wife' so as to include same-sex relationships. It was easily within what could be done with the language, unless you considered that only a man and a woman could live together like a 'husband' and 'wife'.

More dramatic was the control order case of *MB*,[31] when the Law Lords inserted words into the Prevention of Terrorism Act 2005 in order to produce a Convention-compliant interpretation, which was the exact opposite of what Parliament had in fact intended – that is, that a control order could not be confirmed if a fair trial could not be had without disclosure of the secret material; it was still up to the Home Secretary to decide whether or not to disclose, but if he or she failed to do so they would also fail to get the order. It is a remarkable testimony to how things have changed, because of the Human Rights Act, that when the problem came back to the House of Lords in the case of *AF*,[32] the Home Secretary accepted this and did not argue that the Lords' previous interpretation was wrong – despite considerable encouragement from at least one of the Law Lords to ask us to make a declaration of incompatibility instead.[33]

On the other hand, one of my personal low points in the interpretation stakes was the child abuse case of *Re S*.[34] In the Court of Appeal[35] we had tried to say that the Children Act 1989 should be 'read and given effect' under s 3(1) in such a way that the Convention rights of both parents and children were not infringed as result of the local authority's failure to comply with the care plans, which had been approved by the family court in care proceedings. The Law Lords held that we had sinned in two ways: in principle, because s 3 could not be used to contradict a 'cardinal principle' of the legislation – in this case that once a care order was made, the local authority were in charge of its implementation; and technically, because we had failed to identify a particular provision of the 1989 Act which ought to be read in a different way. But we had had in mind not that the Act should be read in a particular way, but that the power to make care orders should be

---

30 [2003] 2 FLR 623.
31 *Secretary of State for the Home Department v MB* [2007] UKHL 46, [2008] 1 AC 440.
32 *Secretary of State for the Home Department v AF (No 3)* [2009] UKHL 28, [2010] 2 AC 269.
33 Ibid. See Lord Scott at para 95.
34 *Re S (Children) (Care Order: Implementation of Care Plan)* [2002] UKHL 10, [2002] 2 AC 291.
35 *Re W and B (Children)* [2001] EWCA Civ 757, [2001] 2 FLR 582.

'given effect' in a particular way – by identifying which parts of the care plan were so crucial to compliance with the Convention rights of the parents or the child that any departure should be brought back to court for explanation. This would have involved reading rather a lot of words into s 31(1)(a) of the Children Act 1989, but if we had realised that it was required we would have done so.

So it seems that if Parliament fails to mention something at all, the courts cannot fill the gaping hole by saying how what Parliament *has* said should be put into practice; whereas if Parliament does say something quite clear and precise which the court thinks incompatible with Convention rights, the court can find a different meaning for it in order to avoid the incompatibility. I wonder whether this is in fact what Parliament intended when enacting s 3(1).

Functions of a public nature

I cannot resist concluding with my own lowest point of all – the majority decision in *YL v Birmingham City Council*.[36] The majority held that it was not a 'function of a public nature' to accommodate an old person in a private care home at public expense under arrangements made with the local social services authority acting under the statutory powers in s 21(1) of the National Assistance Act 1948. This meant that the care home was not a 'public authority' obliged to act compatibly with the Convention rights in this respect. Lord Bingham and I disagreed. The Supreme Court judicial assistants all strongly agreed that this was a low point.

The government had intervened to support the claimant's case but to no avail. The actual decision was rapidly reversed by statute.[37] But the problem remains. When more and more public functions are being outsourced to the private and voluntary sectors, what are the criteria for deciding whether or not theirs is a 'function of a public nature'? Is there anything which is essentially public rather than private? Is coercion the key – so that privatised prisons and psychiatric institutions admitting compulsory patients are still performing functions of a public nature, whereas privatised care homes and medical facilities are not, even if they are paid for through public expenditure? I am still old-fashioned enough to think that the health and social services remain core functions of government, even if outsourced to other bodies.

Conclusion

There have been some notable individual advances because of the Act. It would be good if we could celebrate these, rather than worry about the underlying

---

36 [2007] UKHL 27, [2008] 1 AC 95.
37 Health and Social Care Act 2008, s 145.

constitutional problems of implementation with which I have been concerned in this chapter. It seems a shame that an Act, which appeared to be so clearly drafted and was trying to do such an important but radical thing, has given rise to so many difficult constitutional issues on which we have had to spend so much of our time. Maybe the previous mindset of the practitioners and the courts is more to blame than Parliament and the Parliamentary draftsmen. But there are difficult questions in the relationship between Parliament and the courts and between both of us and Strasbourg. We have still not heard the last word on most of them. I look forward to finding some solutions in the next ten years of the Human Rights Act.

Section 2

Confronting the Human Rights Act as a legal model

4 Human rights protection in Australia

The Commonwealth's odd one out?

Michael Kirby

Dicey's imperial gift

Dicey's constitutional legacy

In the long history of Britain and its laws, there have been a number of general statutes or charters concerning basic rights.[1] However, there had never been anything quite like the Human Rights Act 1998 (UK) ('HRA 1998').[2] That Act represented a shift from what had generally been an approach of scepticism, and even hostility, towards a comprehensive list of enumerated rights. Such an approach was seen as incompatible with two fundamental tenets of the English legal system. These were that the rights (and obligations) of individuals were such as were declared by the sovereign parliament or by the judges in ways not inconsistent with parliamentary law. And that the rights of subjects were unlimited, except to the extent that parliamentary or judge-made laws imposed obligations that restricted the individual's freedom of action.

Those raised in this tradition entertained great confidence in the elected parliament to uphold the traditional rights of the individual. This was true, long before parliaments were elected with a real democratic composition, i.e., well before half the adult population (women) were admitted to the franchise.

The idea of a 'sovereign' parliament – as contrasted to the idea of a sovereign monarch – won many adherents in Britain as a consequence of the two revolutions against the Stuart kings, Charles I[3] and James II.[4] For all of its

---

1 For example, Magna Carta 1215; Habeas Corpus Act 1679 (GB), the Bill of Rights of 1689 (GB); Parliament Act 1911 (UK); and the Statute of Westminster 1931 (UK).
2 The Human Rights Act 1998 (UK) ('HRA 1998') was brought into force on 2 October 2000. See HRA 1998, s 22: A. Lester, D. Pannick and J. Herberg, *Human Rights Law and Practice*, 3rd edn, London: LexisNexis, 2009, (hereafter 'Lester et al.'), p. 15 [146], pp. 101–2 [2.22.1]–[2.22.2].
3 M.D. Kirby, 'Trial of King Charles I: Defining Moment for our Constitutional Liberties', (1999) 73 *Australian Law Journal* 577.
4 Steve Pincus, *The First Modern Revolution*, New Haven: Yale University Press, 2009.

defects, even before the reforms of the nineteenth and twentieth centuries, the Parliament at Westminster was generally careful to respect the traditional rights of the subjects.

It was in this context that, in 1885, A.V. Dicey wrote his influential *Introduction to the Study of the Law of the Constitution*.[5] The whole of Part I of that text was devoted to 'The sovereignty of Parliament'. Whilst Dicey recognised the need for modification of his theory in the case of federal constitutions[6] and for the legislatures of what he called 'non-sovereign law-making bodies' (which included railways corporations, local authorities and the then dominion parliaments within the British Empire),[7] he asserted that (as he put it) 'Englishmen [*sic*] . . . have been . . . accustomed to live under the rule of a supreme legislature . . . [T]he sovereignty of Parliament [is] a salient feature of the English constitution, [and there are] far-reaching effects of this marked peculiarity in our institutions.'[8] The 'Queen in Parliament' was 'absolutely sovereign'. It was this entity alone that had 'the right to make or unmake any law whatever; and, further . . . no person or body is recognised . . . as having a right to override or set aside the legislation of Parliament'.[9]

Throughout the British Empire these principles were taught to law students who later became advocates and judges. The notion that there were universal human rights that Parliament could not override or alter was regarded as heretical. The idea that some such rights inhered in human beings because of their humanness was considered incompatible with the sovereignty of Parliament, as Dicey explained it. It was generally seen as an idea based on natural law concepts that English lawyers attributed to legal doctrines propounded by Europeans, influenced as they were by the natural law teachings of the Roman Catholic Church.[10] Such notions were regarded as alien to the powers and responsibilities of representative parliaments which were the special political heritage of British subjects, together with the pragmatic common law system administered in the courts by independent judges.

In 1960, Dicey's text was an obligatory part of my law school curriculum. A few attentive students of those days might have read the editorial annotation that confessed to the embarrassment of later readers about Dicey's unflattering classification of colonial and post-colonial legislatures in the British dominions beyond the seas, including Australia:[11]

---

5   A.V. Dicey, *Introduction to the Study of the Law of the Constitution*, 1885, 10th edn, London: Macmillan, 1959.

6   Ibid., 'Parliamentary Sovereignty and Federalism'; Part I, Chapter III, p. 138.

7   Ibid., p. 104.

8   Ibid., p. 87.

9   Ibid., pp. 39–40.

10 M.D. Kirby, 'Law Reform, Human Rights and Modern Governance: Australia's Debt to Lord Scarman' (2006) 80 *Australian Law Journal* 299 at 310.

11 See editors' note in Dicey, above note 5, 86.

The reader will not be misled by the examples of non-sovereign law-making bodies which the author uses by way of contrast with a Sovereign Parliament. What he wrote originally in 1885 of the Legislative Council of British India was, of course, obsolete long before India attained independent statehood in 1947. He chose New Zealand as an example of an English colony with representative and responsible government. What follows . . . is only true today of one or two colonies on their way to independence. Paradoxically, New Zealand is the best example within the Commonwealth of a state which has reproduced the purely Dicey doctrine in its entirety, for she has a Parliament which can change any and every law, albeit a uni-cameral legislature.

Even Australian lawyers of 1960 generally thought their own legislatures provisional. Their statutes were subject to any statutory provisions enacted by the Imperial Parliament and extended to it. This was truly the mark of its genuine sovereignty. Its laws were absolute wherever the Union Jack still flew.

The American revolution

The description of parliaments in the Commonwealth of Nations as 'sovereign' is still common and quite popular. Yet even before the current age, there were developments that cast doubts upon the accuracy of Dicey's idea.

In their uprising against the British Crown, the American colonists asserted that they enjoyed fundamental rights to 'life, liberty and the pursuit of happiness'.[12] To a large extent, the American Revolution of 1776 arose from a belief on the part of those colonists that they were being denied in the American settlements the basic rights which British subjects enjoyed at home: not to be taxed except by an elected Parliament; not to be intruded upon in their homes except by authority of a judicial warrant; and not to be subjected to military impositions alien to the fundamental rights of Englishmen. Sir William Blackstone had explained those rights at about the same time.[13] Because the American Revolution of 1776 coincided with (and was partly sustained by) the French Revolution of 1789, the infection of notions of fundamental rights spread to the Americas from Europe, and later far beyond.

Even before 1776, several of the American colonial legislatures had adopted charters of rights, or had enacted legislation which expressed the basic entitlements of the individual, as recognised by the common law. The Constitution of the United States, as originally adopted, did not contain a Bill of Rights.

12 The United States Declaration of Independence. See L. Pfeffer, *The Liberties of an American*, Boston: Beacon Press, 1956 (1963 reprint), pp. 1–8.
13 W. Prest, *William Blackstone: Law and Letters in the 18th Century*, New York: Oxford University Press, 2008.

The proposal that one should be added proved controversial. Initially, it was vigorously resisted by the founding fathers from Virginia. They believed that a Bill of Rights was unnecessary because the new states had their own such charters; the new Constitution created a republic founded on popular sovereignty judged unlikely to abuse its powers; and the federal legislature enjoyed only limited and enumerated rights, obviating the need for a national charter.[14] Reflecting these attitudes, as if part of the English DNA, James Madison, when asked to prepare a draft of the basic rights of Americans, demanded to know who would be so bold as to declare the rights of the people? Yet the first ten amendments to the United States Constitution constituted the model that was to become highly influential in the later development of both national and transnational law.

That model was not at first followed by the emerging British possessions as the Empire evolved into the Commonwealth of Nations. None of the early independence constitutions of Canada (1867), Australia (1901), South Africa (1909), New Zealand (1910) or India (1935) contained an equivalent to the United States Bill of Rights. It was only in the later constitutions of Ireland, India and then the non-settler dominions granted full independence after 1950, that the lawmakers began to enact entrenched human rights provisions, copying the American idea.

At the same time as this post-war legal revolution was occurring in the English-speaking nations, an even greater change was happening in the wider world. During the Second World War, when the leaders of the United States and Britain met to define the Allied war aims in relation to the Axis powers, they included a commitment to the protection of basic rights. Nothing less would have been acceptable, given the influence of United States thinking on the shape of post-war institutions and the widespread evidence of gross oppression and cruelty that emerged about the governmental regimes of their wartime-adversaries.

The commitment to fundamental human rights was reinforced after the war in the Charter of the United Nations (1945)[15] and in the Universal Declaration of Human Rights (1948).[16] The Declaration (UDHR) did much to capture the imagination of people in many lands. It propounded the novel notion that stable conditions of international peace and security could only be achieved by

---

14 H.J. Abraham, 'Bill of Rights' in K.L. Hall, *The Oxford Companion to the Supreme Court of the United States*, New York: Oxford University Press, 1993, p. 52.

15 *Charter of the United Nations* (Preamble 2) 'To re-affirm faith in fundamental human rights, in the dignity and worth of the human person, in the equal rights of men and women and of nations large and small.' See also Art. 1.3 and Art. 55(c). The Charter is contained in F.F. Martin et al. (eds), *International Human Rights Law and Practice: Cases, Treaties and Materials (Documentary Supplement)*, The Hague: Kluwer, 1997, p. 5.

16 Adopted 10 December 1948, GA Res 217A(III), UNDoc A/810 at 71 (1948). See Martin et al., pp. 32ff.

respect for universal rights that were taught to citizens, respected by the powerful and enforced, where necessary, by national and international law.

The Indian Constitution

One by one, the former British dominions and possessions abandoned, or softened, their hostility to human rights charters. The Republic of Ireland was first (1937 and 1948). The Indian Constitution (1950) followed with a substantial chapter (Part III) titled 'Fundamental Rights'. That chapter was divided into sections dealing with the 'right to equality' (Arts 14–18); 'right to freedom' (Arts 19–22); 'right against exploitation' (Arts 23–24); 'right to freedom of religion' (Arts 25–28); 'cultural and educational rights' (Arts 29–30); and 'right to constitutional remedies' (Arts 32–35). In addition, the Indian Constitution contained, in Part II, a substantial section dealing with 'Citizenship' (Arts 5–11). An important section (Part IV) contained 'Directive principles of state policy'. This was copied, in part, from the Irish Constitution of 1937 (Arts 36–51); and later a new section (Part IV-A) was added containing 'fundamental duties'.[17] These provisions were to influence greatly the independence constitutions of the many other countries within the Commonwealth of Nations which gained their freedom in the decades that followed.

The Canadian Charter

In 1960, the Canadian Parliament enacted the Canadian Bill of Rights Act (Can). This was non-constitutional legislation. It set out a list of basic rights as declared by Canada's national legislature. The Act was narrowly interpreted by the courts, basically because it enjoyed no special constitutional provenance.[18] However, in 1982, the Queen, as Queen of Canada, signed into law the Canadian Charter of Rights and Freedoms (the Canadian Charter). This was entrenched as the first part of the Constitution Act 1982 (Can). It provides specified political rights to Canadian citizens and civil rights to all persons in Canada in respect of the actions of government. The Canadian Charter expanded judicial review in Canada and greatly enhanced the role of the courts, especially the Supreme Court. Apart from the political rights of citizens (ss 3–6), there were a number of legal rights (ss 7–14) (including the right to life, liberty and security of the person etc.); equality rights (s 15); and language rights (ss 16–23).

An important innovation of the Canadian Charter was the 'notwithstanding' clause (s 33). This permitted derogations from Charter rights in certain cases

17 H.M. Seervai, *Constitutional Law of India*, 4th edn, Mumbai: Tripathi, 1996, ch.VII–X, vol. 1, pp. 349ff.
18 *Attorney-General of Canada v Lavell* [1974] SCR 1349; cf. *The Queen v Drybones* [1970] SCR 282.

and by specified means. This provision has been invoked by some of the Provinces; but it can only apply to matters that fall within provincial constitutional powers.[19] An important contributor to the Canadian move towards the protection of universal rights was Professor John Humphrey of McGill University.[20] In the 1980s, he was my colleague in the International Commission of Jurists. In 1948, he had led the secretariat of the United Nations working on the UDHR. The Canadian Charter gained widespread popular support. No fewer than 82 per cent of Canadians consulted in 1987 and 1999 expressed the view that the Charter was a beneficial development for Canadian constitutionalism.[21]

The New Zealand Bill of Rights Act

In 1990, the New Zealand Parliament enacted the New Zealand Bill of Rights Act 1990 (NZ). That law was in some ways similar in concept to the statutory enactment in Canada that had preceded the Canadian Charter. The New Zealand Act was designed to protect a number of fundamental rights and liberties from encroachment by government.[22] The Act subjects the three branches of national government (and bodies performing public functions) to judicial review. It obliges the courts, when interpreting and applying other laws, to do so in a way consistent with the Act's provisions. Although it is not expressed in the form of a higher law (nor formally entrenched by popular vote in the law of New Zealand), it has opened up to judicial review a wide range of public actions and the exercise of statutory discretions that were earlier effectively immune. It protects a long list of civil and political rights. It was later supplemented by the Human Rights Act 1993 (NZ). This defines a number of grounds of discrimination that are outlawed in both in the public and private sectors in New Zealand.[23]

The political circumstances that led to the enactment of the New Zealand Bill of Rights Act reportedly included a feeling that the Conservative Government of Sir Robert Muldoon in the 1980s had been 'constitutionally high-handed and repressive'. In particular, strong feelings were engendered in the aftermath of the South African Springbok rugby tour of New Zealand in

19 Thus a law of Alberta, purporting to limit the definition of 'marriage' to opposite sex couples, was of no effect because the legal definition is contained in a Canadian federal law. See *Marriage Act* RSA 2000 C-M–5.

20 J.P. Humphrey, *Human Rights and the United Nations: A Great Adventure*, New York: Transnational, 1984.

21 P. Saunders 'The Charter at 20', *CBC News Online*, 8 April 2002.

22 G. Palmer and M. Palmer, *Bridled Power: New Zealand and Government Under MMP*, Auckland: Oxford University Press, 3rd edn, 1997, p. 264.

23 Supplementing the earlier Human Rights Act 1977 (NZ). See Palmer and Palmer, *Bridled Power*, p. 265.

1981 and in the response of authority to civic protests that took place during that tour.[24] As Sir Geoffrey Palmer (a Labour Prime Minister of New Zealand) observed: 'Although Labour MPs showed no great enthusiasm for the concept then or later, there was a political market for it.'[25]

Perhaps the greatest impact of the New Zealand legislation arose because s 6 of the Act of 1990 contained provisions later to prove influential on the form of s 3 of the HRA 1998. The New Zealand provision states:

> 6. Whenever an enactment can be given a meaning that is consistent with the rights and freedoms contained in this Bill of Rights, that meaning shall be preferred to any other meaning.[26]

Led by Sir Robin Cooke (later Lord Cooke of Thorndon), the New Zealand Court of Appeal, in a series of decisions, gave effect to the Bill of Rights Act by interpreting statutes in ways protective of liberty. This was done, for example, by re-fashioning the previous immunity of the Crown for anything done in discharging, or executing the judicial process.[27]

On the other hand, the interpretative principle expressed in s 6 of the 1990 Act has not always afforded relief to those claiming a breach of their fundamental rights. Thus in *Quilter v Attorney-General (NZ)*,[28] the New Zealand Court of Appeal rejected alternative arguments advanced by a lesbian couple who submitted that the Marriage Act of New Zealand should be construed, in accordance with s 6, so as to require a marriage registrar to record their 'marriage'. If this argument were rejected, the applicants asked the Court to accept their submission that the law discriminated against them so that it could be reconsidered by Parliament with a view to reform of the Act. Unanimously, the Court of Appeal held that the statute did not lend itself to the expansive reading which the applicants sought. Only one judge (Thomas J) concluded that, in denying the couple the right to marry, the legislation was discriminatory.[29] Which goes to show how rights thinking can quickly change.

The South African Constitution

Following the end of the apartheid regime, the South African Parliament enacted the Republic of South Africa Constitution Act 1993 (SAf) (the Interim

---

24 Ibid., p. 267.
25 Ibid.
26 Ibid., p. 273.
27 *Simpson v Attorney-General (NZ) (Baigent's Case)* [1994] 3 NZLR 667. See Palmer and Palmer, *Bridled Power*, p. 275.
28 [1998] 1 NZLR 523; [1998] 3 LRC 119 (NZCA).
29 Cf. M.D. Kirby, 'Same-Sex Relations', in M.D. Kirby, *Through the World's Eye*, Sydney: Fed Press, 2000, pp. 64–7. Contrast *Egan v Canada* [1995] 2 SCR 513; *M v H* [1999] SCR 23.

Constitution).[30] This contained a Bill of Rights designed to apply until Parliament, sitting as a constituent assembly, had drafted a Final Constitution. That process was completed with the enactment of the Constitution of the Republic of South Africa Act 1996 (SAf).[31] That measure likewise contained a Bill of Rights. Substantially, it was the same as in the Interim Constitution of 1993. However, there were a number of important differences. By s 8(1) of the Final Constitution, it is provided that the Bill of Rights applies to all levels of law and binds the legislature, the executive, the judiciary and all organs of state in South Africa. To the extent applicable, it also binds both natural and juristic persons.

Coming later in time, the new South African Bill of Rights contains a wider range of protected and required actions. This was itself a response to the apartheid era. Thus, specific mention is made forbidding derogations from human rights on the basis of sexual orientation. Certain economic and social rights are also expressly protected. These had earlier usually been excluded from such provisions on the basis that they were not legally justiciable.

Reading the later decisions of the South African Constitutional Court, the provisions of the Final Constitution, in particular, stand in marked contrast to the decisions of the Appellate Division in South Africa before the universal rights were protected. In *Sachs v Minister of Justice*,[32] the Appellate Division, then the highest court of South Africa, had said:

> Parliament may make any encroachment it chooses upon the life, liberty, or property of any individual subject to its sway . . . and it is the function of the courts of law to enforce its will.

This was the rule of law as it was then understood in South Africa. It was an understanding perfectly consistent with the writings of Dicey. Yet as Arthur Chaskalson, the former Chief Justice of the South African Constitutional Court, has remarked:

> The apartheid government, its officers and agents were held accountable in accordance with the laws. But the laws were unjust. They failed to protect fundamental rights such as freedom of assembly, and freedom of speech; instead they denied the franchise to blacks, institutionalised discrimination, denied equal education and job opportunities to black persons; made provision for forced removal of black communities from land which they owned and occupied; sharply curtailed freedom of political activity; and vested broad discretionary powers in the executive to enforce these policies. . . . In this setting the law served to reinforce the

---

30 Act 200 of 1993.
31 Act 108 of 1996.
32 1934 AD 11 at 37 per Stratford JA.

belief of whites in their racial superiority, and to that extent legitimised it within the white community . . . .[33]

United Kingdom Human Rights Act 1998

Against the background of these developments in countries whose legal systems were similar to, and largely derived from, that of Britain, the moves in the United Kingdom to adopt statutory provisions for the general protection of fundamental human rights were not surprising. More influential in this development than the steps taken in Commonwealth countries was the pressure exerted from Europe in the form of the European Convention on Human Rights, to which the United Kingdom became a party;[34] the increasing number of decisions of the European Court of Human Rights (several of them adverse to the United Kingdom);[35] the gradual use that was made by British courts of the European jurisprudence;[36] and the support that came to be voiced for 'bringing rights home', in the form of a local British statute.[37]

It is also appropriate to acknowledge the impetus provided by Lord Scarman's Hamlyn Lectures: *English Law – The New Dimension*[38] as well as the determined efforts of Anthony Lester QC (now Lord Lester of Herne Hill) in promoting legislation designed to incorporate the European Convention into the law of the United Kingdom.[39] Within the Commonwealth of Nations, Anthony Lester was equally energetic, helping to secure the adoption of the Bangalore Principles. In these, he promoted the role of judges in construing constitutional and statutory provisions and in resolving ambiguities in the common law by reference to universal principles of human rights.[40] These ideas were to have a considerable influence, which is continuing. Necessarily, common law techniques and individual judicial rulings were no substitute for the passage of a statute of fundamental rights enjoying democratic legitimacy.

In May 1997, the Labour Government of Tony Blair was elected to office in the United Kingdom. The new government was committed to the incorporation of the European Convention in the United Kingdom's domestic law. In pursuit of this commitment, in October 1997, it published a white paper

---

33 A. Chaskalson, 'How About A Bill of Rights', unpublished paper (Fitzgerald Lecture), Griffith University, Queensland, July 2009.

34 Lester et al. op. cit., pp. 4–9 [1.10]–[1.28].

35 Ibid, pp. 9–11 [1.29]–[1.31].

36 Ibid, pp. 11–12 [1.32]–[1.34].

37 Ibid, pp. 12–14 [1.35]–[1.40].

38 1976. See Lester et al., pp. 12–13 [1.35].

39 Lord Lester, 'First Steps Towards A Constitutional Bill of Rights' (1997) EHRLR 124. Cf. Lester et al. 13 [1.40].

40 The Bangalore Principles are set out in M.D. Kirby, 'The Role of the Judge in Advancing Human Rights By Reference to International Human Rights Norms', (1988) 62 *Australian Law Journal* 514 at 531–2.

proposing a Human Rights Act.[41] The proposal gained the support in Parliament of the Liberal Democrats, and several distinguished Conservative backbenchers, as well as many of the Law Lords speaking from the cross-benches. It was opposed at the time by the Front Bench of the Conservative Party[42] together with sections of the media in Britain.[43] Despite this division of opinion, the HRA 1998 was accepted by Parliament. It received the royal assent in November 1998. According to Lord Lester and his colleagues, in the third edition of their book *Human Rights Law and Practice*:

> Ten years later, the Human Rights Act 1998 is deeply embedded in the political and legal fabric of the UK. Its principles have been developed by the judiciary in a way that reflects British values. The courts and legal profession have done their best to ensure that effective legal remedies are provided for breaches of the Convention rights. . . . It is now well recognised that the HRA 1998 has exercised a magnetic force over the entire political and legal system and is of fundamental constitutional importance.[44]

Some of the uncertainty that might have attended the return of the Conservative Party to government in the British general election of May 2010 would seem to be lessened by the coalition which was then forged with the Liberal Democrats. For the immediate future, the central provisions of the HRA 1998 seem safe.

Resisting the magnetic force

Minding the gap

If the United Kingdom was influenced by the magnetic force of the European Convention of Human Rights and if the HRA 1998 incorporates the Convention principles in United Kingdom law, the power of the same forces has yet to be felt in Australia.

Such has been the fascination for English law and traditional English legal values that Australians, in the legal profession and elsewhere, have so far proved resistant to the siren calls for fundamental reforms or modifications.[45] So it has proved in successive endeavours in Australia to introduce national human

---

41 United Kingdom, *Rights Brought Home: The Human Rights Bill* (October 1997), Cm 3782.
42 House of Commons Debates (Hansard), 28 October 2002, 391 *HC Official Report*, Col. 605–49.
43 Lester et al., pp. 14–15 [1.44].
44 Lester et al, p. 15 [1.47].
45 See e.g. M.D. Kirby, 'Overcoming Equity's Australian Isolationism', (2009) 3 *Journal of Equity* 1.

rights legislation to fill the gap that had been felt by lawmakers in Ireland, India, Canada, New Zealand, South Africa and elsewhere during the previous half-century. Australia has adopted no such national law. At a time when Britain is celebrating the first decade of the HRA 1998, Australia is coming to terms with the Government's rejection, on 21 April 2010, of a proposal that it should introduce a law similar to that now operating in New Zealand and the United Kingdom. How has this reluctance played out? What have been the arguments that have prevailed? What are the prospects of change?

Constitutional resistance

When the Australian Constitution was being drafted by successive conventions comprising leading colonial citizens (mostly parliamentarians and all male), the United States Constitution was a common point of reference for their labours. In some respects, as in Chapter III of the Australian Constitution of 1901 which created the Australian Federal Judicature, the founders substantially followed the American precedent. However, they were still influenced by the traditional scepticism that then prevailed amongst English lawyers about incorporating expressly guaranteed rights.[46] Instead, the delegates preferred to rely on their British heritage.

At the Melbourne Constitutional Convention in 1898, when the proposal of A.I. Clark from Tasmania, for a clause to protect deprivation of 'life, liberty or property without due process of law' was debated, most of the delegates were dismissive:

> People would say – 'pretty things these states of Australia, they have to be prevented by a provision in the Constitution from doing the grossest injustice.'[47]

Clark's proposal was eventually rejected by 23 votes to 19. So was a provision, derived from the 14th Amendment to the United States Constitution, forbidding discrimination against people on the ground of their race. This was rejected on the basis that Australians 'are not going to have a civil war here over a racial question'. Perhaps that was so, given the hegemony of the 'white' or settler race in Australia. Isaac Isaacs, later Justice and Chief Justice of the High Court of Australia and subsequently the first locally born Governor-General, opposed the provision. He did so on the basis that it would cut down the legislative power, which he regarded as essential, to make laws with respect to the Chinese in Australia. It would, for example, override laws

---

46 G. Williams, *Human Rights under the Australian Constitution*, Oxford: Oxford University Press, 1999, p. 39, referring to the influence of A.V. Dicey (above note 5); and cf. J. Bryce, *The American Commonwealth*, vol. 1, London: Macmillan, 1888, p. 35.

47 Delegate Alexander Cockburn (former Premier of South Australia) quoted in Williams, *Human Rights*, p. 40.

forbidding 'Asiatic or African alien[s] getting a miner's right . . . on a gold-field'.[48] The result was that the constitutional proposal was rejected. The rejection of this type of constitutional provision was affirmed at the Adelaide session of the Convention in 1897–8.[49]

For three-quarters of the twentieth century, this approach to basic rights in Australia remained substantially unquestioned. Dicey reigned. Imperial pride dismissed any suggested need for constitutional restrictions on the elected parliament. Lesser beings and societies might need these. But not the Australian Commonwealth.

The flavour of the Australian judicial outlook in my youth can be secured by reading some of the earlier judicial opinions. In *Skelton v Collins*,[50] even so considerable a judge as Justice Windeyer wrote in the High Court of Australia:[51]

> Our ancestors brought the common law of England to this land. Its doctrines and principles are the inheritance of the British race, and as such they have become the common law of Australia.

Earlier, to like effect, Sir Owen Dixon had asked why 'should doubt be thrown on the wisdom and safety of entrusting to the chosen representatives of the people . . . all legislative power, substantially without fetter or restriction?'[52] This was thought to be the way British people did government. And, at that time, there was still much evidence to support that belief. Looking around the world, there was much self-satisfaction over the British Empire, and not a little racial superiority in the condemnation of alien ideas. The intellectual elite in Australia formed a bond with the political classes in dismissing the need for an Australian Bill of Rights. A very short list of fundamental rights found their way into the Australian federal Constitution.[53] Even some of these were then so strictly construed by the High Court of Australia as to make their provisions potentially worthless and ineffective.[54]

---

48 Quoted in Williams, *Human Rights*, p. 41.

49 Ibid., p. 43.

50 (1966) 115 CLR 94.

51 (1966) 115 CLR 94 at 134.

52 Quoted in Williams, *Human Rights*, note 45, p. 40.

53 Such as the protection against federal acquisitions of property except on 'just terms'. See *Australian Constitution*, s 51(xxxi). Cf. *Wurridjal v The Commonwealth* (2009) 237 CLR 309, at pp. 424–6 [303]–[309].

54 Such as the right in s 80 to trial by jury of indictable federal offences. It has been held (albeit with a stream of contrary opinions) that this provision in the Australian Constitution does not contain an implied restriction on legislative attempts to render the guarantee nugatory by defining 'indictable' crimes narrowly: see *The King v Archdall: Ex Parte Carrigan and Brown* (1928) 41 CLR 128 at 139–40; *Kingswell v The Queen* (1985) 159 CLR 264 at 276; cf. at 298 per Deane J; *Cheng v The Queen* (2000) 203 CLR 248 at 292; cf. at 306.

Attempts at legal protections

This attitude towards the legal protection of universal 'rights' survived in Australia for most of the twentieth century. In the 1970s and 80s, two attempts were made to introduce federal legislation for a statutory statement of universal human rights, based upon the provisions of the International Covenant on Civil and Political Rights (ICCPR), to which Australia was to become a party.[55] To provide the constitutional foundation for these Bills the external affairs power in the Constitution was invoked.[56] By that provision, the Federal Parliament is empowered to enact laws designed to give effect to Australia's international obligations under treaties that had been ratified by it.[57] Given the broad potential ambit of the proposed federal laws on rights, they proved highly controversial. They were strongly opposed by several of the states. This led to its being stalled in the Australian Senate. When their proponents (respectively Senator L.K. Murphy and Mr G.J. Evans) left politics, the idea of federal legislation for a national statute of universal rights based on the ICCPR moved to the back-burner.

In 1988, an attempt was made to introduce into the federal Constitution a series of guarantees to control state law-makers in ways equivalent to the provisions already appearing in the federal Constitution (trial by jury; religious freedom; just terms for acquisitions of property). However, even this seemingly innocuous provision was rejected at a constitutional referendum held in December 1984. It did not attract a majority in any of the states. The national vote on the proposal was 30.33 per cent of the electors for the amendment and 68.195 per cent against.[58] Securing amendment of the federal Constitution in Australia is notoriously difficult. In part, this is because of the double majority (of the people and of the states) required by s 128 of the Constitution.[59]

Following the federal referendum defeat in 1988, the spotlight for reform, in this respect, shifted to the sub-national jurisdictions of Australia, the states and territories. In 2001, an enquiry was conducted by the Standing Committee on Law and Justice of the New South Wales Parliament. It addressed a proposal that a Bill of Rights should be enacted for that state. The proposal was strongly opposed by the Labor Premier of the state (R.J. Carr). His opposition made its adoption unlikely. So it proved. The Committee acknowledged 'failures by NSW governments to address individual and at times systemic problems'. It agreed that 'the common law is not a sufficient

---

55 Human Rights Bill 1974 (Cth); Human Rights Bill 1984 (Cth).
56 *Australian Constitution*, s 51(xxix).
57 *Tasmania v The Commonwealth (Tasmanian Dam Case)* (1983) 158 CLR 1.
58 Results of the Constitutional Referendum appear in T. Blackshield and G. Williams, *Australian Constitutional Law and Theory*, 3rd edn, Sydney: Federation Press, 2003, p. 1308.
59 Since federation in 1901, there have been 44 proposals considered at referendum and only eight have succeeded. Blackshield and Williams, ibid., p. 1301.

protection of individual rights in the absence of legislative action'.[60] Nevertheless, the Committee did not support the enactment of a statutory Bill of Rights for the state.

Fear was expressed that the introduction of a State Bill of Rights in Australia could politicise the judiciary and, unlike in the past, make future judicial appointments dependent on the judges' political views rather than their legal skills. No satisfactory explanation was given as to how this defect had been avoided in the many other countries which had provided for bills of rights.

This acknowledged defect in the legal position in New South Wales was illustrated vividly in proceedings that came before the High Court of Australia challenging (and seeking to override) the effective 'confiscation' of miners' property without 'just terms' under a state law that lacked the protections required of federal legislation by the national Constitution.[61] Certain mining interests challenged directly the Diceyan theory as it applied to state Parliaments in Australia. The challenge failed. In my reasons, I concluded that the solutions to the complaints were political, not legal.[62] The limits of common law judicial inventiveness had been reached and could not be exceeded. No effective political remedy was available. An arguable injustice attracted no remedy.

Then, in two sub-national jurisdictions of Australia (the Australian Capital Territory[63] and the State of Victoria[64]) the legislature enacted laws similar to the HRA 1998 of the United Kingdom. These laws have attracted a number of cases in the courts. Necessarily, in their application these decisions are confined to the state or territory laws concerned. They do not apply to federal legislation or to federal governmental practices. Apart from the court cases, the obligations in the enactments to procure official certification of charter compliance have proved a useful mechanism for protection of basic rights in practice.

National consultation on rights

To meet the perceived defect in the resulting Australian position, in December 2008, following the election of a new federal Labor Government a year earlier,

60 NSW Parliament, Standing Committee on Law and Justice, Report No.16, *A NSW Bill of Rights* (October 2001), 110 [para 7.3].
61 *Durham Holdings Pty Ltd v State of New South Wales* (2001) 205 CLR 399.
62 (2001) 205 CLR 399 at 427–9 [60]–[66]. See also *Building Construction Employees and Builders' Labourers Federation of NSW v Minister for Industrial Relations* (1986) 7 NSWLR 372 at 404–5 (NSWCA).
63 Human Rights Act 2000 (ACT). See also Human Rights Act 2003 (ACT).
64 Charter of Human Rights and Responsibilities Act 2006 (Vic). A draft Human Rights Bill 2007 (WA) was produced but held over pending the national consultation. It has not proceeded. In 2011, following a change of state government in Victoria, the incoming non-Labor government referred to a parliamentary committee the suggested weaknesses of the State Charter. Reportedly, there is some doubt that the sole State Charter will survive.

the Federal Attorney-General (Robert McClelland), on the sixtieth anniversary of the adoption by the General Assembly of the UDHR, launched a 'national consultation' about the adequacy of Australia's legal recognition and protection of human rights and responsibilities.[65] The government appointed a committee chaired by Professor Frank Brennan (a Jesuit priest and law professor). The task of the committee was to undertake an Australia-wide consultation. Its purpose was to decide whether human rights deserving of protection in Australia were currently being sufficiently protected. If not, the committee was asked to explore how they could be better attained.

Consultation took place over a year, attracting more than 30,000 submissions. All but a small fraction of these were in favour of a recommendation for a national charter of rights. The terms of reference of the committee excluded a proposal for a constitutional model, with power in the courts to invalidate legislation. Effectively, the committee's investigation was limited to whether legislation was required (either a general charter and/or particular statutes) or whether other measures would be sufficient (such as the creation of a parliamentary committee, adoption of educative measures or administrative rearrangements).

The national consultation had before it a commitment expressed in the electoral platform of the Australian Labor Party issued prior to the 2007 election. This obliged the government to 'adhere to Australia's international human rights obligations [and to] seek to have them incorporated into the domestic law of Australia'.[66] As in the case of the New Zealand initiative that led to its Bill of Rights Act, the Australian consultation followed a period where the previous Conservative Government of John Howard was perceived by some as having departed from proper respect for human rights, both in its engagement with multilateral United Nations agencies and in its domestic policy and legislation. Special mention was repeatedly made during the consultation of the treatment of refugee applicants and especially the 2001 *Tampa* affair.[67] Even a noted opponent of a proposed human rights charter in Australia (Cardinal George Pell) conceded that the incident – which involved refusal to receive into Australia refugee applicants rescued on the high seas by a Norwegian vessel – 'highlight[ed] where the limits of the ethic of the fair go among the majority can be encountered'.[68]

---

65 Australia, National Human Rights Consultation, *Engaging in the Debate* (2009), p. 1.

66 Australian Labor Party, *National Platform and Constitution* (2007), Ch.13 [7].

67 The *Tampa* affair is described in M. White, '*Tampa* Incident: Shipping, International and Maritime Legal Issues and Subsequent Legal Issues', *Australian Law Journal* 78, 2004, p. 249.

68 Cardinal G. Pell, 'Four Fictions: An Argument Against A Human Rights Charter' (2008), available online at <http://www.cam.org.au/perspectives/four-fictions-an-argument-against-a-charter-of-rights.html> (accessed 25 October 2011). See National Human Rights Consultation, *Engaging in the Debate* (2009), p. 110.

In the end, reportedly to surprise in some political quarters and to media interests, the national consultation recommended that a national charter of human rights should be enacted by the Federal Parliament. The committee proposed that the legislation should list economic and social rights as well as civil and political rights. However, it proposed that the charter should provide remedies in the courts by way of a declaration in the event that civil and political rights (only) were found not to have been respected. The recommendation also included the legislative enactment, akin to s 6 of the New Zealand Act and s 3 of the HRA 1998, to encourage the interpretation of federal laws consistently with the provisions of the proposed charter.

The Committee's recommendations were criticised by both sides in the debate. Leading state and federal politicians attacked what they saw as an unacceptable attempt to transfer legislative power to the judiciary. Those who hoped for remedies for breaches of economic and social rights were highly critical of the failure of the Brennan committee to include remedies for such breaches in its proposals.[69] Sections of the media which had (for the most part) opposed the idea of a national charter of rights (the publications of News Limited being the most strident) were overjoyed at what they saw as the 'collapse of the push for a national charter of rights'.[70] They repeatedly reported the insignificance of the consultation and what they saw as its lack of political supporters;[71] the lack of any real need for such a measure in a nation so well governed as Australia was said to be; the fear of affording too much power to lawyers and judges; even the suggested isolation of the judges and lawyers in the jurisdictions that had enacted a charter (the ACT and Victoria) and the difficulty they would now have in attaining federal judicial appointment. Inferentially, this difficulty would arise because the law in their jurisdictions was now 'on the nose' and 'out of line' with the orthodoxy of the rest of Australian law.[72]

In the antipathy of the strident campaign waged by such media outlets against a national human rights charter, Australians saw a reflection of some of the debates in Britain at the time of the introduction of the HRA 1998. What was missing in the Australian debates was the presence of a political champion of the measure, the role played in the United Kingdom by the then newly elected Prime Minister, Tony Blair.

The quietus was finally administered to the proposal for an Australian charter on 21 April 2010 when the Attorney-General announced the rejection

---

69 K. Young and R. Thilagaratnam, 'Big Question is Whether Government Will Adopt A Human Rights Act', *Canberra Times*, 10 December 2009, p. 21.

70 G. Henderson, 'Human Rights Act Slips Down the List', *Sydney Morning Herald*, 26 January 2010, p. 11.

71 C. Merritt, 'State Charter Lawyers on Path to Isolation', in *The Australian*, 19 February 2010, p. 27; C. Merritt, 'State out on a Limb, Warns Craven', *The Australian*, 26 February 2010, p. 34.

72 Statement by Attorney-General R. McClelland, 'Australian Human Rights Framework', 21 April 2010 (unpublished).

of the key proposals of the Brennan committee: namely the enactment of a charter of rights and the adoption of the legislative interpretative principle.

Framework not charter

Instead of proposing a charter, the Australian government announced what it described as a 'Framework' for better human rights protection in Australia. This 'Framework' comprised five parts. They were:

1   A re-affirmation of the nation's commitment to international human rights obligations;
2   A new emphasis and expenditure on human rights education across the community;
3   An enhancement of domestic and international engagement on human rights issues;
4   An improvement in domestic human rights protections, including greater parliamentary scrutiny; and
5   The achievement of greater respect for human rights principles within the community, including by the reform of current anti-discrimination legislation.

The expenditure of over $12 million on education initiatives to promote a greater understanding of human rights was welcomed. However, necessarily, it would do nothing to afford redress to those for whom the political process and other present legal remedies were unavailing. The proposed establishment of a new parliamentary joint committee on human rights within the Australian Parliament 'to provide greater scrutiny of legislation for compliance with . . . international human rights obligations'[73] might be welcomed. However, as one commentator, Professor George Williams, observed: 'It will make little difference to the protection of human rights at the community level. It will even more starkly demonstrate how self-regulation by politicians, when it comes to human rights, is the problem, and not the solution.'[74]

The promise of reform of anti-discrimination legislation, including the rationalisation of current laws in a single statute, has obvious advantages. But it was quickly noted that there were no new proposals for protection of minorities presently falling outside federal law, including a general protection against discrimination on the grounds of a person's sexual orientation. The commitment to reinforce engagement with international human rights obligations was certainly to be applauded. However, it could not escape criticism addressed to the suggested difference between governmental rhetoric and the

73 G. Williams, 'Human Rights: People With Power Don't Want To Give It Up', *Sydney Morning Herald*, 27 April 2010, p. 13.
74 Ibid.

actuality. Particularly so because the announcement closely coincided with another, envisaging mandated delays in administrative consideration of refugee applications addressed to applicants originating from Afghanistan and Sri Lanka.

The documentation released by the Brennan committee identified numerous areas of unrepaired discrimination towards minorities in Australia. It did this in the case of indigenous people; racial minorities; non-citizens; people of minority sexual orientation and gender identity; women; and the failure of present protections to address problems of homelessness, police shootings, inadequate health care, prison conditions, arbitrary and extended detention, discrimination in police practice governing the use of arrest, official targeting of particular groups, limitations on free expression and freedom of assembly and association, inequality in the administration of immigration law, defects in protection of children, and significant failings in protection of individual conscience and religion in Australia.

A charter of rights, the interpretive principle and a provision for declaratory orders would not have cured every defect or gap in the Australian legal system. But influential upon the recommendation of the Australian national consultation were the reported findings of the British Institute of Human Rights[75] concerning the material operation of the HRA 1998. This suggested that:

(i) The language and ideas of human rights have a dynamic life beyond the court room and empower a wide range of individuals and organisations to improve people's experience of public services and their quality of life generally;[76]

(ii) Human rights are an important political tool for people facing discrimination, disadvantage or exclusion, and offer a more ambitious vision of equality beyond just anti-discrimination;

(iii) Human rights principles can help decision-makers and others see seemingly intractable problems in a new light; and

(vi) Awareness-raising about human rights empowers people to take action.

Rejection of the charter

So why did politicians on both sides of Australia's major political groupings, supported by large sections of the media, oppose the recommendations proposed by the national consultation? In part, it was probably a resistance to new ideas. In part, it appears to have been traditional hostility to the very

---

75 British Institute of Human Rights, *The Human Rights Act: Changing Times* (2007), p. 10. See *Engaging in the Debate*, above note 65, p. 5.

76 In the Australian Capital Territory, it was recorded that there had been a 'small, but growing impact beyond government'. See ACT Department of Justice and Community Safety, *Human Rights Act 2004 – 12 Month Review – Report* (2006).

notion that human beings have universal rights. In part, it was the objection of non-lawyers to any perceived enlargement of the power of lawyers.

As Professor George Williams put it, in his comment on the outcome of the national consultation, in the matter of human rights protection 'people with power don't want to give it up'. They do not relish the idea of independent courts responding to complaints of otherwise powerless individuals and making interpretative endeavours to respond to their complaints or declarations of a public kind that cannot be easily swept under the carpet.

UN Human Rights Committee

In rejecting the charter idea, the Australian government announced that the proposal would be reconsidered in 2014. In the meantime, Australia has to get by without a human rights charter. Unlike the United Kingdom before 1998, Australia is not subject to any regional human rights treaty for Asia and the Pacific. Alone of the geographical regions of the world, Asia and the Pacific have no human rights treaty, commission or court. Australians are therefore left with a semi-pure Diceyan model of supreme (but not sovereign) legislatures, responding to perceived majority opinion and occasionally (but not necessarily) to minority demands.

The only external human rights stimuli that are provided in the case of complaints against Australia derive from the reports of United Nations human rights rapporteurs and agencies,[77] including the Human Rights Committee established under the International Covenant on Civil and Political Rights (ICCPR). A recent report of that committee provided the opinion of independent external experts about the inadequacy of the present Australian legal 'framework' for upholding the international obligations to which Australia has subscribed under the ICCPR.

The Human Rights Committee found that a communication submitted to it by Mr Fardon was sustained. His continued detention in prison beyond his fourteen-year term of imprisonment was held to be 'arbitrary'. It was thus contrary to Art. 9 para 1 of the ICCPR.[78]

Earlier, in the High Court of Australia, Mr Fardon had challenged the constitutional validity of the Dangerous Prisoners (Sexual Offenders) Act 2003 (Qld) pursuant to which his post-sentence detention was supported. Without a constitutional bill of rights to which he could appeal, Mr Fardon argued that the Queensland statute was incompatible with the Australian Constitution in a particular way. He argued that the law attempted to impose

---

77 Such as the report of the Special Rapporteur on the Human Rights and Fundamental Freedoms of Indigenous People (James Anaya, Geneva, 27 August 2009). See also A. Vivian, 'Some Human Rights are Worth More Than Others: The Northern Territory Intervention and the Alice Springs Town Camps', *Alternative Law Journal* 35, 2010, p. 15.

78 Ibid., para. [7.3].

upon the Queensland Supreme Court an obligation that was incompatible with the judicial function envisaged by the Constitution.

A line of constitutional cases in the Australian courts has decided that state parliaments may not confer on judges of state courts functions that would make them inappropriate receptacles for the conferral of federal jurisdiction under the Constitution.[79]

In the High Court of Australia, I accepted Mr Fardon's submission. I did so, in part, by reference to the exceptional character of the Queensland law providing for a civil commitment to prison (not to a mental hospital or other specialised institution for treatment). But I also referred to the difficulty, or impossibility, of securing an accurate or objective prediction of criminality, whether by a judge or other official.[80] The majority of the Court, however, found no constitutional flaw in the Queensland law.[81]

The Committee simply looked to whether Mr Fardon had suffered double punishment without further determination of any criminal guilt or arbitrary punishment for preventive reasons contrary to the ICCPR. In the result, the Committee concluded that the Queensland law was arbitrary. It therefore constituted a violation of Art. 9 para 1 of the ICCPR.

By the orders of that Committee, Australia was required, within 180 days, to provide information to the Committee on the measures it intended to take to give effect to the Committee's views. Meanwhile, Mr Fardon remained in his prison confinement.

Getting by without a charter

Constitutional implications

Australians must therefore rely on what is still, essentially, the nineteenth-century model favoured by Dicey. This rests on what a former Chief Justice of the High Court of Australia (Sir Anthony Mason) has declared to be a 'romantic' notion about the capacity and inclination of modern parliaments to respond, and to correct, departures from fundamental human rights.[82] This does not mean that they are without any remedies. The courts remain independent of government and sometimes uphold rights based on implications which the judges derive from the express provisions of the Constitution.

Thus, in a case decided shortly before my retirement from the High Court of Australia, *Roach v Electoral Commissioner*,[83] the Court struck down, as

79 *Kable v Director of Public Prosecutions* (NSW) (1996) 189 CLR 51.
80 *Fardon v Attorney-General (Q)* (2004) 223 CLR 575, at p. 637 [163–164].
81 Ibid. p. 593 [23]–[24]; 601–2 [43]–[44]; 619–21 [106]–[118]; 658 [234].
82 A.F. Mason, 'Democracy and the Law: The State of the Australian Political System', *Law Society Journal (NSW)*, November, 2005, p. 69.
83 (2007) 233 CLR 162.

constitutionally invalid, provisions in a federal statute purporting to exclude all prisoners in Australia from the right to vote in federal elections. Although unable to invoke any express provision of the Constitution upholding a right to vote, an inference was drawn from the constitutionally prescribed system of representative government that the ambit of the disqualification imposed by the legislation was too wide.

There were strong dissenting opinions to this outcome in the High Court of Australia. Justices Hayne[84] and Heydon[85] emphatically rejected the references in the majority's opinions to earlier decisions of the Supreme Court of Canada in *Sauvé v Canada (Chief Electoral Officer)*[86] and to the European Court of Human Rights in *Hirst v United Kingdom (No. 2)*.[87] However, the majority of the Court concluded that it was undesirable, in the contemporary world, to close the judicial mind to any arguments expressed on analogous problems in other jurisdictions.

Sometimes, in default of constitutional arguments in Australia, those who seek relief in the courts are pressed back to arguments of statutory construction, addressed to the meaning of the relevant federal or state enactment. This was an issue that arose in *Coleman v Power*.[88] It concerned a provision of the Queensland Vagrants, Gaming and Other Offences Act of 1931. In reaching my view in *Coleman*, I referred to decisions of the House of Lords in *Fitzpatrick v Sterling Housing Association Ltd*[89] and *Ghaidan v Godin-Mendoza*.[90] Australian courts are no longer bound by the decisions of the Privy Council, still less those of the House of Lords (or now the Supreme Court of the United Kingdom). Nevertheless, powerful reasoning in United Kingdom courts, persuasively expressed, continues to have an impact upon judicial minds far away. Such was the case in *Coleman v Power*. The legislation could be read by reference to concepts appearing in the ICCPR. They were not, as such, part of Australian domestic law. But they could help in an understanding of that law.

Strict reading of legislation

A particularly vivid illustration of the difficulties faced by a country without a constitutional or even statutory charter of universal rights arose in the High Court of Australia in *Al-Kateb v Godwin*.[91] That was a proceeding where a

---

84 (2007) 233 CLR 162 at 221 [166]ff.
85 (2007) 233 CLR 162 at 224–5 [181].
86 (2002) 3 SCR 519 at 585 [119]. See (2007) 233 CLR 162 at 177 [13] per Gleeson CJ.
87 (2005) 42 EHRR 41.
88 (2004) 220 CLR 1.
89 [2001] 1 AC 27.
90 [2004] 2 AC 557. See also F.A.R. Bennion, *Statutory Interpretation: A Code*, 4th edn, 2002, p. 779.
91 (2004) 219 CLR 562.

refugee applicant had been detained for five years awaiting final determination of his claim to refugee status in Australia. Eventually, he invoked a provision of the Migration Act 1958 (Cth) by which he could terminate his detention by requesting the Minister to return him to his country of nationality. In the event, the Minister could not do this because, although he had been born in Kuwait, his nationality was Palestinian. Israel would not allow him passage to Gaza. Kuwait would not receive him. Accordingly, on the Minister's theory of the Act, he could be detained in Australia indefinitely.

A minority of the High Court of Australia (Gleeson CJ, Gummow J and I) concluded that the Act should be read so as to be inapplicable to the factual circumstances of Mr Al-Kateb's case. The Act had not dealt specifically with the instance of a stateless person. It should not be taken to apply to a regime involving indefinite detention. If it did, Gummow J and I concluded, it would present serious constitutional difficulties for its validity. The majority of the High Court,[92] however, was unconvinced by these arguments. They rejected the submissions in favour of a narrow reading. By inference, they dismissed any constitutional objection.

Limits to beneficial construction

Sometimes, upon analysis, the provisions of legislation are so clear that even a grave offence to the universal principles of human rights cannot be invoked so as to secure a beneficial or rights-respecting construction. This was the conclusion reached by a unanimous decision of the High Court of Australia in *Minister for Immigration and Multicultural and Indigenous Affairs v B.*[93]

In that case, the Family Court of Australia, acting under the Family Law Act 1975 (Cth), had exercised powers (granted to it in general terms in respect of children) to release children of refugee applicants from detention. Those children had been detained upon their arrival, with their parents, in Australia, without appropriate visas. The Family Court accepted a submission that the otherwise applicable provisions of the *Migration Act* should be 'read down', so as not to apply to the children. In reinforcement of that argument, reference was made by that Court to Australia's ratification of the Convention on the Rights of the Child and the provisions of that Convention providing that any detention of a child must be a 'last resort'.[94] On the Minister's argument, if the federal legislation were valid, it provided for such detention as a 'first resort'.

Attractive though the children's argument might have been to me, there were several legal impediments in the way of its acceptance. The first was that

---

92 McHugh, Hayne, Callinan and Heydon JJ.

93 (2003) 219 CLR 365.

94 *United Nations Convention on the Rights of the Child*, Art. 37(b) ['the detention of a child shall be . . . used only as a measure of last resort and for the shortest appropriate period of time'], see [1991] *Australian Treaty Series* No.4.

the legislation made express and detailed provisions with respect to children in detention. This indicated that Parliament had expressly referred to, and provided for, child detention. As well, the parliamentary record showed that departmental officers had drawn the possible breach of the Child Convention to the notice of Parliament. Yet Parliament had pressed on with the challenged provisions.

In these circumstances, I could not give the legislation the beneficial construction which the Family Court had adopted. Techniques of statutory construction can therefore only take a judicial decision-maker so far. Inclinations protective of human rights can only afford occasional assistance. In the end, if the law is clear, valid and applicable to the case, it is the duty of any court to give effect to it. So, in that case, did I and all other judges of the High Court of Australia.

Common law elaboration

In matters of common law elaboration, the High Court of Australia has frequently endorsed a principle that permits reference to be made to universal human rights when deciding the content of a past rule of the common law. This was done by the court in the important decision in *Mabo v Queensland {No.2}.*[95] That was a challenge by Australian Aboriginals to the earlier holdings of Australian courts, and of the Privy Council,[96] rejecting claims that Australian Aboriginals enjoyed ownership of their traditional land.

In the course of his reasons, upholding the submissions of Mr Mabo that the previous statement of the common law could not stand consistently with contemporary universal principles of human rights as now understood (especially as those principles forbid racial discrimination), Brennan J affirmed the inevitable influence upon the content of Australia's common law of the principles of universal human rights law. In a sense, this opinion was an affirmation of the Bangalore Principles which had been adopted by Commonwealth judges in 1988.[97]

Gaps in legal protection

In a more recent decision, *Wurridjal v The Commonwealth,*[98] the limits of the *Mabo* interpretive rule were revealed. *Wurridjal* was a case that challenged the constitutional validity of federal legislation of 2007 providing for military and police intervention into Aboriginal communities and homes in the Northern Territory of Australia. The challenge came in the form of a demurrer. The High Court of Australia divided. I favoured a view that the Aboriginal

---

95 (1992) 175 CLR 1.
96 *Cooper v Stuart* (1889) 14 App Cas 286 at 291 per Lord Watson, referred to in *Mabo* (1992) 175 CLR 1 at 37ff.
97 (1992) 175 CLR 1 at 42 (with the concurrence of Mason CJ and McHugh J).
98 (2009) 237 CLR 309.

complaints were legally arguable and that the plaintiffs should have their claim heard in full by the court. The majority of the Court rejected the contention. They dismissed the proceedings as legally untenable.

In the course of my reasons, I observed that:

> If any other Australians, selected by reference to their race, suffered the imposition on their pre-existing property interests of non-consensual five-year statutory leases, designed to authorise intensive intrusions into their lives and legal interests, it is difficult to believe that a challenge to such a law would fail as legally unarguable on the ground that no 'property' had been 'acquired'. Or that 'just terms' had been afforded, although those affected were not consulted about the process and although rights cherished by them might be adversely affected. The Aboriginal parties are entitled to have their trial and day in court. We should not slam the doors of the courts in their face. This is a case in which a transparent, public trial of the proceedings has its own justification.[99]

This was the last decision that I delivered in the High Court of Australia, indeed as a member of the Australian judiciary. It involved a case whose order affirmed federal legislation, enacted within eight weeks of the general election in 2007. The legislation was propounded without consultation or expert assessment and was seriously disrespectful of a class of people selected by reference to a racial criterion. When politicians and media interests in Australia assert that the nation does not need a charter or other national protection for human rights, and that all such matters can be safely left to Parliament and to the Australian people as electors, I am afraid that the evidence, including recent evidence, suggests the contrary.

The need for remedies

Empathy towards legal discrimination can derive from sex, race, age, disability, health condition or religion. In my case, it derived from sexual orientation. Those who have never felt discrimination may not always be so alert to the need for remedies. Especially where the remedy proposed reserves the last word to the elected representatives in Parliament, stimulated by the quiet, calm voice of the independent judiciary, it seems difficult to assert that the remedy is excessive or inappropriate or unnecessary to the Australian experience.[100]

I congratulate the Parliament and people of the United Kingdom on the tenth anniversary of the Human Rights Act. I remain of the view that it affords important lessons for a wider world. Those lessons extend to lawyers and judges (and other citizens) in Australia.

---

99 (2009) 237 CLR at 394–5.
100 See now *Momcilovic v The Queen* (2011) 85 ALTR 957, [2011] HCA 34.

5 Inspired by the Human Rights Act

The Victorian Charter of Human Rights and Responsibilities

Diane Sisely

As the title of this chapter suggests, the Victorian Charter of Human Rights and Responsibilities[1] ('the Charter') was 'inspired' by the United Kingdom's (UK) Human Rights Act 1998 (HRA).[2]

The Charter, and those advocating for its development, were inspired in many and varied, sometimes surprising ways. The genesis, content and implementation of the Charter have been and continue to be heavily influenced by the HRA. In Victoria, we learnt from what was occurring in the UK and tried to distil as many lessons as we could. Thus to be complete the ten-year evaluation of the HRA should include consideration of its wider impact beyond the shores of the UK.

The Charter was passed by the Victorian Parliament in July 2006 and became fully operative in January 2008. It is an ordinary Act of Parliament and Victoria is the first state in Australia to introduce such an Act, although the Australian Capital Territory had introduced its Human Rights Act[3] in 2004, which is also substantially based on the HRA.

Australia remains the last major common-law-based country not to have a national human rights charter or Act to ensure that fundamental rights are observed and responsibilities recognised.[4]

For those of us in Victoria campaigning for the protection of human rights, it was not so much a matter of 'bringing the rights home', as it was for the UK, in relation to the European Convention on Human Rights;[5] for us it was establishing recognition of human rights and the need to protect them in the first place.

I will discuss the relationship between the HRA and the Charter under the headings of:

1 Charter of Human Rights and Responsibilities Act 2006.
2 Human Rights Act 1998.
3 Human Rights Act 2004.
4 Department of Justice, *New Directions for the Victorian Justice System 2004–2014: Attorney-General's Justice Statement*, Melbourne 2004.
5 European Convention on Human Rights 1950.

- precursors to and the genesis of the Victorian Charter
- engaging the community on human rights
- the content of the Charter
- applying the Charter.

Precursors to and the genesis of the Victorian Charter

Inadequacy of equal opportunity legislation

From 1994 to 2004, I led the Victorian Equal Opportunity Commission (VEOC) and it was in this role that I became acutely aware of the limitations of our then Equal Opportunity Act 1995[6] (EOA) and its limited capacity to combat discrimination.

The EOA was similar to other anti-discrimination legislation operating in many countries and jurisdictions. It sought to protect equality of opportunity by enabling an individual to seek redress by lodging a complaint of discrimination if they felt they had been subject to unlawful discrimination. The problem with this legislation was that, for most people, lodging a complaint of discrimination was a much too daunting a step for them to take and they didn't take it; they didn't seek redress, they let the perceived discrimination go unchallenged.[7] The reasons for this varied, for example, some feared further discrimination or harassment; some were afraid the process would be too expensive or too drawn out, as many respondents were large multinational companies or government departments with ready access to lawyers and funds; and some gay men and lesbians were afraid of being 'outed' in their local communities.

Furthermore, employers, the overwhelming majority of respondents, appeared not to take their responsibilities seriously, with some 66 per cent not having policies or practices in place to prevent or resolve allegations of discrimination.[8]

The most significant difficulty was that, while the EOA focused on behaviour between one individual and another, the discrimination experienced was more often the result of systemic factors, the result of policies or guidelines or taken for granted 'usual behaviour' that together constituted a discriminatory work environment or practice. In these circumstances it was often hard to identify a compelling individual discriminatory act on which to base a complaint, but discrimination had nevertheless occurred.

This was particularly the case for Indigenous Australians, people with disabilities, women, and gay men and lesbians, and, after the bombing of the

---

6 Equal Opportunity Act 1995.
7 Equal Opportunity Commission Victoria, *The Way Forward: Annual Review*, Melbourne, 2001, p. 10.
8 Equal Opportunity Commission Victoria, op. cit., p. 10.

twin towers in New York on 11 September 2001, muslim Australians and refugees.

It was clear that a new approach was required, an approach that provided proactive protection, that didn't rely on retrospective action by an individual victim, and most importantly we needed an approach that protected all human rights, not just equality rights. We needed an approach that did not place groups of different people in opposition to one another as they struggled for justice. In short we needed to develop a much more mature understanding of human rights and their relevance to our everyday life.

Attorney-General's Justice Statement

The opportunity to put the need for this new approach firmly on the public agenda came in 2002 when the Victorian Attorney-General, Rob Hulls, started preparations for his ten-year plan for the Victorian justice system. He convened a conference comprising the heads of all major justice agencies and courts to discuss what 'A Vision for Justice in Victoria over the next Decade'[9] might look like.

The difficulty for me, as head of the Equal Opportunity Commission, was that there was an implicit assumption that we were considering a ten-year vision for the existing justice system of the law, courts, police and prisons; human rights were not automatically part of the discussion.

Nevertheless I was well aware of the HRA and what was happening in relation to the protection of human rights in the UK and Canada so I put forward the vision that in ten years' time we would have:

- a clear statement on the human rights and responsibilities of all Victorians;
- an annual action plan for the protection of human rights in Victoria;
- annual reporting to Parliament by the VEOC on the enjoyment or otherwise of human rights by the people of Victoria;
- employment equity standards and a compliance and audit regime to ensure proactive compliance.[10]

To expand on this vision and to gather support for it, a public conference, 'From Rhetoric to Reality: Making Human Rights Work',[11] was held in February 2004 and Paul Hunt, the then United Nations (UN) Special

---

9 *A Vision for Justice in Victoria over the next Decade.* Conference convened by the Department of Justice Victoria, Aitken Hill, Victoria, 2002.

10 D. Sisely, *How will the justice system deal with social and human rights in 2012?* Unpublished, 2002.

11 *From Rhetoric to Reality: Making Human Rights Work*, RMIT University, Melbourne, 2004.

Rapporteur on the Right to Health, based at the University of Essex, addressed us and the Attorney-General on the application of human rights.

Fortunately our actions were successful and the Attorney-General's subsequent justice statement, *New Directions for the Victorian Justice System 2004–2014: Attorney-General's Justice Statement*,[12] released in May 2004, proposed a public discussion on whether Victoria needed better protection of human rights and if it did, might this be achieved through a charter of human rights?

The Attorney-General stated his preference for a statutory charter as operating in the UK and New Zealand and noted that 'The aim of the UK legislation is to promote transparency in the way that legislation is enacted and promote public discussion of what the appropriate limits of human rights should be.'[13] He observed approvingly that:

> After two years in the UK, the Lord Chancellor's department found the Human Rights Act had improved public decision-making by harnessing it to a set of fundamental standards. It also improved *'the relationship between Parliament, Government and the Judiciary, so that all three are working together to ensure . . . a culture of respect for human rights'* across society.[14]

We watched what was happening in the UK

The growing number of people in Victoria campaigning for the better protection of human rights recognised that a community consultation on human rights and how to better protect them was a major opportunity, and we seized it. But they were also aware of the attacks on human rights and the HRA occurring in the UK at the time. For example, the calls for the HRA to be abolished or wound back, as it was simply protecting 'terrorists', 'undeserving refugees' and 'criminals'.[15] The populist scare campaigns in the tabloid media that were beginning to undermine respect for the HRA.

As Lord Robert Walker was later to tell us in an address he gave in Melbourne, 'in Britain the UK Act has not had a particularly warm welcome. Prominent members of both the Labour Party and the Conservative Party have recently spoken in favour of repealing it or drastically amending it. The popular press, dominated by Murdoch's *Sun* and Rothermere's *Daily Mail*, regularly deride it. The reasons for this are no doubt complex . . . Does this matter? I think it does, because the effective promotion of human rights

---

12 Department of Justice, Victoria, *New Directions for the Victorian Justice System 2004–2014: Attorney-General's Justice Statement*, 2004, Melbourne.

13 Ibid., p. 55.

14 Ibid.

15 C. Harlow, 'Can human rights survive the war on terror and the war on crime?', *Discussion Paper 21/8, Democratic Audit of Australia*, Australian National University, Canberra, 2006. Online. Available HTTP: <http://www.democraticaudit.anu.edu.au/papers/20060809_harlow_hr_wars.pdf> (accessed 27 January 2011).

depends on winning hearts and minds, as well as on legislation and law enforcement. It does matter that so many British citizens are inclined to feel that the UK Act is threatening, rather than protecting, their liberties.'[16]

We had similar populist scare campaigns operating in Australia, campaigns attempting to mobilise opposition to those seeking to protect rights, repositioning us as privileged elites and ideologues whose interests are inimical to the interests and values of those in the mainstream.[17]

We saw the consequences of introducing the HRA without a functioning human rights commission that could engage the community in a discussion of the issues, undertake community education and present the reasons for the better protection of human rights. We saw the critical importance of ensuring community understanding, engagement and ownership of human rights to lessen the impact of any backlash that might arise.

We studied the report of the UK Audit Commission in 2003 which warned that the implementation of the HRA was 'stalling and the initial flurry of activity surrounding its introduction has waned',[18] warning of public bodies not adopting a strategy for the implementation of human rights, of the HRA 'not leaving the desk of the lawyers'[19] and of not having a clear corporate approach to human rights.[20] This reminded us that meaningful engagement of the public services was critical, not only in gaining support for the better protection of human rights, but also for the implementation of sustained longer term measures to build a culture of respect for human rights.

All of this made our task seem very daunting but it was also immensely helpful; it highlighted what we might expect and potential problems that we needed to guard against, and it provided helpful hints and case studies on best practice.

Engaging the community on human rights

In April 2005, the Victorian Attorney-General announced the appointment of the Human Rights Consultation Committee (Consultation Committee) to conduct a 'conversation' with the Victorian people on the better protection of their human rights. Led by Professor George Williams it was a broadly based

16 R. Walker, 'What Difference can a Human Rights Charter Make?' Melbourne, 2007. Online. Available HTTP: <http://www.hrlrc.org.au/files/RV1EGTE462/Walker%20-%20What%20Difference%20Can%20a%20Charter%20Make.pdf> (accessed 16 June 2011).

17 M. Sawer, *Populism and Public Choice in Australia and Canada: Converting Equality Seekers into 'Special Interests'*, Australian National University, 2003.

18 Audit Commission, *Human Rights: Improving public service delivery*, London, 2003, p. 3. Online. Available HTTP: <http://www.justice.gov.uk/guidance/docs/acrep03.pdf> (accessed 2 February 2011).

19 Ibid., p.7.

20 Ibid., p.10.

committee, including a former opposition party attorney-general and the captain of the 2000 Australian Olympic Team, a basketball player. The Consultation Committee had six months in which to report and there was an election due at the end of the year.

A month later, in May 2005, the Victorian Government set out its preferred position on a human rights model for the State in its *Statement of Intent*.[21] The Government stated that its preference was for a limited set of rights, those contained in the International Covenant on Civil and Political Rights (ICCPR), that it wished to preserve the sovereignty of Parliament, with the courts being given a limited role, and that it was interested in a model like that operating in the UK and New Zealand.[22]

A number of people advocating for the better protection of human rights were disappointed by this *Statement of Intent*, as it was seen as narrowing the conversation before it got started. However, I agree with George Williams when he later observed that:

> By releasing the *Statement of Intent*, the Government went beyond establishing the process merely to gauge community opinion to indicating a preference for a model should, the community be in favour of a bill of rights. This made the *Statement of Intent* influential within Government when the Consultation Committee reported in a form that fell within the preferences expressed in it.[23]

It was an astute political move.

The six months of the consultation were feverish ones. We heeded the lessons learnt in the UK, especially the importance of engaging with people and explaining human rights in terms that were meaningful to them as they went about their everyday lives.

We took note of Frances Butler's warning that, despite examples of the beneficial impact of the HRA,

> many public authorities are having difficulty in understanding how to implement human rights in their decision-making process ... most public authorities have yet to fully appreciate that implementing the Human Rights Act effectively involves leadership from the top and

---

21 Department of Justice, Victoria, *Human Rights in Victoria: Statement of Intent*, Melbourne, 2005. Online. Available HTTP: <http://www.justice.vic.gov.au/wps/wcm/connect/justlib/DOJ+Internet/resources/a/4/a4b8fb00404a3f5ea281fbf5f2791d4a/statement_intent.pdf> (accessed 2 February 2011).

22 Ibid.

23 G. Williams, 'The Victorian Charter of Human Rights and Responsibilities: Origins and Scope', *Melbourne University Law Review*, vol. 30, no. 887, 2006. Online. Available HTTP: <http://acthra.anu.edu.au/articles/The%20Victorian%20Charter%20of%20Rights%20MULR.pdf> (accessed 2 February 2001).

changes in management techniques throughout the organisation. It is not widely appreciated that human rights considerations apply not only to policy-making but to the way in which front-line staff make day-to-day decisions and deliver services.[24]

The Consultation Committee developed a process to give as many Victorians as possible a say about the issues at a community level and met with the judiciary, members of Parliament, government agencies and senior executives of government departments.[25]

At the same time a broadly based coalition of non-government organisations, human rights groups, advocacy organisations, civil liberties groups, community legal centres and some churches mounted an extensive community education campaign, explaining the relevance of human rights, the importance of their protection and encouraging people to express their views to the Consultation Committee. People responded in record numbers, indicating their support for the better protection of human rights.

Report of the Consultation Committee

The Consultation Committee delivered its report to the Government on 30 November 2005. It reported that:

> After six months of listening to Victorians of all ages and backgrounds across the State, it is clear that a substantial majority of the people we heard from want their human rights to be better protected by the law . . . Many people want to see their human rights better protected to shield themselves and their families from the potential misuse of government power. For even more people, however, the desire for change reflects their aspiration to live in a society that continues to strive for the values that they hold dear, such as equality, justice and a 'fair go' for all.[26]

The Consultation Committee recommended that the Victorian Parliament enact a charter of human rights and responsibilities and that it be an ordinary Act of Parliament like that operating in the UK, Australian Capital Territory and New Zealand. The report included a draft bill to do this. The report observed that:

---

24 F. Butler, 'IPPR Report: Improving Public Services: Using a Human Rights Approach', *Institute for Public Policy Research*, London, 2005. Online. Available HTTP: <http://www. edf.org.uk/blog/?p=25> (accessed 2 February 2011).

25 Williams, op. cit.

26 Consultation Committee, *Rights Responsibilities and Respect: The Report of the Human Rights Consultation Committee*, Department of Justice, Victoria, 2005. Online. Available HTTP: <http://www.liv.asn.au/PDF/News/HumanRightsFinalReport2006> (accessed 2 February 2011).

The United Kingdom has a system of law and government similar to Victoria and its Human Rights Act 1998 has been a success without giving rise to the litigation and other problems sometimes associated with the United States Bill of Rights. Its law has also proved effective in balancing issues such as the need to fight terrorism with the democratic and other principles required for a free society.[27]

The Victorian Government accepted this central recommendation of the Consultation Committee on 20 December 2005 and on 2 May 2006 the Charter of Human Rights and Responsibilities Bill was introduced to the lower house of the Victorian Parliament and was passed by the upper house in July 2006. The Charter of Human Rights and Responsibilities Act 2006 came into partial force on 1 January 2007 and full force on 1 January 2008, thereby providing public authorities with a period of time to adjust their practices to be consistent with the Charter, as occurred in the UK.

What does the Victorian Charter contain?

The Charter is an ordinary Act of Parliament and it primarily protects the civil and political rights contained in the ICCPR with some deletions and some additions. For example, the right to self-determination is not included, as it was felt that there was a lack of consensus on this issue amongst the population at the time.[28] The Charter specifically recognises that Aboriginal persons have a right to enjoy their own culture and the preamble recognises them as the descendants of the first people of Australia. Under the Charter, life is seen to begin at birth, and the right to marriage is also not included as this falls within the Australian Commonwealth Government's jurisdiction.

Perhaps because of the backlash against the HRA occurring in the UK, often associated with the trials of alleged terrorists, emphasis in Victoria was placed on the potential transformative effects of the Charter. Stress was also placed on its being designed to prevent human rights breaches arising, on improving how the government and the public service undertake their work, rather than emphasising the potential for litigation based on the Charter.[29] Indeed, it was not envisaged that the Charter would lead to a significant level of litigation.

Similarly to the HRA, the Charter is described as a 'dialogue model',[30] a dialogue that occurs in public between executive government, Parliament and the courts. All new bills are to be consistent with the Charter, all public authorities are to act consistently with the Charter and courts can flag when

---

27 Consultation Committee
28 Ibid.
29 Williams, op. cit., p. 901.
30 Ibid.

legislation is seen to be inconsistent with the Charter. The dialogue model concept has been useful in combating erroneous tabloid headlines about 'unelected judges' usurping the power of Parliament.

In discussing the key features of the Charter, I will adopt the same approach that Lord Bingham used to describe the HRA, when commenting on it in Melbourne in 2008,[31] to highlight the similarities between the two Acts.

First, the cornerstone of the Charter is the provision (s 38) that makes it unlawful for a public authority to act in a way that is incompatible with a human right or, in making a decision, to fail to give proper consideration to a relevant human right. This is similar to s 6(1) of the HRA. As Lord Bingham observed, 'Thus Parliament was requiring compliance with the scheduled Convention rights across the whole spectrum of government.'[32]

A difference is that while the HRA includes a court or tribunal as a public authority, the Charter was thought not to; however, in the recent case of *Kracke v The Mental Health Review Board* (2009)[33] a subtlety on this distinction has emerged. Justice Bell of the Victorian Civil and Administrative Court (VCAT) determined that courts and tribunals are bound to act compatibly with all of the human rights in the Charter when deciding cases that are administrative in nature in the public law sense, as opposed to when they are acting in a judicial capacity; here courts and tribunals are bound to act compatibly only with certain human rights.[34]

The second key feature identified by Lord Bingham is the power conferred on the higher courts in regard to legislation that is inconsistent with the Charter (s 36 of the Charter and s 4 of the HRA). If the Victorian Supreme Court is of the opinion that a statutory provision cannot be interpreted consistently with a human right, the Court may make a declaration of inconsistent interpretation. Such a declaration does not alter the application of the law, nor strike it down, but rather requires the minister administering the statute to prepare a written response to the declaration and lay it before each house of Parliament.

In a recent landmark decision and the first declaration of inconsistent interpretation in *R v Momcilovic* (2010),[35] the Victorian Court of Appeal found that a reverse onus provision, in legislation relating to the finding of illegal drugs,

---

31 Bingham, Lord, *Dignity, Fairness and Good Government: The Role of a Human Rights Act*, Human Rights Law Resource Centre, Melbourne, 2008, pp. 3–4. Online. Available HTTP: <http://www.hrlrc.org.au/files/MBR9WGGYQF/Dignity__Fairness_and_Good_Government__Speech_by_Lord_Bingham.pdf> (accessed 2 February 2011).

32 Ibid.

33 *Kracke v Mental Health Review Board* [2009] VCAT 646 (23 April 2009).

34 For further discussion of this case see the Human Rights Law Resource Centre *Kracke v Mental Health Review Board* [2009] VCAT 646 (23 April 2009).

35 *R v Momcilovic* [2010] VSCA 50 (17 March 2010). This decision is currently under appeal to the High Court of Australia.

infringed the right to the presumption of innocence. Accordingly, the court indicated its intention to issue a declaration of inconsistent interpretation, which would remit the provision to Parliament for reconsideration.

The third feature is the requirement that all existing legislation is to be interpreted consistently with human rights, as far as it is possible to do so consistent with their purpose (s 32 of the Charter and s 3 (1) of the HRA). In the *Momcilovic* case discussed above, the Victorian Court of Appeal also found that s 32(1) of the Charter is not a 'special' rule of statutory interpretation, but rather a statutory directive that requires all persons engaged in the task of statutory interpretation to explore all possible interpretations of the provision(s) in question, and adopt the interpretation which least infringes Charter rights.[36]

The fourth feature of the HRA identified by Lord Bingham is the obligation placed on a minister to make a statement on the compatibility of the provisions of a new bill with the European Convention rights (s 19 of the HRA). The Charter contains a similar provision (s 28): when a bill is introduced into the Victorian Parliament it must be accompanied by a statement of compatibility as to whether, in the member's opinion, the bill is compatible with human rights protected by the Charter, how it is, and if it is not so compatible it must state the nature and extent of the incompatibility.

The fifth feature is the requirement that courts in the UK must take into account judgments and decisions of the European Court.[37] While there is not the close connection to the European Court for the Victorian Charter as there is for the HRA, s 32 of the Charter does refer to international law and judgments of foreign and international courts and tribunals which may be considered by courts in interpreting a statutory provision and they have been used frequently in decisions involving Charter rights.[38]

Unlike the HRA, however, there is no new right of action or avenue for redress under the Charter and for this the Charter has been heavily criticised. If a person has an existing avenue of action they may include human rights issues if they are present. An example occurred in the case of Mr Kracke discussed above. Mr Kracke was a person subject to an involuntary treatment order under the Victorian Mental Health Act (1986) and under this Act he had an existing avenue of appeal to VCAT. He availed himself of this appeal avenue and included human rights issues. VCAT subsequently found that the Mental Health Review Tribunal had breached Mr Kracke's right to a fair hearing.

---

36 The Human Rights Law Resource Centre has a discussion of this case, *R v Momcilovic* [2010] VSCA 50 (17 March 2010).

37 Bingham, op. cit, p. 5.

38 See for example the reasoning of Justice Bell in *Kracke v Mental Health Board* [2009] VCAT 646.

Applying the Charter

The experience gained through the implementation of the HRA in the UK has had a seminal influence on work in Victoria to implement the Charter and to build a culture that champions human rights.

The discussion and teaching of human rights in Victoria and indeed across Australia has until very recently been almost exclusively dominated by consideration of human rights law and the teaching of lawyers. If you asked the 'person in the street' what human rights were about the answer would refer to Somalia, Afghanistan or Rwanda, not to the everyday lives of people in Victoria. There was and still is very little understanding of how human rights apply at a local and community level and we need new ways of thinking and speaking about human rights.[39]

In the very early days of the introduction of the Charter we did not have stories of our own to illustrate how it applied in everyday life so we adopted the stories developed in the UK on the application of the HRA.

We became very familiar with the stories collected by the British Institute of Human Rights (BIHR) in its publication *The Human Rights Act: Changing Lives*.[40] For example, the story of the married woman in Yorkshire with a disability.[41] You may remember that she needed a special bed – a 'profile' bed – to assist with her care, provided by the local authority. She asked for a double 'profile' bed so she could not only be appropriately cared for but also continue to sleep with her husband. She ultimately invoked the HRA and a double bed was provided. Many people in Victoria know of and have been inspired by this woman's story.

I'm pleased to say we are now building our own collection of stories, following the model set by the BIHR, and these can be found on the websites of the Victorian Equal Opportunity and Human Rights Commission (VEOHRC) and the Human Rights Law Centre (HRLC).[42]

In implementing the Charter we not only had the advantage of learning from the British experience, but unlike the UK, we had the advantage of having the established and moderately resourced VEOHRC to authoritatively lead community education on human rights during the development and commencement of the Charter.

As a result of the work of VEOHRC many people in Victoria, especially those in the public services, are very well acquainted with 'FRED', the

---

39 For further discussion of this point see the *National Human Rights Consultation Report* (2009), Barton ACT, Commonwealth of Australia.

40 British Institute of Human Rights, *The Human Rights Act: Changing Lives, Second Edition*, London, 2008.

41 Ibid., p.14.

42 See for example the VEOHRC website <http://www.humanrightscommission.vic.gov.au> and the website of the HRLC <http://www.hrlrc.org.au/content/topics/national-human-rights-consultation/case-studies/>.

acronym Frances Butler used to remind us of the principles underlying civil and political rights – freedom, respect, equality and dignity[43] – or as Alan Johnson, former UK Secretary of State for Health later extended it, 'FREDA', adding autonomy to 'FRED'.[44]

Many people are also well acquainted with the framework developed by the BIHR and the UK Department of Health to guide the development of a human rights-based approach to the provision of health and human services.[45] This framework has been both very useful and – as a consequence – influential. It has been used in our Departments of Health and Human Services and it is also being used in local government. For example, in 2009 at the Australian Centre for Human Rights Education at RMIT University, we developed and ran an 'applied human rights incubator' with 15 members of staff from the Departments of Health and Human Services. The participants were required to develop a human rights-based approach to an aspect of their work using the model developed by the BIHR and the UK Department of Health.

Perhaps the biggest difference between the implementation of the HRA and the implementation of the Charter is the requirement in the Charter for VEOHRC to report to Parliament each year on the operation of the Charter. VEOHRC is also required to assist the Attorney-General with two four-yearly reviews of the Charter.

The Commission has so far delivered three annual reports to the Victorian Parliament on the operation of the Charter, the first in 2008 titled *First Steps Forward*,[46] the second in 2009, *Emerging Change*[47] and the most recent, in 2010, *Making Progress*.[48] The titles give you an idea of the steps being taken and the stage we are at. We are taking small steps, slow steps, but steps that are mostly heading in the right direction to implement the Charter and a culture that supports human rights.

In its most recent report the Commission emphasises that technical compliance (satisfying legal requirements) with the Charter is but a first step. I agree; it is a necessary step but not a sufficient step and it must not be the only step. Implementing the Charter is also about acting consistently with its purpose; it is about adopting a human rights-based approach founded on the principles of participation, accountability, non-discrimination, empowerment and linking

43 Butler, op. cit.

44 Department of Health, *Human Rights in Healthcare A framework for local action*, 2008.

45 Ibid.

46 VEOHRC, *The 2007 Report on the Operation of the Charter of Human Rights and Responsibilities: First steps forward*, Melbourne, 2008.

47 VEOHRC, *The 2008 report on the operation of the Charter of Human Rights and Responsibilities: Emerging change*, Melbourne, 2009.

48 VEOHRC, *The 2009 report on the operation of the Charter of Human Rights and Responsibilities: Making progress*, Melbourne, 2010.

polices and practices to human rights standards; it is about doing things differently.[49]

The Commission gives examples of where this has been successfully under-taken, such as using the Charter to inform the development of the State Plan to Prevent Violence Against Women, designing the Victorian Native Title Settlement Framework to refocus on cultural respect in the resolution of native title claims, and adopting a human rights-based approach to reducing the use of restrictive interventions in the provision of services to people with a disability.[50]

In 2009, people in Victoria participated in vigorous public debates about the protection of human rights across a number of issues, one of which, for example, related to street violence. The Government introduced a bill to give police stronger 'stop and search' powers and its statement of compatibility assessing the human rights impact of the bill was the first such statement to indicate incompatibility with the Charter.[51]

VEOHRC is rightly sharply critical of this bill and stated:

> Recognising that limits on human rights are necessary in certain circum-stances, the Commission's view is that the government failed to demon-strate that the curtailing of rights through these increased police powers would result in a reduction in alcohol-related violence or knife-crime, or lead to an improvement in the safety of the Victorian community.[52]

The Commission also identified a number of matters 'requiring ongoing attention that will be followed up in our 2010 report'. These include the concern that, notwithstanding the role of the Victorian Parliament's Scrutiny of Acts and Regulations Committee (SARC), which has a similar role to the UK Parliamentary Joint Committee on Human Rights, a number of Bills are being introduced into Parliament without sufficient scrutiny and consultation.[53]

The Commission is also concerned that reports from government depart-ments indicate varying levels of integration of the Charter into departmental processes and it suggests that departments could be given 'more responsi-bility' for reporting on human rights-related initiatives. I read this as code for 'government departments should be transparently accountable for their actions under the Charter'. As I said, small steps but in the right direction.[54]

49 VEOHRC, *The 2009 report*.
50 Ibid.
51 For further discussion of this issue from the HRLRC see Summary Offences and Control of Weapons Acts Amendment Act 2009.
52 VEOHRC, *The 2009* Report, op. cit., p. 5.
53 Ibid.
54 Ibid., p.6.

The first of two four-yearly reviews of the Charter was held in 2011 and considered whether economic, social and cultural rights should be included in the Charter, along with self-determination and the protection of the rights of women and children. The recently elected Government of Victoria[55] is critical of the Charter and the Attorney-General has stated that 'in my view this legislation cannot continue in its present form'.[56]

The path towards the establishment of a human rights-respecting community clearly will take many twists and turns and I look forward to continuing to compare notes in future on the implementation of measures to protect human rights by the respective governments of Britain and Victoria.

---

55 The current Victorian Government was elected on 27 November 2010.
56 R. Clark, 'Towards a just and fair Victoria', 2010. Online. Available HTTP: <http://www. robertclark.net/news/towards-a-just-and-fair-victoria/> (accessed 14 February 2011).

Part II

Topical confrontations of the Human Rights Act

Section 1

The Human Rights Act and power

6 Human rights in an age of terror

Irene Khan

When the Human Rights Act (HRA) came into force in 2000, the aspiration of Parliament was that the Act would bring about 'a fundamental transformation of the relationship between individuals and the state, a shift towards "a culture of human rights" '.[1] A decade later, the HRA is one of the most misunderstood and misrepresented pieces of legislation in the UK – criticized by the media and problematized by political leaders, including those who had ushered it in.[2] Even as its tenth birthday is being celebrated, the future of the HRA hangs in the balance in light of the government's proposal to set up a commission to develop a British Bill of Rights.[3]

The birth of the HRA was followed soon after by the attacks of 9/11 which altered dramatically the human rights landscape. The ensuing period has been marked on the one hand by a proliferation of terrorism laws, policies and practices that challenge the premises and provisions of HRA, pitching security concerns against human rights standards and principles, and, on the other, by a stream of political invective playing on popular fears that undermine the credibility and legitimacy of the HRA. Few issues are as controversial in the area of human rights as terrorism and national security – where individual freedom collides with state security, the rights of the guilty are set against those of the innocent, and the dice are heavily loaded against the non-citizen. It is this territory that one must explore to gain a better understanding of why the HRA has become such an object of denigration and how it might be redeemed.

This chapter looks at the first decade of the Act's existence through the prism of counter-terrorism. It focuses on three issues: the erosion of

---

1 Joint Committee on Human Rights (JCHR), *The Human Rights Act: DCA and Home Office Reviews*, HL/278, HC/716, 16 November 2006, para 139. See also Conor Gearty, 'Beyond the Human Rights Act', available at: <http://www.law.leeds.ac.uk/assets/files/research/events/geary-chapter.pdf> (accessed 16 June 2011).
2 *The Observer*, 'Revealed: Blair Attack on Human Rights Law', 14 May 2006.
3 BBC, 'A commission to investigate a British Bill of Rights will be set up "imminently" David Cameron has said', 16 February 2011.

rights, using the prohibition against arbitrary detention and torture and ill-treatment as examples; the struggle to balance security and human rights; and the politicization of the rights discourse and its implications for the future of human rights. Through these issues, it analyses the tension between the political imperative of security and the legal obligation to respect human rights, and the role that the HRA has played in that struggle to protect rights.

The chapter concludes by looking at the risks and opportunities for human rights, as the HRA enters its second decade and the age of security is superseded by the age of austerity.

Human Rights Act: remit and limit

Although the HRA is a frequent whipping boy for unscrupulous politicians, disingenuous media and a discontented public, few among them understand well what the Act does – or does not do. In the words of the Parliamentary Joint Committee on Human Rights (JCHR), '. . . the HRA has been widely misunderstood by the public and has also been misapplied by officials in a number of settings, both phenomena having been fuelled by a number of damaging myths about human rights which have taken root in the popular imagination . . .' [4]

One common myth is that the HRA introduces new rights. In fact, the HRA creates no new rights but instead allows people to access and enjoy existing rights. The UK is a party to various human rights treaties within the framework of the United Nations, the Council of Europe and the European Union. Under UK law, treaties are not self-executing – in other words, they cannot be enforced domestically in a court of law unless they have been incorporated through an Act of Parliament. The HRA incorporates and gives effect to the rights enumerated in the European Convention on Human Rights (ECHR). [5]

The Act makes it unlawful for any public authority to act incompatibly with the Convention rights (unless under a statutory duty to act in that way). It requires all UK law to be interpreted, so far as it is possible to do so, in a way that is compatible with Convention rights. It encourages Parliament and government to make laws and policies consistent with human rights. At the second reading of a Bill, Ministers must make a statement to Parliament as to whether or not the proposed law is in conformity with the Act.

Under the Act, anyone whose rights have been violated can seek legal redress against the authorities in the UK courts. Prior to the adoption of the

---

4 JCHR, op. cit., note 1, para 67. The JCHR statement summarizes the finding of the Review by the Department of Constitutional Affairs.
5 The UK was the first state to ratify the ECHR in 1951, having played a leading role in drafting it.

Act, the only remedy for such persons was in the European Court of Human Rights through a cumbersome, lengthy and expensive process in Strasbourg. The increasing numbers of cases being brought under the Human Rights Act is an indicator of the easing of access to judicial remedy. Perversely, the increase has also led to the criticism that the Act encourages frivolous complaints.[6]

The Act has been described as 'a watershed', aligning domestic law with international obligations, making Convention rights enforceable in domestic courts against all public authorities, and creating a system for the legislature and the executive to improve their compliance with international human rights standards.[7] Such profuse praise, however, needs to be tempered with the recognition that the Act has its limits.

The HRA is not a Bill of Rights. It does not entrench rights. Instead it respects the supremacy of Parliament.[8] Ironically, much of the criticism of the HRA has centred on the misunderstanding that the courts enjoy excessive power. The courts have the power to provide a remedy against a decision by a public authority that is found to be in breach of Convention rights. They do not have the power to strike down a law that they find incompatible with the HRA. If a piece of legislation is in violation of the Act, the courts can declare the law to be incompatible, and it is then up to the government and Parliament to decide whether or not to amend the law.[9]

The Act presumes that no government or Parliament will ignore a declaration by a higher court, and that a process of 'dialogue' between the three branches – government, Parliament and the courts – will lead to a better outcome for rights as well as democracy. There is clearly merit in 'sharing' the responsibility between the political (executive/ legislature) and judicial arms of government, given the dilemmas and hard choices that often have to be made in the context of rights. There is also political wisdom in giving Parliament a central role on human rights in a country where the HRA is looked upon by many with suspicion as having imported 'European rights' even though more than half a century has passed since the UK ratified the ECHR.

It is interesting to note that, in defending the HRA, the JCHR felt compelled to point out that 'the European Convention on Human Rights was

---

6 *The Times*, 'Terrorism and deportation cases have fuelled the first rise for seven years in court cases using HRA', 15 February 2010.

7 B. Berti, 'Securing a Role for International Human Rights Law in Counter Terrorism: The Role of Judicial Review in the United Kingdom', *New England Journal of Political Science*, vol. III, no. 2, 2003.

8 This is in contrast to the European Communities Act 1972, according to which UK law can be overridden if it conflicts with directly enforceable EU law.

9 In *A and Others v Secretary of State for the Home Department*, Lord Bingham described the power of the British courts under the HRA as 'a very specific, wholly democratic mandate' to interpret and apply the Convention but 'not, of course, to override the sovereign legislative authority of the Queen in Parliament' [2004] UKHL 56.

largely drafted by British lawyers, and for the most part contains rights which are in any event recognized in our English common law'.[10] In a similar vein, Lord Hoffman in *A and Others v the Secretary of State for the Home Department* traced the roots of Art. 5 of the Convention to English common law:

> Freedom from arbitrary arrest is a quintessentially British liberty, enjoyed by inhabitants of this country when most of the population of Europe could be thrown into prison at the whim of their rulers. It was incorporated into the European Convention in order to entrench the same liberty in countries which had recently been under Nazi occupation. The United Kingdom subscribed to the Convention because it set out the rights which British subjects enjoyed under the common law.[11]

Appealing to national pride is a good strategy for building popular support and understanding of human rights (by relating people to their local experience), but the very fact of having to do so a decade after the adoption of the HRA and half a century after the ratification of the ECHR indicates that international human rights are still contested territory in the cultural politics of the UK. Lawyers, politicians and journalists continue to debate whether and how global human rights norms should be understood and enacted legally, morally and politically in the UK.[12]

The HRA has set the legal framework but is yet to permeate institutional culture or social values in a meaningful way.[13] While the HRA has brought concrete benefits through litigation, its real potential in terms of promoting and embedding human rights as shared, global values and norms remains to be realized. That is why possibly the biggest misperception is to see the HRA as a technical legal tool rather than as an instrument for transformative social change. For it is the absence of a shared culture of human rights that has made the HRA vulnerable to attack and denigration by vested interests, particularly in the context of national security and counter-terrorism, where nationalistic fears are easily roused.

10 JCHR, op. cit., note 1, para 70.
11 (2004) UKHL 56.
12 Kate Nash, *The Cultural Politics of Human Rights Comparing the US and UK*, Cambridge: Cambridge University Press, 2009. Nash defines cultural politics as 'contests over how society is imagined; how social relations are, could and should be organized'. She concludes that human rights – as global norms, as compared to traditional civil liberties rooted in English common law – are yet to be accepted fully in the UK at the political and people's level.
13 'The challenge for those who would wish to see the firm and enduring establishment of a culture of human rights is to build on the legal basis of human rights provided by the Human Rights Act in such a way as to take concepts of human rights beyond the legal sphere and into the currency of everyday life.' JCHR, op. cit., note 1, para 142.

Fighting terrorism: erosion of rights

The attacks of 9/11 were a decisive turning point for human rights. In the aftermath of 9/11, security concerns acquired legitimacy and dominance over rights in western democracies in a way they had never done before. The US set the tone for the era. In the name of a global War on Terror, the Bush Administration crafted a strategy that attacked the most fundamental human rights principles, including the ban on torture and ill-treatment, the prohibition on arbitrary and secret detention and the guarantees of fair trial. Using the language of war, the Administration justified its actions in terms of the executive power of the President as Commander in Chief.[14] Legal challenges in the courts were brushed off as formalities without substantive effect. 'American exceptionalism' triumphed over human rights.[15]

The Obama Administration promised change, and indeed took some important steps, such as ending the use of torture for interrogation purposes and the denunciation of techniques like water-boarding. But other policies, such as the Guantanamo prison camp, have continued despite the President's decision to close it. Reversing the earlier promise of civilian trials, military commissions have been put into operation to try some of the detainees. The Patriot Act with its harsh measures remains on the statute book. In short, while the worst excesses of the War on Terror have been removed, the overall security strategy persists.

As a global player, the US's policies and practices have had an export value beyond its borders, enticing and implicating its allies. Driven by common military and diplomatic goals and the 'special trans-Atlantic relationship', the UK succumbed to that influence. One example of it has been the UK's complicity in torture and extraordinary renditions.[16] There are also parallels between Guantanamo prison camp and the short-lived regime of arbitrary detention in Belmarsh and Woodhill in that they both sought to place detainees outside the rule of national or international law.

There is, however, a fundamental difference between the US and the UK responses to terrorism. Unlike the US, the UK has not been able to ignore international human rights norms. Because of its membership of the European regional human rights system, 'brought home' through the HRA, the UK has

---

14 US Administration officials argued that the provisions of the UN Convention Against Torture as incorporated in US law could be violated under the discretionary powers of the President as Commander in Chief and using the defence of necessity. US Department of Justice, Memorandum for Jay Baybee, Assistant Attorney General to Alberto Gonzales, Counsel to the President, 1 August 2002.

15 Nash, supra n. 12, pp. 78–93.

16 Amnesty International, *Open Secret: Mounting Evidence of Europe's Complicity in Rendition and Secret Detention*, EUR01/024/2010. Available at: <http://www.amnesty.org/en/library/asset/EUR01/024/2010/en/c70f5d23-cea3-48d3-a768-bc87092cddc8/eur010242010en.pdf> (accessed 17 June 2011).

been compelled to justify its response to terrorism in terms of its international human rights obligations, even though it has continued to contest them in the court of law as well as that of public opinion.

Arbitrary detention, and torture and ill-treatment are two areas where UK governments' security strategies have been tempered – at least to some extent – by judicial and political accountability under the HRA.

Until the 9/11 attacks in the US, the UK's terrorism strategy had been shaped by its experience in Northern Ireland, and checked from time to time by Strasbourg.[17] With the signing of the peace agreement in Northern Ireland in 2000 the UK adopted its first permanent Terrorism Act, which, together with the HRA, set a new legal framework for responding to terrorism. The Terrorism Act was draconian: it widened the definition of terrorism, created new offences of inciting terrorism, enhanced police stop and search powers, increased pre-charge detention from 48 hours to seven days, and outlawed certain groups including al-Qaeda.

Despite the existence of this wide-ranging law, in the weeks following 9/11 the government rushed through Parliament the Anti-Terrorism, Crime and Security Act (ATCSA) to introduce indefinite detention without charge for foreigners suspected of terrorism.[18] Prior to proposing the law, the UK government derogated from Art. 5 of the ECHR and its equivalent provision in the International Covenant on Political and Civil Rights.

A total of 17 foreigners were detained under the ATCSA. The law was challenged in the courts and eventually ended up in the House of Lords.[19] Exercising its powers under the HRA, the court looked at the compatibility of the detention rules with the ECHR as well as the validity of the derogation. While deferring to the Executive on the determination of a clear and imminent danger that necessitated the derogation, the court concluded that by focusing only on foreign nationals the detention provision was both disproportionate and discriminatory, and therefore incompatible with the ECHR.

In response, the government let the law lapse and instead introduced the Prevention of Terrorism Act (PTA) in 2005, which created a regime of control

---

17 Parliament enacted a series of Emergency Provisions Acts (1973–1996) and Temporary Prevention of Terrorism Acts (1974 –1989), which *inter alia* introduced internment and removed trial by jury in Northern Ireland. The UK's policies and practices were challenged several times in the European Court, e.g. *Ireland v United Kingdom* (1978) 2 EHRR.

18 The UK's response to the 9/11 attacks was marked by legislative hyperactivity. In addition to the 2000 TA and the 2001 ATCSA, Parliament enacted the 2005 Prevention of Terrorism Act which introduced control orders, the 2006 Terrorism Act which extended the pre-charge detention period from 14 to 28 days, and the 2008 Counter Terrorism Act which enabled post-charge questioning of terrorist suspects, allowed DNA samples to be taken from individuals subject to control orders and amended the definition of terrorism to include a racial clause. Some of the laws were rushed through Parliament with undue haste. The ATCSA was adopted in a month; its successor, the PTA, in just 17 days.

19 *A v The Secretary of State for the Home Department* (2004) UKHL 56.

orders (of both derogable and non-derogable nature), which the government then used to restrain some of the same individuals who had earlier been subjected to detention without trial. Furthermore, the PTA, respecting the principle of non-discrimination, provided for control orders to be imposed equally on citizens as well as non-citizens – not quite the consequence expected by those who had challenged the ATCSA.[20]

Control orders have been the subject of much controversy, criticism and litigation.[21] The government claims they respect Convention rights. Human rights groups claim they are incompatible with the HRA because they impose essentially criminal sanctions for what are essentially criminal offences based on secret evidence and without the fair trial safeguards required by international human rights law.[22]

The UK's onslaught on Art. 5 of the ECHR was accompanied by a parallel attempt to weaken the prohibition against torture and ill-treatment. Freedom from torture or other ill-treatment is a peremptory norm of international law and a rule of customary international law. It is a clear and unequivocal provision of the ECHR from which there can be no derogation.[23] In *Chahal v UK*, the European Court for Human Rights held that the prohibition on torture and ill-treatment is absolute and that national security considerations do not justify deporting a person to a state where she or he would face torture.[24]

Deportation to torture is a popular counter-terrorism measure because procedural safeguards related to deportation are much lighter than the requirements of fair trial in a criminal prosecution.[25] Very often, however, the countries of deportation tend to be also countries with a poor record on human rights. Under the HRA, UK courts are required to interpret UK law in conformity with the European Convention. They are obliged to apply *Chahal* and block deportation if there is a risk of torture or ill-treatment.

---

20 As at April 2011, there were nine individuals subject to control orders, all of them British citizens.
21 On 1 August 2006, the Court of Appeal affirmed that six control orders made by the Secretary of State under the PTA were incompatible with Art. 5 ECHR: *Secretary of State for the Home Department v JJ and Others* (2006) 3 WLR. See also *Secretary of State for the Home Department v MB* (2007) UKHL 46, (2008) 1AC 440, and *Secretary of State for the Home Department v AF and others* (2009) UKHL 28, (2009) 3 WLR 74.
22 Amnesty International, *United Kingdom: Submission for the Review of Counter-Terrorism and Security Powers*, EUR45/015/2010, 5.
23 ECHR Art. 3.
24 (1997) 23 EHRR 413.
25 E. Metcalfe, 'The future of counter-terrorism and human rights', *JUSTICE*, 2007, pp. 13–14. Available at: <http://www.justice.org.uk/data/files/resources/39/The-Future-of-Counter-terrorism-and-Human-Rights-1-September-2007.pdf> (accessed 17 June 2011).

The then Labour Government tried to overturn European jurisprudence on torture through third-party intervention in an unprecedented manner. In *Ramzy v Netherlands*, the Dutch authorities wanted to deport to Algeria an Algerian national who claimed that he would be tortured on return. The UK government put in a third-party submission to the European Court of Human Rights, arguing that the right of a person to be protected from torture abroad should be balanced against the risk he posed to the deporting state.[26] The UK also intervened as a third party in *Saadi v Italy* with the same argument. In both cases, the European Court rejected the balancing test and maintained the absolute prohibition against return to torture.[27] Both the JCHR and the House of Commons Foreign Affairs Committee subsequently rebuked the UK government for attempting to overturn *Chahal*.[28] The combination of judicial resistance and Parliamentary criticism eventually dissuaded the government from pursuing this route any further.

However, just as the UK was able to achieve detention by another guise (through control orders) when thwarted by the House of Lords in *A and Others*, it has been able to achieve its goal of deportation to torture through the practice of diplomatic assurances. These are formal undertakings by the government of the country concerned that deportees will not be tortured on return. The UK negotiated such assurances from Lebanon, Jordan, Libya and Ethiopia – all countries with credible reports of practice of torture and ill-treatment.

Diplomatic assurances have been strongly criticized by human rights groups, UK Parliamentary Committees and European and UN human rights experts. The UN Special Rapporteur on Torture summed up the concerns succinctly in his report to the UN General Assembly:

> Diplomatic assurances are unreliable and ineffective in the protection against torture and ill-treatment: such assurances are sought usually from States where the practice of torture is systematic; post-return monitoring mechanisms have proven to be no guarantee against torture; diplomatic assurances are not legally binding, therefore they carry no legal effect and no accountability if breached; and the person whom the assurances aim to protect has no recourse if the assurances are violated.[29]

---

26 Italy, Lithuania, Portugal and Slovakia joined the UK's request. In its request to intervene, the UK stated that the Court needs to 're-examine the relationship between the protection from ill-treatment and national security interests'. Observations of the Governments of Lithuania, Portugal, Slovakia and the UK Intervening in Application No. 25424/05, para 27.1.

27 *Saadi v Italy*, Appl. No. 37201/06, European Court of Human Rights, 28 February 2008.

28 JCHR HL278/ HC1716, 14 Nov 2006, para 121; House of Commons Select Comm. On Foreign Affairs, 9th report, session 2007–08, July 9, para 72.

29 Report of the Special Rapporteur on torture and other cruel, inhuman or degrading treatment or punishment, UN Doc A/60/316, 30 August 2005, paras 51–2.

The very fact of seeking an assurance amounts to an admission and a confirmation that the person would be at risk of torture or other ill-treatment in the receiving State if returned. Furthermore, to seek such assurance for deportees could be seen as a tacit acceptance of torture of other cases, thus undermining the overall goal of eradicating torture.

The European Court in *Saadi v Italy* and the House of Lords in *RB (Algeria) and Others v Home Secretary* took a more pragmatic stand. They have not denounced diplomatic assurances as such but instead have held that whether or not an assurance can be relied on is a question of fact to be determined by the decision-maker based on the actual circumstances in that country, and not simply on the accession to international instruments or existence of domestic laws.[30] On that basis, the House of Lords (now the UK Supreme Court) allowed the deportation of individuals to Jordan and Algeria. According to Amnesty International, such judgments have emboldened the government to continue its practice of deportation to torture with diplomatic assurances, despite the risks involved.[31]

In contrast to diplomatic assurances, getting judicial support to weaken the 'exclusionary rule', or the use of information obtained through torture as evidence in judicial proceedings, has proven more difficult. There was an attempt in *A v Secretary of State for the Home Department (No. 2)* to argue that evidence obtained by torture overseas should be admissible in judicial proceedings, as long as UK officials were not directly involved in or had connived at that torture.[32] The Law Lords unanimously rejected the government's proposition, irrespective of where torture occurred in the world, and no matter who carried it out. They rejected national security as a competing consideration.

Lord Bingham stated:

> ... it trivialises the issue before the House to treat it as an argument about the law of evidence. The issue is one of constitutional principle ... the principles of common law, standing alone, in my opinion compel the exclusion of third party torture evidence as unreliable, unfair, offensive to ordinary standards of humanity and decency and incompatible with the principles which should animate a tribunal seeking to administer justice. But the principles of common law do not stand alone. Effect must be given to the European Convention, which itself takes account of the all but universal consensus embodied in the Torture Convention ...

In Lord Hoffman's words: 'The use of torture is dishonourable. It corrupts and degrades the state which uses it and the legal system which accepts it.'

---

30 Supra note 27; (2009) UKHL 10.
31 Amnesty International, *Dangerous Deals: Europe's Reliance on 'Diplomatic Assurances' Against Torture*, EUR01/012/2010.
32 (2005) UKHL 71.

Such strong denunciation of torture by the highest court in the UK sits uneasily with reports and revelations about the involvement of UK officials in cases where individuals claim to have been tortured by US and other intelligence services. Does the participation of UK officials in the interrogation of individuals abroad, knowing that they have been tortured by foreign intelligence agencies, amount to complicity? Is the use by UK state officials of intelligence obtained through torture by others amount to complicity in torture, and so a breach of Convention rights under the HRA? These are not theoretical issues but real concerns that have come to light in the context of cooperation between the UK and US and other intelligence services. The Labour Government's position was so ambiguous, if not prevaricating, that it led the JCHR to conclude:

> . . . the Minister . . . the Director General of MI5 and both the Home and Foreign Secretaries . . . come very close to saying that, at least in the wake of 9/11, the lesser of two evils was the receipt and use of intelligence which was known, or should have been known, to carry a risk that it might have been obtained under torture, in order to protect the UK public from possible terrorist attack. This is no defence to the charge of complicity. We cannot find any legal basis for the Government's narrow formulation of the meaning of complicity . . .[33]

Following the case of *Binyam Mohamed*,[34] in which the disclosure of redacted material shows the involvement (or at least knowledge) of UK officials in the torture of the complainant by US and other foreign intelligence services, the Coalition Government announced in July 2010 that it was establishing an inquiry into the issue of complicity in torture. The outcome is still awaited but there is no doubt that it will raise some complex dilemmas at the heart of the debate about balancing security and human rights.

Balancing human rights and security

Arbitrary detention, complicity in torture and ill-treatment, the use of control orders and diplomatic assurances, an ever widening net of terrorism laws: in each case an Executive determined to push through its security objectives has struggled with a judiciary and civil society groups equally determined not to forsake liberty lightly. In each case, substantial ground has been lost by human rights defenders, if not directly then indirectly. In that process, the HRA, the main instrument of resistance of one side, has become the target for attack by the other.

---

33 JCHR, 'Counter-Terrorism Policy and Human Rights (Seventeenth Report): Bringing Human Rights Back In', HL86/HC111, 13.
34 *Binyam Mohamed v Secretary of State for Foreign and Commonwealth Affairs* (2010) EWCA Civ 65.

Autocratic regimes, whether in Eastern Europe during the Communist era, in Latin America during the military dictatorships of the 1970s and 1980s, or in other parts of the world in the past and currently, have taken the position that human rights considerations cannot be allowed to stand in the way of national security and stability. Democratic governments, subject to judicial scrutiny, parliamentary accountability and the rule of law, do not have the option of jettisoning rights. So they seek to find a balance between rights and security, but there is always an underlying inference that it is the latter that needs to be 'balanced' at the expense of the former.

In the political discourse in the UK, the balance has been articulated as being between 'the ordinary claims of human rights' and 'the extraordinary demands of public safety' or between 'the right to life' and 'all other human rights', or the rights of 'the victims' and the rights of 'criminals and terrorist suspects'.[35] After the 7/7 London bombings in 2005, the then UK Home Secretary, Charles Clarke, stated that 'the right to be protected from the death and destruction caused by indiscriminate terrorism is at least as important as the right of the terrorist to be protected from torture and ill-treatment'.[36] Six years later, a similar message was given by his successor, Theresa May, when she told Parliament that 'the rights of the public come before the rights of the criminals'.[37]

The juxtaposition of the rights of victims with the rights of suspects makes it easier for politicians to gain popular backing for terrorism laws, regulations and policies. Playing on public fears and self-interest can help to push through radical measures such as detention without charge or trial, control orders, deportation to torture, and the use of secret evidence. When human rights advocates and courts intervene in defence of rights, they are discredited as undermining national security. In the media and in the public mind the HRA is seen as 'the charter for terrorists and criminals'.

One of the strongest and most controversial statements against human rights was made by the then Prime Minister Tony Blair. Shortly after the 7/7 attacks in London he declared that 'the rules of the game have changed' and that it might be necessary to amend the Human Rights Act because human rights were hindering efforts to ensure national security.[38] In another [declaration] to Parliament, he stated: 'We will make sure that our human rights legislation does not get in the way of common sense legislation to protect our country.'[39] Such statements, coming from the leader of the Labour Party responsible for the adoption of the HRA, were immensely damaging to the

---

35　Metcalfe, supra note 25, p. 3.
36　Speech to Heritage Foundation, Washington DC, October 2005.
37　BBC, 16 February 2011.
38　Prime Minister's press conference, 5 August 2005.
39　HC Deb 17 May 2006 col. 990.

HRA. It also fed the notion that human rights and security cannot be squared.[40]

Politicizing and problematizing rights has heightened misperceptions about the Human Rights Act, made it more unpopular in the public mind and led to calls from politicians for its repeal or amendment. One tabloid openly campaigned against the Act on the grounds that it frustrates the ability of the government and the will of Parliament to protect citizens.[41]

Calls to scrap the HRA and withdraw from the ECHR are disingenuous.[42] The HRA incorporates the ECHR – so merely repealing or amending the legislation will not let the UK off the hook in terms of its obligations to respect human rights enshrined in the ECHR. Those obligations will remain, as will the possibility for individuals to seek recourse directly from the European Court of Human Rights (as happened prior to the adoption of HRA). Those who propose amending the Act rather than repealing it need to take heed that any amendment would have to be in line with the ECHR – or it could lead to a challenge in the European Court and/or censure by the Council of Europe, under whose auspices the ECHR operates. At the extreme end, there are some politicians who advocate that the UK should withdraw from the ECHR, not just repeal the HRA.[43] This would be 'the nuclear option' as it would require the UK to also withdraw from the Council of Europe and the European Union, the ratification of the ECHR being a prerequisite for membership of both. That is unlikely to happen. What this debate on the HRA is signifying, however, is that though human rights are embedded in UK law, they are not yet a commonly shared value in political discourse.[44]

Draining the hysteria from the political debate requires a better under-standing of the relationship between human rights and security. The two need not be at loggerheads; as a matter of principle, as well as of law, they are not diametrically opposed policy objectives. Lawful counter-terrorism measures and protection of human rights are both vital functions of the state intended to serve essentially the same purpose – the protection of the life and integrity of people – and are recognized as such by international human rights law. As the Joint Committee on Human Rights acknowledged:

---

40 The previous year, the JCHR had rebuked ministers for their unfounded criticism of the HRA. 'In our view public misunderstandings of the effect of the Act will continue so long as very senior ministers fail to retract unfortunate comments already made and con-tinue to make unfounded assertions about the Act and to use it as a scapegoat for admin-istrative failings in their departments.' HL278/HC1716, para 41.

41 *The Sun*, 'Time to Stop the Madness', May 2006.

42 See Gearty, supra note 1.

43 See proposed draft report by Douglas Carswell MP, Minutes of JCHR, 7 November 2006, HL278/HC1716.

44 Nash, supra n. 12, pp. 99–100.

... human rights law itself imposes positive obligations on the State to take active steps to protect people from the real risk of terrorism. Counterterrorism measures may be positively required by human rights law, where they are necessary and proportionate, and human rights law provides the framework within which to assess the important evidential questions about the necessity and proportionality of those measures.[45]

International human rights law recognizes the duty of the state to protect its citizens but requires the state do so within the framework of law and in strict compliance with human rights norms. There are some rights that can never be suspended or restricted, such as freedom from torture and other forms of cruel, inhuman and degrading treatment. But there are many other rights for which restrictions, limitations or derogations are permissible.[46] These are the mechanisms by which conflicts between security and human rights can and should be resolved.

Derogation is an exceptional measure to be adopted in a state of emergency and, as such, it must accord strictly with the principles of legality, proportionality and necessity. That means there must be a public emergency, and that the derogation must be prescribed and determined by law, be necessary to protect a particular public interest, be proportionate to the exigencies of the situation and be compatible with other rights.[47]

The UK has derogated on three occasions since 1974. Between 1974 and 2000, the UK twice derogated from Art. 5 of the ECHR on the basis that the situation in Northern Ireland amounted to a 'public emergency threatening the life of the nation'. The third derogation was in the aftermath of 9/11, when the government submitted a detailed Derogation Order under the ECHR and the International Covenant on Civil and Political Rights in anticipation of the detention provisions under Part 4 of ATCSA. Two of the three derogations were challenged in court. The first case, preceding the

---

45 JCHR, 'Counter-Terrorism Policy and Human Rights (Seventeenth Report): Bringing Human Rights Back In', HL86/HC 111, para 5.

46 Article 15 (1), ECHR: 'In time of war or other public emergency threatening the life of the nation any High Contracting Party may take measures derogating from its obligations under this Convention to the extent strictly required by the exigencies of the situation, provided that such measures are not inconsistent with its other obligations under international law.' Article 4 of the UN Covenant on Civil and Political Rights also contains a derogation clause. By contrast Art. 29 (2) of the Universal Declaration of Human Rights recognizes limitations on rights for the purpose of 'meeting the just requirements of morality, public order and the general welfare in a democratic society'. Such limitations clauses are common in human rights treaties and unlike derogation are not related to emergency situations.

47 J. Fitzpatrick, *Human Rights in Crisis: the International System for Protecting Rights During States of Emergency*, Procedural Aspects of International Law Series, University of Pennsylvania Press, 1994. See also UN Human Rights Committee, States of Emergency, General Comment 29, 24 July 2001.

HRA, was brought before the European Court, which upheld the derogation as lawful.[48]

In the second case, under the HRA, *A and Others v the Secretary of State for the Home Department*, the House of Lords considered in detail the conditions that needed to be fulfilled for derogation.[49] The court noted that the UK was the only European member state to have derogated from Art. 5 of the ECHR, that the Parliamentary Assembly of the Council of Europe had called on member states not to derogate from the ECHR in the fight against terrorism and that the Parliamentary Joint Committee on Human Rights (JCHR) had found no need for derogation based on the information provided by the government to Parliament. Nevertheless, the court felt that the decision of whether or not there was clear and imminent danger to the state was a matter of political judgment for the Secretary of State, not for the court, to make. It therefore deferred to the government on this point. The deference by the courts – both in the UK and in Strasbourg – to the Executive on the security/political dimensions of derogation gives the Executive considerable leeway in terrorism cases.

The JCHR has looked at the issue of derogation on three separate occasions.[50] As a political body, it was less deferential than the judiciary on the government's prerogative to determine 'a public emergency'. While accepting that the UK faces a serious threat from terrorism, the JCHR questioned whether the UK still faced 'a public emergency threatening the life of the nation' eight years after the government first declared such an emergency. Noting the tendency of the government to derogate (or say it will derogate) in response to unfavourable court decisions, the JCHR recommended a statutory framework for derogations.[51] This recommendation, if accepted, would bring much-needed political accountability to the Executive in an area where judicial scrutiny is weak because of the tendency of the judiciary to defer to the Executive.

A maturing process

This selective review of the UK's response to terrorism has highlighted some of the problems in the area of human rights and terrorism between legal obligations and political imperatives. On the plus side, the courts and human rights advocates have fought valiantly, using the ECHR and the HRA as their sword and shield. There has been a powerful subtext of deeply rooted common

---

48 *Brannigan & McBride v United Kingdom* (1993) 17 EHRR 539.
49 (2004) UKHL 56. The House of Lords found the detention provision disproportionate and discriminatory and so incompatible with the ECHR.
50 HL116/HC635 at para 50; LH165-I/HC150–1 at paras 240–3; HL86/HC111 at paras 25–8.
51 JCHR, 'Counter-Terrorism Policy and Human Rights (Seventeenth Report): Bringing Human Rights Back In,' HL86/HC111, paras 13–14.

law principles of liberty and justice, but while the latter have undoubtedly helped – from the perspective of both public mobilization and judicial reasoning – the courts and human rights advocates could not have resisted the onslaught of the Executive and Parliament without the ECHR and its proxy, the HRA.

There is, however, no doubt that rights have been pushed back. Even more dangerously, a negativism about human rights has gained currency with potential damage to democracy, freedom and the rule of law in the longer term. The added value of the HRA is the localization of rights – the embedding of a culture of human rights in state and local institutions – but it is being thwarted in that task by political opportunism that has grown on the back of the security agenda. There is also a dangerous undertone of nationalistic fervour in which human rights are being delegitimized as 'foreign' or 'European' and a narrower concept of civil liberties is being promoted as 'British' and therefore more relevant. It undermines the universality as well as the indivisibility of international human rights.

Against this background, the proposal to set up a Commission to consider a Bill of Rights is both a challenge and an opportunity. There is a risk that the process may damage the HRA without producing a worthy successor. On the other hand, it could also be an opportunity to consolidate rights more firmly – whether in the form of a Bill of Rights or a revised HRA or even a reinvigorated HRA.

Whatever the case may be, there are a number of lessons to be drawn from the HRA's experience with terrorism. The first is the need to entrench rights more firmly. The plethora of terrorism laws enacted in the course of the past decade shows that the Executive is opportunistic and Parliament whimsical. Human rights need to be embedded so firmly that they cannot be overturned or overridden easily.

Secondly, the ECHR standards have been invaluable in the struggle to preserve rights in the face of counter-terrorism measures. But they are focused on civil and political rights. While they remain important, moving from the age of terrorism into the age of austerity requires greater attention to be given to economic, social and cultural rights to which the UK has subscribed internationally but which are still not properly understood or acknowledged as human rights domestically. Making the HRA as relevant to social equity as it is to physical integrity may be a good way to redeem its damaged image.[52]

Thirdly, human rights are global as well as local. The UK's counter-terrorism measures did not only damage human rights at home – they also

---

52 A. Wagner, 'End of the age of terrorism for human rights campaigners', UK Human Rights Blog, 4 August 2010, identifies a range of issues from the removal of a mandatory retirement age to public sector redundancy packages and benefits cuts as possible areas for HRA litigation. Available at: <http://ukhumanrightsblog.com/2010/08/02/feature-end-of-the-age-of-terrorism-for-human-rights-campaigners> (accessed 17 June 2011).

hurt the rights struggle abroad. For instance, complicity in torture set back progress on the global campaign to eradicate torture. There is a link between what the UK does at home and what happens abroad. The UK's promotion of rights internationally can be improved if there is a stronger commitment to accountability at the national level. Similarly, strengthening the UK's domestic record on human rights will give it greater credibility to champion human rights elsewhere. Any future iteration of the HRA should promote better understanding of the global context and universal nature of rights, and increase the synergy between human rights domestically and internationally.

Finally, rights must be locally relevant. Without a broad constituency of support, human rights remain vulnerable to attack and distortion. The UK government introduced the Human Rights Bill in 1998 under the title 'rights brought home', and that is what needs to be done now – through human rights education, local ownership by communities and embedding human rights in local institutions. That would help to create a shared understanding of rights that is now lacking.

The HRA and counter-terrorism have generated a lively political debate in which new understandings and institutions of human rights are likely to be developed. That presents both challenges and opportunities. Looking back in another ten years from now, the HRA – as we know it today – may be seen as the first step in the maturation process of bringing rights home.[53]

---

53 The UK government introduced the Human Rights Act 1998 as *Rights Brought Home: the Human Rights Bill*, Cm 3782, London: The Stationery Office.

7   Doughty defenders of the Human Rights Act

Keith Ewing

Take a random day. 30 March 2011. The day I started writing this chapter. Take a random newspaper on that random day. The one that is delivered to my home six days a week. According to *The Guardian* on that day, there were at least five significant human rights stories worthy of reporting. The first was the inquest into the death of Ian Tomlinson, the news vendor who died after an altercation with a police officer, named in *The Guardian* as PC Simon Harwood.[1] The second was a report about the mass arrest of UK Uncut protestors who had visited Fortnum and Mason during the great TUC march and rally against the cuts on the previous Saturday. The young protestors involved were arrested for aggravated trespass, some of them spending up to 24 hours in custody. The third story was a claim that the Home Office was about to introduce even further controls on political protest, responding to right-wing demands for further restraint. This is despite caution being expressed by a prominent Tory backbencher about introducing yet further controls on freedom of assembly. The fourth was growing concern about so-called super-injunctions, the cover of which is broken only by parliamentary privilege. And the fifth was the ongoing drama of phone hacking by the Murdoch press (a State within a State?). Human Rights Act? 'You're having a laugh,' as they might say on the pages of Rupert's most common title.

Churchill's legacy

But why should we be surprised by any of this? It is true that the Human Rights Act was supposed to make things better, as the midwife of a culture of liberty in the United Kingdom. It was in part New Labour's ironic response to the reactionary laws of the Thatcher and Major years, which saw not only an expansion of State power but also the more visible manifestations of that power.

---

1 An inquest jury was later to find that Mr Tomlinson had been unlawfully killed, after the Crown Prosecution Service (CPS) had decided not to prosecute, and the Independent Police Complaints Authority had found nothing untoward. See *The Guardian*, 4 May 2011.

It was in part also a response to pressure from the judges, who it seems were frustrated by the limited grounds of review of administrative action, and anxious to 'restore this country to its former place as an international standard bearer of liberty and justice'.[2] But for a number of reasons, the wrapping of the Union Jack around the European Convention on Human Rights was never likely to deliver what some people thought it promised, or to meet the inflated expectations of civil libertarians. Not least because – as is being openly acknowledged in a desperate attempt to defend the Act from the 'Tory fundamentalists' – the Act has its roots deep in centre-right (not centre-left) politics and ideology, a point now emerging forcefully as civil liberties activists seek to persuade the 'sensible' Tories that although introduced by New Labour (itself a centre-right ideology), the Human Rights Act was really a Tory instrument in drag.

The point is made elegantly in a major initiative to reclaim the HRA for the Tories by a leading Tory 'thinker' and a leading Tory journalist.[3] In a preface to a pamphlet published by the campaign group Liberty (formed in 1934, ironically to protect communists, trade unionists and the unemployed from police and fascist brutality),[4] Liberty's Shami Chakrabarti wrote that the two authors were:

> extremely well placed to offer a critical conservative analysis of British history and the very important role that centre-right thinking has played in the development of fundamental rights and freedoms. As they have so ably demonstrated, the European Convention on Human Rights, which the Human Rights Act 1998 (HRA) incorporates, largely originated from British common law traditions and it was largely drafted by British conservative lawyers.[5]

This reflects the views of the LSE's Francesca Klug, who claims to have 'assisted the government in devising the model for incorporating the European Convention on Human Rights into UK law', and who 'was a member of the Government's Task Force responsible for overseeing implementation of the Human Rights Act'.[6] Professor Klug now tells us that the Human Rights Act was 'Churchill's legacy'. In her words, 'Winston Churchill was one of the

---

2 See T.H. Bingham, 'The European Convention on Human Rights: Time to Incorporate' (1993) *LQR* 390, at p. 400.

3 J. Norman and P. Oborne, *Churchill's Legacy: The Conservative Case for the Human Rights Act*, Liberty, 2009. Available at: <http://www.liberty-human-rights.org.uk/policy/reports/churchill-s-legacy-the-conservative-case-for-the-hra-october-2009.pdf> (accessed 17 June 2011).

4 See S. Scaffardi, *Fire under the Carpet: Working for Civil Liberties in the 1930s*, London: Lawrence and Wishart, 1986.

5 Norman and Oborne, op. cit., n. 3, p. 5.

6 See LSE Human Rights, 'Who's who: Francesca Klug', available at: <http://www2.lse.ac.uk/humanRights/whosWho/Francesca_Klug.aspx> (accessed 17 June 2011).

main drivers of the convention, it was largely drafted by UK lawyers and the UK was one of the first countries to ratify it in 1951.'[7]

But it is not only the concession that the Human Rights Act has its roots in Tory ideology that should set alarm bells ringing. So should claims that its roots lie also in the common law, which is as compelling an indicator as any that the Act is a force of conservatism rather than progress. The essence of the common law is national security, economic liberty and public order.[8] The common law has not been the friend of political freedom, social equality or popular engagement. Nevertheless, there is a wilful failure on the part of English lawyers to confront the reality of their past. On freedom of expression, for example, it is the common law that created the offences of seditious libel, blasphemous libel, obscene libel and any other kind of libel that you care to mention.[9] Now we are said to have the toughest libel laws on the planet, attracting libel tourists from all over the world,[10] courtesy of the common law. And now we also have the problem of extravagant privacy laws to protect the private lives of the wealthy, who alone have access to the legal system,[11] accompanied by so-called super-injunctions to hide their sexual and other indiscretions, available from the slot machine on the Strand. We now learn, however, that these same super-injunctions are used not only to protect the promiscuous, but also the corporations – such as Trafigura – who in an act of gross impertinence also claim that these injunctions banned the reporting of any discussion about them in Parliament.[12]

Given the history that we care not to confront, why would the present – which in a consistently non-discriminating way we equally care not to confront – be any different? It is true that we have the *A* case, in which the House of Lords ruled that indefinite detention without trial was incompatible with Convention rights.[13] Perhaps shell-shocked by the gravity of their intervention in *A*, the courts appear to have hit the retreat button in the major cases since. So the common law powers of the police to stop people attending meetings have been retained,[14] as have the controversial police powers of containment or

7   *The Guardian*, 16 February 2010.
8   See C. Hill, *Intellectual Origins of the English Revolution*, London: Panther, 1972, p. 256.
9   On common law restraints on free speech, see H. Street, *Freedom, the Individual and the Law*, 3rd edn, London: Penguin, 1972, chapters 5 and 6. See now Criminal Justice and Coroners Act 2009, s 73 (abolishing common law offences).
10 For a good account, see G. Palast, *The Best Democracy Money Can Buy*, New York and London: Plume, 2004.
11 See *Campbell v MGN* [2004] UKHL 22.
12 See *The Guardian*, 13 October 2009, and A.W. Bradley and K.D. Ewing, *Constitutional and Administrative Law*, 15th edn, Harlow: Longman, 2010, pp. 525–6 for a brief discussion of this affair.
13 *A v Home Secretary* [2004] UKHL 56.
14 *R (Laporte) v Gloucestershire Chief Constable* [2006] UKHL [2006] UKHL 55.

'kettling',[15] the decision in the latter case described by Fenwick as 'coming close to political censorship'.[16] Similarly, the stop and search powers in the Terrorism Act 2000 were held not to violate human rights in a case involving their use against a journalist and a student,[17] as were control orders, the ill-begotten issue of the *A* decision, though in the case of the control orders the courts have shown some willingness to police their operation.[18] If *A* is the zenith of judicial achievement, *A (No 2)* must be the nadir,[19] followed closely by the *Abu Qatada* case.[20] Both of these reveal very curious means of expressing disapproval of torture. The former gives the green light to the State to trade in torture, to use evidence obtained by torture, and in some cases (because the burden of proof is set too high) to admit evidence obtained by torture in legal proceedings.[21]

To jaw jaw – but with whom?

Diverting attention away from questions of substantive failure of an instrument now put forward by Tories, public lawyers have urged us to look at what appear to be the procedural advances under the HRA. Fenwick has referred to the 'need for engagement with the idea of a dialogic model of the constitution espoused by a number of current writers'.[22] It is not clear why. The idea is nonsense, devoid of any principled justification or practical evidence that the judges want to engage in this fantasy. Above all, this is simply another attempt to legitimize the illegitimate, and as such is a stunning victory for those who have questioned the propriety of supreme judicial power in a democracy. Clearly unable to defend this position, judicial supremacists are now contending that the judges and the legislature are engaged in some kind of fictional dialogue, raising the question of who gets the last word. But the dialogue metaphor is simply another way of re-heating an intellectual position that has no credibility, and rehearsing an intellectual argument that has

---

15 *Austin v Metropolitan Police Commissioner* [2009] UKHL 5.
16 H. Fenwick, 'Marginalising Human Rights: Breach of the Peace, "Kettling", the Human Rights Act and Public Protest' [2009] PL 737, at p. 763.
17 *R (Gillan) v Metropolitan Police Commissioner* [2006] UKHL 12.
18 *Home Secretary v JJ* [2007] UKHL 45.
19 *A v Home Secretary (No 2)* [2005] UKHL 71.
20 *RB and OO v Home Secretary* [2009] UKHL 10.
21 *A (No 2)*, above, paras 62, 80 (dissenting speeches by Lords Bingham and Nicholls). According to Lord Nicholls, the approach of the majority would 'place on the detainee a burden of proof which, for reasons beyond his control, he can seldom discharge'. Not only would that 'largely nullify the principle, vigorously supported on all sides, that courts will not admit evidence procured by torture', but it 'would be to pay lip-service to the principle', which in his words 'is not good enough'.
22 H. Fenwick, 'Bonfire of the Liberties: New Labour, Human Rights, and the Rule of Law', *Journal of Law and Society* 37, 2010, 682–6.

been lost. In other words, it is simply another way of giving judges a privileged veto in the law-making process, in the sense that the purpose of the dialogue is to restrain the government's scope for manoeuvre in line with judicial perceptions of the legitimate scope of popular power. Until the dialogistic magicians can convince us with a trick about why a group of self-selecting public servants representative of and accountable to no one should enjoy such elevation, they have no claim to be taken seriously.[23]

But that is not the only issue of principle. The dialogicians have even less claim to be taken seriously following the exposure of very different questions of principle on display during the spat between Lord Bingham (then senior Law Lord) and Charles Clarke (then Home Secretary). Frustrated by a number of judicial decisions against him, Clarke asked to engage the judges about what would need to be done to protect legislation from the courts. When the Home Secretary complained about Lord Bingham's resistance to dialogue in evidence to the House of Lords Constitution Committee,[24] he was given the brush-off for a second time, with the Committee remarking that 'his call for meetings between the Law Lords and the Home Secretary risks an unacceptable breach of the principle of judicial independence. It is essential that the Law Lords, as the court of last resort, should not even be perceived to have prejudged an issue as a result of communications with the executive'.[25] For this purpose, there is no reason why it would make any difference whether the dialogue took place face to face privately in an office in Whitehall, in rooms at the Supreme Court, or at arm's length publicly in a courtroom, on display in the reasoning of a court. As put by the Lord Chief Justice, 'judges must be particularly careful not even to appear to be colluding with the executive when they are likely later to have to adjudicate on challenges of action taken by the executive'.[26] The dialogicians want to have another look at the Constitutional Reform Act 2005, s 3.[27]

All this reads to me very much like Public Law 101. But these are by no means the only problems to be overcome by the dialogicians as they crave credibility. There is also the problem that the judges themselves do not seem

---

23 When the TUC was elevated to such a status under a Social Contract with the then Labour Government in the 1970s it was met with feigned constitutional outrage. But why are judges – who speak for no one – any better placed to engage in a dialogue than an organization representing 13 million people?

24 See HL Paper 151 (2006–07), paras 93–7.

25 Ibid., para, 97. The committee thought that the system of judicial preview as practised by some European countries would also be unacceptable (paras 98–106, though compare paras 109–11).

26 As quoted, ibid., para 96.

27 Constitutional Reform Act 2005, s 3: 'The Lord Chancellor, other Ministers of the Crown and all with responsibility for matters relating to the judiciary or otherwise to the administration of justice must uphold the continued independence of the judiciary.'

to be following the script written by the purveyors of the new genre of fiction, whether in the form requested by Mr Clarke or otherwise. A good example is provided by the House of Lords' decision in *R (Wright) v Secretary of State for Health*,[28] where the Lords granted a declaration of incompatibility in relation to the Care Standards Act 2000, s 82(4)(b) on the ground that it violated the right to a fair trial under Art. 6 of the ECHR. It was brought to the attention of the court that the impugned legislation was in any event to be replaced 'by a completely different scheme laid down by and under the Safeguarding Vulnerable Groups Act 2006'.[29] An opportunity for dialogue? Don't be daft. In the words of Baroness Hale:

> I would not make any attempt to suggest ways in which the scheme could be made compatible. There are two reasons for this. First, the incompatibility arises from the interaction between the three elements of the scheme – the procedure, the criterion and the consequences. It is not for us to attempt to rewrite the legislation. There is, as I have already said, a delicate balance to be struck between protecting the rights of the care workers and protecting the welfare, as well as the rights, of the vulnerable people with whom they work. It is right that that balance be struck in the first instance by the legislature.[30]

What we have, in other words, is a dialogue between one party unwilling to speak, and another unwilling to listen and unable to hear. To repeat, in other words it is nonsense. If, nevertheless, the dialogicians are to continue myopically with their fiction, they have some explaining to do about the utility of judicial dialogue, the results appearing to undermine even further (assuming there is any further to go) their claims to be taken seriously. In the new 'culture of liberty' that the Human Rights Act was supposed to launch, we have seen an extension of police powers of arrest and search, the introduction of new statutory powers of surveillance to be exercised by a wide range of public authorities,[31] and the development (without statutory authority) of the largest DNA database in the world.[32] All this is in addition to the enactment of legislation (not brought into force as a result of political pressure rather than judicial resistance) to give effect to government plans for identity cards, which at one time it was intended would be compulsory for everyone in the United Kingdom.[33] At the same time, we had the well-known powers authorizing the indefinite internment of individuals without trial, on the basis of

---

28 [2009] UKHL 3.
29 Ibid., para 39.
30 Ibid.
31 Serious Organised Crime and Police Act 2005.
32 Regulation of Investigatory Powers Act 2000.
33 Identity Cards Act 2006.

secret intelligence which the suspected international terrorist was not permitted to see. When this extraordinary legislation was repealed in 2005, it was replaced in turn with a measure that allowed the Home Secretary to detain people in prison conditions in their own homes under control orders, which the courts accepted did not necessarily infringe the right to liberty under Art. 5 of the ECHR.[34] Dialogue? Control orders for indefinite detention without trial? You must be having an even bigger laugh.

Rights of Man

Faced with the erosion of human rights in the era of the Human Rights Act, there are still those who would argue for even greater judicial power, notwithstanding the evidence about the futility in practice of judicial supremacism, quite apart from its doubtful pedigree from the starting point of constitutional principle. Amongst such counter-intuitive advocates recently is Geoffrey Robertson QC, a human rights lawyer who has argued for a constitution like the US Constitution. According to Robertson:

> Those who want a truly radical and indeed workable solution to the malaise in our liberties should look to a British Bill of Rights embedded in a written constitution, applied by judges who – as in the United States – have the power to ensure that the liberties won by Milton and Cromwell and Wilkes and Paine are not abandoned by MPs more interested in flipping their second homes.[35]

I cannot believe that I am the only person to have thought this to be wholly absurd. Let's move from Public Law 101 to US Politics 101. The United States is perhaps the greatest oligarchy that money can buy. According to the *New York Times*, in 2008 about two-thirds of senators were millionaires (with the average net worth across the Senate being just under $14 million). At the same time about 240 of the 435 members of the House of Representatives were also reported as being millionaires, with the average net worth across the House being a mere $4.6 million.[36]

The United States is also a country of extreme inequality, where 23.5 per cent of annual income is earned by only 1 per cent of households, and where the net worth of the poorest 50 per cent of households is equivalent to the net worth of the 400 wealthiest.[37] It is unlikely that this is the liberty that Tom Paine had in mind, when he railed against the condition of the poor in *Rights*

---

34 Prevention of Terrorism Act 2005.
35 *New Statesman*, 29 March 2010.
36 *New York Times*, 25 November 2009.
37 See Inequality Data & Statistics, available at: <http://inequality.org/inequality-data-statistics/> (accessed 17 June 2011).

of Man.[38] Nor is it likely that he would be sanguine about the fact that the US Constitution has enabled the political system to be captured by these wealthy individuals and their special interests. Nor, indeed, is he likely to have been impressed by the fact that one reason for this is the prohibitive costs of American democracy, which operate to exclude those of modest means from the process. An important reason for this is the Supreme Court's fetish with the First Amendment, which has seen the striking down of various legislative attempts to control the cost of politics. These decisions begin with the landmark *Buckley v Valeo*,[39] where the court has elevated the power of the wealthy over the power of the many,[40] in what was an audacious challenge to various provisions of a federal statute enacted post-Watergate to take the money out of election campaigning. At the heart of the Federal Election Campaign Act of 1974, however, was a cap on election campaign spending by candidates and 'third parties', and a public funding scheme for presidential candidates.

Like it or not, juristocracy breeds oligarchy, with this well-intentioned attempt to control the costs of elections and to promote greater equality between candidates and parties being gutted by the Supreme Court's elevation of the right to free speech over the right to fair elections. According to Mr Justice Powell,

> the concept that government may restrict the speech of some elements of our society in order to enhance the relative voice of others is wholly foreign to the First Amendment, which was designed 'to secure "the widest possible dissemination of information from diverse and antagonistic sources," ' and 'to assure unfettered interchange of ideas for the bringing about of political and social changes desired by the people'.[41]

Little wonder that the majority should draw a strong rebuke from Mr Justice White, who thought it right that 'elections are not to turn on the difference in the amounts of money that candidates have to spend',[42] and according to whom the decision would be seen by many as meaning that 'federal candidates

---

38 T. Paine, *Rights of Man* [1791], London: Penguin, 1976, ch. 5, referring to the poor laws as 'instruments of civil torture' and the 'hearts of the humane' being 'shocked by ragged and hungry children, and persons of seventy and eighty years of age begging for bread', and so on, p. 271.

39 424 US 1 (1976).

40 Some would say that this is a process that goes back to *Lochner v New York*, 198 US 45 (1905), where the Supreme Court struck down legislation regulating working hours in New York state bakeries, and applied the same principles subsequently to strike down minimum-wage laws.

41 *Buckley v Valeo*, op. cit., n. 39, pp. 49–50.

42 Ibid., p. 266.

have the constitutional right to purchase their election'.[43] This, however, is by no means the end of it, with *Buckley* acting as an enema to remove other regulatory blockages to unfair elections.[44] Consequently, we now read reports that the 2010 mid-term elections cost $4 billion and that the 2008 presidential elections cost over $5 billion, a sum that exceeds the GDP of at least 40 of the 180 or so of the world's countries.[45]

Unhappily for Robertson, his call for British judges to have a power like that of their counterparts in the United States was published only a few months after the US Supreme Court had handed down one of its most strongly criticized decisions for some time. This was the decision in *Citizens United*,[46] the latest of the post-*Buckley* issue, which led to the following blistering attack in the pages of the *New York Review of Books*:

> The Supreme Court's conservative phalanx has demonstrated once again its power and will to reverse America's drive to greater equality and more genuine democracy. It threatens a step-by-step return to a constitutional stone age of right-wing ideology. Once again it offers justifications that are untenable in both constitutional theory and legal precedent.[47]

The author of the foregoing passage was not Professor Griffith but Professor Dworkin, himself a celebrated advocate of strong judicial power. Dworkin appeared to be furious that the Court had elevated the First Amendment's protection of money as speech still higher, by holding that global companies (with huge resources) are entitled to the same rights of democratic participation in elections as people (including those of limited resources). According to the Court, 'government may not suppress political speech on the basis of the speaker's corporate identity'.[48] This – it seems – is what it means to have

---

43 Ibid., p. 267. For the treatment of Buckley in the United Kingdom, see *R (Animal Defenders International) v Secretary of State for Culture, Media and Sport* [2008] UKHL 15, where Baroness Hale referred to it as the 'elephant in the room'.

44 See S. Issacharoff, 'Throwing in the Towel: The Constitutional Morass of Campaign Finance', in K. D. Ewing and S. Issacharoff (eds), *Party Funding and Campaign Financing in International Perspective*, Oxford: Hart, 2006.

45 President Obama is planning to raise £1 billion for his re-election (*The Guardian*, 4 April 2011). Only an idiot will be seduced into believing the myth that all this will be supplied by an army of small donors (see *New York Times*, 24 November 2008, "Many Obama Small Donors Really Weren't). See further, R. Hasen, 'The Transformation of the US Campaign Finance System in Presidential Elections', in K.D. Ewing, J. Rowbottom and J.-C. Tham (eds), *The Funding of Political Parties: Where Now?*, London: Routledge, 2011, ch. 13.

46 *Citizens United v Federal Election Commission*, 558 US (2010).

47 R. Dworkin, 'The Decision that Threatens Democracy', *New York Review of Books*, 13 May 2010, p. 67.

48 *Citizens United*, op. cit., p. 30.

'judges with the power to ensure that the liberties won by Milton and Cromwell and Wilkes and Paine are not abandoned'.[49]

From absurd to bizarre

If this is not enough, Robertson's position is all the more bizarre in the light of the position taken by the legal team (of which he was a conspicuously prominent member) in the Julian Assange case. It will be recalled that Mr Assange was catapulted to prominence in the WikiLeaks affair, in the course of which a request was made by the Swedish government for his extradition on matters not directly related to the leaks. According to the subheadline in *The Guardian*, 'Skeleton argument outlined by Australian's defence team claims he could face rendition to US if extradited to Sweden', the report continuing:

> Julian Assange, the founder of WikiLeaks, could be at 'real risk' of the death penalty or detention in Guantánamo Bay if he is extradited to Sweden on accusations of rape and sexual assault, his lawyers claim.
>
> In a skeleton summary of their defence against attempts by the Swedish director of public prosecutions to extradite him, released today, Assange's legal team argue that there is a similar likelihood that the US would subsequently seek his extradition 'and/or illegal rendition', 'where there will be a real risk of him being detained at Guantánamo Bay or elsewhere'.
>
> 'Indeed, if Mr Assange were rendered to the USA, without assurances that the death penalty would not be carried out, there is a real risk that he could be made subject to the death penalty. It is well known that prominent figures have implied, if not stated outright, that Mr Assange should be executed.'[50]

So despite Robertson's desire that we in the United Kingdom should have a constitution similar to that of the United States, where judges have greater power to protect liberty, it would appear after all that the American system may be no more constitutionally literate than those of either the United Kingdom or Sweden. It would also appear after all that the American system, with its Bill of Rights embedded in a written constitution, is thus no better able in practice to safeguard 'the liberties won by Milton and Cromwell and Wilkes and Paine'. So far as the death penalty – referred to in the *Guardian* piece above – is concerned, this primitive and barbaric practice is banned throughout the Council of Europe (even in the United Kingdom). Yet despite

---

49 There will be no need to worry about flipping second homes because only those with second homes will be able to enter the race in the first place.
50 *The Guardian*, 11 January 2011.

extraordinary judicial power vested in the US Supreme Court, there have been 1,234 executions between 1976 and 2010, in the land where the judges have 'the power to ensure that. . .'. Well, perhaps Cromwell might have approved. So far as Guantánamo is concerned, it is true that in a landmark case the US Supreme Court held by a 6:3 majority that detainees could not be denied access to the federal courts.[51] But it is also true that the regime has been described by British judges as 'a monstrous failure of justice'[52] and a 'legal black hole'[53]. One of the same judges warned remarkably that 'We must not allow the smiling charming faces of our American allies to divert us from seeking to discover the reality of what is being done by their interrogators.'[54] (It should not be overlooked, however, that the position was not deemed bad enough as to move the English courts to compel the British government to seek the return of British citizens incarcerated there.)[55]

In the light of the foregoing, it is not clear why we should be seduced by the appeal of the US Constitution. These doubts are reinforced by the fate of Bradley Manning, who is alleged to have leaked the information to WikiLeaks in the first place. So what has happened to Manning? According to *The Guardian*:

> Made to endure strict conditions under a prevention of injury order against the advice of military psychiatrists, he is treated like no other prisoner at the 250-capacity Quantico Brig detention facility in Virginia. Despite that he is yet to be convicted of any crime, for the past 218 consecutive days he has been made to live in a cell 6ft wide and 12ft long, without contact with any other detainees. He is not allowed to exercise or have personal effects in his cell, and for the one hour each day he is allowed free from his windowless cell he is taken to an empty room where he is allowed to walk, but not run.[56]

There are other aspects of this affair which have led to condemnation of the US authorities by members of its own government, and to yet another letter to the *New York Review of Books*.[57]

All of which raises the question: which aspects of the Manning affair – an affair that has led to abuses that the constitution unhelpfully seems powerless to prevent – demonstrate the strengths of the US system? Lengthy detention

---

51 *Rasul v Bush*, 542 US 466 (2004).

52 J. Steyn, 'Guantanamo Bay: The Legal Black Hole' (2004) 53 ICLQ 1, at p. 11.

53 See also *R (Abbasi) v Foreign Secretary* [2002] EWCA Civ 1598, at para 22 (Lord Phillips). See also Lord Hope, 'Torture' (2004) 53 ICLQ 807.

54 Ibid., p. 831.

55 See *Abbasi*, above, and *R (Al Rawi) v Foreign Secretary* [2006] EWCA Civ 1279.

56 *The Guardian*, 4 March 2011.

57 *New York Review of Books*, 10 April 2011.

without trial? The cruel and unusual punishment of detainees? The affair is all the more depressing for taking place not on the watch of Bush and Rumsfeld, but on the watch of Obama, in whom so much hope was (as it now seems) hopelessly misplaced, and upon whom a Nobel Peace Prize was so disgracefully bestowed. The letter to the *New York Review of Books* referred to immediately above was – in the words of *The Guardian* – signed by more than 250 of America's 'most eminent legal scholars', who included Harvard professor Laurence Tribe, significant because Tribe taught Obama constitutional law and was until recently a constitutional adviser in the Justice Department.[58] This 'foremost liberal authority' was quoted by *The Guardian* as complaining that Manning's treatment was 'not only shameful but unconstitutional', and objectionable 'in the way it violates his person and his liberty without due process of law and in the way it administers cruel and unusual punishment of a sort that cannot be constitutionally inflicted even upon someone convicted of terrible offences, not to mention someone merely accused of such offences'.[59] According to the signatories:

> The sum of the treatment that has been widely reported is a violation of the Eighth Amendment's prohibition of cruel and unusual punishment, and the Fifth Amendment's guarantee against punishment without trial. If continued, it may well amount to a violation of the criminal statute against torture, defined as, among other things, 'the administration or application . . . of . . . procedures calculated to disrupt profoundly the senses or the personality'.[60]

And all of this before we even begin to consider the commitment to the rule of law revealed by the events of 1 May 2011, which were said by one leading commentator to represent 'the commission of one crime (torture) [to facilitate] the commission of another crime (assassination)'.[61]

Profligacy with Churchill's legacy

There will almost certainly not be a US-style Bill of Rights in the United Kingdom, even though the US experience provides a nice snapshot of what it means to locate human rights in a centre-right political environment. The penny has dropped nevertheless, with the Tories having at long last accepted the arguments being urged upon them by the civil liberties lobby. Albeit

---

58 *The Guardian*, 10 April 2011.
59 Ibid.
60 For the text of the letter, see 'Private Manning's Humiliation', *The New York Review of Books*, available at: <http://www.nybooks.com/articles/archives/2011/apr/28/private-mannings-humiliation/> (accessed 17 June 2011).
61 J. Waldron, 'Letter to the Editor', *The Guardian*, 5 May 2011. See also the equally powerful letter by Professor Richard Overy in the same edition.

belatedly, the little Englanders in the Tory party have realized that it is not the Human Rights Act that is the enemy at the door, but the European Court of Human Rights in Strasbourg. For however much the Tories – along with those cosying up to them – may claim that that the Strasbourg system is 'Churchill's legacy', the fact is that the Strasbourg court has long broken free of its alleged moorings in centre-right politics, and certainly of the extraordinarily arrogant assumption that what the Europeans needed most to protect them from the thrall of Bolshevism was a strong dose of the English common law. Social democratic Europe has produced a different breed of judges from that to be found in the United Kingdom or the United States, and the Strasbourg court has performed a remarkable role in stamping a European solution on human rights problems. As a result, the European centre of gravity usually spins some way in advance of the position in the United Kingdom, and some way in advance of anything to be found in the Land of the Free, where the Supreme Court so conspicuously serves corporate masters.

It has long been thus, with the Strasbourg court having held against the United Kingdom in a number of high-profile decisions going back as far as the 1970s. A striking feature of many of these cases is that the Strasbourg court was concerned with failures of the common law, in the sense that some of the restraints on human rights complained of were complaints imposed by the common law, while some reflected a failure of the common law to develop adequate grounds to scrutinize executive action.[62] The complaints cover a wide range of issues, though the early cases are dominated by the conflict in Northern Ireland, with the United Kingdom being found in breach of Art. 2 (on the right to life no less) in a case about the shooting to kill of IRA suspects in Gibraltar while the latter were believed to be on 'active service'; and subsequently in another case involving the failure to investigate the killing of a death at the hands of the police.[63] Other notable cases involved breaches of Art. 3 (in a case brought unusually by the Republic of Ireland about alleged torture by the armed forces of the State, and the inhuman and degrading treatment of nationalist detainees); Art. 5 (in a case about legislation permitting arrested suspects to be held for up to seven days on ministerial authority, without being brought before a court); and Art. 6 (in a case about denying suspects in police custody access to a lawyer for up to 48 hours).[64]

But it is not only in relation to terrorist-related activity that the Strasbourg court has been a source of protection for British human rights. The court has

---

62 Notably *Sunday Times v United Kingdom* (1979) 2 EHRR 245, and *Lustig Prean v United Kingdom* (1999) 29 EHRR 548 respectively.

63 Respectively, *McCann v United Kingdom* (1995) 21 EHRR 97, and *Jordan v United Kingdom* (2003) 37 EHRR 52.

64 See, respectively, *Republic of Ireland v United Kingdom* (1978) 2 EHRR 25, *Brogan v United Kingdom* (1988) 11 EHRR 117, and *Murray v United Kingdom* (1996) 22 EHRR 29.

transformed the law (if not the practice) of the British security state after decades of indifference from the domestic judges,[65] and has been the principal reason why the security and intelligence services have been placed on a statutory basis, and why their powers are now governed by legislation.[66] Inadequate though the latter may be, it is better than the unregulated regime that operated before, when the forces of the State had no legal recognition whatsoever. Yet, it is not only in relation to Northern Ireland or in relation to the security and intelligence agencies that the benefits of the Convention have been seen in domestic law, with many disadvantaged, oppressed or marginalized groups finding the long road to Strasbourg a great deal more rewarding than the short ride to the House of Lords (as it then was) in London. This would be true of gays (including gays in the military),[67] trade unionists and political activists,[68] as well as the victims of the immigration authorities. In view of recent rabid attacks on the Strasbourg court by the right-wing press, it is moreover most paradoxical that newspapers have also benefited, not only challenging common law rules about contempt of court and breach of confidence in two landmark cases,[69] but also securing victories for free speech in important decisions on libel damages and the protection of journalists' sources.[70]

As if to ram home the point that it is the European Convention on Human Rights and not the Human Rights Act that has been most responsible for the protection of human rights, the enactment of the latter has by no means eliminated the need to go to Strasbourg. The statistics relating to human rights adjudication in the domestic courts are alarming, with Poole and Shah revealing that only one in three human rights cases led to findings in the House of Lords (now the Supreme Court) of a human rights violation.[71] The decisions of the domestic courts are equally alarming, on as wide a range of issues as anyone would care to imagine – from the treatment of terrorist suspects, criminal justice and prisoners' rights, freedom of assembly, trade union rights, and freedom of expression. It has been left to Strasbourg to sweep up some of this mess, finding that the DNA database is a violation of the right to privacy when it stores the data of the innocent, holding that

65 See *Malone v Metropolitan Police Commissioner* [1979] Ch 344, and *Attorney General v Guardian Newspapers Ltd* [1987] 3 All ER 316.
66 Interception of Communications Act 1985, Security Service Act 1989, Intelligence Services Act 1994, and now Regulation of Investigatory Powers Act 2000.
67 See for example *Dudgeon v United Kingdom* (1981) 4 EHRR 149, and *Lustig Prean v United Kingdom* (1999) 29 EHRR 548.
68 See *Wilson v United Kingdom* (2002) 35 EHRR 523, and *Bowman v United Kingdom* (1998) 26 EHRR 1.
69 *Sunday Times v United Kingdom*, above, and *Observer v United Kingdom* (1991) 14 EHRR 153.
70 See *Tolstoy Miloslavsky v United Kingdom* (1995) 20 EHRR 442, and *Goodwin v United Kingdom* (1996) 22 EHRR 123.
71 [2009] PL 347.

random police powers of stop and search violate the right to freedom of assembly, and taking a tough line on the use of secret evidence in terrorist trials.[72] It has also been left to the Strasbourg court to address the wholesale disenfranchisement of prisoners – regardless of the nature or length of the offence and regardless of the circumstances in which it was committed. This was said to be a violation of Art. 3 of the First Protocol to the Convention.[73]

'Repatriating' Churchill's legacy

Like the New Labour Government before it, the Tory-led government in the United Kingdom would doubtless like a new form of human rights adjudication. The true inheritors of Churchill's legacy would no doubt like a human rights jurisprudence that reflected rather than challenged the common law, and which was more understanding of the burdens and responsibilities of government. One that is tough on terrorism and terrorist suspects, strong on criminal justice and prisoners' rights, and regressive on social and economic rights, including trade union rights. To this end, the right-wing think tank Policy Exchange produced a paper in 2011 entitled *Bringing Rights Home*, which proposed that the United Kingdom should review its relationship with the court, arguing that:

> The time has now come for the UK government to consider whether or not it wishes to remain tied to an inefficient, unaccountable and remote court, or whether our own constitutional reforms have done enough to ensure that the British judiciary is itself capable of considering these questions as the final appellate court. Just as Commonwealth countries have evolved and developed their legal systems to a level where they have felt capable of dealing with all cases that come before their courts domestically, so the UK should now ask itself the same question.[74]

Also part of a comprehensive script was a proposal that Convention rights should be more narrowly construed, and that national courts should be allowed greater scope in interpreting the Convention, without the risk of being challenged in Strasbourg.[75]

These proposals are endorsed in a foreword to the Policy Exchange document penned by Leonard Hoffmann, as a means whereby 'we can repatriate our law of human rights'.[76] But there are many who would see 'repatriation' as

---

72 See respectively *S and Marper v United Kingdom* [2008] ECHR 1581, *Gillan and Quinton v United Kingdom* [2009] ECHR 28, and *A v United Kingdom* [2009] ECHR 301.
73 *Hirst v United Kingdom (No 2)* [2005] ECHR 651.
74 M. Pinto-Duschinsky, *Bringing Rights Home: Making Human Rights Compatible with Parliamentary Democracy in the UK*, Policy Exchange, 2011, p. 70.
75 Ibid., pp. 71–2.

a synonym for 'weakening' our human rights standards, Lord Hoffmann railing also against the tragedy that 'the very concept of human rights is being trivialized by silly interpretations of grand ideas',[77] without giving examples of the decisions of which he disapproves.[78] It is perhaps understandable that judges should align themselves so closely with right-wing think tanks, given that they have been reduced to following 'in the wake of Strasbourg' since the enactment of the Human Rights Act.[79] What is less understandable, however, is the hypocrisy of the right-wing press which has put its weight behind the Tory campaign for repatriation (an unfortunate choice of language given its connotation in Tory politics) of human rights which Lord Hoffmann has endorsed. Indeed such is the depth of stupidity which this debate has plumbed that the attack on the Strasbourg court has been led by *The Sunday Times*,[80] once a great newspaper which was at the front of the queue on the road to Strasbourg when its own Convention rights were threatened in the thalidomide affair.[81] There was no complaint from *The Sunday Times* when conservative common law judges were put in their place by the Strasbourg court, or when the Contempt of Court Act 1981 was passed to trump the common law.[82]

Irrational and ill-conceived though much of this politically driven criticism appears to be, it is almost certain to become even more intense. One subject which is calculated to make the Tory fundamentalists take even greater leave of their senses than prisoners' rights is the rights of trade unions. In a number of recent decisions, the Strasbourg court has held that the right to freedom of association includes not only the right to bargain collectively and the right to strike,[83] but (at least in the case of the former) at a level set in International Labour Organization (ILO) Conventions.[84] The Court of Appeal has so far set its face against these developments and has refused to apply

76 Lord Hoffmann, in M. Pinto-Duschinsky, *Bringing Rights Home*, p. 8, though there is no reason why they should simply follow in the wake of Strasbourg. The HRA, s 2 gives them the opportunity to step out beyond the shadow of Strasbourg, an opportunity they have failed to grasp.

77 Ibid., p. 7.

78 He does, however, in the following paragraph of his foreword condemn the decision on prisoners' right to vote.

79 Lord Hoffmann, in Pinto-Duschinsky, op. cit., p. 7.

80 *The Sunday Times*, 13 February 2011.

81 *Sunday Times v United Kingdom*, above.

82 Like the rest of the media *The Sunday Times* is deeply troubled by the rise of super-injunctions and the elevation of the right to privacy over the right to free speech. But it seems rather bizarrely to overlook the fact that this is a British-led problem, for which the European Court of Human Rights provides the best solution.

83 *Demir and Baykara v Turkey* [2008] ECHR 1345, and *Enerji Yapi-Yol Sen v Turkey*, Application No. 68959/01.

84 *Demir and Baykara*, above, paras 157, 166.

Convention jurisprudence on Art. 11,[85] leaving undisturbed the most restrictive labour laws in Europe. However, the RMT, the NUJ and Unite the Union have all made separate complaints to the Strasbourg court about the tight restrictions under which their members labour. These include the unparalleled notice and ballot provisions which must be satisfied before industrial action can be called, the absolute ban on all forms of solidarity action, and the lack of adequate protection from punitive action by employers when workers participate in lawful strike action. Expect the temperature to rise to boiling point if (as is expected) these claims succeed, and a Tory or a Tory-led government is required as a result to roll back decades of anti-union laws. Votes for prisoners is one thing; rights for trade unionists is something quite different in the rabid minds of the neo-liberals.

We are thus back to the politics of human rights and a willingness to accept a human rights system that produces the 'right kind' of human rights outcomes. British judges on the whole can be trusted to deliver these human rights outcomes (as seen again in the recent right to strike cases), unlike Johnny Foreigner in Strasbourg (who has been a source of major irritation for governments for some time). This is the politics of human rights that leads this country to eschew social and economic rights, and to fall a long way behind international human rights standards. So we are happy to sign up to the European Social Charter (the ECHR's conjoined twin, ratified by the UK's Tory government in 1962), and happy (perhaps even proud) to be condemned regularly by the Council of Europe's supervisory bodies for failing to comply with the standards we have accepted. But we will do absolutely nothing to address the findings that we have violated 10 of the 13 provisions recently examined by the Social Rights Committee, on some occasions (relating specifically to core labour rights) on multiple grounds.[86] Nor will we contemplate ratifying the Revised European Social Charter, which would enable complaints of social rights violations to be made to the Strasbourg authorities by trade unions and other NGOs, as happens in other Council of Europe states under the so-called Collective Complaints procedure introduced in 1995. The little Englander approach to human rights obligations implied by Tory plans for repatriation comes at a heavy cost to human rights protection.

Conclusion

I completed this paper on 7 May (I am a slow writer). The newspaper dropping through my door on that day was full of the Lib Dem wipe-out at the

---

85 *Metrobus Ltd v Unite the Union* [2009] EWCA Civ 829.

86 See European Committee of Social Rights, *Conclusions XIX-3* (2010) (United Kingdom). Available at: <http://www.coe.int/t/dghl/monitoring/socialcharter/Conclusions/State/UKXIX3_en.pdf> (accessed 17 June 2011).

local government elections, the extraordinary rise of Alex Salmond, and the defeat of the 'Yes' camp in the AV referendum. In the previous six weeks, however, grim stories had continued to be reported. We learned that an inquest jury found that Ian Tomlinson had been unlawfully killed at the G20 demonstration;[87] more about super-injunctions, of which there were thought to be about 30, including the one obtained by BBC journalist Andrew Marr 'to protect his family';[88] and about the arrest of anti-monarchists for 'conspiracy to commit a public nuisance', detained by the police to prevent protests at the royal wedding on 29 April.[89] There were also fresh proposals from prominent Tories for further restrictions on freedom of association, these Tories including a prominent backbencher who had written about *The Assault on Liberty* before the election in 2010.[90] And, of course, there was the British government's celebration of the events in Pakistan on 1 May 2011 when a man was assassi-nated by US special forces,[91] in as flagrant a violation of the rule of law as it is possible to imagine. So much for the heirs to Churchill's legacy.

And so it goes on. There is no need for any formal repatriation of human rights: the United Kingdom will not leave the Council of Europe, it will not denounce the European Convention on Human Rights, and it will not remove the right of individual petition to the European Court of Human Rights. Attempts will nevertheless be made to secure a measure of repatriation by informal means, as Tory ministers seek to exert political pressure to 'reform' the Court,[92] and there are no doubt various ways by which the centre-right governments now dominating Europe will be able in the long run to have an impact on its jurisprudence. So while human rights activists have no cause to celebrate the Human Rights Act ('what is there not to like?'), they should be cautious about embracing the Strasbourg court too tightly, even though it provides the best example of human rights protection by a court anywhere in the world. Let the European Court of Justice (ECJ) be a salutary warning, having been once held up as a great paragon of progressive virtue, particularly in its development of the law relating to equality. No more, the reputation of the Court having been tarnished beyond repair by its well-known decisions in

---

87 *The Guardian*, 3 May 2011.
88 *The Guardian*, 26 April 2011. The story was given by Mr Marr to *The Daily Mail* (26 April 2011) in the first instance.
89 *Cambridge News*, 29 April 2011. There are also concerns about the alleged use of stop and search powers on the day. *The Guardian*, 29 April 2011.
90 Dominic Raab MP; *The Times*, 26 April 2011.
91 *The Guardian*, 2 May 2011: 'David Cameron hailed the death of Osama bin Laden as a "massive step forward" in the fight against terrorism.'
92 See *The Daily Telegraph*, 6 May 2011 ('British courts to regain power to deport terrorist suspects'). See also *Daily Mail*, 28 April 2011. It is not yet clear whether the other 46 member states of the Council of Europe will oblige, or whether the judges themselves will accept the script being written in Whitehall.

Viking and *Laval* and their progeny, which have led one senior scholar to reflect on the ECJ's 'Lochner moment'.[93]

Perhaps the lesson for human rights activists everywhere is a very simple one. Always be suspicious of government, of course; but always be sceptical of courts, as well. Above all, however, be scornful of the professor who elevates the raw politics of human rights into ethereal technical jargon called constitutional principle, which only those suitably trained can understand, and with which only those appropriately qualified can engage. Constitutional principle is no substitute for political power. Indeed, constitutional principle may be a tool of the politically powerful, a point brought home to me most forcefully by the recent attempts by the insurance companies (so far unsuccessfully) to challenge an Act of the Scottish Parliament designed to compensate the victims of pleural plaques.[94] And be scornful too of those who claim that 'out there' in the ether somewhere is a dialogue between judges and politicians which will protect our liberties, even though it is a conversation so rarefied that none of us will understand, and so exclusive that none of us will be permitted to participate, in the unlikely event that we were even able to locate the great conversation taking place. Delusion is no substitute for democracy.

---

93 D. Nicol, 'Europe's Lochner Moment' [2011] *PL* 308. On *Lochner*, see footnote 40 above. The United Kingdom had its own Lochner moment before Lochner: *Taff Vale Railway Co Ltd v Amalgamated Society of Railway Servants* [1901] AC 426. For discussion, see K.D. Ewing, 'Judiciary', in M. Flinders et al. (eds), *The Oxford Handbook of British Politics*, Oxford: Oxford University Press, 2009, ch 15.

94 *Axa General Insurance Ltd v Lord Advocate* [2011] CSIH 31 – not yet Scotland's Lochner moment.

Section 2

The Human Rights Act and the socio-economic perspective

8 Limits and achievements of the Human Rights Act from the socio-economic point of view

The HRA, poverty and social exclusion

Alice Donald and Elizabeth Mottershaw[1]

Introduction

It is tempting to ask whether the Human Rights Act (HRA), in its first decade, had an impact on poverty and social exclusion in the UK. In this chapter, however, we go further. Given that the HRA was meant to create a 'culture of human rights'[2] we ask whether human rights, more broadly, achieved this aim.

Comparative experience outside the UK demonstrates that anti-poverty actors use human rights to hold governments accountable both via litigation and by other forms of social action.[3] These include 'shadow reports' to United Nations human rights monitoring bodies and using human rights to scrutinise the conduct and impact of legislation, policy and budget-setting. In addition, governments and others who perceive themselves as 'duty-bearers' sometimes use human rights to shape anti-poverty strategies and legislation.

This applied human rights work commonly sees outcome and process as interdependent: human rights standards help define desirable outcomes (such as the realisation of the right to an adequate standard of living) and human rights principles inform the process by which those outcomes are achieved (such as realising the right to participation). Also prevalent is a multidimensional conception of poverty that encompasses a low income, isolation from civic participation and a loss of dignity and respect.

We argue that, in the UK, efforts to use the HRA directly to tackle poverty have been episodic; litigation has had limited impact on policy and practice, and we examine why this might be so. However, we further argue that to focus only on such *direct* use of the HRA neglects an embryonic but growing

1 We are grateful to Professor Philip Leach of the Human Rights and Social Justice Research Institute at London Metropolitan University for his comments on an early draft of this chapter.
2 Joint Committee on Human Rights, *The Case for a Human Rights Commission*, Sixth Report of Session 2002–3, vol. I, 2003, pp.11–12.
3 A. Donald and E. Mottershaw, *Poverty, inequality and human rights: Do human rights make a difference?* York: Joseph Rowntree Foundation, 2009.

body of practice *outside* the courtroom, using human rights principles and international human rights law, and sometimes also the HRA, to confront the causes and consequences of poverty.[4]

Holding government accountable through litigation

It is beyond our scope to offer a comprehensive analysis of relevant HRA case law.[5] Rather, we present an illustrative selection of cases that demonstrate the potential of the HRA to tackle aspects of poverty and social exclusion. In some instances, evidence is available as to the impact of the cases on policy, practice and substantive outcomes – and the barriers to impact.[6]

The case of *Limbuela* concerned state failure to provide support to late asylum applicants.[7] The case established the principle that where the fate of individuals is in the hands of the state – because it denies them support and bars them from working – severe destitution that results constitutes inhuman or degrading treatment under Art. 3 of the European Convention on Human Rights (ECHR). *Limbuela* had a direct and immediate impact on the policy of denying support to late applicants, with a marked drop in the numbers deemed ineligible for support; however, the case had no impact on government policy towards the rising incidence of destitution among failed asylum seekers.[8]

The *Bernard* case used Art. 8 on the right to private and family life to argue that a local authority had a positive obligation to improve the housing situation of a severely disabled woman who had been confined to a single room with no access to a toilet for two years.[9] However, this case had no generalised impact on policy or practice among local authority housing or social care departments, including in the defendant authority, or at a national policy level.[10]

---

4 In this chapter, we draw on evidence gathered in 2008–9 for research projects commissioned by the Equality and Human Rights Commission and the Joseph Rowntree Foundation, including interviews with public authorities and civil society organisations across the UK.

5 See E. Palmer, *Judicial Review, Socio-Economic Rights and the Human Rights Act*, Oxford: Hart Publishing, 2007.

6 See A. Donald and E. Mottershaw, *Evaluating the impact of selected cases under the Human Rights Act on public services provision*, London: Equality and Human Rights Commission, 2009.

7 *R (Limbuela and Others) v Secretary of State for the Home Department* [2005] UKHL 66.

8 In 2003, 9,410 late applicants were denied support. A survey by refugee agencies found that some 70 per cent of these people were destitute. In 2004, the number of late applicants denied support fell to 1,360; in 2005 it was 335; Donald and Mottershaw, op. cit., note 6, pp. 65–77.

9 *R (Bernard) v Enfield LBC* [2003] HRLR 4.

10 Donald and Mottershaw, op. cit., note 6, pp. 94–103.

Article 8 has also featured in several cases concerning Gypsies and Travellers and local authorities' application and enforcement of planning controls and homelessness applications.[11] Cases have confirmed that local authorities need to take Art. 8 into account in their decisions. They have established the principle that authorities must consider whether the removal of Gypsies or Travellers from a site is proportionate to the public interest in preserving the environment; and that 'respect' for private life, family life and home includes the positive obligation to act so as to facilitate the Gypsy and Traveller way of life, without being under a duty to guarantee it to an applicant in any particular case.[12] Clements and Morris note that the judgment in the consolidated appeals case known as *South Bucks District Council v Porter* reflects the findings of their own research – that the judiciary has absorbed the 'cultural and constitutional significance' of the HRA.[13] However, their survey of local authorities found that barely a third had reviewed their policies in relation to travelling people for compliance with the HRA.

In another instance, the HRA was used – with qualified success – to challenge discrimination against homeless people in the benefits system. The case of *RJM* concerned the practice of denying the disability premium – a component of income support – to individuals who were 'without accommodation'.[14] RJM contended that this practice amounted to discrimination in the right to 'peaceful enjoyment of . . . possessions' (Art. 1 ECHR, Protocol 1). The court accepted that the disability premium fell within the ambit of Art. 1, Protocol 1[15] and that homelessness was an 'other status' – that is, a ground on which discrimination is prohibited. Although it recognised these significant principles, the court went on to find that the justifications for the policy of disallowing the disability premium were not unreasonable and that 'the court should be very slow to substitute its view for that of the executive'

---

11 For example: *Wrexham County Borough Council v Berry, South Buckinghamshire District Council v Porter and another, Chichester District Council v Searle and others (Consolidated Appeals)* [2003] UKHL 26; *R (Margaret Price) v Carmarthenshire County Council* [2003] EWHC 42 (Admin); *South Buckinghamshire District Council and another v Porter* [2004] 1 WLR 1953; *First Secretary of State, Grant Doe and Others v Chichester District Council* [2004] EWCA Civ 1248. See *also Manchester City Council v Pinnock* [2010] UKSC 45 for a consideration of proportionality in the context of eviction of a person who was not a Gypsy or Traveller.

12 F. Klug and H. Wildbore, *Equality, Dignity and Discrimination under Human Rights Law; selected cases*, London: LSE, Centre for the Study of Human Rights, 2005, pp. 15–16.

13 L. Clements and R. Morris, 'The Millennium Blip: Local Authority Responses to the Human Rights Act 1998', in S. Halliday and P. Schmidt (eds), *Human Rights Brought Home: Socio-Legal Studies of Human Rights in the National Context*, Oxford: Hart Publishing, 2004, p. 229.

14 *R (on the application of RJM) v Secretary of State for Work and Pensions* [2008] UKHL 63.

15 The same principle was subsequently applied to income support for a pregnant student nurse (*CM v Secretary of State for Work and Pensions* [2009] UKUT 43 (AAC)).

(para 56). This presents an evident hurdle to future claimants since, even where policies discriminate (or differentiate), the government may often meet the required standard of its policies having reasonable justification.

Barriers to the impact of HRA litigation

While cases may have provided redress to claimants in specific circumstances, established important principles, and/or explicitly recognised as applicable principles previously established by the European Court of Human Rights, their impact is highly variable and may not be generalised across public authorities. We suggest below a number of barriers to wider impact.

Access to Justice

Multiple barriers prevent people affected by poverty and social exclusion from asserting their rights using legal process.[16] These include low awareness about human rights; an ingrained feeling of powerlessness; unwillingness to complain for fear of retribution; barriers inherent in the civil justice system itself, including its adversarial nature; and a lack of cohesion and resources to instigate group action when administrative or corporate decisions require collective, rather than individual challenge. To overcome these barriers, Clements adds, 'third party assistance is essential'; yet evidence suggests that restrictions in state funding for legal aid and variations in the availability of legal representation or advocacy had already under the Labour Government put the civil justice system beyond the reach of many people experiencing social exclusion.[17]

It is striking that the issue of impaired access to justice appeared only sporadically in Labour Government documents about social exclusion, suggesting a disjuncture between the largest reform in fifty years of the legal aid system (the creation of the Community Legal Service in 2000) and the concurrent pursuit of anti-poverty, social inclusion and human rights policies.[18] The Equality and Human Rights Commission's Human Rights Inquiry concluded:

> There are problems of a lack of local access to advice centres . . . a shortage of resources to train advisers on human rights law . . . a scarcity of

---

16 L. Clements, 'Winners and Losers', *Journal of Law and Society*, 2005, vol. 32, no. 1, 34–50; Joint Committee on Human Rights, *A Life Like Any Other? Human Rights of Adults with Learning Disabilities*, Seventh Report of Session 2007–8, Vol. I, London: The Stationery Office, 2008.

17 Ibid; see also J. Stein, *The Future of Social Justice in Britain: A New Mission for the Community Legal Service;* Centre for Analysis of Social Exclusion paper 48, 2001.

18 Clements, op. cit., pp. 44–9.

expert advisors to assist the resolution of cases involving human rights issues without litigation, and to bring ... cases to court where necessary.[19]

One survey reveals that lawyers, as well as potential claimants, encounter (or perceive) barriers to using the HRA to tackle poverty.[20] Solicitors in the Cynon Valley, a deprived area in south Wales, spoke about uncertainty about how to access rights under the HRA; lack of training; difficulty in securing public funding for cases; and perceptions that courts were unreceptive to human rights arguments or that the HRA benefited only 'undesirable' groups.

Another factor limiting access to the HRA is the loophole which, as a result of restrictive judicial interpretation of the meaning of 'public function' in s 6 HRA, excludes public services provided by the voluntary and private sector from responsibility under the Act.[21] The loophole was partially closed in 2008 to bring people with publicly-funded care home places into the ambit of the Act, though not self-funders.[22] Older people and people with disabilities using domiciliary care, looked-after children, tenants in some housing association properties and children with special needs in private schools are among those left without effective redress under the HRA.

The law itself

The HRA does not contain socio-economic rights that might underpin a strong egalitarian or redistributive agenda. However, the demarcation between civil and political and socio-economic rights is not firm and the cases above show that civil and political rights *can* be used to address policy issues associated with poverty and social exclusion.[23] Yet the impact (where it is known) has been circumscribed or peripheral. For example, neither the

19 Equality and Human Rights Commission, *Human Rights Inquiry*, London: Equality and Human Rights Commission, 2009, p. 106.
20 R. Costigan and P.A. Thomas, 'The Human Rights Act: A View from Below', *Journal of Law and Society*, 2005, vol. 32, no. 1, pp.51–67.
21 *Heather & Ors, R (on the application of) v Leonard Cheshire Foundation & Anor* [2001] EWHC Admin 429; *YL (by her litigation friend the Official Solicitor) v Birmingham City Council and others* [2007] UKHL 27; *Johnson & Ors v London Borough of Havering* [2006] EWHC 1714.
22 A. Donald with P. Leach and J. Watson, *Human Rights in Britain since the Human Rights Act 1998: a critical review*, London: Equality and Human Rights Commission, 2009, pp. 188–9.
23 The jurisprudence of the European Court of Human Rights is a source for further understanding the scope for rights contained in the ECHR (and, thus, the HRA) to be used to tackle poverty and social exclusion. For a review of Strasbourg jurisprudence, and also relevant European Community and European Union law, see Palmer op. cit., note 5, Chapter 2.

Limbuela judgment nor the UK government's policy response to it established the very existence of destitution as a violation of Convention rights.[24]

Further, as Palmer notes, the potential of the HRA to impact on socio-economic rights, and issues of poverty and social exclusion, has been limited, in the Act's first decade, by judicial interpretation of the limits on its scope of intervention. In disputes where resource allocation may be at issue, 'developments have been constrained by judicial deference to the authority of the executive and other public authorities'.[25] In the case of *RJM*, above, the judgment is explicit in declining to substitute the court's view for that of the executive. These factors suggest that there are limitations to the impact that litigation on civil and political rights can have in confronting economic and social insecurity or degradation in the UK, especially where problems are structural or systemic.

Translating law and legal judgments into policy and practice

People facing social exclusion, who lack an effective means of remedying the wrongs they experience, can only benefit from the HRA if – at minimum – public authorities review their policies and practice for non-compliance.[26] Further, realisation of a human rights culture requires public authorities to see the HRA not merely as a matter of 'tick box' compliance but also as a matter of aspiration – recognising and acting upon their positive obligations not just to refrain from harm, but also to take steps to prevent harm. As Murray Hunt, Legal Adviser to the parliamentary Joint Committee on Human Rights (JCHR) argues:

> . . . human rights law doesn't just contain lines you can't cross but aspirations you've got to strive to achieve . . . [like] a magnet pulling policy in a certain direction.[27]

24 In fact, the *Limbuela* judgment (para 7) explicitly notes, '(a) general public duty to house the homeless or provide for the destitute cannot be spelled out of article 3'. Subsequent to *Limbuela*, the JCHR accused the UK government of 'practising a deliberate policy of destitution' at all stages of the asylum claim process in a manner that 'falls below the requirements of the common law of humanity and of international human rights law'; Joint Committee on Human Rights, *The Treatment of Asylum Seekers*. Tenth Report of Session 2006–7, London: The Stationery Office, 2007, p. 41.

25 E. Palmer, 'Memorandum to the Joint Committee on Human Rights' in *A Bill of Rights for the UK?* Twenty-ninth Report of Session 2007–8, Volume II, Oral and Written Evidence, London: The Stationery Office, 2008, p. 161. See also Palmer, op. cit., note 5, for a detailed examination of judicial deference, the boundaries of judicial interpretation, and the complex way this impacts on implementation of human rights law.

26 Clements, op. cit., p. 42.

27 A. Donald with P. Leach and J. Watson, op. cit., p. 38.

There is a growing body of evidence that, where public authorities implement this approach, significant benefits accrue both to staff and users of services.[28] However, in most public authorities, institutional and attitudinal barriers have prevented more systematic application. In interviews we conducted with public authorities, we found both positive and negative views about human rights and the Act at different levels of seniority, with implications for the extent to which legal judgments translate into changes in either institutional or individual behaviour. Some had experienced human rights as the basis for unrealistic or unfounded claims to services. Others spoke positively about using HRA case law to approach seemingly intractable problems (such as the moving of morbidly obese patients) and as a framework within which to resolve competing interests (for example, between care staff and the people they care for).

Clements and Morris suggest that for local authorities:

> . . . not being proactive may indeed be the most attractive political option . . . Put simply, there are few votes to be gained by elected members actively promoting policies on behalf of unpopular causes.[29]

A significant barrier to applying the lessons of case law systematically is the actual or perceived need for additional resources (for example, the cost of a social care budget) or additional capacity (for example, housing stock that is accessible to disabled people). In some cases, public authorities appear to develop ways of interpreting the obligations they might be expected to take on as a result of case law to fit within available resources. For example, a regional asylum policy officer told us that hard-pressed local authorities with large numbers of destitute failed asylum seekers effectively apply a higher threshold for community care than neighbouring authorities with fewer claimants. In other instances, case law concerned with a minimum level of decency and respect for a claimant's human rights can struggle to gain purchase in a system which is primarily organised around the equitable and transparent *rationing* of resources. A case like *Bernard* may be a salient reminder of the 'bottom line' but may not assist an authority to make decisions about allocating housing stock in a context where not everyone's needs can be met. Further, the HRA and case law are commonly viewed as peripheral to stronger drivers of policy and practice – or simply irrelevant ('it couldn't happen here').

28 Office for Public Management, *The Impact of a Human Rights Culture on Public Sector Organisations: Lessons from practice*, London: Equality and Human Rights Commission, 2009; Scottish Human Rights Commission, *Human Rights in a Health Care Setting: Making it Work for Everyone: an evaluation of a human rights-based approach at The State Hospital*, Glasgow: SHRC, 2009.
29 Clements and Morris, op. cit., p. 222.

The impact of a legal decision may depend upon the extent to which it clearly articulates a discrete principle with broad potential application. It may also depend on how far a judgment determines the extent of the obligation on public authorities to take positive steps to secure human rights. This may in turn discourage public authorities from identifying generalisable principles in case law and encourage them to await further legal challenges in order to determine the impact on, and relevance to, new situations. Francesca Klug advocates a process of 'smart compliance' – providing guidance to public authorities on the implications of human rights case law that extend beyond the public authority and specific facts raised by a particular case.[30] The absence until 2007 of a commission in Britain charged with 'translating' the lessons of case law into effective practice may have led to the HRA being under-sold and under-exploited.

Using human rights to pursue accountability outside the courtroom

In this section, we analyse the use of human rights by community-based organisations and NGOs concerned with poverty or social exclusion; we also present examples of work within the academic community where it interacts directly with government and/or civil society.

From 2008 to 2010, the British Institute of Human Rights (BIHR) supported six London-based organisations working with and for people facing social injustice in using human rights to strengthen their influence with national and local policy-makers.[31] Some used human rights to seek to influence specific aspects of public policy and practice. These included the practice of waking rough sleepers in the night and hosing down their sleeping areas; the lack of 'joined-up' services resulting in high numbers of women becoming homeless on release from prison; and policies which result in social services departments refusing to support undocumented migrant families and threatening to take their children into care due to the family having no recourse to public funds.

The Participation and the Practice of Rights project (PPR) in north Belfast provides a further example of using the normative content of human rights to frame advocacy on poverty-related issues and pursue accountability. Using participatory methods, PPR has pioneered the development – by communities affected by poverty – of indicators and time-bound targets to measure the realisation of their human rights. Tangible improvements have resulted. In one initiative, families affected by disproportionately high rates of suicide and

---

30 F. Klug, *Establishment of the Commission for Equality and Human Rights: implications for the public sector*, Westminster Explained 36: An assessment of the impact of the HRA, 7 December 2004.

31 See the BIHR website: <http://bihr.org.uk/projects/poverty> (accessed 17 June 2011).

self-harm secured policy change across Northern Ireland on follow-up appointments for mental health service users.[32] In another, residents in a housing estate devised indicators to measure whether a regeneration project fulfilled the state's obligation to progressively realise their rights to work, education, adequate housing and the highest attainable standard of health. Residents secured improvements relating to the prompt clearing of pigeon waste, rehousing families out of unsuitable accommodation and preventing sewage flowing into bathrooms; however, progress on indicators relating to residents' involvement in decision-making was minimal.[33] For PPR,

> . . . a rights-based approach acknowledges the systematic and institutional exclusion of disadvantaged communities from participation in decisions of resource allocation and service delivery. It also implies that in order to achieve sustainable change, the processes of changing power relationships are as important as 'getting the result'.[34]

Like PPR, the Poverty Truth Commission in Scotland embraced the human rights principles of participation and dignity. The Commission, based on the principle of 'nothing about us without us is for us', brought together people experiencing poverty to testify about their experiences and develop policy to address poverty. Human rights language was not expressly used – according to one of its founders, it was not a familiar frame of reference for participants – however, a human rights-based approach to poverty was strongly evident in the testimonies of those living in poverty. Participants rejected models that viewed them as supplicants for charity, rather than individuals claiming justice; as one noted, 'This is not Victorian England in which the upper class claims it knows what is best for us.'[35]

The potential for pursuing accountability outside the courtroom was further explored from 2008 to 2010 by Queen's University Belfast (QUB) in a project that analysed public expenditure in Northern Ireland using a framework based on the International Covenant on Economic, Social and Cultural Rights (ICESCR).[36] Its activities included a human rights-based analysis of

---

32 F. V McMillan, N. Browne, S. Green and D. Donnelly, 'A Card before You Leave: Participation and Mental Health in Northern Ireland', *Health and Human Rights*, 2009, vol. 11, no. 1, pp. 61–72

33 Participation and the Practice of Rights, *Seven Towers Monitoring Group: Fourth Report on Progress of Human Rights Indicators*. Belfast: PPR, 2009.

34 D. Donnelly, 'Project puts rights tools into practice', in *Action on Poverty Today*, Combat Poverty Agency, Spring 2007, no. 16, p. 13.

35 P. Chapman, *'Put Yourself in My Shoes . . .': Poverty Truth Commission*, weblog, 21 March 2009. Available at <http://povertytruthcommission.blogspot.com/2009/05/put-yourself-in-my-shoes.html> (accessed 17 June 2011).

36 QUB Budget Analysis Project, *Budgeting for Economic and Social Rights: A Human Rights Framework*, Belfast: QUB School of Law, 2010.

budgetary aspects of social housing.[37] Among other findings, it concluded that there had been retrogression in the fulfilment of the right to housing in Northern Ireland and that government needed to increase its expenditure on new social housing to comply with its human rights obligations. Further, the project analysed *how* the resources allocated to housing were used, concluding, for example, that the practice of purchasing land at market value meant that a valuable resource (land) had been used to benefit already advantaged groups, rather than maximising the resources available for the progressive achievement of everyone's right to adequate housing.

The QUB project expanded the understanding and application of these obligations in the context of budget-setting in the UK. As Nolan and Dutschke argue:

> There is a growing recognition of the importance of budgetary decisions in terms of achieving the realisation of [economic and social rights]. These factors combine to produce a strong inducement – and perhaps a compulsion – to evaluate budgets from an [economic and social rights] perspective.[38]

Some UK civil society organisations have participated in international human rights accountability mechanisms. When the Committee on Economic, Social and Cultural Rights (CESCR), which monitors implementation of the ICESCR, considered the UK's record in 2009, no fewer than 31 organisations submitted 'shadow reports', which are considered by the Committee alongside the UK government's official report.[39] These included organisations expressly concerned with human rights, but also groups working on health, housing, family planning and the arts and working against discrimination, marginalisation and poverty among particular groups – women, children, failed asylum seekers, migrant workers and people from ethnic minorities. Many of the issues raised in shadow reports were reflected in the Committee's concluding observations.[40] These observations have, in turn, been used as an advocacy tool, including by the BIHR poverty and human rights initiative described above.

---

37 QUB Budget Analysis Project, *Budgeting for Social Housing in Northern Ireland: a human rights analysis*, Belfast: QUB School of Law, 2010.

38 A. Nolan and M. Dutschke, 'Article 2(1) ICESCR and states parties' obligations: whither the budget?', *European Human Rights Law Review*, 2010, 3, p. 289. See also C. Harvey and E. Rooney, 'Integrating Human Rights? Socio-Economic Rights and Budget Analysis', *European Human Rights Law Review*, 2010, 3, 266–79.

39 Notably, half of the submissions were from groups in Northern Ireland, indicating the disproportionate prevalence of human rights (and, particularly, socio-economic rights) language in Northern Ireland compared to other parts of the UK.

40 All submissions and the Committee's concluding observations are available online at <http://www2.ohchr.org/english/bodies/cescr/cescrs42.htm> (accessed 17 June 2011).

Similarly, when, in 2008, the UK was reviewed by the Human Rights Council under the Universal Periodic Review mechanism, 25 civil society organisations made submissions. The submissions covered not only civil and political rights but also discrimination and inequality, child poverty, the right to an adequate standard of living and the right to education.[41] Poverty was also prominent among the concerns of the children's commissioners in the UK, who submitted a joint shadow report to the UN committee monitoring implementation of the Convention on the Rights of the Child (UNCRC) in 2008.[42]

Much of this work draws on underlying principles of human rights, international human rights law and international mechanisms. However, there is also evidence, collated by BIHR, that the HRA itself has been used in advocacy to tackle social exclusion and poverty without recourse to legal process. BIHR details examples of carers, advocates and professionals raising arguments around dignity, inhuman and degrading treatment, and the right to private and family life to secure changes in the practices of local authorities, care homes and hospitals.[43] In one instance, a support group used human rights to challenge a decision to remove children from a mother living in poverty, who was in temporary accommodation to escape an abusive father.[44]

Governments and other 'duty-bearers' using human rights to shape anti-poverty strategies

The early years of the Labour Government will be remembered in part for its expansive declarations of intent to transform society. In 1999, Tony Blair promised to 'end child poverty for ever' within a generation and presented a blueprint for a 'popular welfare state' which would tackle the fundamental causes of poverty, social exclusion and community decay.[45] At the same time, the (then) Home Secretary Jack Straw spoke about the government's vision for the HRA:

41 Human Rights Council, *Summary prepared by the Office of the High Commissioner for Human Rights, in accordance with paragraph 15(C) of the Annex to Human Rights Council Resolution 5/1: United Kingdom of Great Britain and Northern Ireland* (UN Doc. A/HRC/WG.6/1/GBR/3), 2008.

42 UK Children's Commissioners, *The UK Children's Commissioners' Report to UN Committee on the Rights of the Child*, 2008.

43 British Institute of Human Rights, *The Human Rights Act: Changing Lives* (Second Edition), London: BIHR, 2008.

44 Ibid., p.18.

45 T. Blair, 'Beveridge revisited: a welfare state for the 21st century' (Beveridge Lecture, 18 March 1999) in R. Walker (ed.), *Ending Child Poverty: Popular welfare for the 21st century*, Bristol: Policy Press, 1999, p.7.

> The Human Rights Act . . . confirms an ethical bottom line for public authorities. It provides a fairness guarantee, if you like, for the citizen . . . There's a new system of ethical values here which everyone can sign up to. Unifying, inclusive and based on common humanity.[46]

However, what is striking about these two narratives is how they were largely disconnected from each other by government, both rhetorically and in public policy. The twin aspirations to promote human rights and tackle poverty were like trains on parallel tracks, at times accelerating and at other times slowing down or reversing, but with no shared timetable and only rare exchanges of passengers. We have found no express reference to the HRA in key documents setting out government strategy or charting progress in relation to poverty and social exclusion. Reports after 2007 refer to the creation of the Equality and Human Rights Commission (EHRC) but there is no indication that human rights were a significant driver of strategy. Some documents refer to 'rights and responsibilities' (the two terms invariably being bracketed together) but this is primarily in the context of compulsion and conditionality in relation to welfare benefits. Similarly, documents explaining the HRA to public authorities or reviewing its implementation make no express reference to poverty or social exclusion, suggesting that the framers of the Act and those charged with promoting its application did not aspire for it to improve the lives of communities affected by structural deprivation.[47]

The Child Poverty Act (CPA) 2010 illustrates the way in which the Labour Government largely kept human rights and poverty apart.[48] Although aspects of the CPA contribute to the realisation of some socio-economic rights, as Ellie Palmer states,

> questions of state obligations to make adequate provision for human needs are seldom debated as human rights issues . . . the language of human rights is absent from the moral justification for prioritising the

---

46 J. Straw MP, Constitution Unit Annual Lecture, 27 October 1999, pp. 5–6.

47 See, for example: Department of Constitutional Affairs, *Review of the Implementation of the Human Rights Act*, London: DCA, 2006.

48 The Apprenticeship, Skills, Children and Learning Act 2009 is a rare example of a piece of Westminster legislation that both explicitly embraced obligations to fulfil a social or economic right – in this case, the right to education – and was recognised as doing so in government analysis of the Bill. Murray Hunt points out that generally, even where a Bill includes measures that contribute to the implementation of human rights obligations, this 'does not feature in [the government's] own analysis of the Bill's human rights implications'; M. Hunt, 'Enhancing Parliament's role in relation to economic and social rights', *European Human Rights Law Review*, 2010, 3, pp. 242–50.

needs of children and families in the Government consultation that preceded the Act.[49]

It should also be noted that in at least one policy area – that of asylum – the 'human rights' and 'anti-exclusion' trains travelled in entirely opposite directions, producing a grotesque disparity between the language of universal rights and the deliberate dehumanisation of an already impoverished and demonised group. Shami Chakrabarti observes that the early infancy of the HRA coincided with a policy of 'deliberate, targeted and forced destitution' towards asylum seekers and with sustained attacks on their access to legal process.[50]

The UK parliament's Joint Committee on Human Rights (JCHR) has contributed to coordinating our two trains. It sought to enhance parliament's role in relation to economic and social rights by means of thematic reports containing discussion of these rights; legislative scrutiny and scrutiny of the UK's compliance with international human rights treaties.[51] However, as Hunt notes, there is scope to expand parliament's role: scrutiny has largely been limited to looking at the obligation not to interfere with the realisation of a right, rather than extending into obligations to protect and fulfil that right.[52] Budget scrutiny processes have made no reference to the programmatic duties of progressive realisation of socio-economic rights imposed by the UK's international obligations; nor does parliament have experience of considering the implications of the principle of non-retrogression, according to which progress towards the realisation of socio-economic rights cannot be reversed without compelling justification. Hunt calls for a re-evaluation of the UK parliament's role in order to ensure 'the democratic legitimacy of implementing measures and full accountability for their adequacy'.[53]

A stronger connection between human rights and poverty has been made in the devolved administrations. The 2003 Homelessness etc. (Scotland) Act, while not explicitly referring to *human* rights, resulted from a policy commitment to using legally enforceable rights to tackle homelessness.[54] The Act has been described as 'the closest thing to the practical implementation of the

49 E. Palmer, 'The Child Poverty Act 2010: holding government to account for promises in a recessionary climate?', *European Human Rights Law Review*, 2010, Issue 3, p. 307.
50 S. Chakrabarti, 'Rights and Rhetoric: The Politics of Asylum and Human Rights Culture in the United Kingdom', *Journal of Law and Society*, 2005, vol. 32, no. 1, pp. 131–47.
51 Hunt, op. cit.
52 Hunt, op. cit., p. 250.
53 Ibid.
54 Donald and Mottershaw, op. cit. note 3, p. 36.

right to housing the world has yet seen'.[55] It identifies specific rights and correlative obligations held by specific entities; by 2012, all unintentionally homeless people in Scotland will have the right to a permanent home. Crucially, the Act also gives individuals the right to sue if they believe their rights are not being respected.

The Welsh Assembly Government has formally adopted the UNCRC as the basis for its policy-making on children and young people. Its strategy on child poverty is 'built on a set of core values in line with the [UNCRC]' and highlights the rights to social security and an adequate standard of living, as well as participation and equality.[56] In January 2011, the Welsh Assembly Government passed a Measure imposing a duty upon Welsh Ministers and the First Minister to have due regard to the rights and obligations in the UNCRC and its Optional Protocols when making policy decisions of a strategic nature. The Measure requires ministers to prepare a children's scheme and to produce reports about compliance with the duty, along with promoting understanding of the UNCRC and amending legislation to give better effect to the Convention and its Optional Protocols.

Using human rights to inform policy and strategy is also evident in the work of development organisations that have extended their programmes into the UK. Development organisations increasingly view themselves as 'duty-bearers' with human rights obligations, if not, strictly, legal ones.[57] For Oxfam, human rights principles compel it and similar agencies to:

> 'raise the bar' on their own accountability, lest they unwittingly perpetuate outmoded notions of charity, overlook discrimination and exclusion, and reinforce existing imbalances of power.[58]

Oxfam International's strategic plan for 2007–12 is grounded in five rights, including the right to a sustainable livelihood, the right to basic social services and the right to be heard.[59] Oxfam UK has adopted this strategy in its

55 E. Tars and C. Egleson, 'Great Scot!: the Scottish plan to end homelessness and lessons for the housing rights movement in the United States', *Georgetown Journal on Poverty Law & Policy*, 2009, Vol. XVI, No. 1, p. 190.

56 Welsh Assembly Government, *A Fair Future for our Children: The Strategy of the Welsh Assembly Government for Tackling Child Poverty*, 2005, p. 9.

57 CARE, Oxfam, Save the Children, ActionAid, Concern and Plan are among the larger agencies committed to using human rights in their anti-poverty work. See P. Gready and J. Ensor, *Reinventing development?: Translating rights-based approaches from theory into practice*, London: Zed Books, 2005.

58 D. Green, *From Poverty to Power: How Active Citizens and Effective States Can Change the World*, Oxford: Oxfam International, 2008, pp. 27–8.

59 Oxfam International, *Demanding Justice: Oxfam International Strategic Plan 2007–2012*, Oxford: Oxfam, 2007.

anti-poverty work in the UK. In 2007, it was among the civil society actors that submitted a shadow report to the CESCR, stating that:

> across the UK . . . people experiencing poverty frequently lack access to a range of economic and social as well as civil and political rights.[60]

Barriers to using human rights outside the courtroom

Outside the UK, communities experiencing poverty and social exclusion have identified advantages that human rights afford over 'top-down', discretionary approaches by shifting the debate from needs to socially and legally guaranteed entitlements and from charity to duty.[61] Within the UK, the JCHR has stated that 'a rights-based approach can assist government in addressing poverty and Parliament and civil society in scrutinising its success in doing so'.[62] Yet, as the evidence above indicates, work in the UK to integrate human rights and strategies to combat poverty and social exclusion is in its infancy, and is fragmented both geographically and in terms of the actors involved.

Further, where human rights and anti-poverty work *have* been connected, implicitly or explicitly, the impact of this work has not always been identified and evaluated. For these reasons, it is premature to make definitive judgments about whether the approaches and beneficial impacts identified in some non-UK contexts might be replicable in the UK. However, we offer some tentative conclusions about the barriers facing any such efforts and how they might be (or have been) overcome.

Participants in our research projects did not have a uniform view of the value of the HRA – and human rights more broadly – to combat poverty. This variation is partly explained by the distinctive political environments that have developed in the UK since devolution. In particular, human rights 'literacy' among civil society organisations in Northern Ireland is greater than that elsewhere due partly to the extensive consultation on a Bill of Rights, led by the Northern Ireland Human Rights Commission (NIHRC) and involving a wide range of actors.[63] Socio-economic rights featured prominently in these

---

60 Oxfam GB, *Comments on the UK's 5th Periodic Report under the International Convention* [sic] *on Economic Social and Cultural Rights*, 2007, p. 1.
61 Donald and Mottershaw, op. cit., note 3.
62 Joint Committee on Human Rights, *The International Convention on Economic, Social and Cultural Rights*, Twenty–first Report of Session 2003–4, London: The Stationery Office, 2004, p. 38.
63 A. Donald, with the assistance of P. Leach and A. Puddephatt, *Developing a Bill of Rights for the UK*, London: Equality and Human Rights Commission, 2010, pp. 17–21.

debates, and in the advice document presented to the UK government by the NIHRC in 2008.[64]

Attitudes varied within as well as between the four nations of the UK, suggesting that geographical differences should not be overstated. Some participants in each nation viewed the language of human rights and guaranteed entitlements as politically ineffective in a policy environment dominated by notions of conditionality, compulsion and personal responsibility. They suggested that introducing human rights might risk sabotaging policy goals through the undue legalisation of process and the association of the HRA with groups perceived as 'undeserving'. In one snapshot, the Rural Community Network in Northern Ireland said it avoided talking about human rights because rural communities see them as 'technical, inaccessible and oppositional rather than being about solutions and relationships'. However, other participants had found human rights to be persuasive and revelatory to particular audiences. One voluntary organisation supporting people with sight loss in Wales said rights language was a 'very powerful tool', increasing confidence and a sense of entitlement among individuals living on benefits.

Perceptions of human rights and the HRA as being irrelevant or ineffective, then, are neither universal nor immutable. Moreover, some participants suggested that resistance by advocacy organisations to using human rights and the HRA may not necessarily reflect the degree to which human rights resonate at community level; advocacy groups concerned with political positioning vis-à-vis policy-makers may wittingly or unwittingly act as 'gatekeepers', inhibiting or masking the use by particular communities of human rights as a language with which to articulate their conditions and claims.

Many participants expressed the need for evaluative work that identifies the 'added value' of connecting human rights and anti-poverty work. This evidence base is necessary to answer the critiques of human rights as a framework for tackling poverty; for example, that human rights are ill-suited to deal with the deferred progress inherent in much anti-poverty work. We suggest that evaluative work should be premised on an understanding that human rights are not a panacea; using human rights is not a one-way street but, rather, requires an exchange between human rights supporters and anti-poverty actors who may be unfamiliar with each other's habitual frameworks.

---

64 Northern Ireland Human Rights Commission, *A Bill of Rights for Northern Ireland: Advice to the Secretary of State for Northern Ireland*, Belfast: NIHRC, 2008. The NIHRC justified the inclusion of social and economic rights in its advice on the grounds that (among other criteria) they arose from the particular circumstances of Northern Ireland, were not already adequately protected, and reflected the principles of mutual respect and parity of esteem between the two main communities. The Northern Ireland Office responded by stating that socio-economic rights are common across the UK and should be addressed as part of consultation on a UK Bill of Rights; Northern Ireland Office, *Consultation Paper – A Bill of Rights for Northern Ireland: Next Steps*, London: NIO, 2009, pp. 19–20.

Notwithstanding these challenges, what was striking in our discussions was the suggestion that introducing socio-economic rights – and civil and political rights as an anti-poverty tool – more visibly into public debate may help challenge perceptions that human rights benefit only certain groups. Some participants argued that the notion of human rights as empowering communities to find solutions to poverty and social exclusion challenged the assertion (made, for example, by senior Conservative politicians[65]) that the HRA creates an individualistic or infantilising culture. Further, opinion surveys suggest that economic and social rights are generally popular with the UK public, though there is low awareness of the trade-offs they might require in public policy.[66]

Conclusion

Participants we interviewed across the UK in 2009 expressed an appetite for a 'new paradigm' to shape public debate and policy around poverty and social exclusion (an appetite that may be assumed to have sharpened in the context of fiscal austerity heralded by the 2010 Comprehensive Spending Review). Some said human rights could help provide this new narrative by promoting the dignity and participation of affected communities, and by pushing to the fore the human rights principle of accountability in relation to public expenditure and revenue-raising. By this account, the HRA and international human rights treaties provide a coherent and transparent framework with which to scrutinise legislation and policy for both their immediate and cumulative impact on the vulnerable and marginalised.[67]

For some authors, legally enforceable socio-economic rights represent the gold standard of human rights protection and would permit people experiencing poverty to challenge gaps and inadequacies in the protection afforded by existing domestic law.[68] This might be achieved either by incorporation of the ICESCR (as the CESCR has recommended) or, as the JCHR has proposed, the inclusion in a new UK Bill of Rights of the rights to health, education, housing and an adequate standard of living, by means of a duty on the government to

---

65 David Cameron, speech to Conservative Party Conference, 2008.

66 P. Vizard, *Should economic and social rights be included in a Bill of Rights? An analysis of public attitudes*, Research Report, Centre for the Analysis of Social Exclusion, London School of Economics, 2010.

67 Palmer, op. cit., note 49; R. Balakrishnan and D. Elson, 'Auditing economic policy in the light of obligations on economic and social rights', *Essex Human Rights Review* 2008, 5, no. 1; R. Balakrishnan, D. Elson and R. Patel, *Rethinking Macro Economic Strategies from a Human Rights Perspective: Why MES with Human Rights II*, New York: Marymount Manhattan College, 2009.

68 G. Van Bueren, 'Including the Excluded: The Case for an Economic, Social and Cultural Human Rights Act', *Public Law*, 2002, pp. 456–72.

achieve the progressive realisation of these rights, by legislative or other means, and to report to parliament on its progress.[69]

However, others place greater emphasis on the moral and political dimension of human rights as a challenge to structural deprivation and inequality – not least because of the degree of judicial deference shown to the executive where questions of resources are at issue and the unlikelihood that a government of any political hue would allow the courts greater scrutiny of health and welfare legislation in accordance with human rights standards than is afforded under the HRA.[70]

Our review of the impact of the HRA on the lives of people experiencing poverty and social exclusion is a reminder that human rights law alone cannot promulgate values or change cultures in the absence of concerted social and political action to secure its implementation. Such action must embrace both the UK's domestic and international human rights obligations. It must include civil society action, involving communities affected by poverty and their allies. Further, there must be action to strengthen the implementation of human rights by public authorities, beyond merely negative compliance. In addition, there is potential to use human rights to enhance parliamentary scrutiny of law and policy that might serve either to perpetuate or reduce poverty and social exclusion in the UK.

69 Joint Committee on Human Rights, *A Bill of Rights for the UK?*, Twenty-ninth Report of Session 2007–8, London: The Stationery Office, 2008, pp. 53–6.
70 C. Gearty and V. Mantouvalou, *Debating Social Rights*, Oxford: Hart Publishing, 2010.

9   The Human Rights Act and assisted dying

The (most) unkindest cut of all?[1]

Jo Milner and Lisbeth Bourne

Introduction

The year 2010 saw the tenth anniversary of the United Kingdom Human Rights Act 1998 (HRA), and recently the announcement and publication of the Coalition Government's Comprehensive Spending Review (CSR)[2] in autumn 2010. This has been widely criticised by socio-economic analysts,[3] disability groups[4] and research organisations[5] alike, including the Institute for Fiscal Studies,[6] for cutting health and social welfare spending to a point not seen since the Second World War, where it disproportionately impacts on those at the bottom end of the income distribution, especially older and/ or disabled people, including those who have progressive, life-threatening illnesses.

---

1 W. Shakespeare, *Julius Caesar*, Act 3, Scene 2.
2 Available at: <http://cdn.hm-treasury.gov.uk/sr2010_completereport.pdf> (accessed 24 June 2011).
3 'Of the £80 billion a year spending cuts announced in the Comprehensive Spending Review, £18 billion will be found from cuts in welfare spending by 2014–15', N. Yates et al. (eds), *In Defence of Welfare: The Impacts of the Spending Review*, Social Policy Association, 2011, available at: <http://www.social-policy.org.uk/downloads/idow.pdf> (accessed 24 June 2011).
4 United Kingdom Disabled People's Council (UKDPC), *A Report on Benefit Reform Proposals by the Coalition Government*, 2011. Available at: <http://www.ukdpc.net/library/UKDPC%20Report%20on%20Benefit%20Reform%20Proposals%20by%20the%20Coalition%20Government1.pdf> (accessed 27 June 2011).
5 The 'research [study] showed that far from being protected from the worst of the cuts, disabled families across the country faced significant reductions in their household income. Losses of two to three thousand pounds over the course of the next parliament were typical and overall, [it was] estimated that disabled people would lose over £9 billion in welfare support in the next five years', C. Wood and E. Grant, *Tracking the Lives of Disabled Families through the Cuts*, London: Demos, 2011, Available at: <http://www.demos.co.uk/files/Destination_unknown_Spring_2011_-_web.pdf?1305026600> (accessed 27 June 2011).
6 M.Brewer and J. Browne, 'The New Politics of Welfare: Cuts to Welfare Spending', in Yates et al., op. cit., n. 3.

A key plank of the welfare reforms will soon, for example, see the phasing out of the Disability Living Allowance (DLA), which was designed to meet the additional costs of living with a disability, that is, cover what Sen calls the 'Conversion Handicap',[7] and its replacement with the Personal Independence Payment, with a view to saving 20 per cent of the original DLA budget. Yet, in February 2011, the Disability Rights Partnership[8] conducted a survey of 900 disabled people to gauge their views about the removal of the DLA, and found such a profound level of uncertainty and apprehension on the respondents' part, that '9 per cent said losing DLA may make life not worth living'.[9] This suggests that without what Wood and Grant[10] describe as:

> the only benefit . . . which takes into account personal, practical and social barriers that effectively 'disable' an individual with an impairment, many such people may be so economically pressurised by this potential loss of their independence, and hence, the level of personal choice and control over their lives that death may 'sometimes seem a rational refuge'.[11]

Indeed, the link between incidence of suicide, and lack of social integration and support, was established as far back as 1897, in the seminal work on the subject by Sociology's founding father, Emile Durkheim.[12]

This changing backdrop of extreme austerity measures and cutbacks in public expenditure, which severely disadvantages people with long-standing illnesses and disabilities, therefore casts the current topical campaign for legalisation of assisted suicide and voluntary euthanasia, led by such prominent supporters as author Terry Pratchett, and lobbying groups including Dignity in Dying, in a very different light, and one which may separate the

---

7 A. Sen, *The Idea of Justice*, London: Allan Lane, 2009, p. 258, pointed out that disabled people 'are often the poorest in terms of income, but in addition, their need for income is greater than that of able-bodied people, since they require money and assistance to live normal lives and attempt to alleviate their handicaps. The Impairment of income-earning ability, which can be called "the earning handicap", tends to be reinforced and much magnified in its effect by "the conversion handicap"; the difficulty in converting incomes and resources into good living, precisely because of disability'.

8 Comprising Disability Alliance, the National Centre for Independent Living (NCIL) and the Royal Association for Disability Rights (RADAR).

9 Disability Rights Partnership, *End of a Lifeline?: Ending Disability Living Allowance to Introduce Personal Independence Payment*, 2011. Available at: <http://www.disabilityalliance.org/r68.pdf> (accessed 27 June 2011).

10 Wood and Grant, op. cit., n. 5, p. 28.

11 M. Epstein, 'Legitimising the Shameful: End of Life Bioethics and the Political Economy of Death', *Bioethics*, 21 (1), January 2007, pp. 23–31, p. 25.

12 E. Durkheim, *Suicide: A Study in Sociology*, London: Routledge & Kegan Paul, 1952.

rich from the poor, that is, those who have the financial resources[13] to exercise choice over the manner of their death by facilitating a final trip to the Dignitas clinic in Switzerland, or by challenging the 1961 Suicide Act, which rules that it is an offence to assist another person to die by suicide under s 2(1), using Art. 8[14] of the European Convention of Human Rights (ECHR),[15] as Debbie Purdy did in 2008 in the High Court,[16] and later the House of Lords in 2009.[17]

This chapter will therefore examine the legal context on the one hand, as illustrated by the House of Lords ruling in 2009 – which, notwithstanding its dismissal of Debbie Purdy's claim, looked sympathetically on her situation by holding that the issue of ending suffering by means of assisted suicide was 'conduct ... many might regard as ... to be commended rather than condemned,'[18] but, however, noted that this should be subject to a change in legislation by Parliament – and the position of people vulnerable to coercion and/or despair, who, in a time of rapidly diminished public spending in health and welfare, have little choice, on the other.

The Human Rights Act and assisted dying

At its inception, the HRA was an ambitious attempt to 'bring rights home', that is, to base the UK legal system on a clear and definitive statement of citizens' rights and entitlements, with a view to building a better, fairer and more just UK society. Over a decade has now elapsed since it came into force, and notwithstanding earlier predictions that it would radically transform the delivery of health and social welfare in the UK, it is now possible to gauge the level of impact the HRA has had on medical law to date, and the key decisions about resource allocation which underpin it.

13 Campaigning organisation 'Care not Killing', opponents to 'Dignity in Dying' (formerly the Voluntary Euthanasia Society) point out that both key cases, Pretty and Purdy, were financed by Dignity in Dying: 'BBC assisted suicide programme', 7 June 2011. Available at: <http://www.carenotkilling.org.uk/?show=931> (accessed 27 June 2011).

14 1. 'Everyone has the right to respect for his private and family life, his home and his correspondence. 2. There shall be no interference by a public authority with the exercise of this right except such as is in accordance with the law and is necessary in a democratic society in the interests of national security, public safety or the economic well-being of the country, for the prevention of disorder or crime, for the protection of health or morals, or for the protection of the rights and freedoms of others.'

15 The 1998 Human Rights Act incorporates Arts 2–18 (excluding Art. 13) of the European Convention of Human Rights 1950 into domestic law.

16 *R (On the Application of Purdy) v DPP* [2008] All ER (D) 284 (HC; 2/3 October 2008).

17 *R (On the Application of Purdy) v DPP* [2009] EWCA Civ 92 (30 July).

18 Ibid., para 83.

Yet, although many of these HRA-instigated changes have been viewed as limited, and as 'incremental and apparently piecemeal,'[19] it is in the area of end-of-life decisions and rights of non-interference,[20] 'negative rights' (rather than 'positive rights',[21] rights of entitlement), especially assisted suicide legislation, that the HRA has had the most transformative effect. As Mason and Laurie note,

> although human rights instruments . . . identify protections that are considered to be of core value to our society, these do not deserve protection at any cost, and exceptions are possible. The starting point is, however, that fundamental rights should be protected and, and the onus is on those who interfere with such rights to justify such interference.[22]

For just as improved medical technologies and interventions have served to extend life expectancies and prolong life (even if the corollary is a drop in quality), and have strengthened the control of doctors, who can make decisions to hasten death which are held to be in the patient's 'best interests', such as the doctrine of 'double effect', or 'medical futility' and the withdrawal of life-saving treatments, so the idea of the patient regaining control over end-of-life decisions has developed, including 'the right to die' at a point and in a manner of one's choosing.

Underlying this process of decision-making is the principle of self-determination, which hinges on the central concept of 'autonomy', the subject of much debate, especially within the extensive literature surrounding the ethics of legalising assisted suicide and/or voluntary euthanasia. Yet, as Epstein argues,[23] this understanding of 'autonomy' 'pertains to "negative rights" only, freedom from interference, as "positive rights", rights to specified goods and services, are more routinely dealt with within the framework of an allegedly separate discourse, that of "distributive justice" '. Therefore, the decision to consent to or refuse treatment rests solely with the patient, and indeed, the right to (informed) refusal is now so entrenched a principle, that it now ranks on a par with the legal doctrine of (informed) consent, and is such a guiding factor, that it has been described by Mason and Laurie 'as a cult of self-determination',[24] for once it has been competently expressed 'the doctor is

---

19 L. Terry, 'Ethical and Legal Perspectives on Human Rights' in A. Leathard and S. McLaren (eds), *Ethics: Contemporary Challenges in Health and Social Care*, Bristol: Policy Press, 2007, p. 132.
20 Entailing, for example, the right to consent to refuse treatment.
21 Entailing, for example, the right to have treatment.
22 J.K. Mason and G.T. Laurie, *Mason and McColl Smith's Law and Medical Ethics*, 8th edn, Oxford: Oxford University Press, 2011, p. 44.
23 Epstein, op. cit., n. 11, p. 27.
24 Mason and Laurie, op. cit, n. 22, p. 582.

now bound, both legally and professionally, to accept a refusal' or alternatively risk being found unfit to practise.

So while the HRA has a positive obligation to safeguard life, under Art. 2, 'The right to life', it was ruled that, in two cases, *NHS Trust A v M*, and *NHS Trust B v H*,[25] resting on whether artificial nutrition and hydration could be removed from patients held to be in a 'permanent vegetative state', that although Art. 2 imposed a positive obligation to give treatment, this was only applicable where it is considered by medical opinion to be in the 'best interests' of the patient, and not where it would be futile. Further, the European Court of Human Rights (ECtHR) ruled in *Osman v United Kingdom*[26] that Art. 2 obligations to preserve life are also subject to financial constraints:

> bearing in mind the . . . operational choices which must be made in terms of priorities and resources, such an obligation must be interpreted in a way which does not impose an impossible or disproportionate burden on the authorities.[27]

The principle that autonomy works only in one direction, in favour of non-interference rights, was further established in *R (on the application of Burke) v General Medical Council*,[28] which overturned the decision in the Court of Appeal that where a severely disabled person sought positive confirmation that artificial nutrition and hydration would not be withdrawn against his stated wishes, if he became incompetent at the end of his life. Lord Philips clearly articulated the limits to the right to self-determination, which stop short of positive entitlement to rights:[29]

> The proposition that a patient has a paramount right to refuse treatment is amply demonstrated by the authorities cited by Munby, J. The corollary does not, however, follow, at least as a general proposition. Autonomy and the right of self-determination do not entitle the patient to insist on receiving a particular treatment regardless of the nature of the treatment.

The concept of 'autonomy' which underpins the HRA, especially as it relates to end-of-life rights-based claims, is clearly fettered, as freedom of choice is constrained by a lack of entitlement to resources, and therefore, as Epstein highlights, 'the meaning and social role of a right to die with dignity depend foremost on the absence or presence of a positive right to live with dignity.'[30]

---

25 [2001] Fam 348.
26 (2000) 29 EHRR 245.
27 Ibid., para 116.
28 [2005] EWCA 1003.
29 Ibid., under subheading 'Best interests and Autonomy' p. 10.
30 Epstein, op. cit., n. 11, p. 27.

Indeed, until the implementation of the HRA, recognition of non-interference rights in terms of the 'right to die' did not extend to assisted dying, including, most notably, assisted suicide. However, this has recently been transformed by both the Pretty[31] and, later, the Purdy litigation.[32]

The discussion will first consider the key human rights implications surrounding Diane Pretty's case. Pretty, although unsuccessful in her attempt to persuade the Director of Public Prosecutions (DPP) that if her husband was to help her assisted suicide he would not be prosecuted under s 2(1) of the Suicide Act 1961, then took her case to the House of Lords,[33] and later the European Court of Human Rights (ECtHR), invoking a number of Convention articles, particularly Art. 2 ('right to life'), Art. 3 ('right not to suffer torture and inhumane treatment'), Art. 14 ('right to non-discrimination'), and also her Art. 8 'right to respect for a private and family life'. While both the House of Lords and the ECtHR ruled that Art. 2 did not also include a correlative right to die in the manner of her choosing, that is, suicide, and also did not agree that her Art. 3 rights were contravened by failing to allow her husband to assist her suicide, the ECtHR,[34] unlike the House of Lords, did accept that a right to a private life concerns the 'quality of life' and so also covers matters pertaining to dying and death, by conceding that, 'in an era of growing medical sophistication combined with longer life expectancies, many people are concerned that they should not be forced to linger on in old age or in states of advanced physical or mental decrepitude which conflict with strongly held views of self and personal identity'. However, the European Court held that even if Pretty's Art. 8(1) rights were interfered with, her Art. 8(2) rights could be justified as being in accordance with the interests of the state on the basis that it prevented vulnerable people from being taken advantage of by others and coerced into committing suicide.

The Purdy[35] judgment also resulted in a number of important ramifications, which impacted on the interface between criminal and medical law to such an extent that the DPP's policy guidelines, required as an outcome of the ruling (with the aim of detailing the criteria determining culpability in assisting or encouraging suicide), were described by Keown as 'unsound, if

31 *R (on the application of Pretty) v DPP* [2002] 1 AC 800, [2002] 1 All ER 1; *Pretty v UK* Application 2346/02 2FCR 97, [2002] FLR 45.
32 S. McLean, *Assisted Dying: Reflections on the Need for Reform*, London: Routledge-Cavendish, 2007, points out that 'in the case of *Pretty v UK* [2002], the ECtHR, which adjudicates on Convention rights, accepted that assisted dying had been legalised in some Council of Europe Member states . . . using its margin of appreciation policy', p. 14.
33 Her argument was rejected in the House of Lords on the basis that the DPP did not have a legal power to issue an immunity from prosecution.
34 *Pretty v UK*, op. cit, para 65.
35 *R (On the Application of Purdy) v DPP* [2009] EWCA Civ 92 (30 July).

not unconstitutional'[36] and later by Williams as 'totally unacceptable' as this ' "passes the buck" on an issue which requires parliamentary engagement and consultation'.[37] Accordingly, this judicial direction was swiftly followed by the publication of interim guidelines[38] which were subject to public consultation, and the Policy for Prosecutors in Respect of Cases of Encouraging and Assisting Suicide[39] in February 2010. To Williams,[40] this move represents a clear departure from a democratic process determining legislature, towards what she calls a 'quasi-judicial' agency, that is, the Crown Prosecution Service (CPS) and the DPP, which serve as a 'kind of lower court of justice',[41] who have control over the decision as to whether or not to prosecute a defendant referred by the police. She further points out that the rationale of this decision-making process is far from transparent, as although the DPP Guidelines are available to the public, prosecution decision-making is also based on further sources of policy guidance, which are 'restricted and concealed from public view', so prohibiting access to the very people 'who may be affected by the decisions'.[42]

For Rogers,[43] a further constitutional problem also arises from the restriction of scope within the DPP's policy to only cases of assisted suicide, rather than 'applying coherently to substantive law as a whole,'[44] as some 'cases hover ambiguously on the borderline between assisted suicide and murder, for example if D opens V's mouth for her (which V cannot do) and puts in the overdose of pills, which V then voluntarily swallows'.[45] Hence, as murder and attempted murder is not within the scope of this DPP policy, it does little to allay the fear of prosecution by relatives such as the mother of Lynn Gilderdale,[46] who helped administer a final dose of morphine to her 31-year-old daughter who had been bedridden with chronic ME since her early teens. Furthermore,

---

36 J. Keown, 'Dangerous Guidance', *New Law Journal*, Volume 159 (7397), 2009.

37 G. Williams, 'Assisting Suicide, the Code for Crown Prosecutors and the DPP's Discretion,' *Common Law World Review*, Volume 39, 2010, p. 183.

38 Crown Prosecution Service, *Interim Policy for Prosecutors in respect of Cases of Assisted Suicide*, 2009. Available at: <http://www.cps.gov.uk/consultations/as_consultation.pdf> (accessed 27 June 2011).

39 Available at: <http://www.cps.gov.uk/publications/prosecution/assisted_suicide_policy. html> (accessed 27 June 2011).

40 Williams, op. cit, n. 37, pp. 181–203.

41 Ibid., p. 182.

42 Ibid.

43 J. Rogers, 'Prosecutorial Policies, Prosecutorial Systems, and the Purdy Litigation', *Criminal Law Review*, Volume 7, 2010, pp. 543–64.

44 Ibid., p. 555.

45 Ibid.

46 S. Laville, 'Trapped by ME, Lynn Gilderdale made it clear she wanted to die', *Guardian Newspaper*, 25 January 2010. Available at: <http://www.guardian.co.uk/society/2010/ jan/25/lynn-gilderdale-me-assisted-suicide> (accessed 31 October 2011).

as Rogers[47] points out, although the details of the Gilderdale case conformed to all the 'anti-prosecution' factors in the policy, she was still prosecuted for attempted murder, but later acquitted by the jury who found in her favour.

However, Ost[48] asks whether, by spelling out the public interest arguments for and, especially, against prosecution, the DPP's public documents now actually serve to promote the interests of proponents of assisted suicide? Indeed, just as it is now evident following the DPP policy, as Mullock[49] points out, that although (since the first suicide tourist, Reginald Crew, travelled to Switzerland in 2003), no one who has travelled abroad for the purposes of assisting suicide has yet been prosecuted, so any remaining uncertainty as to whether it is an offence under the 1961 Act to travel abroad to assist another's suicide has now been much reduced, as long as sufficient 'compassion'[50] is evidenced as the primary motive. Accordingly, if the factors against prosecution are clearly present, this has led to the effective decriminalisation of assisting suicide in terms of the application of the law, in direct contrast to the strongly worded prohibition in the 1961 Act, which to Ost amounts to a 'marked discrepancy between on the one hand, the law on assisted suicide as laid down by statute and on the other, the law as applied in practice'.[51]

This has led to an 'unsatisfactory' legal limbo, and given the well-documented public support[52] for relatives either assisting in the suicide, or carrying out the voluntary euthanasia or 'mercy killing' of severely disabled people,[53] has reignited often highly emotive debates played out in the public spotlight as to whether or not to legalise 'the right to die' in the UK.

47 Rogers, op. cit., n. 43.
48 S. Ost, 'The De-medicalisation of Assisted Dying: Is a Less Medicalised Model the Way Forward?', *Medical Law Review*, Volume 18 (4), 2010, p. 531.
49 A. Mullock, 'Overlooking the Criminally Compassionate: What are the Implications of Prosecutorial Policy on Encouraging or Assisting Suicide?', *Medical Law Review*, Volume 18, 2010, p. 447.
50 DPP (2010), op. cit, n. 39, states under note 2 of 'Public interest factors tending against a prosecution', that 'a prosecution is less likely if the suspect was wholly motivated by compassion'.
51 Ost, op. cit., n. 48, p. 14.
52 E. Elery, S. McLean and M. Philips, 'Quickening Death: Euthanasia Debate', in P. Alison et al. (eds) *British Social Attitudes Survey: 23rd Report*, London: Sage, 2007, which demonstrated that a majority of the public surveyed in 2005 would support legal change in favour of the decriminalisation of assisted dying, if the victim had a terminal, incurable or painful illness. Public support is directly correlated to the severity and progressiveness of the illness or disability of the victim.
53 Laville, op. cit, n. 46 re the trial of Kay Gilderdale, mother of Lynn, who was found not guilty by a sympathetic jury.

Reframing the debate: assisted dying and economic stress

This chapter now takes as its starting point the cogent argument advanced by Epstein, who points out that, notwithstanding the voluminous writing on the theme of end-of-life decisions, especially assisted dying, one critical and highly sensitive issue is notable for its absence in this socio-legal and ethical debate, and that is the effect of the 'economic environment', and the extent to which economic factors might determine the relative value of human life.

To Epstein,[54] on the one hand, although this 'silent argument' so clearly underpins all these issues, and is an invisible yet dominant force, on the other, the lack of explicitness as to just how and in what ways economic factors might serve to 'provide motivations for hastening the death of patients . . . actually legitimises economic pressures and reaffirms their original causes, whatever they might be', as they fail to be taken into account, and so remain critically unchallenged.

We will now move on to re-frame the assisted dying debate in the light of the economic considerations which, although so evident in discussions of health care rationing and resource allocation, are dropped from the agenda at the point of end-of-life decisions. Therefore, although, as shown in the foregoing discussion, end-of-life decisions within a clinical context, such as treatment withdrawal or Do Not Attempt Resuscitation orders (DNAR), have resource implications which are highlighted in judicial reasoning, these are not generally regarded as impinging in any way on patient self-determination in cases involving competent patients.

Epstein attributes this reluctance to include economic factors within these debates to two key reasons, first, and perhaps most importantly, to a moral rejection of their dark heritage, where medical ethics and economics were used to justify the large-scale physician-assisted euthanasia and eugenics movements during the era of the Third Reich in the mid-twentieth century, which systematically removed those considered as having devalued, 'economically unproductive' lives, who were classed as a drain on scarce financial resources; the so-called 'life unworthy of life'. Hence, this position rejects as abhorrent any link between end-of-life decisions and private business profit.[55] The second explanation suggests that there is less a rejection of economic considerations as they relate to such debates, and more that 'the silent argument' is a useful 'ideological smokescreen', which conceals the extent to which such economic considerations, particularly in times of economic austerity and the rolling back of state support, inform government legislative and policy decision-making, and also public attitudes to end-of-life, including the 'right to die' issues. As Epstein points out, such socio-economic pressures:

---

54 Epstein, op. cit., n. 11, p. 24.
55 As Epstein, op. cit, n. 11 notes, 'with the exception of the private funeral industry', p. 24.

force people to reduce the value of almost anything, including life, to exchange value. Further, to the degree, to which this is so, people will also be inclined to perceive life without such value as a burden, which may be relieved by hastening death.[56]

The 'slippery slope' debate

Advocates of the 'right to die' campaign to legalise assisted suicide argue that whilst suicide was decriminalised in the Suicide Act 1961, s 2 (1), at the same time, to preserve the sanctity of life doctrine, it also created a crime of assisting in suicide, and so automatically denied choice to people (who although competent) may be so physically debilitated that they are unable to take their own lives, and rely on the help of other people to do so. This prohibition therefore places the very group of people who, as McLean points out, might 'positively wish their lives to be ended . . . [and who are] most likely to endure a long drawn out even undignified dying process',[57] in an unenviable position.

Opponents of the legalisation of assisted suicide often draw on the so-called 'slippery slope' argument, which holds that 'once an exception to a moral norm is permitted, it will inevitably lead to further erosion of the modified norm';[58] that is, as McLean[59] explains, if ('acceptable' option) A is undertaken, this will inevitably lead to B ('less acceptable'), and so on, to a point where the ('completely unacceptable') end of the slope is reached, and 'once introduced on compassionate grounds [assisted suicide] will lead to death on request, or euthanasia without consent'[60] for those judged to have lives that are not worth living.

This risk was very thoroughly covered in the 'Assisted Dying for the Terminally Ill' Bill (the second of three of Lord Joffe's Private Members' Bills),[61] which was referred to the House of Lords Select Committee for Medical Ethics for full evaluation.[62] However, it was also evident from Lord Joffe's contribution to the debate, that he did, indeed, envisage that the application of the Bill's scope would be extended to include those experiencing

---

56 Epstein, op. cit, n.11, p. 26.
57 McLean, op. cit., n. 32, p. 17.
58 Mason and Laurie, op. cit., n. 22, p. 568.
59 McLean, op. cit., n. 32, p. 49.
60 C. Odone, *Assisted Suicide: How the Chattering Classes have got it Wrong*, London: Centre for Policy Studies, 2010.
61 In 2003, Lord Joffe introduced his first private members' bill, 'The Patient (Assisted Dying) Bill', which would legalise physician-assisted suicide, but it did not progress beyond the second reading.
62 It ran to three volumes of evidence drawn from a wide spectrum of experts, but was prevented from progressing further by the dissolution of Parliament in 2005 for the General Election.

'unbearable' suffering, and yet not terminally ill.[63] Ost[64] has offered a strong critique against legal recognition of the concept of 'unbearable suffering', arguing that this shifts the parameters towards those who simply may have 'life fatigue'.[65] To Ost, in 'a further related danger in extending the criteria to non-medically based suffering, society risks encouraging an assisted dying culture, with an assisted death being seen as an option whenever life becomes taxing or difficult'.[66]

Indeed, a logical development of this understanding of a gradual incremental drift to the bottom of the slope is that this will further serve to legitimise discrimination against vulnerable groups, whose lives are seen as of less value. This perspective has been raised by Mullock,[67] who pointed out that the interim DPP guidelines which were published (following the Purdy ruling) highlighted that if the victim had 'a terminal illness, a severe and incurable illness or a severe degenerative condition', this factor would weigh against prosecution. Yet this direction was later dropped from the 2010 DPP policy guidelines, in the light of public consultation where over 1,500 respondents viewed this provision as discriminatory, for this implied that such a motivation may be benign if it was considered that disabled people have lives of less value, and thus should be helped and relieved of their burden. Mullock cites a quote from Greasley, who observed that 'the law cannot impose value of life thresholds in assisted suicide, without by extension engaging in value of life comparisons directed not just at individuals, but whole groups of sufferers'.[68] However, as Mullock explains, notwithstanding their lack of reference to disability, this assumption still remains implicit in the text of the 2010 DPP Guidelines, which state that 'if the suspect was wholly motivated by compassion', this counts against prosecution, and raises the question 'can any understanding of compassion exclude considerations of the victim's health?'[69]

A further important mitigating factor in the DPP Guidelines rests on the principle of autonomous choice, that is, whether 'the victim had reached a

---

63 '... when we considered the opposition to the previous Bill, we felt that there was such strength of feeling in the debate about extending it to younger people who had a long lifetime ahead of them that we thought it wise ... To limit it to terminally ill patients who were already suffering terribly and had a short time to live. But I can assure you, I would prefer that the law did apply to patients who were younger and not terminally ill but who were suffering unbearably, but if there is a move to insert that into the Bill I would certainly support it', para 92.

64 Ost, op. cit., n.48, p. 527.

65 S. Templeton, 'Woman commits suicide to avoid old age', *Sunday Times*, 3 April 2011, To avoid what she described as 'prolonged dwindling' in old age, Nan Maitland travelled to Switzerland, where assisted death is legal as long as it is not selfishly motivated.

66 Ost, op. cit, n. 48, p. 12.

67 Mullock, op. cit., n. 49, p. 461.

68 Ibid., p. 461.

69 Ibid., p. 462.

voluntary, clear, settled, and informed decision to commit suicide'. And yet, as Epstein emphasises, as long as the foregoing provisions are apparent,

> all conceivable values – including all values that are implicit in patients' motivations for hastening death, must be respected, irrespective of the conditions that might have induced them. Moreover, economic pressures . . . are not considered 'truly coercive' as to render the patient's decision heteronomous and hence ethico-legally invalid.[70]

This is therefore consistent with the foregoing discussion, which shows that 'autonomy' within this context is based on a negative, rather than positive rights-based obligation, and therefore may be either directly or indirectly shaped by lack of sufficient resources to make life subjectively worth living.

The same line of argument was also adopted by the Disability Rights Commission in their representation to Lord Joffe's Assisted Dying for the Terminally Ill Bill, which stated

> the odds are currently stacked against people's positive choices to have access to treatment/services; and in favour of people's right to refuse them . . . any increase in rights to refuse treatment or die would tilt the balance still further. In the view of the DRC, the priority lies in establishing genuine choice, to ensure that people have rights to agreed standards of palliative care and rights to independent living – i.e. rights to be supported to live (and die) at home (where possible), rights to respite services such that relatives are not exhausted, rights to the type of support that can make life worth living.[71]

Health and welfare resource allocation and rationing

The discussion will now move on to examine the wider socio-political context, and the role of resource allocation and rationing within health and social welfare, which, especially as it relates to the former, inevitably relies on decision-making based 'on the application of some sort of productivity test',[72] which can hinge on social value judgments as to where the threshold lies.

Resource allocation and rationing are a clearly evident and inescapable fact, for example the use of Quality Adjusted Life Years (QALY) in health care decision-making processes. QALY assess the benefits gained from health care interventions in terms of quality of life and survival for the patient. When

70 Epstein, op. cit., n. 11, p. 27.
71 House of Lords, Select Committee on the Assisted Dying for the Terminally Ill Bill, *Volume II: Evidence*, London: House of Lords, p. 223.
72 Epstein, op. cit., n. 11, p. 29.

combined with the cost of providing such interventions, cost utility ratios indicate how much it will cost to provide a perfect year of health, so comparisons can be made between interventions and those that have a relatively low cost can be prioritised over those that are more expensive.[73] The result may be that some patients will not be offered treatment. John Harris contends that people's moral claim to health care resources should not be diminished by how old they are, how rich or poor, powerful or weak or, particularly, by the quality of their lives. He adds that any principle of justice 'worth its salt' covers both young and old, sick or healthy, regardless of race, creed, colour and sex but also of quality of life and life expectancy. To Harris, the principle aim of the NHS should be to protect the lives and health of all, offering treatment based on individual need so that all have an equal chance of flourishing to the extent that their personal health allows.[74]

Further to this, Herring[75] points out that one particular concern is that the QALY indeed works very harshly against older people, in that an older person who has a low life expectancy will find it very hard, if not impossible, to claim a higher value of QALY than a younger person in a similar situation. Opponents of age as a relevant factor argue that it is extremely unjust to place more value on the life of a younger person than on the life of an older person. The use of age reinforces the notion that the elderly are simply a 'waste of space'.[76] Not only this, but there is also concern that for those who are seriously ill, any treatment that will only be able to offer a slight increase in life expectancy or some minor improvement in the quality of their life may be deemed to be futile. Other objections to the QALY approach are unacceptable results that consider such concepts as dignity to be of little importance,[77] particularly at a time when complaints about the lack of dignity accorded to patients in the NHS have been investigated by the Health Service Ombudsman[78] and it has found, in some quarters, to be wanting. Moreover, patients who suffer from a disability unconnected with their medical condition would be disadvantaged, or subject to what Harris calls 'double jeopardy',[79] meaning that those with disabilities may be seen by health

73 C. Phillips, 'What is a QALY?' *Health Economics*, 2nd edn, London: Hayward Medical Communications, 2009, pp. 1–5.

74 J. Harris, 'The rationing debate: Maximising the health of the whole community: the case against: what the principal objective of the NHS should really be', *British Medical Journal*, 314, 1997, pp. 669–71.

75 J. Herring, *Medical Law and Ethics*, 3rd edn, Oxford: Oxford University Press, 2010, pp. 78–9.

76 Ibid.

77 Ibid.

78 A. Abraham, *Care and compassion? Report of the Health Service Ombudsman on ten investigations into NHS care of older people*, London: Routledge, 2011.

79 J. Harris, 'Double Jeopardy and the Veil of Ignorance: A Reply', *Journal of Medical Ethics*, 21, pp. 151–7.

care professionals as having a poorer quality of life and therefore benefiting less than those who after treatment could be returned to a full state of health.[80]

Yet Herring observes that there are those who promote the benefits of QALY.[81] The main benefit is their ability to provide a way of considering the quality of life that treatments can offer, as well as the length of time a person may gain in years. They also provide a method of comparing treatments for different conditions and the cost effectiveness of treatments, which is necessary in a climate of reduced resources. Age discrimination is also defended. Quality Adjusted Life Years is probably the most popular way of determining the cost effectiveness of treatments, and the National Institute for Health and Clinical Excellence (NICE) frequently uses this concept for decision-making in cases where rationing is required.[82]

In defence of age discrimination, NICE makes it clear that 'health should not be valued more highly in some age groups than others' but that 'where age is an indicator of benefit or risk, age discrimination is appropriate'.[83] Lockwood,[84] however, goes even further in defence of ageism, and takes the view that QALY are not ageist enough, on the grounds that a 40-year-old should have a greater priority than an 80-year-old, as an 80-year-old has already had a 'fair innings'.[85] Surely this must then mean that some older and disabled patients are left with very little choice or hope of accessing medical services?

So clearly, if applied to end-of-life decisions and resource allocation, this legitimisation of discrimination as shown by the QALY approach to ethical decision-making processes also raises the highly politically sensitive issue, articulated by Huxtable, that some groups may be more vulnerable to exploitation, and coerced either directly or indirectly into 'choosing' to hasten their

---

80 J. Harris, 'QALYfying the Value of Life', *Journal of Medical Ethics*, 13(3), 1987, pp. 117–23.

81 Herring, op. cit., n. 75, p. 77.

82 NICE, *Social Value Judgements: Principles for the development of NICE Guidance*, London: NICE, 2005.

83 Ibid., p. 24.

84 M. Lockwood, 'Quality of Life and Resource Allocation', in J.M. Bell and S. Mendus (eds) *Philosophy and Medical Welfare*, Cambridge: Cambridge University Press, 1988.

85 John Harris discusses the 'fair innings' argument in *The Value of Life*. This argument takes the view that there is a span of years that is considered to be a reasonable life (he suggests 70) – in other words, a fair innings – and that those who do not reach this suffer the injustice of being cut off in their prime. On the other hand, those who do must consider any additional years to be a bonus. Everyone must be given an equal chance to reach the threshold, but having reached this, they must forfeit additional years to help others to reach the threshold. He suggests that this argument becomes a reason for preferring to save younger rather than older people. He argues that it is always a tragedy to die when one wants to live; it is, however, not a tragedy to die in old age, but it is both a tragedy and a misfortune to be cut off prematurely. See J. Harris, *The Value of Life*, London and New York: Routledge, 1985, pp. 91–3.

death.[86] Indeed, his point that resource limitations, in particular, might mean that the elderly would come to be seen, whether by their doctors or themselves, as 'candidates for euthanasia', has already been suggested by Baroness Warnock in the case of people with dementia.[87] Warnock, who is a prominent 'right to die' supporter, makes explicit 'the silent argument'[88] by linking economic pressures, economic productivity, the relative value of life, and euthanasia, stating:

> If you're demented, you're wasting people's lives, your family's lives, and you're wasting the resources of the National Health Service . . . I'm absolutely, fully in agreement with the argument that if pain is insufferable, then somebody should be given help to die, but I feel there is a wider argument that if somebody absolutely, desperately wants to die because they're a burden to their family, or the state, then I think they should be allowed to die.[89]

Revealingly, the same article continues, 'Figures show there are 700,000 people with degenerative diseases such as Alzheimer's in Britain. By 2026, experts predict there will be one million dementia sufferers in the country, costing the NHS an estimated £35 billion a year.'[90]

This argument which was once silent has now become an explicit economic rationale for supporting the assisted dying of groups judged to have such a low value of life that they are no longer considered worthy of state support. Although Mclean sees this line of argument as the most 'compelling rhetoric' against the legalisation of assisted suicide, she also claims that it is an 'untestable presumption'.[91]

However, research undertaken by Golden and Zoanni shows that this economic argument in favour of hastening the death of 'socially disadvantaged people who have less access to medical resources and who already may find themselves discriminated against in the health care system' – people who may be deemed expensive in terms of investment of resources – is very much in evidence in the state of Oregon.[92]

Indeed, Oregon introduced the Death with Dignity Act in 1994, legalising assisted suicide, and in the same year it also introduced what Mason and Lurie

---

86 R. Huxtable, *Euthanasia, Ethics and the Law: From Conflict to Compromise*, London: Routledge-Cavendish, 2007, p. 17.

87 M. Beckford, 'Baroness Warnock: Dementia Sufferers May Have a "Duty to Die" ', *Daily Telegraph*, 18 September 2008.

88 Epstein, op. cit., n.11.

89 Ibid.

90 Ibid.

91 McLean, op. cit, n. 32, p. 50.

92 M. Golden and T. Zoanni, 'Killing us Softly: The Dangers of Legalising Assisted Suicide', *Disability and Health Journal*, Vol. 3, January 2010, pp. 16–30.

describe as 'the first exercise in public consensus healthcare rationing . . . available under Medicaid and business related private insurance arrangements . . . according to a priority list of services to which more individuals who cannot afford private health insurance could have access'.[93] The drawback was that some groups became worse off, at the expense of everyone. The rationing process was undertaken by the Oregon Medical Assistance Programme (OMAP), which stopped funding for 167 of 700 health services four years on, once the Death with Dignity Act was enforced. At this point, OMAP Directors put lethal prescriptions on the list of 'treatments' categorised as 'comfort care'. It should be noted that the cost of such lethal medications is far less, at $300, than alternatives such as palliative care and home-based support services. Further, Golden and Zoanni show that the Health Care plan guidelines state that:

> it will not cover the cost of surgery, radiotherapy or chemotherapy for patients with less than a 5 per cent expected five-year survival. However, such patients are eligible to receive comfort/palliative care which includes 'services under the Oregon Death with Dignity Act, [that is] physician assisted suicide' to include but not be limited to the attending physician visits, consulting confirmation, mental health evaluation and counselling, and prescription medication.[94]

Golden and Zoanni also demonstrate that end-of-life palliative care has been cut back at the same time, so highlighting that 'real' patient choice, far from being enhanced, as proponents of assisted suicide argue, has, for those who lack the economic resources to take alternative options, actually diminished. [95]

The foregoing evidence supports Gill's assertion that assisted suicide will further divert limited resources away from vulnerable groups on the basis that:

> expanding our culture's comfort with letting go of 'suffering people' will ultimately lead to less support for our lives, whether it involves an antibiotic that is withheld, a ventilator that is withdrawn or a message about being a burden that takes away one's will to live. The decriminalisation of assisted suicide has already begun to increase the broken body count far beyond countable incidents of assisted suicide.[96]

93 Mason and Laurie, op. cit., n. 22, p. 42.
94 Golden and Zoanni, op. cit., n. 92, p. 19.
95 Ibid.
96 C.J. Gill, 'No we don't think our doctors are out to get us: Responding to the straw man distortions of disability rights arguments against Assisted Suicide', *Disability and Health Journal*, Vol. 3, Issue 1, January 2010, p. 34.

Public sector spending cuts: 'doing the bed-run'[97]

This final section will now move on to show, by drawing on current research into health and social welfare, the extent to which the current 'swingeing' public sector cuts will further serve to not only exacerbate the fears of vulnerable older and disabled people of losing what remaining choice and control they have over their lives, but will indeed demonstrate that such fears, far from being unfounded, are in fact a daily reality for a now rapidly growing number of people.

In this period of fiscal constraint, the government aims to meet the financial challenges presented by the current economic downturn by achieving unprecedented 'efficiency gains' of £80 billion cuts to public spending in health and social welfare,[98] comprising £18 billion which will be found from welfare in 2014–15[99] and £15 to £20 billion from the NHS.[100] When Andrew Lansley, Secretary of State for Health, set out his vision for the future of public health policy, at the same time as placing greater emphasis on individual and social responsibility[101] he highlighted the need to '[recognise] the additional demands facing the NHS in the coming decades – an increasing and ageing population, costly advances in treatment and rising expectations – we simply can't go on like this'.[102] Hence a key thrust to the reforms is to reduce debt while at the same time meeting the existing and future costs of the rapidly changing demographic shift towards an increased proportion of older and disabled people and accompanying technological innovations.[103]

---

97   This subheading derives from the personal experience of one of the authors, who was told by a member of staff working for the care agency that cared for her relative that, in order to meet the contracted schedule, she was working on the 'bed-run', meaning that some of the clients would need to be put to bed at 6pm because of a shortage of staff. Visits the following morning started at 9am so the presumption then, is that those clients who are immobile and dependent on carers to get them out of bed are left stranded for many hours at a time with no assistance.

98   Yates et al, op. cit., n. 3, p. 4.

99   Ibid.

100 Department of Health, *Equity and Excellence: Liberating the NHS*, 2010.

101 As a means of addressing social problems, such as alcohol dependence or obesity, which are seen as deriving from 'unhealthy lifestyles', and so a matter of behavioural control and self-discipline.

102 A. Lansley, Secretary of State for Health's Speech to the UK Faculty of Public Health Conference – 'A new approach to public health', Department of Health, 7 December 2010. Available at: <http://www.dh.gov.uk/en/MediaCentre/Speeches/DH_117280> (accessed 19 June 2011).

103 The population of the UK is becoming increasingly older and while this may be a cause for celebration it also presents new challenges, for example an increasing demand on access to local services, housing and health and welfare services. Ageing of the UK population is projected to continue with the number of people aged 65 and over increasing by nearly two-thirds to reach 15.8 million by 2031, when those aged 65 and over will account for 22 per cent of the UK population. The largest population increases are

Yet Wilkinson and Pickett found evidence in their international analysis of inequality of 'a social gradient in health running right across society . . . [showing that] where we are placed in relation to other people matters; those above us have better health, those below us have worse health, from the very bottom to the very top'.[104] This is also borne out by research undertaken by both the Disability Rights Commission[105] and Mencap,[106] which found that protected equality characteristics are no guarantee of equality of treatment, and inequalities based on, for example, disability interact with socio-economic status and significantly impact on health.

Current research shows that the public spending cuts will disproportion- ately affect vulnerable and frail older and disabled people, leaving them without the necessary vital home-based care.[107] Moreover, as Walker points out, there is already evidence of a substantial shortfall in the provision of existing Adult Social Care services without factoring in the future cuts. The current needs-supply 'care' gap shows that although the largest proportion of older people, approximately 5.5 million older people, do not need adult social care services, only three out of five of the remaining 1.4 million who have low level needs, and 0.9 million who have high level needs, 'receive any formal support either in their own homes or in residential care/nursing homes'.[108] Indeed, Walker further adds that just to stay at the current level and stand still requires an increase of funding 'by 3.5 per cent per annum'[109] and states that if just 6.5 per cent were cut in 2010/11, this would amount in 2012/13 to 'the further exclusion of around 170,000 of those with high needs from full

projected for the oldest of the older age groups, resulting in a 77 per cent increase in those over the age of 75 and a 131 per cent increase in those aged 85 and over. Women in older age groups currently outnumber men because, on average, they have a greater life expectancy, but with improvements in male life expectancy this differential is pro- jected to decrease. By 2031, the number of women over 65 is expected to increase by 54 per cent alongside an expected increase of 74 per cent for men. This is even more pro- nounced for the 'oldest old', with a projected increase of 93 per cent in women aged 85 and over, compared with a 220 per cent increase in men of the same age. J. Bayliss and F. Sly, *Ageing Across the UK*, London, Office of National Statistics, 8 June 2010. Available at: <http://www.ons.gov.uk/ons/rel/regional-trends/regional-trends-online-tables/2010/regional-trends-42---ageing-across-the-uk.pdf> (accessed 1 November 2011).

104   R. Wilkinson and K. Pickett, *The Spirit Level: Why More Equal Societies Almost always do Better*, London: Penguin, p. 76.

105   Disability Rights Commission, *Equal Treatment: Closing the Gap, Part 1*, London, DRC, 2006, pp. 33–40. The DRC has now been amalgamated into the Equality and Human Rights Commission.

106   Mencap, *Death by Indifference*, London: Mencap, 2007, pp. 18–24.

107   J. Forder and J.L. Fernandez, *The impact of a tightening fiscal situation on social care for older people*, Personal Social Services Research Unit and Age UK, 2010, London. Available at: <http://www.pssru.ac.uk/pdf/dp2723.pdf> (accessed 19 June 2011).

108   A. Walker, 'Social Care', in Yates et al., op. cit., n. 3, p. 23.

109   Ibid.

support, and a reduction of all recipients of state support by around 490,000'.[110] Age UK also found that each older and disabled person, especially over the age of 75, who relies on £18,000 worth of public services per year, will lose over a third of this, whilst people who rely on state support in the 65–75 age range will lose up to 29 per cent.[111]

This is a pattern which is now cascading across all local authorities in England and Wales. To make cuts of 6.1 per cent from £212 million to £199 million, for instance, West Sussex Council has raised the threshold for priority intervention, and now excludes adults defined as having 'moderate' needs to concentrate on those regarded as having 'substantial' or 'critical' needs.[112] To save nine million pounds from the Adult Social Care budget, Bradford Council plans to close a centre for disabled patients, and has already increased the cost of Meals on Wheels.[113]

Moreover, even the watchdog body, the Care Quality Commission (CQC), which was developed to oversee and regulate care standards, has now seen its role severely undermined by a 30 per cent budget reduction and so has 'cut its inspections by 70 per cent, taking a minimum of 70 days to register new homes. Its 900 inspectors are expected to cover more than 8,000 GP practices as well as 400 NHS trusts, 9,000 dental practices and 18,000 care homes'.[114] In the light of such cuts, the CQC failed to follow up a whistleblower who spoke out against staff at Winterbourne View, a private care home facility in Bristol for 24 adults with varying degrees of learning disability and autism, which was later revealed by an undercover BBC documentary to show adults with varying degrees of learning disabilities being cruelly goaded, humiliated and abused by untrained care workers.[115]

The lack of adequate regulation of care standards at the time of writing is further evidenced by the publication of the interim results from a large-scale

---

110 A. Walker, 'Social Care' in Yates et al., op. cit., n. 3, p. 23.

111 T. Horton, *How the government's planned cuts will affect older people*, London: Age UK, 2010.

112 Birmingham City Council's plans to save £17.5 million by restricting social services to adults whose needs are defined as 'critical' was ruled as unlawful on 19 May 2011 in a case brought by the families of four disabled people whose needs would no longer be considered. Mr Justice Walker declared that both Birmingham City Council's budget setting and its decision to change its eligibility policy were unlawful on the grounds that they did not promote equality under s 49A of the Disability Discrimination Act 1995 and their attempts at consultation were flawed. EHRC Media Centre Briefing available at: <http://www.equalityhumanrights.com/news/2011/may/commission-comment-on-birmingham-council-care-ruling/> (accessed 19 June 2011).

113 *The Independent*, 'Elderly will suffer as cuts force councils to slash care services', 2 June 2011, p. 4.

114 P. Toynbee, 'Public tolerance has now been tested to destruction', *The Guardian*, 4 June 2011.

115 P. Kenyon and J. Casey, 'Undercover Care: Abuse Exposed', BBC *Panorama*, shown 31 May 2011.

research project undertaken on behalf of the EHRC, which took place at a time which pre-dates the most severe of the public sector cuts, which will be implemented from 2012 to 2014.[116] The study found that the standard of state-provided care for older people at home can be of such poor quality that examples of neglect and human rights abuses include people being left in bed for 17 hours or more between care visits, failure to wash people regularly, failure to provide people with the support they need to eat and drink, and people being left in soiled beds and clothes for long periods.

However, although the foregoing discussion highlights the very real (negative) quality of life issues arising from the financial impact of the cuts, one recent survey also demonstrated the implications of the cuts for the morale and emotional health of those on the receiving end. Indeed, the Disability Rights Partnership (DRP), a coalition of three long-standing and prominent disability rights organisations, comprising the Royal Association for Disability Rights (RADAR), the National Centre for Independent Living (NCIL) and Disability Alliance, published the results of their survey of just under 2,000 disabled people, 'of which 82 per cent were receiving or caring for someone using Disability Living Allowance', in early 2011.[117] The findings showed that it was what was termed the 'human costs' that were perhaps the most critical issue raised in the report, for when the DRP asked respondents, as an open question, to describe 'the impact of losing some or all of the DLA support . . . 9 per cent of the first 900 respondents cited death and suicide as possible outcomes'.[118] Verbatim quotes by respondents in the survey perhaps exemplify and render transparent a now demonstrable and deadly link between economic pressures and pressure to depart life prematurely. To many, DLA support was so critical that it makes the difference between a life worth living and one which is not, as illustrated by one person who stated, 'I would kill myself to stop being a burden on my family. If I didn't do this, I would end up homeless and in an inevitable decline anyway. Might as well get the horror over with';[119] and a further person who pointed out, 'I would not be able to go to work, I would not be able to see my family or friends. Therefore, I would not want to live'.[120] Another person despaired, saying 'It would add an extra

---

116 Equality and Human Rights Commission, 'Inquiry reveals failure to protect the rights of older people receiving care at home'. Available at: <http://www.equalityhumanrights.com/news/2011/june/inquiry-reveals-failure-to-protect-the-rights-of-older-people-receiving-care-at-home> (accessed 19 June 2011). The survey participants comprised 54 per cent of local authorities, 250 home care providers in England and Wales, 503 written submissions in response to a call for evidence, including 344 responses from individuals (older people, their friends and family), 58 from organisations, and 101 from home care staff.
117 Disability Rights Partnership, op. cit, n. 9.
118 Ibid., p. 22.
119 Ibid.
120 Ibid.

burden on me which I couldn't cope with. I would probably have to think about ending it all'.[121]

Clearly, this critically challenges the concept of 'autonomy' and self-determination applied in human rights law, as it illustrates that for the third of disabled people who live in poverty in the UK,[122] who are most subject to the foregoing 'economic stress', any real level of choice relating to end-of-life decisions is contingent upon sufficient resources to render life worth living.

Conclusion

This chapter has argued that the HRA has had a transformative effect on medical and criminal law, as it has led, through the judicial rulings in Pretty and Purdy, and the DPP guidelines, to the effective decriminalisation of assisted suicide if factors against prosecution are evidenced (in the application of the law, if not in statute). The HRA-led entrenchment of the legal doctrine of patient 'autonomy' and self-determination relating to end-of-life decisions within medical settings has now extended from the right to refuse or withdraw treatment to the right, in principle, for severely disabled and/or older people, with the support of relatives and sufficient financial resources, to now purchase a legal exit abroad, and exercise a modicum of control over the manner and timing of their death (with less fear of their relatives being prosecuted for breaking the law).

This incremental shift towards the potential future legalisation of assisted suicide is now a hotly debated and highly controversial topic which is played out in the public spotlight of the press and media in the UK. 'Right to die' proponents passionately hold on to the position that, until assisted suicide is legalised, severely disabled and/or older people will be denied the option of circumventing what could be a long, drawn-out and painful departure.[123] Their argument hinges on 'autonomy', and the idea that disabled people are discriminated against in this context, as they are a group who may have most cause to want to hasten their departure through suicide, but who are physically unable to do so, in contrast to non-disabled people. Yet it has been shown that the only rights which have been endorsed within the legal doctrine of 'autonomy' have been negative, non-interference rights, and not positive rights of entitlement to medical treatment and resources. Therefore, the legal 'rights-based' concept of 'autonomy' may be severely compromised by lack of resources, as disabled people or older people experiencing severe economic stress, as a result of the current economic downturn and public sector cuts,

---

121 Disability Rights Partnership, op. cit., n. 9.
122 Ibid., p. 16.
123 In the case of the terminally ill, or a life robbed of quality, in the case of extreme physical debilitation.

may lack sufficient resources to live a life of dignity, and so may turn to what may be less a 'choice' and more a 'duty', and hasten their death.

The foregoing argument shows how the deadly economic equation between economic scarcity and severe resource rationing particularly discriminates against vulnerable disabled and older people, who, at a point in life when they may place greater demands upon an already overstretched health and social welfare system, may be directly or indirectly steered towards a cost-saving therapeutic and untimely death, for want of 'expensive' resource-consuming realistic alternatives.

Part III

Activist confrontations

Section 1

Confronting the Human Rights Act from the feminist perspective

10 What potential does the Human Rights Act hold for domestic violence groups?

Ronagh McQuigg

Domestic violence is an issue that affects vast numbers of women throughout the world. It seems to constitute a clear violation of Arts 2, 3 and 8 of the European Convention on Human Rights, but it has only been recognised as being a human rights issue relatively recently. Indeed, until 2007 domestic violence had not been directly addressed by the European Court of Human Rights. However, the European Court has now clearly established that domestic violence constitutes a human rights abuse, as highlighted by recent judgments such as *Bevacqua and S v Bulgaria*;[1] *Opuz v Turkey*;[2] and *E.S. and Others v Slovakia*.[3]

This chapter will assess the potential held by the Human Rights Act 1998 for groups working in the area of combating domestic violence. The question of whether domestic violence has been recognised as being a human rights issue by the courts in the United Kingdom will be assessed. Potential difficulties will also be analysed, for example the deferential approach adopted by the judiciary in questions surrounding the allocation of resources and the problems involved in using the Human Rights Act in relation to an 'unseen crime' such as domestic violence. In addition, the chapter will examine the question of whether other human rights law mechanisms, such as the Optional Protocol to the United Nations Convention on the Elimination of All Forms of Discrimination against Women, hold greater potential as regards the issue of domestic violence.

The European Court of Human Rights and domestic violence

The European Court of Human Rights has clearly recognised that domestic violence is a human rights issue. For example, in *Kontrova v Slovakia*[4] the

---

1 Application No. 71127/01, 12 September 2008.
2 Application No. 33401/02, 9 September 2009.
3 Application No. 8227/04, 15 December 2009.
4 Application No. 7510/04, 24 September 2007.

applicant had been subjected to domestic violence by her husband. She alleged that the police had failed to take appropriate action to protect her children's lives under Art. 2 and her private and family life under Art. 8 of the Convention, despite knowing of her husband's abusive behaviour. He had threatened to kill himself and their two children and he had in fact carried out this threat. Under domestic law in Slovakia, the police had various specific obligations, such as accepting and registering the applicant's complaint; launching a criminal investigation; and commencing proceedings against the applicant's husband immediately. However, they had failed to comply with any of these obligations.

In holding that there had been a breach of the children's right to life, the Court re-iterated the principle that Art. 2

> enjoins the State not only to refrain from the intentional and unlawful taking of life, but also to take appropriate steps to safeguard the lives of those within its jurisdiction . . . It also extends in appropriate circumstances to a positive obligation on the authorities to take preventive operational measures to protect an individual whose life is at risk from the criminal acts of another individual.[5]

The applicant alleged that the violation of Art. 2 also constituted a violation of her own private and family life under Art. 8; however, the Court held that in the light of the finding of a violation of Art. 2, it was not necessary to examine the case under Art. 8 also.

In *Bevacqua and S v Bulgaria*,[6] the applicants were a victim of domestic violence and her young son. It was argued that there had been violations of Arts 3 and 8 of the Convention, as the authorities had failed to protect the first applicant against the violent behaviour of her former husband and had failed to take the necessary measures to secure respect for the family life of both applicants. The Court examined the complaints under Art. 8, but not under Art. 3. In holding that there had been a violation of Art. 8, the Court stated that:

> At the relevant time Bulgarian law did not provide for specific administrative and policing measures (in relation to domestic violence) and the measures taken by the police and prosecuting authorities on the basis of their general powers did not prove effective . . . In the Court's view, the authorities' failure to impose sanctions or otherwise enforce Mr N.'s obligation to refrain from unlawful acts was critical in the circumstances of this case, as it amounted to a refusal to provide the immediate assistance the applicants needed. The authorities' view that no such assistance was due as the

---

5 Application No.7510/04, para 49.
6 Op. cit., note 1.

dispute concerned a 'private matter' was incompatible with their positive obligations to secure the enjoyment of the applicants' Article 8 rights.[7]

In *Opuz v Turkey*,[8] the applicant alleged that the authorities had failed to protect herself and her mother from domestic violence, which had resulted in the death of her mother and her own ill-treatment. She complained that the authorities had failed to safeguard the right to life of her mother, who had been killed by the applicant's husband, in violation of Art. 2 of the Convention. The Court concluded that 'The criminal law system, as applied in the instant case, did not have an adequate deterrent effect capable of ensuring the effective prevention of the unlawful acts committed by (the applicant's husband).'[9] There had thus been a breach of Art. 2.

The applicant also alleged that she had been subjected to violence, injury and death threats but that the authorities were negligent towards her situation, which caused her pain and fear in violation of Art. 3 of the Convention. She argued that the injuries she had suffered amounted to torture within the meaning of Art. 3. The Court held that the violence suffered was sufficiently serious to amount to ill-treatment within the meaning of Art. 3, although it did not specify whether it amounted to torture, as opposed to inhuman or degrading treatment. The Court concluded that there had been a violation of Art. 3 'as a result of the State authorities' failure to take protective measures in the form of effective deterrence against serious breaches of the applicant's personal integrity by her husband'.[10] In addition, the applicant claimed that there had been a breach of Art. 14 of the Convention, an argument which was also upheld by the Court. The applicant demonstrated through statistical data that domestic violence affected mainly women, and established that judicial passivity in Turkey created a climate conducive to domestic violence. It was stated that, 'Bearing in mind . . . that the general and discriminatory judicial passivity in Turkey, albeit unintentional, mainly affected women, the Court considers that the violence suffered by the applicant and her mother may be regarded as gender-based violence which is a form of discrimination against women.'[11]

In *A v Croatia*,[12] the applicant was again alleging that the state had failed to protect her adequately from domestic violence on the part of her former husband. Although the Croatian courts had ordered measures such as periods of detention and fines, many of these had not been enforced. It was held that the authorities' failure to implement these measures had resulted in a violation of the applicant's Art. 8 rights. The applicant also argued that there had

---

7 Application No.71127/01, para 83.
8 Op. cit., note 2.
9 Ibid., para 153.
10 Ibid., para 176.
11 Ibid., para 200.
12 Application No. 55164/08, 14 October 2010.

been a violation of Art. 14. However, the Court held that, unlike the applicant in *Opuz v Turkey*, she had not given sufficient evidence to prove that the measures or practices adopted in Croatia against domestic violence were discriminatory. This case therefore emphasises the point that if a victim of domestic violence wishes to argue that there has been a breach of Art. 14, it will be necessary for her to produce evidence such as reports or statistics to demonstrate the presence of discrimination.

In *E.S. and Others v Slovakia*,[13] the applicants were a mother and her three children. All four applicants had suffered abuse from the first applicant's husband. The Court held that the Art. 3 and Art. 8 rights of all four applicants had been violated due to the failure of the authorities to protect them in an appropriate manner from the treatment to which they had been subjected.

Finally, in *Hajduova v Slovakia*,[14] the applicant's former husband had been convicted after he had attacked her and repeatedly threatened to kill her and also several other persons. The national court had ordered that he be detained for psychiatric treatment. However, the treatment was not carried out. He was released and he subsequently renewed his threats against the applicant. It was argued that the state had failed to fulfil its positive obligation to protect her from her former husband, in violation of Art. 8. The European Court held that insufficient measures had been adopted and that there was therefore a breach of the applicant's Art. 8 rights.

Overall, it can be seen from these cases that states clearly have positive obligations to ensure that their criminal justice systems are of a certain standard in dealing with domestic violence. In these cases, particular attention was paid to the response of police forces to the issue. The fact that the European Court has now directly addressed the problem of domestic violence is a crucial development in itself, as it underlines the fact that it is a human rights issue. It is only relatively recently that domestic violence has been recognised as such, as evidenced by the fact that it took until 2007 for a domestic violence case to come before the European Court. However, what has been the approach of the domestic courts under the Human Rights Act in this area?

Has domestic violence been recognised as a human rights issue in the United Kingdom?

By acknowledging the horizontal effects of the Human Rights Act, the courts have laid the doctrinal foundations for using the Act to provide assistance to victims of domestic violence. However, has domestic violence actually been recognised by the courts as being a human rights issue?

13 Op. cit., note 3.
14 Application No. 2660/03, 30 November 2010.

In *McPherson v Secretary of State for the Home Department*[15] the appellant came to the United Kingdom from Jamaica. She was convicted of supplying a Class A controlled drug and a deportation order was signed by the Home Secretary. She claimed that deporting her to Jamaica would breach her rights under Art. 3 of the European Convention, as she feared violence on the part of her former partner.

It was held by the Court of Appeal that the appellant's claims should be remitted to another adjudicator, due to a procedural matter. However it was commented that:

> If the appellant were able to show to the requisite standard of proof that the remedies provided under the law of Jamaica against domestic violence are unlikely to be an effective deterrent . . . she would have shown that her removal from the United Kingdom to Jamaica would violate her rights under Art 3 of the European Convention on Human Rights.[16]

The judgment of the European Court in *Osman v United Kingdom*[17] was cited, in which the Court stated that 'the State's obligation . . . extends beyond its primary duty to secure the right to life by putting in place effective criminal law provisions to deter the commission of offences against the person'. The Court of Appeal stated that the requirement that the provisions of the law safeguarding the right to life must be 'effective' applied equally to the right to be free from torture and inhuman and degrading treatment under Art. 3, as both Arts 2 and 3 are non-derogable rights and that 'to be "effective", measures for the purpose of Art. 3 must be those which attain an adequate degree of efficacy in practice as well as exist in theory'.[18]

The *McPherson* case clearly illustrates the fact that the UK courts have recognised domestic violence as being a human rights issue. At first glance, it would appear that *McPherson* displays a willingness to use the Human Rights Act in an effective manner, and this case does accord some hope in relation to how the courts might apply the Act in a case of domestic violence, in that it is acknowledged that domestic violence constitutes a violation of Art. 3 of the European Convention. It is also stated that, not only must states take measures to prevent violations of Art. 3, these measures must have 'an adequate degree of efficacy in practice'. It could therefore be argued, for example, that not only must it be possible for a victim to have her abuser prosecuted, it must also be ensured that police, prosecutors and judges act in such a manner as to make the system effective and efficient.

15 [2001] EWCA Civ 1955.
16 At para 38.
17 [1999] 1 FLR 193 at 222.
18 Ibid., para 38.

The deference shown by judges in questions surrounding the allocation of resources

However, a number of problems remain. It has been commented that it is social support measures that constitute the primary need of victims of domestic violence[19] and it seems that the judiciary displays a deferential attitude in relation to questions surrounding the allocation of resources. The argument is put forward that judges do not have the expertise to assess sufficiently the issues involved in such cases. In *R (on the application of Douglas) v North Tyneside Metropolitan Borough Council and another*[20] it was stated that:

> It is not for the courts to interfere with the Secretary of State's funding arrangements provided they are lawfully made and applied . . . The courts have to be careful when considering an issue of justification . . . not to trespass into the discretionary area of resource allocation. That is an area that is not justiciable.[21]

Oxfordshire County Council v R (on the application of Khan) and another[22] involved an applicant who was a national of Pakistan. She was granted leave to enter the UK to join her husband, but she then suffered severe domestic violence. The police intervened and she took a place in a refuge. The Oxfordshire County Council undertook an assessment of her needs, and it was decided that Mrs Khan needed safe and secure accommodation, legal advice and finances. However, the Council stated that she did not meet the criteria for such social support, as she was not suffering from a physical disability, learning disability or mental health condition.

Arguments were made under Arts 3 and 8 of the European Convention and it was considered whether s 3 of the Human Rights Act required the relevant legislation to be interpreted in such a way as to avoid violations of the Convention rights. The Court of Appeal emphasised 'the extremely limited scope for the operation of Articles 3 and 8 in this area.'[23] It was stated that:

> while Strasbourg has recognised the possibility that Art 8 may oblige a State to provide positive welfare support in special circumstances, it has made it plain that neither Art 3 nor Art 8 imposes such a requirement as a matter of course.[24]

---

19 For example, E.M. Schneider, *Battered Women and Feminist Lawmaking*, New Haven: Yale University Press, 2000, p. 52.
20 [2004] 1 All ER 709.
21 Ibid., para 62.
22 [2004] EWCA Civ 309.
23 Ibid., para 52.
24 Ibid., para 52.

It was decided that s 3 of the Human Rights Act did not require the relevant legislation to be interpreted in any special manner.

This case indicates that the UK courts may be reluctant to hold that the state has a duty under the Convention rights to provide accommodation, financial resources or child care facilities to victims of domestic violence. The Court of Appeal in *Khan* appeared to be strongly opposed to the view that the state may be under an obligation to provide such social support measures.

In *Re Limbuela*[25] the House of Lords held that the state had a duty to provide accommodation and support to asylum seekers in a state of destitution, if their circumstances fell within the category of inhuman or degrading treatment under Art. 3 of the European Convention on Human Rights. This case does give some hope that the Supreme Court could potentially hold that the state has a duty to provide support to victims of domestic violence. Nevertheless, it must be remembered that the respondents in this case were each suffering or facing 'a life of extreme deprivation, sleeping rough on the streets of London, not permitted to work and denied all support'.[26] The House of Lords was making its decision based on these very extreme circumstances and it seems that the case does not therefore automatically indicate that the courts would be willing to place obligations on the state to provide social support measures to all victims of domestic violence.

Similar difficulties arise as regards the case law of the European Court of Human Rights on the issue of domestic violence. In these cases, the Court's attention was focused on the responses of police forces to the issue. In a small number of cases, the European Court has established that in certain circumstances the state has a duty to provide resources to individuals to prevent violations of their rights. The seminal case in this area is still the well-known case of *Airey v Ireland*.[27] In that case, the applicant alleged that her husband had subjected her to physical violence. The issue revolved around the fact that legal aid was not available in Ireland for the purpose of seeking a judicial separation. The Court held that there had been violations of Arts 6 and 8. However, although the Court did hold that ensuring effective access to particular means of protection may in certain situations entail the expenditure of monetary resources, the Court did not actually hold that civil legal aid must be granted in such situations as that which arose in the case. The Court just stated that there must be effective access to the protective measure of a decree of judicial separation. This obligation could have been fulfilled by other means, such as simplifying the procedures. It seems therefore that it cannot be

---

25 *R (on the application of Limbuela) v Secretary of State for the Home Department; R (on the application of Tesema) v Secretary of State for the Home Department; R (on the application of Adam) v Secretary of State for the Home Department* [2005] UKHL 66.

26 Ibid., para 80.

27 (1981) 3 EHRR 592.

argued on the basis of *Airey* that the state has an obligation to provide victims of domestic violence with social support measures.

In general terms, it is much more difficult for courts to order that affirmative programmes be put in place than it is for them to hold that certain practices be stopped. Nevertheless, it is not impossible for courts to make such affirmative orders. The Court does seem to be prepared to move with the times and there is a growing consensus that an important counter to domestic violence is the provision of social assistance.

The ability of law to deal with an 'unseen' crime

Violence against women taking place in the home constitutes an 'unseen' crime, which victims are often too frightened or ashamed to report. This creates a difficulty for the effectiveness of a litigation approach in relation to domestic violence. It is widely recognised that only a minority of cases of domestic violence ever come to the attention of the police. Many incidents are never reported. In an ongoing cycle of domestic abuse, it is unlikely that the police will be called to every violent incident. If they are called and prove to be unhelpful, it is improbable that the victim will contact them again. The British Crime Survey found that the police come to know of fewer than one in four of the worst cases of domestic violence.[28] Even if victims do report incidents of domestic violence, they may wish to take matters no further.

Under the Human Rights Act, the test of standing is very narrow. The person wishing to bring a case under the Act must be a victim. For human rights law to be used effectively to protect victims of domestic violence through a litigation approach, victims themselves must be willing to take cases to court. This test of standing is thus problematic when dealing with an 'unseen crime' such as domestic violence, where a high percentage of victims simply may not wish to engage in litigation. The same difficulty also arises as regards taking a case to the European Court of Human Rights.

These problems lead one to consider whether other human rights mechanisms, such as the Optional Protocol to the UN Convention on the Elimination of All Forms of Discrimination against Women (CEDAW) may hold greater potential as regards the issue of domestic violence.

The Optional Protocol to CEDAW

The CEDAW Convention does not make any explicit reference to domestic violence. However, the UN Committee on the Elimination of Discrimination against Women (CEDAW Committee) has interpreted the Convention in such a way as to cover the issue of domestic violence. The CEDAW Committee

---

28 *Domestic violence, sexual assault and stalking: Findings from the British Crime Survey*, Home Office Research Study 276, 2004, p. 97.

produced its General Recommendation 19 in 1992. This was an extremely important document as it officially interpreted CEDAW as prohibiting violence against women, in both public and private contexts. The General Recommendation stated that 'The full implementation of the Convention required States to take positive measures to eliminate all forms of violence against women.'[29] It also established that:

> The definition of discrimination includes gender-based violence, that is, violence that is directed against a woman because she is a woman or that affects women disproportionately. It includes acts that inflict physical, mental or sexual harm or suffering, threats of such acts, coercion and other deprivations of liberty. Gender-based violence may breach specific provisions of the Convention, regardless of whether those provisions expressly mention violence.[30]

The document stated that gender-based violence may breach *inter alia* the right to life; the right not to be subject to torture or to cruel, inhuman or degrading treatment or punishment; and the right to liberty and security of person.[31] It was emphasised:

> that discrimination under the Convention is not restricted to action by or on behalf of Governments . . . Under general international law and specific human rights covenants, States may be responsible for private acts if they fail to act with due diligence to prevent violations of rights or to investigate and punish acts of violence, and for providing compensation.[32]

In this way, the concept of state responsibility was used to great effect to transcend the public/private divide that has posed substantial difficulties for the effectiveness of human rights law in relation to issues such as domestic violence. The General Recommendation recognised that:

> Family violence is one of the most insidious forms of violence against women. It is prevalent in all societies. Within family relationships women of all ages are subjected to violence of all kinds, including battering, rape, other forms of sexual assault, mental and other forms of violence, which are perpetuated by traditional attitudes.[33]

29 General Recommendation No.19, Committee on the Elimination of Discrimination Against Women, UN Doc A/47/38 (1992) at para 4.
30 Ibid., para 6.
31 Ibid., para 7.
32 Ibid., para 9.
33 Ibid., para 23.

The Optional Protocol to CEDAW came into force in December 2000 and the UK acceded to the Protocol in December 2004. This Protocol allows individuals or groups to submit claims of breaches of the Convention to the CEDAW Committee. Essentially, the Protocol gives to every woman in states that have ratified it an opportunity to go to the CEDAW Committee and say that the state is failing to protect her rights under the Convention. The Preamble to the Optional Protocol states that it is a reaffirmation of states' 'determination to ensure the full and equal enjoyment by women of all human rights and fundamental freedoms and to take effective action to prevent violations of these rights and freedoms'. Article 2 of the Protocol allows individuals or groups of individuals who are victims of any breaches of CEDAW to submit complaints to the Committee. Crucially, communications may also be submitted on behalf of individuals with their consent, unless acting on their behalf without their consent may be justified. This is a much wider test of standing than that which is contained in the European Convention on Human Rights or the Human Rights Act. Under both these instruments the person bringing the case must be the actual victim; however, under the Optional Protocol a communication may be made on behalf of an individual or a group of individuals. For example, a domestic violence group could make a communication alleging that the state has failed to fulfil its positive duties under CEDAW in the area of violence against women in the home.

Under Art. 7 of the Protocol, when a communication is submitted, the Committee should bring it to the attention of the state in question. The state then has six months to submit an explanation to the Committee. Communications are considered by the Committee in closed meetings. The views of the Committee are then transmitted to the parties. The state is required to respond in writing within six months, including a description of any action it has taken on the matter.

The Optional Protocol procedure does bear similarities to a litigation process. However, in crucial respects the procedure under the Optional Protocol may hold more potential in the area of domestic violence than does a traditional litigation approach. For example, the CEDAW Committee has stated in General Recommendation 19 that states should provide social support measures for victims of domestic violence and implement public awareness campaigns, and it seems that it has no hesitation in reiterating this in dealing with communications under the Optional Protocol. Generally, traditional courts must restrict their judgments to the actual case scenario that is before them; however, in dealing with communications the Committee is free to take a broader approach.

Nevertheless, although the communications procedure allows the CEDAW Committee to make recommendations as to the measures that should be adopted to remedy a breach of the Convention, it has no means of forcing the state concerned to comply with these recommendations. Similar enforcement difficulties arise in relation to the Optional Protocol as arise concerning the main CEDAW provisions. However, the Optional Protocol procedures may provide an incentive for states to comply more fully with their obligations under CEDAW. Perhaps the most valuable aspect of the Optional Protocol is the potential it holds for increasing international pressure on states to comply with their duties.

AT v Hungary

AT v Hungary[34] was the first decision of the CEDAW Committee on the merits of a communication under the Optional Protocol. The views of the Committee were adopted in January 2005. It was stated that Hungary was in violation of CEDAW for failing to take sufficient measures to protect a victim of domestic violence. There were no protection orders or suitable shelters available to the victim and no specific legislation had been enacted to deal with domestic violence. The CEDAW Committee made recommendations concerning the author of the complaint specifically, and also more general recommendations. The Committee commented that the state should take effective and immediate measures to ensure Ms AT's safety and give her a safe home, child support and legal assistance, in addition to reparation for the violation of her rights. In general, the Committee stated that Hungary should 'assure victims of domestic violence the maximum protection of the law by acting with due diligence to prevent and respond to such violence against women'.[35] The state should also provide regular training on CEDAW to judges, law enforcement officials and lawyers. All allegations of domestic violence should be investigated in a thorough manner and victims be provided with sufficient access to justice.

Goekce v Austria

In August 2007, the CEDAW Committee examined two more communications surrounding the issue of domestic violence. *Goekce v Austria*[36] concerned a victim of domestic violence who had eventually been killed by her husband. The communication was brought by the Vienna Intervention Centre against Domestic Violence and the Association for Women's Access to Justice, on behalf of the family members of the deceased. The Committee stated that the police and the Public Prosecutor had failed to respond in an adequate manner to protect the victim, despite knowing that she was in serious danger. The victim had called the police several hours before she was killed and the Committee stated that, in the light of the long record of domestic violence, by not responding immediately the police had failed to exercise due diligence to protect the victim. The police had requested that the victim's husband be

---

34 Communication No 2/2003, views adopted 26 January 2005.
35 Ibid., para 9.6(II)(b).
36 Communication No 5/2005, views adopted 6 August 2007.

arrested after earlier incidents of domestic violence, but the Public Prosecutor had denied these requests. The Committee commented that, although it was

> necessary in each case to determine whether detention would amount to a disproportionate interference in the basic rights and fundamental freedoms of a perpetrator of domestic violence, such as the right to freedom of movement and to a fair trial, . . . the perpetrator's rights cannot supersede women's human rights to life and to physical and mental integrity.[37]

The Committee found that Austria was in violation of the victim's rights to life and to physical and mental integrity under CEDAW and recommended that the state act with due diligence to prevent and respond to violence against women and prosecute perpetrators of domestic violence in a vigilant manner. The state should 'ensure that criminal and civil remedies are utilized in cases where the perpetrator in a domestic violence situation poses a dangerous threat to the victim'.[38] It should also ensure enhanced coordination among law enforcement and judicial officers, and strengthen training programmes on domestic violence for judges, lawyers and law enforcement officials.

Yildirim v Austria

Yildirim v Austria[39] also concerned a victim of domestic violence who had eventually been killed by her husband. Again the communication was brought by the Vienna Intervention Centre against Domestic Violence and the Association for Women's Access to Justice, on behalf of the family members of the deceased. The victim had been in ongoing contact with the police and had authorised the prosecution of her husband. The CEDAW Committee stated that the Public Prosecutor's denial of the requests of the police to arrest the victim's husband and place him in detention constituted a violation of the state's due diligence obligation to protect the victim. Again the Committee emphasised that 'the perpetrator's rights cannot supersede women's human rights to life and to physical and mental integrity'.[40] The recommendations which had been made to the state in *Goekce v Austria* were then reiterated.

In its consideration of the complaints surrounding the issue of domestic violence, the Committee has clearly emphasised that not only must an adequate legal framework be in place, but that this framework must be implemented in a substantive and meaningful way by the relevant officials, such as police and prosecutors. However, it seems that there remains a general lack of awareness of the Optional Protocol and its potential. To date, only eleven

---

37 Communication No 5/2005, para. 12.1.5.
38 Ibid., para. 12.3(b).
39 Communication No 6/2005, views adopted 6 August 2007.
40 Ibid., para. 12.1.5.

communications have been considered by the Committee, three of them relating to domestic violence and the remainder relating to other issues.

Conclusion

In conclusion, therefore, domestic violence has been recognised as being a human rights issue by the UK courts. However, there are a number of difficulties involved in using the Human Rights Act in relation to this issue. It appears that the judiciary adopts a deferential approach in questions regarding the allocation of resources. This is a major drawback in relation to the use of the Human Rights Act in relation to domestic violence as it has been argued that the most pressing needs of victims of domestic violence are for adequate measures of social support. In addition, the effectiveness of a litigation approach depends largely on the willingness of victims to bring cases before the courts. This is problematic as regards the issue of domestic violence, which is largely an 'unseen' crime.

These difficulties appear to be surmounted by the Optional Protocol mechanism. However, the enforcement difficulties which surround this procedure may prove problematic. Although the CEDAW Committee may make recommendations as to the measures that should be adopted to remedy a breach of the Convention, it has no means of forcing the state concerned to comply with these recommendations. Similar enforcement difficulties arise in relation to the Optional Protocol as arise concerning the main CEDAW provisions.

Nevertheless, there are signs of hope. The European Court of Human Rights has now clearly stated that domestic violence constitutes a human rights violation under the European Convention. The domestic courts are under a duty to take account of the Strasbourg jurisprudence and it is not inconceivable that this may, however subtly, alter the attitudes of national courts in this area.

11 Feminism, women, rape and social change

Catherine Little and Kate Cook

Introduction

Many survivors of rape in England and Wales who report their rape to the police feel that the criminal justice system has failed them and that their needs are not adequately met by State provision.[1] In many instances, support offered to rape survivors by Sexual Assault Referral Centres (SARCs) is good, but does not necessarily provide the level and type of support that women most want. The desire to discover what women tell us about their experiences of rape, reporting to the police, and the type of support they would like, led a feminist activist group (Campaign to End Rape) to conduct a piece of research. This chapter examines some initial findings from that research on what should be done about rape. It reports on some results within this new research into women's views on rape. These views are examined here in the contexts which led to the new study. While considering these findings the chapter also measures the human rights response against a feminist anti-rape approach. It also considers whether a human rights claim, under Art. 3 of the Convention, might aid change which could fit with women's demands.

This chapter focuses on the promise of a human rights approach, but this chapter comes from a different tradition. It argues that the human rights discourse, and by extension, the Human Rights Act 1998 (HRA), has not changed the position of women who have survived rape. Instead this chapter considers the choice of radical feminist activism as the most useful avenue for change for these women and argues that this is because that approach is rooted in the concept of women's consciousness. We outline the roots of this anti-rape feminist activist position and compare these to a liberal legal, or human rights-based approach. The chapter argues that a feminist activist interrogation could produce a very different set of responses to rape, given that it would place women's experience at the centre. The traditional discourses on rape and the criminal justice process are seen as treating women's experiences of rape as

---

1 L. Kelly, *A Gap or a Chasm? Attrition in Reported Rape Cases*, London: Home Office, 2005.

an object to be resolved, but not one to be opened up and examined. However, we note that there has been a glimmer of support for the dignity of rape survivors, in a recent suit, using the right to freedom from inhuman or degrading treatment. The possibilities of expanding on this avenue are therefore examined.

The chapter reflects on what we know about rape and how this has changed since feminists such as Brownmiller,[2] Russell[3] and Griffin[4] began writing about rape in the early 1970s. At that time, the dominant understanding of rape was that it was an aberration, a rare event. Since then great progress has been made, within feminist activism, in listening to survivor testimony about the reality of rape. Yet, within the mainstream it is apparent that attitudes and institutions remain resistant to change. The chapter examines these trends and draws on the authors' experience of being members of the Campaign to End Rape (CER) involved in lobbying for social and legal reform. It reviews some recent government initiatives on rape and considers how these might be constrained by the legal/social model of human rights. However, it also draws on knowledge from the recent CER survey on women's views on rape, to consider future calls for change.

The chapter outlines the method of this study and considers where this activist-based call for change might lead to different ideas for the future. The initial findings of the study argue for women-only provision; properly funded support; flexible reporting possibilities; and more information/education across the board. These are presented here and mapped against the possibilities for an improvement in women's experiences as rape survivors.

Comparing approaches

This discussion considers the problems which the human rights discourse presents for rape survivors. However, it is perhaps worth starting with a brief outline of the radical feminist approach to rape. This perspective draws its knowledge from women's and girls' testimony. It considers the term 'rape' to encompass all the violations which these women and girls name as rape. This produces a broad and flexible definition, which considers rape, sexual abuse, sexual assault, pornographic rapes and rape in the lives of sex workers and asylum seekers. All of these are part of the term 'rape' no matter what age, race, ability, sexuality or class the women or girls are.

By contrast, of course, traditional legal approaches, including the human rights perspectives, define rape using legal definitions, which tend to be inflexible and are drawn much more closely. Within these traditional theoretical

---

2 S. Brownmiller, *Against our Will: Men, women and rape*, Harmondsworth: Penguin, 1977.
3 D. Russell, *The Politics of Rape: The Victim's Perspective*, New York: Stein & Day, 1975.
4 S. Griffin, *Rape: The Power of Consciousness*, New York: Harper and Row, 1979.

approaches, ideas from great thinkers (very often men) are utilised by others to create an agenda for change. This is clearly so within the liberal tradition, drawing on ideas which can be traced back to Hobbes, Locke and John Stuart Mill to measure the levels of freedom experienced by individuals. The human rights formulation, whilst appearing to have a fresher face than traditional liberalism, draws on the same roots.[5] This comes with a number of difficulties from a feminist anti-rape standpoint.

Firstly, that same tradition has created the problems which women experience today, with regard to rape. Patriarchal liberal theory does nothing to disturb these trends. These can be briefly summarised as: rape is very common; rape complaints tend to be treated with scepticism; and rape has horrific effects on women's sense of self. A need to break with this tradition (the radicalism of radical feminism) was therefore established within the beginnings of the women's liberation movement in the US.[6]

Secondly, the framework of liberalism or human rights tends to focus on the rights of the individual as pitted against those of the State. The right to liberty and security of person (Art. 5) or to respect for private life (Art. 8) both illustrate this understandable tradition, which remains problematic for women claiming rape. The women are often understood as having interests coinciding with those of the State, as the criminal law (in the common law tradition) is a function of public law. The State prosecutes criminal wrongs on behalf of the public, against the individual wrongdoer. This effectively puts the complainant women into the 'other' category, from a liberal standpoint.

In reality, feminism has been able to show that women's position is markedly different to that of the State, and this third status (not defendant, not prosecutrix, but witness) can be seen as emblematic of the problems women who are raped face, in law. Consider, for example, the claim of accused rapist 'A', that the attempt to limit his right to ask questions about the female witness's sexual history[7] contravened his right to a fair trial, under s 3 of the HRA.[8] Here a liberal attempt to limit sexual history questioning was attacked, using the HRA, since the right of the witness to protection from insidious questions was seen as coinciding with the State's attempt to prosecute. For survivors of abuse, the reality of human rights legal interventions tends to be that their interests are conflated with those of the State. In other cases, aggrieved parents have claimed an infringement of the right to privacy, when the State has attempted to investigate claims of child abuse. The rights of the (possibly abused) children are wrongly conflated with the interventions of a State power,

---

5 A. McColgan, *Women under the Law: The false promise of human rights*, Harlow: Pearson, 2000.

6 Brownmiller, op. cit., note 2.

7 Under the Youth Justice and Criminal Evidence Act 1999, s 41.

8 *R v A (No 2)* [2002] 1 AC 45.

which is claimed to be inappropriate.[9] Even if the children in the case were, in fact, safe, the cumulative effect of actions of this kind is to subsume the position of survivors of abuse with that of a rights-abusing State power.

Thirdly, in considering the rights of women survivors of abuse, it is also fair to say that women who are raped are also often badly let down by the State. The State has positive obligations, including a duty to investigate cases, and where it fails to do so adequately it may be deemed to have breached a person's human rights. This is illustrated by the first case of its type, where a woman who was raped was paid £3,500 by Cambridgeshire Police in an out of court settlement.[10] Catherine was raped twice by a man whom she had allowed into her home. She later reported this but the police entirely failed to investigate as they did not record her allegation as a crime. The basis of her claim was that under Art. 3 of the Convention, in which no one should be subject to inhumane and degrading treatment, the State has a duty to investigate a case. There was a fundamental failure on the part of Cambridgeshire Police to do this and although no liability was admitted, they paid her the out of court settlement. This may well pave the way for further challenges and so this chapter returns to consider this possibility, in due course.

The law and social responses to rape purport to offer a framework for women to access, using support services, medical interventions and the Criminal Justice System, to provide redress and response. Each of these interventions remains modelled upon a liberal, rational, male response to rape, which is based in a liberal or rights-based discourse where women and women's experience are not central. To begin to explore what difference it makes to use a different approach, feminist activism starts in another place altogether. The notion of the idea filtered down from a great thinker, which is so strong in many strands of theory (Marxism being another clear example), is rejected by radical feminism, which works from the bottom up.

Feminism and knowledge about rape

Feminist knowledge on rape comes from a process called 'consciousness-raising' which Catharine MacKinnon has described as the 'method' of feminism.[11] The process of consciousness-raising occurs when women uncover their experiences of being women and, through that process, experience a change in their sense of self. This process also brings recognition of the

---

9 For example: *Dolhamre v Sweden* (67/04) European Court of Human Rights, 8 June 2010, where the State's intervention was upheld.

10 Reported in *The Daily Mail*, 'Police pay £3,500 to "rape" victim after officers forgot to investigate her allegations", 1 December 2009, available at: <http://www.dailymail. co.uk/news/article-1232270/Rape-complainant-wins-landmark-settlement-police-neglect-investigate-case.html> (accessed 26 January 2011).

11 C.A. MacKinnon, *Toward a Feminist Theory of The State*, London: Harvard University Press, 1989.

commonality of their experiences as women, under patriarchy. Their awareness of themselves as women within a patriarchy is thus changed. When women come together and take part in this process the effects have been very rewarding both for the individuals concerned and for feminism. The power of this process can be seen in comments women have posted on Facebook recently, in response to the CER study that we discuss later:

> This is the first time I've been asked to narrate the experience . . . THANK YOU for the opportunity.
>
> Thank you for this opportunity to be heard even though I found it difficult to really express my feelings because they are confused, contradictory and often painful. May you be successful in the campaign.
>
> Please give me a copy of my results . . . this cause is so fantastic . . . END RAPE TODAY![12]

Research into rape can create space for individual women to grow, by giving them a voice through which they can contribute to change. The radical version of feminism aims to take the knowledge produced by consciousness-raising and distil it into theory, which will in turn inform action.

Early on in the Women's Movement, in 1960s America, consciousness-raising was often undertaken in 'rape' groups but sometimes the public process of the 'speak-out' was used:

> The first rape speak-out was held in January 1971 with free entry for women and an entrance fee for men (who could only attend if accompanied). Over 300 women attended and at least 30 testified to their different and compelling experiences of forced sex. To a generation raised on *Oprah* and the many other versions of the televised 'speak-out', it is hard to imagine the power and significance of this meeting. Here was the truth of the slogan 'the personal is political'. Women's stories (of their own violations) came together to create a powerful force for change. The day produced knowledge and impetus which (Susan) Brownmiller says left the participants reeling. A future conference on rape was quickly in the pipeline. Brownmiller herself went on to produce *Against Our Will: Men, Women and Rape* (1976), still the starting point for feminist consideration of rape, some 30 years after its production.[13]

So, from this beginning, rape research began and studies by Diana Russell[14] and others demonstrated that rape was commonplace; writing and theorising

---

12 Comments posted in 2009, no longer available online.
13 H.D. Jones and K. Cook, *Rape Crisis: Responding to Sexual Violence*, Lyme Regis: Russell House Publishing, 2008, p. 4.
14 Russell, op. cit., note 3.

around rape myths also followed on with Susan Brownmiller[15] and Susan Griffin[16] putting together significant early works. In addition, the rape crisis movement was also founded, in Washington DC around 1972.[17] The first centre started small and operated from a shared house, where one of the women in the group lived.[18]

All of this took place in the US, but the ideas and the models soon transferred to the UK. Rape crisis centres opened here[19] and some research began to take place; theorists such as Liz Kelly[20] and Elizabeth Wilson[21] started to look at questions of rape and sexual abuse from a British feminist perspective. The processes of listening to women, creating theory and building an agenda for activism are, therefore, inextricably linked, within this strand of feminism.

In addition to the developments in feminist activism, feminist theory was also developing to provide us with the concepts to explain violence against women in the context of patriarchy. Some of the issues relating to violence against women are treated as separate issues, e.g. domestic violence, child sexual abuse, rape and sexual assault, as if they are not connected. Liz Kelly's concept of the 'continuum of violence' allows us to look at many of these issues, and more, as part of male power and control. The continuum includes pornography, prostitution, sexual harassment and even sexual murder and covers a range of behaviour that shares the same basic common characteristics that instil fear in women and keep them in an oppressed state.[22]

The Campaign to End Rape is a radical feminist campaign which emerged from the rape crisis movement and from knowledge of women's problems with responses to rape. It was founded in 1996, following a workshop at a women's conference in Brighton.[23] The campaign was invited to contribute to the Sexual Offences Review, which preceded the Sexual Offences Act 2003, so it was quickly given a chair at the table in terms of discussing responses. It continues to be involved in lobbying and discussion with government and various departments about responses to rape. The small group of academics and activists who currently make up the campaign's core group decided to embark on a fresh piece of research into women's views on rape and began drafting a questionnaire during 2009.

As this illustrates, the radical approach has succeeded in putting rape onto the public agenda and has provoked successive reforms of the law on rape, in

15 Brownmiller, op. cit., note 2.
16 Griffin, op. cit., note 4.
17 Jones and Cook, op. cit., note 13.
18 Ibid.
19 Ibid.
20 L. Kelly, *Surviving Sexual Violence*, Cambridge: Polity, 1988.
21 E. Wilson, *What is to be Done About Violence Against Women*, London: Penguin, 1983.
22 Kelly, op. cit., note 20.
23 K. Cook, 'Raging against Rape', *Trouble and Strife* 35, 1997, pp. 23–9.

the UK and elsewhere. However, much of the testimony used has become a little older and there has always been a lack of large-scale UK rape studies. These issues led CER to decide to undertake this new piece of work. The new CER study continues in this consciousness-raising tradition, asking women about their experiences and views. Before examining that study further, the next discussion puts that research into perspective, by examining some previous British studies and by looking at recent policy developments.

Developments in research, legislation and policy

This entire strand of research owes its existence to the radical feminist method just discussed. Earlier research into rape, which can be seen as stemming from a traditional liberal concern for victims, merely posed questions about victim culpability or precipitation[24] using official records to examine the rape event. The idea of asking women themselves was a radical departure.

The largest pieces of research into women's experiences of rape conducted in this country have been the *Ask Any Woman* survey, from 1986[25] with 1,236 responses and Kate Painter's 1991 study[26] which surveyed 1,007 women. In addition, *An Exploratory Study of Sexual Abuse in a Sample of 16 to 21-year-olds* asked 1,244 young people about their experiences of unwanted sex.[27]

The oldest of these studies, *Ask Any Woman* used a questionnaire to ask women whether they had experienced rape, and for their views on rape. The questionnaire was called the *Women's Safety Survey* and the research was conducted by *Women Against Rape*, an activist group.[28] It began by asking questions about women's fears, showing, for example, that women were most afraid when at home alone.[29] The survey moved on to ask questions about incidence of rape, showing that 17 per cent had experienced rape and 20 per cent had experienced attempted rape.[30] This gave an early estimate of the prevalence of rape; later research has only tended to show that rape is even more common than this.[31] Towards the end, the survey asked some questions based on opinion, such as question 62, which asked: 'Do you think it is rape if a woman is forced to have sex with her husband against her will?' Although rape in marriage was not a crime in 1985, 83 per cent of respondents thought

24 M. Amir, *Patterns of Forcible Rape*, Chicago: University of Chicago Press, 1971.
25 R.E. Hall, *Ask Any Woman: A London Inquiry into Rape and Sexual Assault*, Bristol: Falling Wall Press, 1985.
26 K. Painter, *Wife Rape, Marriage and Law: Survey Report, Key Findings and Recommendations*, Manchester: Manchester University, 1991.
27 L. Kelly et al., *An Exploratory Study of the Prevalence of Sexual Abuse in a Sample of 16–21 year olds*, London: University of North London, 1991.
28 R.E. Hall, op. cit., note 25.
29 Ibid. 81 per cent of respondents to question 1 were sometimes frightened.
30 Ibid.
31 Painter, op. cit., note 26; Kelly et al., op. cit., note 27.

it should be a crime. Since then the law has moved on considerably and women's views have too, but we do not have recent research on women's opinions, except where it is related to government agendas. CER decided to aim to change this, by embarking on a new survey of women's views.

The new CER survey is also a questionnaire, which asks about experiences of rape, but also about women's views. Our survey was distributed via the internet, using the *Survey Monkey* web tools and with email, web and e-newsletter bulletins raising awareness and asking women to complete the survey.

As a result a large number of women did complete the questionnaire, in a very short period of time. Over 1,200 women completed the survey and most of this data is still being analysed. The precise figures from these previous pieces of research are quoted here, simply because the new survey is already rivalling these, in scale, after being available for completion for only a few weeks. Clearly then, the internet is an extremely useful tool in data collection. Arguably, however, the passage of time may also mean that feminist ideas about rape are more imbued into female populations and so women are more able to speak of rape.[32]

The information produced in the 1970s, 80s and 90s really began to have some impact with the government in the past 12 years or so. This has included legislation on procedure[33] and on the substance of the law[34] as well as numerous reviews of procedure and practice.[35] We have also seen some use of feminist research methods, within evaluation reports published by government.[36] The *Gap or Chasm* research is one of the most definitive studies on attrition to date and was conducted on behalf of the Home Office by researchers at the Child and Woman Abuse Studies Unit.[37] This was a large-scale piece of research which adopted methods, and asked questions, that were sympathetic to women's experiences. Women who completed the telephone survey were also invited to face-to-face interviews conducted in various locations (sexual assault referral centres, women's own homes or premises of counselling services).[38] One of the main areas of focus was on what victims of rape/sexual assault need

32 More recently there has also been some data distilled from a far larger sample, that of the British Crime Survey. This, clearly useful information, is nevertheless quite different from a dedicated study on rape. A. Myhill and J. Allen, *Rape and Sexual Assault of Women: findings from the British Crime Survey*, London: Home Office, 2002.

33 Youth Justice and Criminal Evidence Act 1999.

34 Sexual Offences Act 2003.

35 For example, HMIC & HMCPSI report, *Without Consent*; Feist et al., *Investigating and Detecting Recorded Offences of Rape*, London: Home Office, 2007.

36 Kelly, op. cit., note 1 and L. Kelly et al, *Section 41: an evaluation of new legislation limiting sexual history evidence in rape trials*, London: Home Office, 2006.

37 Kelly, op. cit., note 1.

38 Ibid.

and how their experiences compared with this.[39] The researchers also asked women how the process could be improved.

This research has marked a process of integration and/or assimilation, whereby feminist researchers have tried to take feminist method into the 'malestream' of liberal social and legal responses, in order to make a difference. The process has been one which workers in the field tend to find personally draining and exhausting, since their ideas are endlessly misunderstood by a framework that does not acknowledge the inherent value of women's views.

It becomes clearer over time that some more radical departure would need to be achieved to create real change. A way to incorporate women's experience of rape within the human rights-based language of the modern law is required as it does not currently differentiate women's needs from those of the State.

What we notice, though, is a closing down of the agenda. So, whilst a feminist consciousness-raising exercise might ask women 'What should we do about rape?' a government-funded piece of research is more prone to ask 'How did you feel about the police response?' Further context, below, shows how those police responses and other public initiatives have been framed in recent years.

Recent government initiatives

Successive governments tend to focus on rape as an equality issue based on liberal principles of fairness and justice. This is represented by the focus on how rape complaints are handled in the criminal justice system (CJS); a focus on performance of police service in terms of service delivery and the need to develop a consistent approach. Obviously, these are important issues, as implementation of law is necessary for justice to be delivered, but these types of reviews tend to focus on what needs to be done with little reference to women's experiences. Sandra Walklate sums up this position:

> . . . modernist principles reflect principles of justice that assume a majoritarian worldview. In other words, justice is not only in all our interests, but it is something that we can all agree upon, but with one key caveat: the legal subject, the rational man of law, must remain intact. This is the story of the last 25 years in responding to violence against women.[40]

The women who experience this violence are failed, or they may achieve the legal version of justice, but this may not be experienced as justice, while the women are not at the centre of the endeavour. There is often little

39 Kelly, op. cit., note 1.
40 S. Walklate, 'What is to be Done About Violence Against Women', *British Journal of Criminology* 48(1), January 2008, p. 51.

opportunity for women's voices and experiences to be heard and incorporated into law and policy changes. This makes the CER survey distinct from the government agenda as the key focus of our survey is to provide an opportunity for women to tell about their experiences and views of what they think women want/need. Consequently, this provides an opportunity for a more 'transformative' agenda. To illustrate this point it is useful to focus on some recent government initiatives.

The Stern Review

The latest investigation into rape instigated by government was the review led by Baroness Vivien Stern, a cross-bench peer, which reported during 2010. The remit of this review was to:

> look at how public authorities, including the police, local authorities, health providers and the Crown Prosecution Service respond to rape complaints and interact with each other.[41]

Its terms of reference were:

> To examine the response of the public authorities to rape complaints and examine how more victims can be encouraged to report;
> To explore ways in which the attrition rate in criminal cases can be reduced and, how to fairly increase the conviction rate;
> To identify how to increase victim and witness satisfaction, and confidence in the CJS in addressing rape;
> To explore public and professional attitudes to rape and how they impact on outcomes;
> To utilise findings and information available from other relevant work, particularly the work on victims' experience being led by Sara Payne and the Department of Health Taskforce led by Professor Sir George Alberti, avoiding unnecessary duplication;
> And to make recommendations, with particular reference to improving the implementation of current policies and procedures.[42]

By definition, then, this was a non-radical intervention. It aimed to work within the system and to look for changes to improve implementation. It involved asking survivors for their views, within the existing framework. It did not ask survivors for their ideas for a new approach.

---

41 Baroness V. Stern, *The Stern Review: An Independent Review of How Rape Cases are Handled by Public Authorities in England and Wales*, London: Home Office, 2010, p. 6.
42 Ibid.

Almost inevitably, the foremost conclusion of this review was that the 'policies are right'.[43] Recommendations were made which could prove helpful to survivors, if implemented. However, they are clearly rooted within the status quo:

> A national communications strategy to challenge attitudes towards violence against women, including rape and other forms of sexual violence;
>
> The inclusion of gender equality and violence against women in the school curriculum for Personal, Social, Health and Economic (PSHE) lessons;
>
> A further £3.2 million of funding to help establish more Sexual Assault Referral Centres (SARCs).[44]

Interestingly, the investment in (professional, mainstream) SARCs has already been abandoned, by the Coalition Government, in favour of funding for (independent, feminist) rape crisis centres.[45] The 'Victims' Champion', Sara Payne, was also asked to collate a review, from the perspective of victims, which then fed into the Stern Review. This report, *Rape: The Victim Experience Review*,[46] aimed to:

> understand from the victim's point of view . . . how the system was measuring up and how it was letting them down. This was an opportunity to understand what could be improved at the point at which various agencies interacted with the victim, rather than trying, from an organisational standpoint, to understand what a victim might want and then consider how it could be delivered.[47]

This quotation illustrates how Payne's report, although useful, contrasts with the CER survey which focuses precisely on what women want.

Two key themes emerged from the Payne review of women's experiences of rape which accord with findings from the CER study. These are: a lack of belief; and inconsistent treatment by the CJS agencies. Additionally, Payne's review outlined victims' needs in rape cases as: to be believed; to be treated with dignity; to be reassured that it was not their fault; to feel safe and comforted; to not to feel like a 'victim'; services that support them and their family; to feel in control; and to be able to make informed choices. Again, this is further backed up by general findings from the CER survey.

43 Stern, op. cit., note 41.
44 Ibid.
45 Ministry of Justice, press release, available at: <www.justice.gov.uk/news/newsrelease 280111a.htm> (accessed 8 March 2011).
46 Home Office, 'Review of rape victims' experiences welcomed', available at: <http://www. homeoffice.gov.uk/about-us/news/review-rape-victims-experiences> (accessed 8 March 2011).
47 S. Payne, *Rape: The Victim Experience Review*, London: Home Office, 2009, p. 6.

Unlike our own research, the position that emerged from the Stern Review and Sarah Payne's work is to focus on how to improve what is already in place rather than change it or replace it with something else.[48]

Clearly this position is different from our own agenda, which is to challenge existing practice and improve the experiences of women by asking them to identify their needs and suggest ways of improving services to women survivors of rape. Our view is that women should not have to use human rights provisions to seek compensation for the failure of the police to investigate but that the State could quite easily serve women well if only it started from a position of belief. Seeking redress through human rights provision is costly, time-consuming and does not necessarily deliver what women tell us they need; that is, support rather than compensation.

CER study

This project came into being because the group of researchers, who are all members of the campaigning group CER, considered that feminist ideas on rape have been co-opted into a governmental agenda and so perceived a need to take those ideas back. The idea behind this research has been outlined above and so the remaining discussion here simply outlines what CER undertook and how the study has progressed and provides a little insight into the different agenda which women produce, when asked for themselves about rape and the law.

This activist approach is capable of asking women larger questions, such as 'What might be done about rape' rather than focusing on the small-scale 'How did the police treat you?' questions of review studies. As a result, this piece of research goes back to the beginning in questioning the framework of social responses, rather than in simply examining their implementation.

The survey was completed using a fairly lengthy questionnaire (maximum 80 questions, depending upon a woman's personal experiences), and this was piloted in early 2009 via colleagues at Manchester Metropolitan University and women at Manchester Rape Crisis. The style and content were dictated by CER interests in allowing women to respond to the questions as fully as they wished, and in exploring the current legal framework. However, the questionnaire included questions which sought women's wider ideas, and it is results from one of these questions which are discussed further below.

The survey was delivered via the internet and was launched online on 24 October 2009, with a measure taken at 20 November 2009 to allow CER to submit something to the Stern Review. The study was then reopened to allow more women to take part and was finally closed at the end of 2009.

---

48 This is despite the fact that more recently there seems to be some commitment to listening to victims' views and experiences, which is also illustrated by the *Together We Can End Violence Against Women and Girls Strategy*, released at the end November 2009.

Analysis of the full sample of answers is now under way and this will be reported further in the future.

The survey asked women for their views and could be understood as a form of opinion survey. However, it also asked women to indicate which experiences they were basing their answers on. It opened with the question:

> First of all, please help us to understand what experiences you are telling us about:
>
> Are you telling us about what you did when you were raped or what you think you would do if you were?

The data therefore contains subsets of information from survivors and from women who have not identified as survivors. For the purposes of the remaining discussion, however, the whole of the sample is relevant.

What should be done about rape?

Finally then, this chapter examines one of the open questions within the survey, to see what the first 600 respondents had to say. The analysis here is partial; it was undertaken quickly, in an attempt to contribute something radical to the Stern Review. The inclusion of the discussion here is to give an indication of the different sorts of responses to rape which women are now capable of looking for. Question 80 asked:

> What do you think should be done to make the reporting process better for women who report rape?

Below is a section from just one of the responses:

> There should be immediate support available to the woman at the time of reporting. This may help the woman to understand better the situation she has come to be in due to no fault of her own, and to understand the role of the police and investigating officers. Investigating officers should also continually be made aware that women should not be interrogated while they are trying to collect evidence of the crime reported. They should be clear with the women what the reasons are for every step they take during this process. Campaigns and other forms of communication about the issues that surround sexual violence should continue, and individuals within various and relevant agencies should be held accountable . . .

This partial response is included here to give a feel of the lists of ideas that women came up with. Of course, some responses were simply 'I don't know' and many were shorter than this example. However, a good proportion of the women completing this question clearly had a lot of ideas about what might be done to improve the system.

This discussion reports on the ideas which were repeated most frequently, to give an idea of the strength of women's views and the clear gap that remains between what does happen when women report rape, and what women want. However, it is worth commenting that some very strong ideas were given in just one woman's response and so CER will spend some more time working through these responses to ensure that they are distilled to summarise everything that women have thought of. It would be easy to assume that the most important ideas are those that are repeated often, yet feminist method insists that all women's experience should be examined and this can mean that one woman's idea may help everyone. For example, one woman suggests customer satisfaction surveys for all women who make rape complaints. These, she says could be linked to information to allow a women to make a complaint, if that is necessary. This has provoked us to have a look at the information available for women who report since the suggestion does not seem too radical a departure from modern-day practice. However, it does not appear to apply as routine to systems responding to rape.[49]

We summarise below the most common responses, grouped under the headings of 'education', 'support' and 'other issues', but starting with the reporting process itself. In terms of reporting rape to the authorities women asked for a number of things which are summarised in Figure 11.1.

In total, 23 women wanted to be able to make a confidential report, clearly having concerns about being identifiable though the process. Seventy-seven talked about aspects of flexibility in reporting: variety of media for reporting

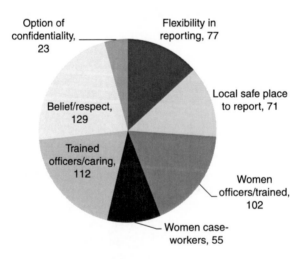

Figure 11.1 Reporting process.

49 It is however possible to provide feedback to the CPS: <http://www.cps.gov.uk/contact/feedback_and_complaints> (accessed 11 November 2011).

through (email, letter, helpline) but also a helpline, dedicated, 24-hour and allowing for discussion of what to do, who to talk to, without having to make a formal report. Women also specifically raised the possibility of making an informal complaint; 71 wanted a local safe place to report: this is a local welcoming place with childcare, which is not a police station. This place might well be staffed by women, since 102 suggested that women victims want to talk to trained women officers. A further 55 talked about the importance of a dedicated woman case-worker, throughout the Criminal Justice process, while 112 talked more generally about the importance of sympathetic and caring, trained officers.

Finally, and this was the largest group of responses to question 80, 129 simply want belief and respect from the police and CJS regardless of what women are wearing, or what they have had to drink (echoing findings by Sara Payne).

Clearly then this group of responses suggests a major shift from the current approach to reporting rape, which is to be taken to a police station and/or sexual assault referral centre. These places are not often local to women's homes; they are not the child-friendly centres which women feel might be suitable for such a purpose.

Another group of responses from women centred on issues about information and education, as shown in Figure 11.2. Women wanted the public in general to have better knowledge about the reporting processes, including an advertising campaign telling women that they will be believed. This was to assist those reporting, but also the people around them, so needed to be directed very broadly. Still on the general population, women also called for public education on the reality of rape and on gender stereotypes. This education should challenge the idea that sex is a man's right and the idea that women are liars.

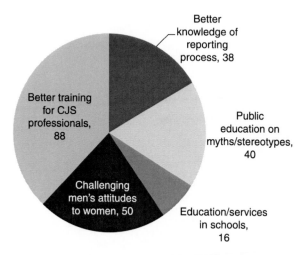

Figure 11.2 Education.

Women also wanted this education to start young, with education in schools and someone in every school for children to talk to. Again, this is related to one of the conclusions discussed earlier. However, the women's view here is that there needs to be a safe person in every school, so this is joined-up thinking, recognising that children need to learn about rape, but knowing that some of the same children will already have their own personal knowledge. Finally, 88 women wanted better training for all within the CJS who may come into contact with victims.

Another tranche of responses, shown in Figure 11.3, centred on support. Women asked for Independent Sexual Violence Advocates (ISVA) to be truly independent and to have them or another support worker at interview when women go to the police. This reveals a high level of understanding of the existing systems, where the ISVA role is funded from government and so might not be truly an independent advocate. No work has yet been done to analyse the sample of women who completed the questionnaire, but the methods of distribution used mean that those already involved within rape crisis and similar groups will be represented. This response draws our attention to that level of expertise.

Similarly, the women called for more and better funded rape crisis centres and more generally for more specialist support (again echoing the Stern Review conclusions). Women also asked for more Sexual Assault Referral Centres but added in some cases that SARCs need to be more welcoming and have better trained staff. Finally, 17 women pointed out that police could have better links with support services so that women can be offered immediate support.

The final chart shown in Figure 11.4 highlights a group of other responses which attracted nine or more responses. These concern improvements in the conviction rate, but again include a call for a woman-centred criminal justice system.

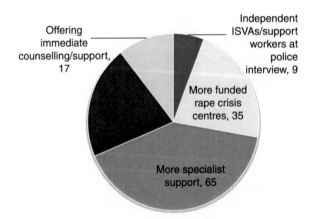

Figure 11.3 Support.

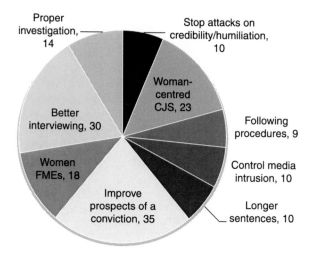

Figure 11.4 Other issues.

Conclusions

As this chapter has illustrated, the CER survey contains a great deal of data which has yet to be analysed. However, these preliminary results, in relation to just a partial sample of responses to one question, provide a new insight into women's views on rape. Women are now able to articulate a wish for women-only professionals and services and for safe, non-stigmatising places in which to receive information and decide whether to report. These results are beyond the range of anything yet achieved by the human rights discourse. That traditional, liberal approach has not been able to create radical insights such as this, nor arguably deliver what women want.

The figures within the CER survey so far remind us that the rapes that are reported are not representative of the whole story and so we need to pay attention to this when working to improve conviction rates. Women who report rape are more likely to be young, to have been raped by someone they did not know and to have experienced an isolated rape. Older women who are raped in marriage or in relationships, perhaps many times over, are less well served by the liberal establishment. It is important therefore, that the whole of women's testimony is incorporated into plans for change.

These groups of women, excluded from 'malestream' support, are often better served by rape crisis centres and other independent women's groups. It may be, then, that the current Coalition Government will, admittedly surprisingly, serve women better because the idea of the 'Big Society' is based upon 'grass roots' activity, the model of the rape crisis movement.

Properly independent support can achieve a feminist model, which allows for the whole of women's stories of rape to be listened to, with respect and belief.

Catherine's recent victory in a case where her word had been wholly disrespected[50] does, however, give a glimmer of hope for the intractable cases where it has proven very difficult to ensure that the authorities pay attention. If other women can use Human Rights provisions to ensure that investigation takes place, then the lessons which the CER survey and other sources of testimony are producing can help us to use the Human Rights Act in new and more radical ways.

50 See n. 10 above.

Section 2

Confronting the Human Rights Act from the activist perspective

12 Testimony, tolerance and hospitality

The limitations of the Human Rights Act in relation to asylum seekers

Suryia Nayak[1], Revive and The Salford Forum for Refugees and People Seeking Asylum United for Change Campaign Group[2]

Introduction

In an old joke from the defunct German Democratic Republic, a German worker gets a job in Siberia; aware of how all mail will be read by the censors, he tells his friends: 'Let's establish a code: if a letter you get from me is written in ordinary blue ink, it's true; if it's written in red ink, it's false.' After a month, his friend gets the first letter, written in blue ink: 'Everything is wonderful here: the shops are full, food is abundant, apartments are large and properly heated, cinemas show films from the West, there are many beautiful girls ready for an affair – the only thing you can't get is *red ink*.'[3]

---

1 I am extremely grateful to Professor Erica Burman, Professor of Psychology and Women's Studies, Manchester Metropolitan University and Dr Daniela Caselli, Lecturer in Twentieth-Century Literature, Culture, English and American Studies, School of Arts, Histories and Cultures, University of Manchester, for their comments on an early draft of this chapter.

2 See the Forum's website at: <http://www.salfordrefugeeforum.org.uk/> (accessed 27 June 2011). The following summary was taken from the website: 'The seeds of Salford Forum for Refugees and People Seeking Asylum were planted in 2009 when Salford CVS came together with Community Pride Unit in order to establish a refugee and asylum seeker network in Salford. The forum concentrates on identifying ways in which refugee and asylum seeker groups can be brought together to support each other as a network. The developing work of the forum includes campaigning, signposting, training, information sharing at regular meetings, joint working, and representation within key decision making structures.' Revive's website is available at: <http://www.revive-uk.org/> (accessed 27 June 2011). The following summarises the organisation's activities: 'Revive (est. 2002) is a Christian organisation supporting refugees and people seeking asylum. We work directly with refugees, asylum seekers and the most vulnerable in society. Our service is free as many of those that we work with are destitute or on voucher systems. Revive offers emotional support, specialised case works and advocacy services to asylum seekers and refugees.'

3 S. Žižek, *Welcome to the Desert of the Real*, London and New York: Verso, 2002, p. 1.

Unlike the German worker in relation to his friend, the 'refined conditions of liberal censorship'[4] in the UK fall short of supplying the asylum seeker with the code of what blue and red ink signify, so that the UK's offer of tolerant hospitality to the foreigner who seeks asylum masks contradictions, ambivalence, limitations and regulation. So that the letter might read something like:

> Everything is wonderful here; we subscribe to the 1951 UN Convention for Refugees and have added further legal protection through the Human Rights Act 2000 (HRA), which applies to everyone in the United Kingdom, regardless of citizenship or immigration status. On this basis we promise dignity, fairness, equality and respect – a very tolerant and hospitable society.

Women asylum seekers involved in writing this chapter responded to and believed in the UK's offer of asylum from their situations of degradation, danger to life, torture and threat to family life in the Congo, Zimbabwe, Cameroon, Ghana, Kenya, Eritrea, Afghanistan, Iraq, Angola, Rwanda, Burundi, Gambia and South Africa. These women had no blue and red ink code to forewarn them of destitution, no recourse to public resources including health and social care, no right to work and vouchers.

> No one tells you what is really going on, you just find out the hard way, then they get you for not knowing fast enough, they are calling you a liar because you did not know what they did not tell you.

> I feel like, since I have arrived here, that I don't know what words to trust.

> It is like this, if you can imagine, you are hungry, I invite you to my house to eat, but I do not give you my address, or directions and then when you arrive late I am offended, when you do not know how to eat in my house I am offended, when you do not take off your shoes and you do not know to do this because I didn't tell you and you couldn't guess it right, I am offended. This is what it is like to come here as an asylum seeker.

In relation to the UK Human Rights Act (HRA) 1998[5] with specific reference to, and co-written with people seeking asylum, this chapter is interested in Žižek's metaphorical red ink; it is concerned to decode that which 'operates normatively; and how its normativity is rendered oblique almost to the point of invisibility'.[6] In particular, the aim is to decipher how notions of

---

4 Žižek, op. cit., note 3, p. 2.
5 The HRA entered into force in 2000.
6 W. Brown, *Regulating Aversion Tolerance in the Age of Identity and Empire*, Princeton: Princeton University Press, 2008.

hospitality, tolerance and the epistemology of testimony underwrite the HRA. The theoretical method adopted here is an analysis of the intersection of hospitality, tolerance and testimony, drawing on principles of Crenshaw's theory of 'intersectionality',[7] and applying them to a conceptual analysis of the HRA. Here, intersectionality is at once a tool for analysis and the subject under analysis. Even though the HRA is broken down into specific articles concerning specific violations, all violations of human rights violate other intersecting vectors of a person's identity; the cumulative effects of exploitation, destitution, torture, degradation, lack of liberty and family intersect.[8] The reductionist move where 'becoming a stranger can . . . reduce us to the visible signs of sex or race'[9] constitutes the asylum seeker into a recognisable form; the act of diminishing the complexity of an asylum seeker's identity diminishes her claim to human rights. Butler explains how this reductionism functions as Žižek's unavailable red ink,

> producing what will and will not count as a viable speaking subject . . . under social conditions that regulate identifications . . . the line that circumscribes what is speakable and what is livable also functions as an instrument of censorship.[10]

In response, our specific attention is on the 'interlocking and mutually reinforcing vectors'[11] of hospitality, tolerance and testimony. Just as Crenshaw argued that the 'intersectional experience is greater than the sum of racism and sexism' in her critique of 'single-axis' anti-discrimination law,[12] this chapter argues that the intersectional experience of the excess of hospitality,

---

7 Kimberlé Williams Crenshaw is Professor of Law at UCLA and Columbia School of Law, and a founder and leader of the critical race theory movement.
8 P. McDonald and M. Coleman, 'Deconstructing hierarchies of oppression and adopting a multiple model approach to anti-oppressive practice', *Social Work Education*, vol. 18, no. 1, 1999.
9 J. Still, *Derrida and Hospitality Theory and Practice*, Edinburgh: Edinburgh University Press, 2010, p. 6.
10 J. Butler, *A Precarious Life: the Powers of Mourning and Violence*, London: Verso, 2004, p. xix.
11 J. Nash, 'Re-thinking intersectionality', *Feminist Review*, 89, 2008, pp. 1–15. See also B.A. Arrighi, *Understanding Inequality: the intersection of race/ethnicity, class, and gender*, New York: Rowman & Littlefield, 2001; P.H. Collins, *Gender, Black Feminism, and Black Political Economy*, Annals of the American Academy of Political and Social Science, 568, 2000, pp. 41–53; V. Hunt and A. Zajicek, 'Strategic Intersectionality and the Needs of Disadvantaged Populations: An Intersectional Analysis of Organizational Inclusion and Participation,' *Race, Class and Gender*, vol. 15, no. 3, 2008, pp. 180–203; J. Siltanen and A. Doucet, *Gender Relations in Canada: Intersectionality and Beyond*, Toronto: Oxford University Press, 2008.
12 K. Crenshaw, *Demarginaliizing the intersection of race and sex: a black feminist critique of antidiscrimination doctrine, feminist theory, and antiracist politics*, Chicago: University of Chicago Legal Forum, 1989, pp. 140–9.

the supplement of tolerance and the circuitry of evaluating trustworthiness[13] in testimony is greater than the sum of these. In summary, what is being proposed is that the HRA rests on concepts such as hospitality, tolerance and the element of establishing trustworthiness in the epistemology of testimony. It will become evident that these concepts are intrinsically problematic: Derrida talks about the impossibility of hospitality,[14] Brown examines the anxious ambivalence of tolerance[15] and Dotson analyses the 'epistemic partiality in testimony'.[16] These problems, contradictions and paradoxes are experienced, personified and performed within the situation of seeking asylum. The objective here is not to expose a conspiracy or to offer an alternative to the flaws and failures of the HRA. Rather the objective is to go beyond the 'repressive hypothesis'[17] in order to apprehend that which is disavowed and attend to the function of that disavowal. Indeed, it becomes apparent that the manoeuvres and function of the disavowal are contingent upon and constituted by each other and by shared anxieties and threats. Censorship, production, function, constitution and contingency are interdependent and intersect. Žižek's blue and red ink refer and defer to each other.

Critical situated knowledge

If 'the space and place we inhabit produces us'[18] and if 'knowledge is situated',[19] questions concerning production, with specific reference to the space and place of seeking asylum within the UK, raise theoretical and practical issues of fundamental aspects of the HRA. In and of itself there is nothing suspect about the HRA functioning as a tool of the state to interpellate, constitute and construct particular identities, positions and discourses. Indeed it could be argued that this is a core function and outcome of the HRA in relation to fairness, equality, dignity and respect. The situation becomes more dubious when the interpellation, constitution and constructions are injurious.[20]

13 K. Lehrer, 'Testimony and Trustworthiness', in J. Lackey and E. Sosa (eds) *The Epistemology of Testimony*, Oxford: Clarendon Press, 2006, p. 144.
14 M.W. Westmoreland, 'Interruptions: Derrida and Hospitality,' *Kritike*, vol. 2, no. 1, 2008, pp. 1–10.
15 Brown, op. cit., n. 6, p. 25.
16 K. Dotson, 'On Epistemic Partiality in Testimony', PhD Thesis, Tennessee: The University of Memphis, 2008.
17 M. Foucault, *The History of Sexuality, The Will to Knowledge*, trans. R. Hurley, Harmondsworth: Penguin, 1978, p. 13.
18 E. Probyn, 'The Spatial Imperative of Subjectivity', in K. Anderson, M. Domosh, S. Pile and N. Thrift (eds), *Handbook of Cultural Geography*, London: Sage, 2003.
19 P. Hill Collins, *Black Feminist Thought: Knowledge, Consciousness, and The Politics of Empowerment*, London: Unwin Hyman, 1990.
20 J. Butler, *The Psychic Life of Power*, Stanford: Stanford University Press, 1997, p. 105.

This chapter is written with women asylum seekers as a lens of critical situated knowledge. These co-writers are members of the campaign group United for Change, within the Salford Forum for Refugees and People Seeking Asylum and the charitable organization Revive, based in Salford, Greater Manchester. The origin of this relationship began when these asylum seekers gave testimony to their experience at a conference about the HRA.[21] The paradox is that within the context of the conference the credibility of these asylum seekers' testimonies as a critical lens was contingent on the fact and consequences of the lack of credibility of their testimony within the legal and state processes that establish the authenticity of their request for asylum. The decision that they were assessed as inauthentic made them authentic witnesses. Indeed, incorporating the element of testimony in the conference represented inclusivity of the 'Other', an antidote to accusations of exclusivity and the rubber-stamping voice that authenticates. Insisting on the problematic of 'authenticism or the authority of authenticity',[22] Spivak argues that 'the *mechanics* of the constitution of the Other' and 'invocations of the *authenticity* of the Other'[23] are used to circumvent the difficulties inherent in representation. Picking up Said's notion of the violence of relentless fetishisation of difference,[24] Griffiths states that 'a fetishised cultural commodity', may be employed 'to enact a discourse of "liberal violence" [*sic*], re-enacting its own oppressions on the subjects it purports to represent and defend'.[25] Similar tensions had to be explored and not necessarily resolved in co-writing this chapter with asylum seekers.[26] In particular, consideration of how inclusion of testimony in this chapter re-enacts the mastery of the host in the dynamics of hospitality and the regulatory function of tolerance continues to be grappled with. The words of asylum seekers in this chapter function as metaphorical red ink: to interrupt, disturb and dislocate theoretical perspectives and interpretations.

---

21 'Ten Years On: A Multi-Perspective Evaluation of the Human Rights Act', held at the University of Salford, June 2010.

22 A. Sanchez Arce, 'Authenticism or the Authority of Authenticity', *Mosaic*, vol. 40, no.3, 2007, pp. 139–55.

23 G. Spivak, 'Can the Subaltern speak?' in C. Nelson and L. Grossberg (eds) *Marxism and the Interpretation of culture*, Basingstoke: Macmillan, 1988, p. 294.

24 E. Said, 'Representing the Colonized: Anthropology's Interlocutors', *Critical Inquiry*, vol.15, 1986, pp. 205–25.

25 G. Griffiths, 'The Myth of Authenticity,' in C. Tiffin and A. Lawson (eds) *De-Scribing Empire*, London: Routledge, 1994, p. 241.

26 The process involved weekly meetings of consultation, negotiation, knowledge exchange and editing during a nine-month period. Process generally does not in and of itself reconstitute power differentials. Within the particular process of co-writing this chapter with women in the campaign group United for Change the Foucauldian power/knowledge relation was at once a tool of analysis and the subject under analysis. The women in United for Change actively engaged with and shaped the conceptual framework and methodology adopted in this chapter and this is evident in their words and how they use their words in the text. Neither the individual names of the women in United for Change nor the term 'asylum seeker' appear against their words; this is deliberate and represents a conscious tactic to underscore the presence of the 'absolute unknown, anonymous other' in the text.

In short, the words of asylum seekers in this chapter function to transgress the hierarchical relations of host/guest, tolerate/tolerated, known/unknown.

> It's crazy, I am not welcome in your country, I am told to leave, but I am welcome in your conferences and now in one of your books; make up your minds, do you want me or not?

> If and when I am forced to leave the UK, I will still remain here on shelves in this book and maybe when someone reads this chapter that we are writing and I may be gone I will still be here.

> I wonder, would my words have power without the words of Derrida, Wendy Brown, Homi Bhabha and others in this writing? I mean they freely give their names, I cannot afford to have my name printed, too dangerous, do we need these other words, I do not want to be a ventriloquist's puppet.

The episteme and intersectionality

An obvious question is: how does the UK commitment to the HRA exist with the UK's policy, practice and experience of asylum seekers? To highlight just a few examples, how can Art. 3, freedom from degrading and inhumane treatment, sit with destitution, living off vouchers, detention, dawn raids and Home Office interviews? How can Art. 4, freedom from forced labour, sit with no right to work, which pushes people into exploitative and unregulated labour? How can Art. 5, the right to liberty and security, sit with detention, the insecurity and risk inherent in destitution particularly, when those who are destitute are suffering the physical and psychological effects of trauma? How can Art. 8, a right to respect for private and family life, sit with families split up due to detention, enforced separated dwellings, taking children into the care of the state because of the consequences of seeking asylum, and untreated, misunderstood and misdiagnosed trauma? How can Art. 14, which states that the enjoyment of the rights shall be secured without discrimination on any ground such as sex, race, colour, language, religion, political or other opinion, national or social origin, association with a national minority, property, birth or other status sit with the discriminatory treatment of those people seeking asylum in the UK?

Drawing on Foucault's 'episteme', which refers specifically to the coexistence, alignment and legitimatisation of contradictory and incongruous discursive frameworks that share underlying presuppositions and, significantly, have a shared function, this chapter is concerned with 'ensembles of discourse . . . the play of rules, of transformations, of thresholds . . . their clusters and relations'.[27] Of particular interest is how incongruent conflicting, contradictory discourses

---

27 M. Foucault, *Discipline and Punish: The Birth of the Prison*, Harmondsworth: Penguin, 1991, p. 55.

and practices intersect, become congruent, harmonious and complementary in their function to provide contingency, foreclosure and regulation. The theoretical method of intersectionality applied to Foucault's 'episteme' reveals something of how the internal tensions and instability within the discourse of human rights and asylum calibrate not only to censor and mask, but also to produce. Answering the question of what is produced, masked and censored with reference to tolerance, hospitality and testimony uncovers an 'ideological quilt' where 'the quilting performs the totalization by means of which this free floating of ideological elements is halted, fixed – that is to say, by means of which they become parts of the structured network of meaning'.[28] The quilt is produced to fix, halt or censor ambivalence and contradictions and mask anxiety and instability.

Deconstructing the edifice of the HRA reveals foundations, supporting walls and rolled steel joists (RSJs) manufactured from the building blocks of tolerance, hospitality and testimony. The rationale for investigating the alignment of these conceptual elements is that they are constituted and function in similar ways. Tolerance, hospitality and testimony share a quality of internal instability, they function on paradox, they interpellate,[29] position and legitimise. Each concept – tolerance, hospitality and testimony – intersects and re-inscribes the others to form a scaffolding or perform the 'totalization' that bears the weight of tensions within the HRA that threaten to bring the house down. Žižek explains that 'the first task of the analysis is therefore to isolate, in any given ideological field, the particular struggle which at the same time determines the horizon of its totality'.[30]

This chapter draws on a body of multidisciplinary scholarship which uses the metaphor of hospitality,[31] the politics of tolerance[32] and the epistemology

28 S. Žižek, *The Sublime Object of Ideology*, London: Verso, 1989, p. 95.

29 L. Althusser, 'Ideology and ideological state apparatuses', in *Lenin and Philosophy and Other Essays*. London: New Left Books, 1971, pp. 170–86.

30 Žižek, op. cit., n. 28, p. 97.

31 P. Lynch, J. Germann Molz, A. McIntosh, P. Lugosi and C. Lashley (ed) 'Theorizing hospitality', *Hospitality and Society*, vol. 1, no. 1, 2011. See also S. Ahmed, *Strange Encounters*, London: Routledge, 2000; Z. Bauman, *Paradoxes of Assimilation*, New Brunswick: Transaction Publishers, 1990; J. Derrida, 'Hospitality, Justice and Responsibility: A Dialogue with Jacques Derrida' in R. Kearney and M. Dooley (eds) *Questioning Ethics: Contemporary Debates in Philosophy*, London: Routledge, 1989; J. Derrida, 'Hostipitality', *Angelaki Journal of the Theoretical Humanities*, vol. 5, no. 3, 2000, pp. 3–18; S. Gibson, 'Accommodating Strangers: British Hospitality and the Asylum Hotel Debate', *Journal for Cultural Research*, vol. 7, no. 4, 2003, pp. 367–86. See also S. Gibson, 'The Hotel Business is About Strangers: Border Politics and Hospitable Spaces in Stephen Frears's *Dirty Pretty Things*', *Third Text*, vol. 20, no. 6, 2006, pp. 693–701; M. Rosello, *Postcolonial Hospitality: The Immigrant as Guest*, Stanford, CA: Stanford University Press, 2001.

32 J. Horton and S. Mendus (eds) *Aspects of Tolerance: Philosophical Studies*. London: Methuen, 1985. See also D. Heyd, (ed.) *Toleration: An Elusive Virtue*, Princeton: Princeton University Press, 1996; S. Mendus, (ed.) *The Politics of Tolerance in Modern life*, Durham, NC: Duke University Press, 1999; I. Creppell, *Toleration and Identity: Foundations in Early Modern Thought*, New York: Routledge, 2003.

of testimony[33] to theorise the social, economic and political dynamics of crossing and setting borders, the question of citizenship, human rights, the position and treatment of the foreigner. Of particular interest is how the conjunctive and disjunctive of hospitality, tolerance and testimony act as tools of social control. The offer of asylum to those who claim need of a place of safe refuge could be rephrased to say: the offer of tolerant hospitality to the foreigner who testifies to claim of needing hospitality that tolerates. The idea, politics and practice of tolerance is required in order to sanction hospitality and is required in order to maintain and sustain hospitality. They supplement each other and function as supplements in their own right.[34] Tolerance and hospitality of the foreigner is mediated through the question of how the host hears the speech act of the foreigner seeking hospitality. In the context of asylum seekers the speech act takes particular forms, including testimony required in Home Office interviews.

Testimony

Testimony is at the core of whether an asylum seeker is granted leave to remain or not. The framework that adjudicates the question of honesty and dishonesty, belief and disbelief, authenticity and inauthenticity rests on testimony. The outcome of the adjudication gestures to the idea of tolerance and positions the believed, the honest, the authentic asylum seeker on the 'to be tolerated' bench and the disbelieved, dishonest and inauthentic asylum seeker on the 'not to be tolerated' bench. 'The tolerated' are granted hospitality and 'the not tolerated' are not granted hospitality. The reasonableness of this sequence is quickly undone with slight probing into the intersubjective encounter between speaker and hearer in the speech act of testimony, the relation between host and guest, and the dynamic of tolerator and tolerated.

The space and place of testimony, tolerance and hospitality exposes the shifting instability of credibility and recognition. This is exemplified in the switch from dishonest to honest, disbelieved to believed, and inauthentic to authentic, in the shift from the space and place of the asylum process, where the same asylum seekers who were not tolerated or given hospitality are tolerated and hosted within a conference on the HRA, and in this chapter reviewing the

33 P. Lipton, 'The Epistemology of Testimony', *Studies in History and Philosophy of Science*, vol. 29, 1989, pp. 1–31. See also J. Lackey, 'Testimonial Knowledge and Transmission', *Philosophical Quarterly*, vol. 49, 1999, pp. 471–90; P. Faulkner, 'The Social Character of Testimonial Knowledge', *Journal of Philosophy*, vol. 97, 2005, pp. 81–601; M. Weiner, 'Accepting Testimony', *Philosophical Quarterly*, vol. 53, 2003, pp. 256–64.

34 Brown, op. cit., n. 6, p. 70. See also J. Derrida and J. Caputo, *Deconstruction in a Nutshell: A Conversation with Jacques Derrida*, New York: Fordham University Press, 1997, reprinted 2006, p. 110; B. Honig, *Democracy and The Foreigner*, Princeton: Princeton University Press, 2001, p. 3.

HRA. Žižek unravels the logic of this 'in the negation of the negation; the negativity preserves all its disruptive power; the whole point is just that we come to experience how this negative, disruptive power, menacing our identity, is simultaneously a positive condition of it'.[35] The negation of the negation in relation to asylum seekers could be represented by their participation in a conference on the HRA and in co-writing this chapter, or indeed in general terms, in the encounter between those who are negated through the negation of their human rights, and those who champion the rights of the negated. Žižek explains how this works: 'the very identity of our position is structured through a negative relationship to this traumatic figure.'[36] Thus it is much more subtle than a switch from negative to positive, for example, in the movement from disbelief to belief, dishonesty to honesty and inauthentic to authentic. It is not as straightforward as a switch or shift; the negation of the negation means that any positive stance, identity or identification is contingent on and structured through negativity. Hillis Miller describes 'a paradoxical action which is negative and positive at once'.[37] Picking up the crucial elements of space and place, Žižek comments: 'While in the "negation of the negation", negativity is *in a way prior to what is being negated*, it is a negative movement which opens the very place where every positive identity can be situated.'[38]

Just as tolerance 'requires in advance what it also promotes',[39] testimony requires in advance what it needs to establish legitimacy and credibility. Thus it could be said that testimony situates before it situates. Testimony's adjudicating function is in process prior to the act of giving testimony; indeed without this 'prior', 'the testimony in itself does not constitute evidence'.[40] Lackey comments, 'One of the main questions in the epistemology of testimony is how we successfully acquire justified belief or knowledge on the basis of what other people tell us.'[41] Or, rephrased, the main question for asylum seekers becomes the following;

On the basis of what we tell you how do you believe us?

Is justified belief really on the basis of what we say or is there some other basis?

OK, you tell me something, do I believe you or not and if I do believe you then how and why do I believe you?

35 Žižek, op. cit., n. 28, p. 199.
36 Ibid.
37 J. Hillis Miller, *The Critic as Host: Deconstruction and Criticism*, New York: Continuum, 1979, reprinted 2004, p. 205.
38 Žižek, op. cit., n. 28, p. 200.
39 Brown, op. cit., n. 6, p. 154.
40 Lehrer, op. cit., n. 13, p. 149.
41 J. Lackey, 'Introduction', in J. Lackey and E. Sosa (eds), *The Epistemology of Testimony*, Oxford: Clarendon Press, 2006, p. 2.

I think that this word 'acquire' is most interesting: it is as if to believe cannot stand on its own, it has to be 'justified', so my question is, even around this table we are all from different places, different languages, so what I mean by 'successfully acquire justified belief' is going to be different to you and you and you.

I have not been believed so many times that now, today, here, I do not know what would make them believe, I could not tell you.

I had to flee for my life because the truth I was saying was called a lie, I came here and was called a liar, they did not believe me, I have no trust left in anything, this trust thing is slippery.

The basis of what these and other failed and destitute asylum seekers 'tell' is constructed and constituted by ideology that undermines, discredits and invalidates before testimony begins. Thus the sequence of testimony gesturing to the idea of tolerance which then positions the tolerated and not tolerated as a welcomed guest or an unwelcomed, parasitic intruder is disrupted. The function of testimony as adjudicator is dislocated due to the 'prior' and the prior is contingent on tolerance and hospitality. The conditions of subject formation are prior to and beyond the control of the subjects[42] within each role designated and performed in and through tolerance, hospitality and testimony; the conditions and its subjects are 'always already' interpellated.[43]

In addition, the process of providing testimony – testimony where the objective is to acquire justified belief of the experience and situation of the trauma that necessitated the seeking and provision of asylum – re-traumatises. Lackley's question becomes even more complicated because the recognised basis for successful acquisition of justified belief is undermined at every level, due to the extraordinary and unrecognisable physical and emotional presentation of the testifier,[44] who happens to be foreign, who also happens to be traumatised, most often without documentation. Lackley argues for 'an alternate view of testimonial justification that goes beyond the reductionist/non-reductionist dichotomy'.[45]

Putting the element of trustworthiness into the equation brings with it the problem of relationality. Lehrer explains:

42 J. Butler, 'Giving an account of oneself', *Diacritics*, vol. 31, no. 4, 2001, pp. 22–40.
43 L. Althusser, 'Ideology and ideological state apparatuses', in *Lenin and Philosophy and Other Essays*, London: New Left Books, 1969, pp. 170–86.
44 J. Lewis Herman, *Trauma and Recovery from Domestic Abuse to Political Terror*, London: Pandora, 2001.
45 J. Lackey, 'It Takes Two to Tango: Beyond Reductionism and non-Reductionism in the Epistemology of Testimony', in J. Lackey and E. Sosa (eds), *The Epistemology of Testimony*, Oxford: Clarendon Press, 2006, p. 160.

I must evaluate the trustworthiness of others to evaluate their testimony. This leads to the question of whether I am trustworthy in my evaluation of their trustworthiness. This leads to the further question of how I am to evaluate my own trustworthiness without appeal to the intersubjective constraint based on the testimony of others. If, however, I must evaluate my own trustworthiness of others before accepting their testimony, and I must evaluate my own trustworthiness by appeal to the testimony of others, then I am involved in a circle of evaluation from which there is no exit.[46]

Rather than seeing the intersubjectivity as a 'constraint' and the circuitry 'no exit' as a cul-de-sac, Butler proposes that acknowledgement of the

> limits of self-knowledge can work in the service of a conception of ethics and, indeed, of responsibility. If the subject is opaque to itself, it is not therefore licensed to do what it wants or to ignore its relations to others. Indeed, if it is precisely by virtue of its relations to others that it is opaque to itself, and if those relations to others are precisely the venue for its ethical responsibility, then it may well follow that it is precisely by virtue of the subject's opacity to itself that it sustains some of its most important ethical bonds.[47]

Constituent parts of the HRA are defined, qualified and exist on the basis of recognition of relationality, yet this relationality produces 'opacity' and has the potential, as Butler points out, to be a basis for ethical responsibility which causes anxiety. Opaque borders – not only between peoples but in terms of national, political and ideological boundaries – are resisted at every level and with every tool available, including the HRA. Thus, the opportunity to enable 'opacity' to work for justice is missed.

Tolerance and hospitality

The question of to whom hospitality and tolerance are granted, and on what basis, is pivotal. The point of the parable of the Good Samaritan is precisely that the Samaritan was good because he did not have a defined 'whom' and 'basis' for his hospitality and tolerance; it was unconditional. The HRA applies to everyone in the United Kingdom, regardless of citizenship or immigration, and Art. 14 states that the enjoyment of the rights shall be secured without discrimination on any ground such as sex, race, colour, language, religion, political or other opinion, national or social origin, association with a national minority, property, birth or other status. Thus Art. 14 should be

---

46 Lehrer, op. cit., n. 13, pp. 145–59.
47 Butler, op. cit., n. 42, p. 22.

applied without reference to geographical, identity, ideological, economic or political borders, divisions and differences. However, this same Art. 14 within the edifice of the HRA, which speaks of universal and absolute rights, rests on the supporting walls of hospitality and tolerance. The paradox is that tolerance and hospitality are configured on, produce and respond to geographical, identity, ideological, economic or political borders, divisions and differences. The invocation of the proprietor, whether named as host or that which tolerates, is not compatible with Art. 14's request not to discriminate, neither is it compatible with the HRA's instigation of absolute and universal rights. To be hospitable and to tolerate is to discriminate; quite incongruent with concepts such as universal and absolute. Derrida states:

> The law of hospitality, the express law that governs the general concept of hospitality, appears as a paradoxical law, pervertible and perverting. It seems to indicate that absolute hospitality should break with the law of hospitality as a right or duty, with the 'pact' of hospitality. To put it in different terms, absolute hospitality requires that I open up my home and that I give not only to the foreigner (provided with a family name, with the social status of being a foreigner, etc.), but to the absolute unknown, anonymous other, that I let them arrive, and take place in the place I offer them, without asking of them either reciprocity (entering into a pact) or even their names.[48]

Tolerance is also governed by paradoxical, pervertible and perverting laws. 'The pronouncement "I am a tolerant man" conjures seemliness, propriety, forbearance, magnanimity, cosmopolitanism, universality, and the large view.'[49] The problem that hospitality and tolerance share is the arrival and non-reciprocal accommodation of the 'absolute unknown, anonymous other'. Whether opening up 'my home' refers to the house of national borders, ideological, political or economic territories, hosting or tolerating the 'absolute unknown, anonymous other' contradicts the laws that govern the concept and act of hosting and tolerating.

Asylum seekers are people who have applied for refugee status in a country and are waiting for a decision about their legal right to remain in that country.[50] In other words, until this decision is made the asylum seeker is the 'absolute unknown, anonymous other'. The 1951 UN Convention on the Status of Refugees defines a refugee as:

48 J. Derrida, *Of Hospitality: Anne Dufourmantelle Invites Jacques Derrida to Respond*, trans. R. Bowlby, Stanford, CA: Stanford University Press, 2000, p. 25.

49 Brown, op. cit., n. 6, p. 178.

50 *A Place of Refuge: A positive approach to asylum seekers and refugees in the UK*. Report commissioned by the Church of England's Mission and Public Affairs, Church House Publishing, 2005.

A person who is outside his/her country of nationality or habitual residence; has a well-founded fear of persecution because of his/her race, religion, nationality, membership in a particular social group or political opinion; and is unable or unwilling to avail himself/herself of the protection of that country, or to return there, for fear of persecution.

Thus the refugee is clearly not the unknown anonymous other. The identity and status of the refugee is neither unconditional nor fully representative. Butler comments:

Perhaps we make a mistake if we take the definitions of who we are, legally, to be adequate descriptions of what we are about. Although this language may well establish our legitimacy within a legal framework ensconced in liberal versions of human ontology, it does not do justice to passion and grief and rage, all of which tear us from ourselves, bind us to others.[51]

The legal definition of the status of the refugee is conditional and these conditions happen to be the same conditions required for hospitality, tolerance and testimony. In terms of hospitality, the refugee must be outside of their own residence or territory, and, unable to return, seeks sanctuary on the basis of being recognised, knowable and defined because of their race, religion, nationality, or membership in a particular social group or political opinion. In terms of testimony the conditions have to be well founded, believed and trustworthy. In terms of tolerance, the need for refuge is based on a lack of tolerance. The 1951 Convention works on the binary of tolerant and intolerant, hospitable and inhospitable, well founded and not well founded.

The problem is that refugee status is reliant on testimony, hospitality and tolerance and these are contingent on identity and identification. The establishment, verification and trustworthiness of identity and identification are key issues for the epistemology of testimony.[52] Identity and identification are fundamental to tolerance because 'tolerance is generally conferred by those who do not require it on those who do'.[53] It follows that 'that which tolerates is not eligible for tolerance'.[54] In terms of hospitality, 'A host is a host only if he owns the place, and only if he holds onto his ownership, if one *limits* the

---

51 Butler, op. cit., n. 42, p. 25.
52 G.E.M. Anscombe, 'What Is It to Believe Someone?' in C.F. Delaney (ed), *Rationality and Religious Belief*, Notre Dame: University of Notre Dame Press, 1979; D. Bartolomey, 'Cross-racial identification testimony and what not to do about it: A comment on the cross-racial jury charge and cross-racial expert identification testimony', *Psychology, Public Policy, and Law*, vol. 7, no.1, 2001, pp. 247–52.
53 Brown, op. cit., n. 6, p. 186.
54 Ibid., p. 187.

gift.'[55] Thus the problem of an unconditional absolute unknown, and anonymous other, for tolerance and hospitality, is not just a matter of ambivalence or anxiety as to what is foreign. A hospitality and tolerance contingent upon an 'absolute unknown, anonymous other' would reconstitute the terms, alter their function and obliterate any border between known and unknown. In other words the 'absolute unknown, anonymous other' threatens the very existence and viability of hospitality and tolerance. Pursuing the question of what is impossible in the impossibility of hospitality, Keating asks:

> Is absolute hospitality, what must be given prior to identification, impossible because of the impossibility of not posing questions to the foreigner, not translating their language and subsuming their identity into something that is not 'strange' any more? No question to the stranger is pure because we already assimilate their being into terms that we can arrange into our own conceptions of being. This seems to be a factual impossibility, which is the empirical impossibility of experiencing or giving unconditional hospitality.[56]

The function of testimony within the asylum process is to make the unknown known. The foreigner presented through the speech act, often mediated through an interpreter, speaks in an unrecognisable tongue; an unrecognisability exacerbated by trauma and disorientation is made recognisable, familiar and identifiable. The asylum process functions to censor the impasse or 'red ink' of undecidability and indeterminacy. This is why Derrida referred to the 'pervertable' and 'perverting', 'express law that governs the general concept of hospitality'.[57] Drawing on Kant,[58] Keating explains that 'the unconditioned needs the conditioned: because the conditioned is constitutive of the unconditioned'.[59] Actually, the aporia of unconditional hospitality towards the absolute unknown and anonymous other, and the need for a legal, political and economic identity conditioned within the legally defined territory recognised as the UK, are mutually contingent:

> The conceptual and practical impossibility of unconditional hospitality could then be its original singular existence. It exists dependently in an aporia. The relationship between impossible and conditional hospitality

55 Derrida and Caputo, op. cit., n. 34, p. 110.
56 P. Keating, 'The Conditioning of the Unconditioned: Derrida and Kant', *Borderlands*, vol. 3, no. 1, 2004.
57 Derrida, op. cit., n. 48, p. 25.
58 I. Kant, 'Groundwork of the Metaphysics of Morals', in *The Cambridge Edition of Practical Philosophy*, ed. M.J. Gregor, Cambridge and New York: Cambridge University Press, 1999. See also I. Kant, *Critique of Pure Reason*, eds P. Guyer and A.W. Wood, Cambridge and New York: Cambridge University Press, 1998.
59 Keating, op. cit., n. 56.

is one of mutual fecundity and corruption. And yet, the demand for the laws is constitutive for the law of unconditional hospitality. So while the conditional offer of amnesty to refugees by a government may in fact sully a true ethic of unconditional hospitality, the latter requires such examples of conditions on hospitality for its existence. The existence of unconditional hospitality seems to be the requirement for critique of the legal and political laws of conditioned hospitality.[60]

Thus, tolerance and hospitality 'deconstructs itself in being put into practice'.[61] In practice this is translated and experienced as:

They decided what I am even before I spoke.

You call me asylum seeker. I don't like that word, I have come not to like it, you call me that so you can know who I am, but I have a name, but let's forget that for a minute; I am a human being, I have a heart, I need to eat, sleep, drink water just as you do, I may be a stranger, of course you do not know me, but we are not so different, you know.

The 'Manichean rhetorical scheme' within the discourse and practice of tolerance to make the unknown known relies on a codification of differences into hierarchicalised binaries of 'fundamentalist/intolerant/free' on the one side and 'pluralist/tolerant/free' on the other.[62] This binary is distilled into the known and unknown, recognised and unrecognised, tolerant and intolerant, and skates over the complexity that is inherent in all identities and identifications, Hall explains how this works:

Identities are constructed through, not outside, difference. . . . it is only through the relation to the other, the relation to what it is not, to what has been called its 'constitutive outside' that the positive meaning of any term – and thus its identity – can be constructed. . . . identities function as points of identification and attachment only because of their capacity to exclude, to leave out, to render 'outside', abjected. The unity, the internal homogeneity, which the term identity treats as foundational is not natural, but a constructed form of closure.[63]

The real predicament is that that the act of recognition simultaneously involves a dynamic of misrecognition.[64] The notion of a stable, unified identity and

60 Keating, op. cit., n. 56.
61 Derrida, op. cit., n. 31.
62 Brown, op. cit., n. 6, p. 190.
63 S. Hall, 'Who needs identity?' in P. du Gay, J. Evans and P. Redman (eds), *Identity: A reader*, London: Sage, 2000, reprinted 2009, p. 18.
64 M. Pêcheux, 'The mechanism of ideological (mis)recognition', in S. Žižek (ed.), *Mapping Ideology*, London: Verso, 1994.

identification as host, guest, tolerator, tolerated, known, unknown, anonymous and other is destabilised because it is constituted by what is outside, what it is not. Derrida comments that 'inclusion and exclusion are inseparable in the same moment'.[65] This is precisely what is disavowed; the general law governing hospitality and tolerance is designed to resist instability of identity and identification. Žižek's blue ink censors the fact that 'The language of tolerance is part of what sanctions the state violence that itself reproduces and mobilizes the "difference" that becomes the occasion for tolerance in the first place.'[66]

The foreigner question

Derrida deconstructs the question of the foreigner 'As though the foreigner were being-in-question, the very question of being-in-question, the question-being or being-in-question of the question.'[67] Asylum seekers report that their experience of the asylum process here in the UK brings into question their very being; the questioning works performatively to locate the 'questioning' in the being of the questioned.

> I look at a photograph I have of myself and my family when I was back home and I do not recognise that person anymore, I do not see myself in the photograph of myself, I do not know who I am any more, I could not say to you I am that person.

Here the violence of 'the very question of being-in-question' reconfigures her to the extent that she does not even recognise herself. Being-in-question is traumatic; it lays trauma on top of the trauma that forced this woman to seek the sanctuary of asylum. Lewis Herman comments that 'at the moment of trauma, almost by definition, the individual's point of view counts for nothing ... The traumatic even thus destroys the belief that one can *be oneself* in relation to others.'[68]

Honig invites us to

> switch the question that has long dominated our thinking about foreignness. Rather than 'How should we solve the problem of foreignness?' and 'What should "we" do about "them"? ... the question ... is what problems does foreignness solve for us? Why do nations or democracies rely on the agency of foreignness at their vulnerable moments of (re) founding, at what cost and for what purpose?[69]

65 Derrida, op. cit., n. 48, p. 81.
66 Brown, op. cit., n. 6, p. 105.
67 Derrida, op. cit., n. 48, p 3.
68 Lewis Herman, op. cit., n. 44, p. 53.
69 Honig, op. cit., n. 34, p. 4.

Honig's switching of the question indicates that this construction is malleable, unstable with the potential for (re)founding. The characterisation of the foreigner as a 'problem' enables the host to circumvent the anxiety of the 'anonymous', 'unknown', transforming that which is unrecognisable and without name to a recognisable 'problem'. 'Problem' is a handy catch-all term recognised from a political, social, cultural and economic perspective. 'Problem' simultaneously enables identification and the disavowal of the uncomfortable 'constitutive outside'. Problem enables the episteme to coalesce around a common function of tackling the problem. Asylum seekers personify the problem,

> I feel like I am the problem.

> Do you know what it feels like to be a problem? It gets into you, you start to believe it; why should my life, my children, my need for a place to stay, something to eat, to be safe be a problem? I am a prickle, a thorn, I am seen as negative and this does something to you.

The words of the two destitute asylum seekers quoted above answer Butler's question, 'What does it mean for a word not only to name, but also in some sense to perform and, in particular, to perform what it names?'[70] The embodiment of 'problem' reinscribed repeatedly through the discourse and practice of the asylum process constitutes and informs a particular interpretation of the potential problem of the asylum seeker. Honig comments, 'Again and again, I find foreignness used in familiar ways, as a device that gives shape to or threatens existing political communities by marking negatively what "we" are not.'[71] Representing asylum seekers as a problem to be solved is more comfortable than the excess of extending hospitality to the absolute unknown or of confronting that the 'we' is constituted through and therefore inextricably bound to the 'not'. Wilkinson and Kitzinger comment that 'Representation is never merely descriptive; it serves also a constitutive and regulatory function which is obscured in (but not absent from) accounts relying upon the conventions of representational realism.'[72] There is nothing original, alternative or specific about pejorative claims and derogatory tropes representing asylum seekers as lazy, illegal parasites flooding in, stealing jobs and resources, which work on real conventional stereotypes, fears and pressures.

The etymology of tolerance and hospitality further complicates the problematic. Hospitality is explained in John Caputo's commentary on the 1994 round table discussion with Derrida:

70 J. Butler, 'Burning Acts, Injurious Speech', in S. Salih (ed.) *The Judith Butler Reader*, Oxford: Blackwell, 2004 p. 214.

71 Honig, op. cit., n. 34, p. 3.

72 S. Wilkinson and C. Kitzinger, *Representing the Other; A Feminism and Psychology Reader*, London: Sage, 1996.

... the word 'hospitality' carries its opposite within itself ... the word hospitality derives from the Latin *hospes*, which is formed from *hostis*, which originally meant a 'stranger' and came to take on the meaning of the enemy or '*hostile*' stranger (*hostilis*) + *pets* (*potis, potes, potentia*), to have power. 'Hospitality', the welcome extended to the guest, is a function of the power of the host to remain master of the premises.[73]

Seeking asylum as distinct from economic migration is not a voluntary choice in order to seek a more prosperous life. Asylum seekers are forced to seek asylum because they are perceived and treated as a hostile enemy within the hostile conditions of their own country or habitual residence. The etymology of hospitality demonstrates that hospitality in the form of providing asylum and conferring refugee status performs the very same dynamics that necessitated asylum in the first place.

The Latin root of tolerance is '*tolero*', derived from the Greek verb '*talao*', which means 'to bear' and 'to endure', invoking a moral and power differential that positions that which endures and that which has to be endured. Brown picks up three particular angles presented in the *Oxford English Dictionary*'s definition: '(1) 'the action or practice of *enduring* pain or hardship'; (2) 'the action of *allowing*; license, permission granted by an authority'; (3) '*the disposition to be patient with or indulgent to* the opinions or practices of others.'[74] From every angle, the condition of seeking asylum concerns tolerance, and lack of tolerance; for example, the configuration of the intolerance of the persecutor, the asylum seekers' inability to tolerate persecution, and the potential tolerance or intolerance of the host. However, the supplement tolerance is not neutral: 'In every lexicon, tolerance signifies the limits on what foreign, erroneous, objectionable or dangerous element can be allowed to cohabit with the host without destroying the host.'[75]

Excess

Now to the problem of the supplement and excess. Any qualification, limitation or restriction on human rights that are not deemed absolute, inalienable and inherent must be exacted proportionately or not excessively; ergo to be disproportionate is to be excessive. Here the theory of tolerance and hospitality raises a further problem – the problem of excess – because there is nothing proportionate about tolerance and hospitality. The tension between the impossibility of absolute, inalienable tolerance and hospitality and limited, qualified and regulatory tolerance and hospitality produces excess. The excess of hospitality is deconstructed as:

73 Derrida and Caputo, op. cit., n. 34, p.110.
74 Brown, op. cit., n. 6, p. 25.
75 Ibid., p. 27.

this tension built into 'hospitality', this 'aporia' or 'paralysis' . . . what Derrida calls the impossible (the im-possiblity of hostil-pitality) . . . Hospitality really starts to happen when I push against this limit, this threshold, this paralysis, inviting hospitality to cross its own threshold . . . that requires that the host, in a moment of madness, tear up the understanding between him and the guest, act with 'excess', make an absolute gift of his property, which of course is impossible. But that is the only way the guest can go away feeling as if he was really at home.[76]

So we have the asylum seeker knocking at the door of the UK, seeking asylum, the absolute unknown, the 'anonymous other' without identity documents; no passport or birth certificate, verification of identification for recognition, seeking hospitality on the basis of universal, inalienable and inherent human rights. The anxiety on the part of the host (UK) is twofold, contingent on the anonymous unknown that pushes at the threshold of recognition and misrecognition and the need for mastery over space and place. Put in simple terms, the UK is anxious to be recognised and identified as a distinct bounded nation state that is known for its hospitality, tolerance and human rights. However, 'the language of tolerance, which always signals the undesirable proximity of the Other in the midst of the Same',[77] ensures that the Other remains Other. The problem is that the 'Same' and the 'Other' constitute each other in unbearable relationality;[78] this is as close as proximity gets, and herein lies the excess. Hillis Miller's deconstruction of the simultaneous relation of intimate kinship and enmity is condensed in the phrase, 'There is no parasite without its host.'[79] The excess is about the threat of proximity and disavowal of the interdependency of difference. This disavowal undermines the potential for the interdependency of difference performing a key role in the formation of ethical responsibility.

Bhabha's analysis of the mimicry of colonisation, founded on 'the desire for a reformed, recognizable Other, as a subject of a difference that is almost the same, but not quite',[80] provides a nuanced analysis of the excess of hospitality and tolerance. It is in the gap between 'almost the same but not quite' that the ambivalence, indeterminacy and disavowal of the impossibility and excess of hospitality and tolerance exists. The theoretical stage of colonisation, hospitality and tolerance perform similar scripts with similar actors. Bhabha speaks of 'a flawed colonial mimesis, in which to be Anglicized is emphatically not to be English'.[81] Brown says, 'Political and civic tolerance, then, emerges when a group difference that poses a challenge to the definitions or binding features of the whole must be incorporated but also must be sustained as a difference:

76 Derrida and Caputo, op. cit., n. 34, p.111.
77 Brown, op. cit., n. 6, p. 73.
78 Butler, op. cit., n. 42.
79 Hillis Miller, op. cit., n. 37, p. 178.
80 H.K. Bhabha, *The Location of Culture*, London: Routledge:, 1984, pp. 85–92, at p. 86.
81 Ibid., p. 87.

regulated, managed, controlled.'[82] In other words, the incorporation must be partial, incomplete and a resemblance in order to maintain the binary of coloniser/colonised, host/guest, tolerator/tolerated; and the nauseous, partial nature of the incorporation needs to be evacuated and hidden. The situation of *hôte* (host) as guest and guest as *hôte* (host)[83] is experienced as an indigestible violence that 'turns the home inside out'.[84] In relation to failed and destitute asylum seekers excess would be Žižek's unavailable red ink; the lie that exists but is unavailable. Žižek comments:

> . . . one starts by agreeing that one has all the freedoms one wants – then one merely adds that the only thing missing is the 'red ink': we 'feel free' because we lack the very language to articulate our unfreedom. What this lack of red ink means is that today, all the main terms we use to designate . . . human rights, and so on – are false terms . . . in this precise sense, our freedoms themselves serve to mask and sustain our deeper unfreedom.[85]

The legal duty in the HRA to be proportionate demonstrates the internal contradictions and instability of the construction of the HRA, founded on the excess of hospitality and tolerance, the paradox of proportionality resting on disproportionality. Perhaps the unavailable red ink masks the lie of proportionality and tries to hide the violent and inhuman excesses in the discourse and practice of the UK asylum process. Excess is articulated both in terms of 'too much', 'indulgent', 'over the top' and its opposite, to restrict, regulate, and withdraw, as manifest in the voucher scheme, no recourse to public funds, and the withdrawal of health and social care services.

Derrida examines the state response to the rapidly evolving technological advances in communication, information sharing and globalisation, surveillance, policing of the shifting borders and the space and place of the state and comments:

> The state, suddenly smaller, weaker than these non-State powers, both infra- and supra-state – the classical State, or cooperation of classical States – makes excessive efforts to catch and monitor, contain and reappropriate to itself the very thing that is escaping it as fast as possible. This sometimes takes the form of a rearrangement of the law, of new legal texts, but also of new police ambitions attempting to adapt to the new powers of communication and information, in other words also to new spaces of hospitality.[86]

82 Brown, op. cit., n. 6, p.71.
83 J. Derrida, *Adieu*, trans. P.A. Brault and M. Naas, Stanford: Stanford University Press, 1999.
84 Westmoreland, op. cit., n. 14, p. 6.
85 Žižek, *Welcome to the Desert of the Real*, op. cit., n. 3, p. 2.
86 Derrida, op. cit., n. 48, p. 57.

Derrida's analysis resonates with Foucault's notion of governmentality.[87] The HRA places a duty on all public authorities in the UK to act in a way that respects and fits with the rights in the European Convention.[88] The contradictions, paradoxes and predicaments of tolerance and hospitality become exacerbated as the territory of the host is under continual transition through globalisation, virtual technologies, revolution and ecology. Here the seminal work of Menzies Lyth[89] on the functioning of social systems as a defence against anxiety could be translated, to enable a detailed analysis of the social and psychic manoeuvres deployed by the state to disavow anxiety. These manoeuvres include fragmentation of the subject and increasing proximity, to create a sense of distance through the use of officialdom, uniforms, the removal of proper names in place of a diagnosis, and disrupted lines of responsibility and accountability. Menzies Lyth's study is based on a large teaching hospital where patients are referred to by their diagnosis rather than their actual name, for example identified and referred to as 'the liver in bed three'; nurses' uniforms and systems operating within the hospital are designed to disavow 'the constituent outside' and to diminish any opacity of the subject. This could be understood as the common function of the episteme. In other words, the quite contradictory, incongruent practices and ideology of the Home Office, immigration, interpretation and application of the HRA align for a common function. The common function is 'of the power of the host to remain master of the premises',[90] where the unknown is made known, dressed up in the language of human rights.

The master's tools will never dismantle the master's house[91]

To conclude, in this chapter the object under analysis is also the tool for analysis. The method of using a multi-dimensional theoretical lens to focus in on the detail of the conceptual foundation of the HRA enables the microscope of theory to expose how the limits of the HRA are constituted. Attending

87 M. Foucault, 'Governmentality', in G. Burchell, C. Gordon and P. Miller (eds), *The Foucault Effect: Studies in Governmentality*, Chicago: University of Chicago Press, 1991.

88 British Institute of Human Rights, *A guide for Refugees and Asylum Seekers*, 2006. Available at: <http://www.bihr.org.uk/documents/guides/a-guide-for-refugees-and-asylum-seekers> (accessed 27 June 2011).

89 I. Menzies Lyth, 'The Functions of Social Systems as a Defence Against Anxiety: A Report on a Study of the Nursing Service of a General Hospital', *Human Relations*, vol.13, 1959, pp. 95–121.

90 Derrida and Caputo, op. cit., n. 34, p.110.

91 A. Lorde, 'The Master's Tools Will never Dismantle the Master's House', comments at The Personal and the Political Panel, Second Sex Conference, New York, 29 September 1979, reprinted in A. Lorde, *Sister Outsider: Essays and Speeches*, Trumansburg, NY: Crossing Press, 1984, p. 110.

with rigour to the detail of the constituent parts – here the parts are the concepts of tolerance, testimony and hospitality – enables the specificity of and bridges between the concepts, to produce the tools for analysis. Analysis of the situatedness of knowledge; of the particular space and place each concept inhabits within the construction of the HRA, produces a critical lens. For example, taking the concept of hospitality, the impossibility of unconditional hospitality opens up the possibility of tracing and critiquing the legal and political conditions of hospitality. Thus, rather than impossibility as fore-closure, impossibility becomes a tool that opens up a critique of legal and political conditions. Another example is that of the 'constitutive outside', where the space and place of the other produces 'opacity' not only of the subject but of all kinds of borders operating within the context of globalisa-tion. Rather than opacity as foreclosure, it becomes a tool for constructing a basis for ethical responsibility. The situation of asylum seekers in relation to the HRA challenges the very core of its ethics as translated in and through the practices and policy of UK state apparatus. The question of the foreigner, personified by asylum seekers and experienced as 'being-in-question of the question', where they are the subject under question, could become a tool for 're-founding' or reformulating some basic concepts, such as the concept of borders. Perhaps borders in all of their forms (not just in the form of hospi-tality, tolerance or testimony) should be at once the subject under and the tool for analysis as articulated by Ngugi Wa Thiong'o:

> When we think of borders, we think of divisions. But, if a border marks the outer edge of one region, it also marks the beginning of the next region. As the marker of an end, it also functions as the marker of a begin-ning. Without the end of one region, there can be no beginning of another. Depending on our starting point, the border is both the begin-ning and the outer edge. Each space is beyond the boundary of the other. The border in between serves as both the inner and the outer of the other. It is thus at once the boundary and a shared space.[92]

92 N.W. Thiong'o, 'Borders and Bridges: seeking Connections Between Things', in F. Afzal-Khan and K. Seshadri-Crooks (eds), *The Pre-occupation of Postcolonial Studies*, Durham, NC: Duke University Press, 2000, p. 120.

13 The politics of protest and the Human Rights Act

Peter Tatchell[1]

I'm very glad to join you here today and want to thank Salford University for organising this conference. It's always very valuable to bring together human rights defenders, and those who think, write and organise around human rights, so that we share our experiences and learn from each other – both within this country and with our friends and comrades internationally.

As you all know, I'm involved in a wide range of human rights campaigns, in the United Kingdom and worldwide including in Palestine, West Papua, Russia, Zimbabwe, Iran and Pakistan, to name just a few. These campaigns are all about international solidarity to support the brave and courageous human rights defenders in those countries, who are often operating in conditions of great tyranny and oppression. During the struggle against apartheid, it was very important to South Africans who were struggling for freedom to know that the world was on their side. The international campaign against apartheid was a very important and valued counter to the apartheid regime, and a very important argument to the internal struggle by the South African people themselves.

I guess I'm best known for my work on lesbian, gay, bisexual and transgender human rights. It is this work that I want to share with you today, and rather than say lesbian, gay, bisexual and transgender every time, I will just abbreviate it to LGBT.

I began campaigning for LGBT human rights way back in 1969 at the age of 17. I'd already been active in various other human rights work but it was then that I realised that I was gay. I can remember, very clearly, in late 1969, making a conscious decision that I would do something – although I initially didn't know what – to help progress the cause of LGBT freedom. I didn't have any model, I didn't have a template. I didn't come from a political family. I came from the suburbs, from a very conservative working-class background.

1 This is the transcript of the paper delivered at the Salford Human Rights Conference 2010. For more information about Peter Tatchell's human rights campaigns and to make a donation: <www.petertatchell.net>.

Nothing prepared me for this decision that I'd made, but I did have an awareness of the history of some key social justice struggles; in particular the struggles of the suffragettes, who I felt a great emotional and political connection with, and also the struggle of the black civil rights movement in the United States, which was contemporary to my awareness of my own sexuality.

During the 1960s, the nightly TV bulletins were filled with news about the Freedom Riders in the Deep South, about the Black Panthers, Malcolm X, Martin Luther King, and their historic, momentous struggle for black freedom in the United States. I was able to look at this struggle and take inspiration from it, to see the methods that black communities in America were using to fight for their freedom. I asked myself: why couldn't we use similar methods to fight for queer freedom as well?

So I began this LGBT activist journey, inspired by the suffragettes and the black civil rights movement. The more I learned, the more inspiration I got. I read about Gandhi, and sought to adapt his ideas about non-violent civil disobedience to the contemporary struggle for LGBT human rights. I can remember thinking in this period, late 1969, that I had three basic aims. The first was to take LGBT rights from the margins to the mainstream, the second was to make LGBT human rights acceptable and respectable, and the third was to end legal discrimination against LGBT people in the UK – and in the process to change public consciousness, to change hearts and minds, to change public opinion. I understood that it was no use having perfect equality laws, if popular attitudes remain homophobic.

So those were the three aims that I began with. I remember thinking: 'I wonder how long this is going to take?' I studied other movements and I thought that if we were lucky, maybe we would get legal equality within fifty years. In the end I was proven somewhat pessimistic, because it only took forty years to end nearly all homophobic legal discrimination in the UK. This goal had been achieved by 2009, forty years from 1969 when I began.

Over the last decade, since 1999, when the ban on lesbian and gay people serving in the armed forces was lifted, since then virtually every homophobic law in Britain has been repealed. This is an astonishing, extraordinary pace of change; the fastest, most successful law reform campaign in this country's history. Britain, in the 1980s, had more homophobic laws than any other country on earth, even more than the communist bloc, and some of these laws dated back not decades but centuries. The law that sent Oscar Wilde to prison in 1895, the law against so-called gross indecency between men, was only repealed in 2003. The main anti-sodomy law, enacted at the time of King Henry VIII, in 1533, was only finally repealed in 2003. So, the last decade has been a very momentous period of LGBT law reform and social change.

I mentioned that nearly all homophobic laws have been repealed. The one major discrimination that remains on the statute books is, of course, the ban on same-sex civil marriage. Now, in Britain, we have same-sex civil partnerships, which do remedy many of the injustices and inequalities that faced same-sex couples who, until 2005, had no legal recognition or rights whatsoever. Up until that point, relationships, love and commitment between people of the same sex, did not legally exist and were not acknowledged in British law. Civil partnerships changed that. I would not for one moment wish to diminish the significance, importance and value of that change. But having said that, civil partnerships are not equality. The only true equality is same-sex civil marriage. I say that as someone who shares the feminist critique of marriage, and who personally would not want to get married. Nevertheless I defend, absolutely, the right of other people to make that choice. That choice should be available to everyone, regardless of gender or sexual orientation.

Many people, even in the LGBT movement and community, ask: 'What's the fuss about? Civil partnerships include almost all the rights that go with civil marriage. So why make a fuss?' Well, I think that's the old 'separate but equal' argument, or rather, 'separate but not equal' argument. Black people in South Africa fought against apartheid because there were separate laws for black and white. They said, quite rightly: 'There should be one law for everyone; everyone should be equal regardless of race.' To me, the distinction between civil partnerships and civil marriage – where civil marriage is reserved for heterosexual couples and civil partnerships are reserved for same-sex couples – is a form of sexual apartheid: a differentiation in law based on sexual orientation which flies in the face of the democratic ethos that we should all be equal before the law. It concerns me greatly that we now have a situation where the homophobia of the ban on same-sex civil marriage is now compounded and extended by the heterophobic ban on opposite-sex civil partnerships. Because just as a same-sex couple cannot have a civil marriage, an opposite-sex couple cannot have a civil partnership. I think we need to say very loud and clear: 'Two wrongs do not make a right.' Just as a same-sex couple should have the option to have a civil marriage, so a heterosexual couple should have the option to have a civil partnership. I know quite a few of my feminist friends who would be delighted to be able to choose to have a civil partnership, rather than what they see as the baggage of patriarchy that goes with traditional marriage.

In terms of how we got here, to this place of near equality, it was a long, arduous struggle. Lesbian and gay human rights were, back in the 1950s, not deemed acceptable or respectable. Politicians and political parties almost universally ignored the issue right through to the 1990s. To get any debate in parliament was impossible. MPs were not willing to debate LGBT human rights because they were not deemed to be legitimate rights. They were regarded as contemptible, immoral and beyond the pale. Homosexuality, even in terms of rights and welfare, was seen as being too disgusting to bring before the House of Commons. Even in the 1980s, attempts to get parliament to debate LGBT equality were rebuffed. You had a handful of parliamentarians, and I mean literally a handful – only about four or five MPs and a similar number of Lords – who would raise LGBT issues. Nearly always, government ministers would bat them away. When MPs tried to get statistics on how many lesbian and gay people were being drummed out of the armed forces, they'd have to pressure and pressure ministers to get an answer. So often, the government regarded this issue as unseemly. Homosexuality was so reviled that our allies in parliament found great difficulty in getting the statistics. Eventually they did, through the persistence of a few dedicated MPs. That's how we learned the true scale of the homophobic persecution of military personnel.

The same goes for the number of LGBT people arrested for consenting sexual offences. For years, the Home Office, in effect, covered this up. We eventually discovered that, far from decreasing after the partial decriminalisation of male homosexuality in 1967, the number of arrests and convictions for consenting same-sex behaviour increased. In fact, in the early 1970s, the conviction rate for 'gross indecency' was four times greater than in the mid–1960s, before so-called decriminalisation. The LGBT community had a limited decriminalisation that was followed by ever greater repression.

As for the media, if it wasn't overtly and viciously homophobic, it would just ignore LGBT issues. Even Britain's main liberal paper, *The Guardian*, has a less than honourable record in terms of covering LGBT human rights abuses. It's only in the last fifteen or twenty years that *The Guardian* has begun to report these issues in a more objective and reasonable way. In the 60s and 70s, there were dozens of queer-bashing murders which *The Guardian* failed to report. You had thousands of gay men being arrested for victimless behaviour, which *The Guardian* mostly reported, if at all, in the tiny 'news in brief' section. By the 1980s, it gave prominent coverage to racist attacks and racial discrimination but its reportage of homophobic violence and arrests remained very poor.

In 1989, the number of gay and bisexual men convicted for the consenting offence of 'gross indecency' – an offence that only applied to sex between men – was almost as great as in 1954/55, in a period when homosexuality was totally illegal, and when the country was gripped by a McCarthyite homophobic witch-hunt. *The Guardian* gave hardly any coverage to these large-scale prosecutions. I had to plead and beg to get a story published. The paper seemed to not regard homophobic persecution as worthy of reporting.

Even mainstream human rights organisations were not always supportive of LGBT equality. Hats off to Irene Khan and others who have taken a stand, but let's not forget that, right up until the early 1990s, Amnesty International refused to campaign against homophobia and for people who were jailed on account of their homosexuality. Refused! Myself and my colleagues from the LGBT direct action group OutRage! had to blockade the headquarters of Amnesty International and chain the doors locked to pressure Amnesty to eventually change its stance.

We had similar experiences with many other human rights organisations: embarrassment, indifference, neglect and inaction. Until the early 90s, they seemed reluctant to campaign on LGBT human rights.

In the end, we did change Britain's laws, values and institutions. How? Lobbying mostly failed, at least initially. From the 1960s to the 1990s, we lobbied the police, judiciary, courts, politicians, churches and newspaper editors, without much success. We did try changing things from within the system: meeting with MPs and very occasionally with government ministers. We met police commissioners and so on. The results were pretty miserable. So, in desperation, we resorted to direct action. There were two objectives in mind. One was to expose, shame and embarrass those in power, who were enforcing homophobic laws and supporting homophobic discrimination. The other was, through high-profile spectacular protests, to put these issues in the news to get people thinking and talking about them, to raise public consciousness.

In the early 1990s, I did a research project to uncover the true scale of arrests and convictions for consenting homosexual behaviour. When it was publicised, the reaction from most people, even those who were quite homophobic, was: 'We had no idea, we had no idea.'

These revelations of police and judicial homophobia prompted a wave of enraged protests, spearheaded by OutRage! These included the famous 'kiss-in' in Piccadilly Circus in 1990. This was during a period when same-sex couples were being arrested, taken to court and convicted for kissing, touching, holding hands or cuddling in public places. No heterosexual couples were being arrested for this kind of affectionate behaviour, but lesbian, gay, bisexual and transgender people were, right up until the 1990s. When we held that kiss-in, first of all it drew public attention to the fact that these arrests and convictions were taking place. Secondly, it put the police on the spot. The kiss-in involved 300 couples daring the police to arrest them. One hour before the kiss-in began, I received a message, presumably with the authorisation of the then Metropolitan Police Commissioner, Sir Paul Condon, saying that as of five o'clock that day no same-sex couple would be arrested for merely kissing, cuddling or holding hands in the Metropolitan Police district.

We won even before the kiss-in took place. So it was with all the other issues around policing. We tried negotiating with the police. We had meetings in New Scotland Yard. The police would sit there, smile, shake our hands, give us tea and sandwiches, and then go away and order another series of raids. After three or four months of this charade, we decided that lobbying wasn't working. The meetings were just a PR exercise by the Metropolitan Police. We took inspiration from the Black movement, which had fought a long battle against the 'sus' laws and other racist policing policies.

From their experience, we knew that sometimes it is necessary to confront those in power, so that's what we did. We began a high-profile campaign of disrupting the press conferences of Sir Paul Condon, invading and occupying police stations that were organising raids and entrapment operations, and exposing the 'pretty police' – the agents provocateurs that the police were using to lure and arrest gay men. The police in those days used to send young, handsome officers, dressed in tight white jeans, black leather jackets and boots, into public toilets and parks. They'd play with their willies and any man who responded would get arrested. So we'd covertly photograph these officers and then staple their photos on trees in parks or fly-post them inside public toilets, warning people that these men were police agents provocateurs. Within three months of this campaign, the police were begging for us to come back to New Scotland Yard to resume negotiations. Being ever generous, we did. We came back with a set of demands, a set of concrete policies for a non-homophobic policing policy. Within one year, the Metropolitan Police had agreed to three-quarters of our demands. One thing they said in retrospect, not at the time but some years afterwards, was that our protest campaign was deeply embarrassing and created incredible discomfort at higher levels. Our key campaign message was: 'Why are the police wasting all these resources on arresting gay and bisexual men for victimless behaviour, where no one has complained and no one has been harmed, when they so often pleaded insufficient resources to deal with really serious crimes like armed robberies, street assaults, racist attacks, domestic violence, rapes, queer bashings and so on?' Why were they putting so many officers into policing victimless crimes when they should be putting them into tackling crimes with victims? These arguments were really embarrassing for the police. They helped us win public opinion on our side. Most ordinary people, even if they didn't agree with homosexuality, felt that this inordinate focus on policing consenting gay behaviour was a misplaced policing priority. In the end, the police did change. Within a year, three-quarters of our demands for a non-homophobic policing policy were adopted. Within three years, the number of gay and bisexual men convicted for the consenting offence of 'gross indecency' fell by two-thirds – the biggest, fastest fall ever recorded. This literally saved thousands of gay and bisexual men from arrest, conviction and all the adverse follow-on consequences like, in those days, losing your job and, if the person was married, the break-up of their marriage. It was a classic example of how direct action worked when negotiations and lobbying had failed.

The other thing the police later confided in retrospect was that we weren't just protesting. We were not just oppositionists and negative. When we came back into those negotiations with the police we had a set of concrete, practical policies – well-thought-out proposals on how the police could shift to a non-homophobic policing policy. We adapted some of these proposals from the experience of the Netherlands, Denmark and other countries in Europe that had already reformed the way they policed the LGBT communities. Presenting the police with tangible, alternative policies was also a very important factor in convincing them to change.

I'll just finish with just one other example of a successful direct action campaign. You may recall the outing of the bishops in 1994, when OutRage! named ten Anglican bishops and called on them to 'Tell the Truth'. We outed them not because they were gay and not because they were in the closet, but because they were hypocritical homophobes. They went along with the church's anti-gay policies in public while having gay relationships in private. It was their double standards and two-facedness that motivated us to name them.

Outing the bishops was not a method of first resort. It was one of last resort. We had long pleaded with the church to reconsider its homophobic policies. We asked for meetings with the then Archbishop of Canterbury, Dr George Carey. He refused to meet us. So we decided to up the ante. Our gripe was that the church was pursuing homophobic policies, not only condemning homosexuality and sacking gay priests, but supporting homophobic laws. The leadership of the Church of England was opposing gay equality in the 1990s. The Archbishop of Canterbury was against an equal age of consent, against legal recognition of same-sex relationships, against lesbian and gay couples being allowed to foster or adopt children and so on.

We gave the church a warning: 'If you don't stop this homophobia, do not be surprised if we retaliate. We know there are key people in high positions in the church who are homophobic in public, but homosexual in private. We will expose their hypocrisy if they don't stop their homophobia.' The church hierarchy was so arrogant. It didn't think we'd dare carry out this threat. But we did. We named those ten bishops on the opening day of the General Synod in London in late 1994.

It caused shockwaves, not only throughout the church but throughout the wider society too. The end result was positive. As far as I know, every single one of those ten bishops ceased publicly endorsing homophobic discrimination. Two went on to become allies of the LGBT community. Subsequently, a month later, the House of Bishops passed what is, to this day, one of its strongest condemnations of homophobic discrimination – something it would have never done, if we had not outed those bishops.

On that positive note, I thank you all and leave you with this one final thought: it takes many small streams to make a mighty river. I am very proud to have been one of the thousands of small streams that have helped make the mighty river for queer freedom.

14 Blacklisting of trade unionists

What is the point of human rights law?

Dave Smith and Keith Ewing

> The Consulting Association files are blatant evidence of systematic victimi-
> sation but this is not about being a victim. This is about justice for honest
> building workers who raised genuine concerns about safety or complained if
> they were not paid. This is about multinational companies not being above
> the law. This is about human rights for trade unionists.
>
> Steve Kelly, blacklisted construction worker

Introduction

Millions of people around the world are members of a trade union. In its
simplest form, a trade union is a free association of individuals working in the
same workplace or industry who cooperate in order to present a united voice
to their employer.

They believe that the most effective way to improve living standards, safety
and equality is by working people joining together in some form of collective
activity rather than dealing with issues on a purely individualistic basis. Their
actions are a manifestation of the old slogan: Unity is Strength.

In the UK alone, hundreds of thousands of individuals have taken up the
unpaid role of union representative, assisting and organising workers with
grievances in occupations as diverse as airline pilots, professional footballers,
nurses, teachers, actors, engineers, scientists, refuse collectors, civil servants
and care workers, to name but a few.

In a globalised society increasingly dominated by trans-national corporations, trade unions often provide the only credible counterbalance to the
power of Capital. Whilst trade union influence may have declined over the
recent period, unions remain the largest voluntary campaigning organisations
in the UK, with the Trades Union Congress (TUC) representing some six and
a half million people.

Trade union rights are human rights

Trade union rights are enshrined in a vast range of international human
rights instruments. Indeed the volume of the provision is matched only by the

ignorance of human rights lawyers as to its content, though there are also human rights organisations that appear disinclined to talk about trade union rights. So toxic is the brand, and so unpopular the cause, that even well-known human rights organisations are to be seen jostling at the back of the crowd, rather than in its vanguard, when it comes to defending trade unions and their members.

No doubt to the great embarrassment of the soft liberal centre, trade union rights are protected by the Universal Declaration of Human Rights,[1] as well as by the International Covenant on Civil and Political Rights[2] and its cold war sibling, the International Covenant on Economic, Social and Cultural Rights.[3] Freedom of association underpins the UN's International Labour Organization (ILO), the core right to organise and collective bargaining conventions of which have been ratified by the United Kingdom.[4]

There are also important regional treaties, notably the European Convention on Human Rights (ECHR), Art. 11 of which grants 'everyone the right to Freedom of Association and Assembly with others, including the right to form and to join trade unions for the protection of his interests'. The latter has been greatly enriched by recent decisions of the European Court of Human Rights, which has read this guarantee widely to include the right to bargain collectively, and the right to strike,[5] guided in part by ILO Conventions and the European Social Charter of 1961.[6]

---

1 UDHR, Art. 23(4): 'Everyone has the right to form and to join trade unions for the protection of his interests.'
2 ICCPR, Art. 22(1): 'Everyone shall have the right to freedom of association with others, including the right to form and join trade unions for the protection of his interests.'
3 ICESCR, Art. 8(1)(a): 'The right of everyone to form trade unions and join the trade union of his choice, subject only to the rules of the organization concerned, for the promotion and protection of his economic and social interests. No restrictions may be placed on the exercise of this right other than those prescribed by law and which are necessary in a democratic society in the interests of national security or public order or for the protection of the rights and freedoms of others.'
4 Freedom of Association and Protection of the Right to Organise Convention, 1948 (Convention 87); Right to Organise and Collective Bargaining Convention, 1949 (Convention 98); Workers' Representatives Convention, 1971 (Convention 135).
5 See especially *Demir and Baykara v Turkey* [2008] ECHR 1345. See also *Enerji Yapi-Yol Sen v Turkey*, Application No. 68959/01, 21 April 2009.
6 On which see Art. 5: 'With a view to ensuring or promoting the freedom of workers and employers to form local, national or international organisations for the protection of their economic and social interests and to join those organisations, the Contracting Parties undertake that national law shall not be such as to impair, nor shall it be so applied as to impair, this freedom. The extent to which the guarantees provided for in this article shall apply to the police shall be determined by national laws or regulations.' The same is reproduced in the Revised Social Charter, 1996, which the United Kingdom has not ratified.

But human rights are meaningless unless they can be enjoyed by those to whom they are addressed. We can have treaty after treaty, but all are simply rusting monuments to the vanities of lawyers, politicians and statesmen if they are honoured only in the breach. This chapter is concerned with a group of workers from the UK construction industry who have been victimised over many years in a particularly cowardly way and we invite human rights lawyers to reflect more seriously on the universality of their discipline. This is what happens when we pick and choose our human rights.

From the Economic League . . .

Before the activities of the Consulting Association were exposed, blacklisting was associated with an organisation called the Economic League that was set up in 1919 to 'reinforce support for democracy, personal freedom and free enterprise',[7] or in the view of some 'to fight Bolshevism'.[8] Well known for having maintained a blacklist of trade unionists, the Economic League was said to have 'had 40 current Labour MPs on its files, including the [then] chancellor, Gordon Brown, and prominent trade unionists, as well as journalists and thousands of shopfloor workers'.[9]

An investigation by the House of Commons Employment Committee in 1991 heard from the TUC that the 'unsavoury', 'sinister' and 'all too often inaccurate' practice of blacklisting 'affects the job prospects of thousands of individuals', referring to evidence from former employees of the Economic League, former personnel managers of firms that had used the League's services, and blacklisted employees themselves. According to the TUC, this evidence 'bears witness to the inaccurate and unreliable nature of much of the League's information'.

The TUC also noted that the League 'makes no attempt to check the accuracy of its records', with individuals being branded as unsuitable for employment on the basis that 'they attended meetings of unions or voluntary organisations, or if they wrote to a newspaper, or their name appeared on a petition'. The TUC was equally concerned that employers using the services of the League did not check the information supplied; they 'do not ask what information is held, but reject applicants simply on the ground that they are on the League's files'.[10]

These concerns were echoed by the Committee in its report, which referred to the evidence it had received about 'inaccurate information being handed out in secret, with employers rejecting applications simply on the basis that

---

7 K. D. Ewing, *Britain and the ILO* (1994), London: Institute of Employment Rights, pp. 11–12.
8 *The Guardian*, 9 September 2000.
9 Ibid.
10 TUC, *Memorandum by the TUC: Inquiry into Recruitment Practices*, HC 176-II (1990–91).

the League had information about them, rather than weighing carefully what the information was, and information being kept [about] many more than the 10,000 individuals quoted by the League'.[11]

The Economic League was given a very uncomfortable time by the Select Committee, oral evidence being taken from its Director General and its Director of Information and Research. Although acknowledging that they had 10,000 names on their list (including MPs), they were reluctant to say who their clients were or how much they paid, though it transpired at a subsequent oral evidence session with the Ford Motor Company that the latter had been clients and had paid £25,000 in the previous year, after their representative was pressed hard to provide this information.[12]

The League's records were kept in manual files at a time when the Data Protection Act 1984 applied only to computerised records. For its part however, the League said that 'they will provide any applicant with the information held on them, if any. To do this [the League] request[s] from the applicant full details of their past employment, National Insurance numbers, etc.', though the Select Committee pointed out that 'this has given rise to the suspicion that this information will be added to the League's records'.[13]

Clearly unimpressed, the Committee recommended that legislation should be introduced to give workers the same rights as consumers turned down by credit reference agencies. Thus, information supplied to employers about potential employees would be passed to the employee refused employment, and the employee given a chance to refute the information. In addition, it was proposed that organisations that provide information about employees should have to be licensed and subject to a code of practice, modelled on the Employment Agencies Act 1973.[14]

But, although falling a long way short of a recommended ban on blacklisting, even the notions of transparency and accountability on the part of those who operated blacklists was too much for the government of the day. This is despite the fact that the Employment Act 1990 had made it unlawful to refuse to employ someone because of trade union membership, a provision that would have been more effective if blacklisting was also unlawful, as demanded by the ILO.[15]

---

11 House of Commons Select Committee on Employment, *Recruitment Practices*, HC 176 (1990–91), para 42.
12 House of Commons Employment Committee, Minutes of Evidence, 17 October 1990, HC 176-II (1990–91), Q 842–4.
13 House of Commons Select Committee on Employment, *Recruitment Practices*, above, note 11, para 40.
14 Ibid., paras 46 and 47.
15 Case No 1618 (283rd Report of the Freedom of Association Committee (Interim Conclusions)), and 287th Report of the Freedom of Association Committee. See Ewing, above, note 7, pp. 11–12.

. . . to the Consulting Association

The Economic League has, however, since disbanded, and although no one knows what happened to its database, there has been some speculation. . . . Fast forward to 6 March 2009, when the UK data protection watchdog, the Information Commissioner's Office (ICO), published a report into a previously unknown organisation called The Consulting Association.[16] John McDonnell MP described the findings in the ICO report as 'one of the worst ever cases of organised abuses of human rights in the UK' and has called for a full public inquiry.[17]

For decades The Consulting Association had operated a secret blacklisting operation on behalf of 44 multinational building contractors. The companies identified by the ICO are all household names including:

Amec, Amey, B. Sunley & Sons, Balfour Beatty, Balfour Kilpatrick, Ballast Wiltshire, Bam Construction (HBC Construction), Bam Nuttall (Edmund Nutall Ltd), CB&I, Cleveland Bridge UK Ltd, Costain UK Ltd, Crown House Technologies, Carillion, Tarmac Construction, Diamond M & E Services, Dudley Bower & Co. Ltd, Emcor (Drake & Scull), Emcor Rail, G. Wimpey Ltd, Haden Young, Kier Ltd, John Mowlem Ltd, Laing O'Rourke, Lovell Construction (UK) Ltd, Miller Construction Limited, Morgan Ashurst, Morgan Est, Morrison Construction Group, N.G. Bailey, Shepherd Engineering Services, Sias Building Services, Sir Robert McAlpine Ltd, Skanska (Kaverna/Trafalgar House Plc), SPIE (Matthew Hall), Taylor Woodrow Construction Ltd, Turriff Construction Ltd, Tysons Contractors, Walter Llewellyn & Sons Ltd, Whessoe Oil & Gas, Willmott Dixon, Vinci PLC (Norwest Holst Group).[18]

The ICO investigation discovered a centralised database holding personal sensitive information on 3,213 individuals; the vast majority of the information related to trade union membership or workers raising concerns about safety issues. The information on this database was covertly shared among the

16 Available at <http://www.ico.gov.uk/news/current_topics/consulting_association.aspx> (accessed 23 June 2011). See also *The Guardian*, 6 March 2009 for an excellent article co-written by journalist Phil Chamberlain who had done much to expose the practice. Some of the issues in this section are also considered in D. Smith, 'Deliberate and Vindictive Victimisation', 16 *International Union Rights* 28, 2009; D. Smith 'Not Safe to be a Safety Rep', *TSSA Journal*, December 2009/January 2010, and D. Smith, 'Notes on a Scandal', *Safety and Health Practitioner*, 26 May 2010.

17 *Morning Star*, 25 February 2011. The matter was also pursued in Parliament by Michael Clapham MP, and was considered by the Joint Committee on Human Rights: see HL Paper 5–1; HC 64–1 (2009–10).

18 ICO press release, 'ICO seizes covert database of construction industry workers', 6 March 2009. Available at: <http://www.ico.gov.uk/news/current_topics/-media/documents/pressreleases/2009/TCA_RELEASE_060309.ashx> (accessed 24 June 2011).

building firms to prevent these trade union members from gaining employment on their projects, the construction firms each paying a £3,000 annual subscription fee to The Consulting Association for this service.[19]

The written constitution of The Consulting Association makes it clear that the body was not merely a company providing facilities to the building industry but rather it was an 'unincorporated trade association' actually owned and controlled by its member companies. Quarterly meetings took place, with representation required at director level.[20] While staff at the The Consulting Association collated the blacklist, the organisation did not employ spies on every building site; instead specific entries recorded on files were supplied by senior managers of the major contractors.

The latter forwarded information on any employees, workers or subcontractors regarded as 'troublemakers'.[21] Each file entry is dated and accompanied by a reference number denoting the company that supplied the information. File entries included workers' names, addresses and National Insurance numbers, and also photographs, work history, press cuttings, medical information, discussions about family relationships and political leanings, and sometimes wildly inaccurate malicious gossip.[22] Some of this material is now in the public domain as a result of the tribunal cases discussed below.

Whilst the majority of files are only one page with a few personal notes attached, there are a number of files that take up many pages: these are reserved for workers prepared to become elected unpaid union representatives, and to raise issues on behalf of their co-workers. Some of the files are up to 49 pages long. Entries on individual files refer to workers raising concerns about unpaid wages or an employer's failure to adhere to nationally negotiated agreements. Safety representatives are targeted for speaking to managers about asbestos, near fatal accidents, electrical safety or poor toilet facilities.

Official union safety reps' credentials (which are intended to provide some legal protection) have been photocopied and appear in the files. Files of other victimised workers have entries such as:

DO NOT EMPLOY UNDER ANY CIRCUMSTANCES
need to monitor route onto projects via Employment Agencies.
would not employ – active in trade union

---

19 BIS, *The Blacklisting of Trade Unionists: Revised Draft Regulations*, December 2009, p 9. Available at: <http://www.bis.gov.uk/files/file53734.pdf> (accessed 28 October 2011).
20 The Consulting Association, *Constitution* (as agreed and amended after meeting of 7 February 2002).
21 A good account of how the system worked in practice is provided by the Employment Tribunal in the *Willis* case below, where a particular manager was said to have introduced the company in that case to the Consulting Association.
22 Some detail of the content of the personal files is provided in K.D. Ewing, *Ruined Lives: Blacklisting in the UK Construction Industry*, Institute of Employment Rights, 2009.

It is apparent that on some occasions individuals have been followed, and telephone calls have been made to their spouses. A report in the *Daily Mirror* raised possible links to the Special Branch.[23]

The mechanics of blacklisting took place by means of individual checks on job applicants. Senior managers supplied The Consulting Association with the names of workers applying for employment on their projects. If a name appeared on the database, this information was passed back to the company and the worker was simply not employed (or was dismissed if already engaged). This was mainly completed by telephone to avoid a paper trail, but occasional faxes have been retained and supplied as employment tribunal evidence.

Each name check cost £2.20. Between April 2006 and February 2009 the construction companies paid in total more than £450,000 to use the service. Invoices seized show that, in 2008 alone, one division of the Scandinavian giant Skanska was billed £28,000. This equates to thousands of checks on individual workers. Given the simplicity of the process and the scale of the 44 companies involved, it is hardly surprising that their systematic black-listing had such a devastating impact upon employment prospects.[24]

During an unprecedented building boom lasting from 1996 to 2008, when the industry was desperate for skilled labour, many blacklisted workers found it almost impossible to gain work. Steve Acheson (a blacklisted electrician) has been unemployed for eight out of the past ten years, with numerous entries on his blacklist file every time he attempted to gain fresh employment. Hundreds of skilled and highly trained workers either suffered repeated dismissals, and prolonged periods of unemployment, or else were forced to leave the industry altogether in order to meet their housing costs.

The ICO's raid led to the prosecution of a man called Ian Kerr, who had played a prominent part in its activities. The action was brought under the Data Protection Act 1998 for processing data without having first registered with the Commissioner as required by the Act.[25] Although Mr Kerr's conviction was applauded, many in the construction industry were surprised by the leniency of the £5,000 fine handed down by Knutsford Crown Court,[26] to which the case had been committed by the Macclesfield Magistrates' Court on the ground that the maximum fine they could impose was 'wholly inadequate'.[27]

But what about the multinational construction companies, the household names that had used the blacklist over many years and on an industrial scale? Here we encounter the limits of the Data Protection Act 1998, with the ICO pointing out on 4 August 2009 that 'it is not a criminal offence to breach the data protection principles, which is why the ICO chose only to prosecute Ian Kerr for failing

---

23 *Daily Mirror*, 20 January 2010.
24 ICO press release, above, note 18.
25 Data Protection Act 1998, ss 17–19.
26 On which see D. Smith, 'Blacklisting', *Socialist Lawyer*, February 2001, p. 23.
27 *Construction News*, 23 July 2009.

to notify as a data controller'.[28] Under the Act, the Information Commissioner can only issue an enforcement notice – which effectively means 'stop doing it', and only if you don't will it be a criminal offence. What is surprising, however, is that enforcement notices were issued against only 14 companies.[29]

The impact of being blacklisted for trade union membership

Steve Acheson, Graham Bowker and Colin Trousdale

Steve Acheson, who feared he had been on a blacklist, said he was 'absolutely thrilled' by the findings of the information commissioner's investigation.

The electrician, 55, from Denton, south Manchester, said: 'I've been angry for so long. It affects your character and demeanour – it's the fact it's so blatantly unjust. I'm hoping that because of this brilliant success I'll be able to get my family life back and it will open the doors for me and others to get back to work.'

He suspects that being blacklisted for his trade union membership is the reason why he has only had 36 weeks' employment in the last nine years. He believes he was blacklisted after winning three separate employment tribunals and felt he had been punished for those victories.

'Up to 2000 I'd be getting a couple of job offers a week from agencies. I was a supervisor on the Channel Tunnel, I worked all over the Middle East. I should be securing £40,000 a year but I've not had an employment agency phone me in nine years.'

Graham Bowker, from Oldham, has only worked for five months since winning an employment tribunal case along with Acheson in 2006. The electrician, who has been in the industry since 1971, believes he deserves compensation. He said: 'I've been at snapping point a few times. You've got a job, then you haven't got a job. You get to the stage where you think, should

---

28 Information Commissioner, 'Trade in personal data jeopardised employment prospects', press release, 4 August 2009. Available at: <http://www.ico.gov.uk/upload/documents/library/data_protection/notices/construction_firms_040809_final.pdf> (accessed 28 October 2011).

29 The companies were told that they must: 'Refrain from using, disclosing or otherwise processing any personal data obtained from Mr Kerr unless the processing is necessary for the purpose of complying with any obligation under the Act or by law or for obtaining legal advice or for the purpose of, or in connection with, any legal proceedings; Ensure that if any personal data relating to recruitment is obtained from a source other than the data subject, the data subject is, in so far as is practicable, provided with the information specified in paragraph 2(3) at Part II of Schedule 1 to the Act in accordance with the First Data Protection Principle; and ensure that if any personal data relating to recruitment is disclosed to a third party for use in connection with the recruitment of workers, the data subject is, in so far as is practicable, provided with the information specified in paragraph 2(3) at Part II of Schedule 1 to the Act in accordance with the First Data Protection Principle.'

I bother? As soon as I've phoned and given my national insurance details, they don't call back. I'm going to ask my MP, Michael Meacher, to see if I can get my NI number changed.'

Colin Trousdale, 50, from Bacup, Lancashire, has found work hard to come by since he spoke up for colleagues who were sacked two years ago. Trousdale, who has 35 years' experience as an electrician and is an active trade union member, believes he is on a blacklist. He said the information commissioner's action . . . made him very happy.

The pressure of not finding work contributed to the breakup of his marriage and forced him to move out of Manchester to find work, he said. 'I had to move away because employers would look at the postcode and think I was a troublemaker,' he said.

The Guardian, 6 March 2009

The futility of the Human Rights Act

So much for Kerr and the multinationals. But what about the victims? The Consulting Association blacklist represents secret, centrally orchestrated and repeated victimisation over a prolonged period. As such it appears to provide prima facie evidence of deliberate systematic breaches of Art. 11 of the European Convention on Human Rights. One of the first questions to be answered is: what in practice does Art. 11 of the ECHR cover?

While everyone has the right to be a member of a trade union, does this right only cover union membership or does it extend to protect workers who play a more active role in the union? Could an employer reasonably argue that they are not victimising anyone for being a member of a trade union per se but they are inoculating themselves against union 'militants' who would disrupt their production? This question has been answered in the famous *Wilson and Palmer* decision at the European Court of Human rights,[30] which concludes that:

> . . . it is of the essence of the right to join a trade union for the protection of their interests that employees should be free to instruct or permit the union to make representations to their employer or to take action in support of their interests on their behalf. If workers are prevented from so doing, their freedom to belong to a trade union, for the protection of their interests, becomes illusory. It is the role of the State to ensure that trade union members are not prevented or restrained from using their union to represent . . .[31]

30 [2002] ECHR 552.
31 Ibid., para 44.

The ruling of the Strasbourg court in *Wilson and Palmer* emphasises the right for a worker not only to be a passive member of a trade union, but also to be free to play an active role and receive full representations without fear of victimisation or discrimination.[32] There is also an ILO Convention on Workers' Representatives that requires states that have ratified the Convention to take action to provide 'effective protection' for such representatives.[33] This is in addition to the protection already provided by ILO Convention 98.[34] ILO Conventions are important sources, which have been used recently by the Strasbourg court to inform the content of Convention rights.[35]

But although blacklisting appears to constitute a breach of Art. 11, there is not much that the blacklisted construction workers could do about it under the Human Rights Act. As the organisations that are breaching the convention rights are private companies, it is not possible to make a direct claim against them under the HRA.[36] And although the courts have developed a domestic law of privacy from Art. 8 of the Convention to protect the super-rich by means of super-injunctions and the like,[37] there are few who would put money on the courts developing similar rights to protect the privacy of the construction workers who built the homes in which the celebrities live.

This is not to say that the Human Rights Act is wholly irrelevant to the claims of blacklisted construction workers, with two provisions highly significant to legal proceedings under other legal instruments, such as the Trade Union and Labour Relations (Consolidation) Act 1992, ss 137 and 152, which are considered below. The first is s 2, which requires the employment tribunals and other courts in any such cases to have regard to Strasbourg jurisprudence when applying domestic law, which would mean reading domestic law widely to embrace the decision in the *Wilson and Palmer* case.

Also important is s 3, which provides that 'So far as it is possible to do so, primary legislation and subordinate legislation must be read and given effect

---

32 Thereby contradicting a decision of the House of Lords to the contrary: *Wilson v Associated Newspapers Ltd* [1995] 2 AC 454.
33 ILO Convention 135, Art. 1: 'Workers' representatives in the undertaking shall enjoy effective protection against any act prejudicial to them, including dismissal, based on their status or activities as a workers' representative or on union membership or participation in union activities, in so far as they act in conformity with existing laws or collective agreements or other jointly agreed arrangements.' See also ILO Recommendation 143.
34 See note 4 above, referring especially to Art. 1.
35 See ILO Convention 98, Art. 1: 'Workers shall enjoy adequate protection against acts of anti-union discrimination in respect of their employment.' See also Case No. 1618 (283rd Report of the Freedom of Association Committee (Interim Conclusions)) and 287th Report of the Freedom of Association Committee.
36 Despite the fact that in some cases it is likely they would be working on public projects with public money.
37 *HRH The Prince of Wales v Associated Newspapers Ltd* [2006] EWHC 522 (Ch).

in a way which is compatible with the Convention rights.' As is well known to human rights lawyers, this is a provision that has been widely construed, it having been said in the Court of Appeal in the important labour law case, *X v Y*,[38] that:

> the interpretative duty imposed by section 3 applies to the same degree in legislation applying between private parties as it does in legislation which applies between public authorities and individuals. There is nothing in the HRA which, either expressly or by necessary implication, indicates a contrary intention. If the position were otherwise, the same statutory provision would require different interpretations depending on whether the defendant was a public authority or a private individual.[39]

And as is well known to labour lawyers, the relationship between legislation relating to unfair dismissal (highly germane to the position of some blacklisted workers) and the HRA was expressly considered in the same case. There Lord Justice Mummery recommended that it was advisable for employment tribunals to deal with points raised under the HRA in unfair dismissal cases between private litigants in a structured way. He suggested the following framework of questions:

1   Do the circumstances of the dismissal fall within the ambit of one or more of the articles of the Convention? If they do not, the Convention right is not engaged and need not be considered.
2   If they do, does the state have a positive obligation to secure enjoyment of the relevant Convention right between private persons? If it does not, the Convention right is unlikely to affect the outcome of an unfair dismissal claim against a private employer.
3   If it does, is the interference with the employee's Convention right by dismissal justified? If it is, proceed to (5) below.
4   If it is not, was there a permissible reason for the dismissal under the ERA, which does not involve unjustified interference with a Convention right? If there was not, the dismissal will be unfair for the absence of a permissible reason to justify it.
5   If there was, is the dismissal fair, tested by the provisions of section 98 of the ERA, reading and giving effect to them under section 3 of the HRA so as to be compatible with the Convention right?[40]

---

38 [2004] EWCA Civ 662, [2004] ICR 1634.
39 Ibid., para 66 (Dyson LJ).
40 Ibid., para 64.

Colin Trousdale

I was costing companies thousands and impacting on the profits. They would say to the client these are the risks that are involved and this is the safety equipment we will provide in order to negate those risks. But then to maximise profits they will circumvent the risk assessments and not provide the safety equipment.

So then I'll come along as safety officer and say, 'I'm reading your risk assessment, you said you'll provide this, where is it? We're not doing that job until you provide that.' So that then is impacting on their profits because they had to go out and buy all the safety equipment that they costed for in the first place.

If companies weren't cutting corners to maximise output it could be a much safer industry. It might take a week longer, but nobody's going to die. How can you put a price on life?'

Manchester Mule, March 2011

The Employment Tribunal lottery

So, faced with a breach of Convention rights but no means to enforce them, the only option for blacklisted construction workers was in the employment tribunals, with claims under the Trade Union and Labour Relations (Consolidation) Act 1992, s 137 which makes it unlawful for an employer to refuse to employ someone because of trade union membership; and s 152 of the same Act, which makes it unfair to dismiss an employee because of trade union membership or activities.

In a few cases, the tribunal process has had positive outcomes. In one case,[41] Phil Willis was able to claim that he had been refused employment by CB&I (UK) Ltd after it had consulted the database.[42] Willis had applied for a job at the Isle of Grain and had submitted his CV to a Mr Ron Barron, the senior HR and employee relations manager, who – according to the employment tribunal – regularly consulted the Consulting Association (CA) database. Indeed, he was said by the tribunal to have consulted it 984 times between April and September 2007 at a cost of over £2,000.[43]

---

41 Case No 1101269/09 (30 November 2010).
42 Employing roughly 13,000 employees worldwide, London based CB&I 'is one of the world's leading engineering, procurement and construction companies and a major process technology licensor'. On its website it also states that 'Ensuring the health and safety of our employees, our customers and the public – and protecting the environment – are core values of CB&I. We uphold these values in the same way that we ensure the quality of our work – by implementing rigorous controls through every phase of our projects': <http://www.cbi.com/about-cbi/hse> (accessed 28 October 2010).
43 Case No 1101269/09 (30 November 2010), para 10.

Although the company claimed that the CA was used 'simply to assist with reference check', this was not believed by the tribunal, which also expressed surprise that Mr Barron had failed to attend as a witness, thought to be strange in view of 'his crucial position in the context of the case'.[44] No satisfactory explanation was provided for Mr Barron's absence,[45] it being noted, however, not only that it was Mr Barron who had introduced the blacklist to the respondent company,[46] but that Mr Barron 'contributed to the blacklist by updating details of the respondent's employees and those who had applied for jobs' (including Mr Willis).[47]

In this case the employment tribunal thought it highly likely that Mr Barron had consulted the CA about Mr Willis's application; it rejected evidence for the company that the claimant's job application was rejected because there was no vacancy. It also reproduced extracts from Mr Willis's CA file, which contained personal information about him, as follows:

> . . . '*involved in one day strike of steel erectors*' and a reference to him as '*a wolf in sheep's clothing. A lovely chap on the surface but able to stir*'. The entry said that he '*Claimed unfair dismissal for trade union activities*' and that he '*will sit in the background and "wind up" in other forums, is very clever, covers himself well*'. In the last part of the entry he is stated to be '*Part of a militant conspiracy*', and '*He has had recent successful claim at IT for discrimination on grounds of TU membership. Wife, Cathy Willis, is similarly militant*' . . . '*Tactic is to get someone onto a site – this opens door to other extremist colleagues*'.[48]

In this case the complaint under s 137 was upheld, and Mr Willis was awarded compensation of £18,375, which included £4,000 for injury to feelings, and another £2,000 aggravated damages, to reflect the fact that the employer had not only consulted the blacklist but had contributed to it, and had added information about Mr Willis which 'he could not challenge any more than he could challenge what was already there'.[49] By all accounts a fine outcome, and indeed Phil Willis has not been alone in successfully using s 137.[50]

---

44 Case No 1101269/09, para 8.
45 Ibid.
46 Ibid., para 11.
47 Ibid., para 12.
48 Ibid., para 22.
49 Ibid., para 35.
50 An employment tribunal in Ashford found that Paul Tattersfield had been refused employment by Balfour Beatty Engineering Services Ltd because he was on The Consulting Association's blacklist. He was awarded just under £24,000, including loss of earnings, injury to feelings and aggravated damages. 'Anti-blacklist demo targets Olympic site', *Blacklist blog*, available at: <http://www.hazards.org/blacklistblog/2011/03/03/anti-blacklist-demo-targets-olympic-site/> (accessed 24 June 2011).

Unfortunately, however, this has not been the experience of the vast majority of the construction workers who have pursued tribunal claims, with most having been thrown out without even reaching a full-merits hearing. References to the Human Rights Act by counsel representing the workers have had little if any discernible impact in these cases, with tribunals adopting a fairly predictable approach, and for the most part probably having little room for manoeuvre.[51] These problems have been encountered particularly in the cases under the Trade Union and Labour Relations (Consolidation) Act (TULRCA) 1992, s 152.

In March 2010, *Dooley v Balfour Beatty* became the first unfair dismissal claim to reach a full-merits hearing at Employment Tribunal.[52] Despite documentary evidence that Balfour Beatty had supplied information to the blacklist database (which the judge described as 'ghastly'),[53] a majority found in favour of the company. The blacklisting evidence was not disputed by Balfour Beatty, who themselves provided the blacklist file as part of *their* bundle of documents, arguing that the information on the file was justification for a dismissal in the early 1990s.

Unlike TULRCA s 137, which applies to a 'person', s 152 applies only to 'employees',[54] and it was held that Dooley was not an employee of Balfour Beatty. *Dooley* is likely to be typical of many of the blacklisting cases because of the specific employment relationships that exist in the UK construction industry, which differ substantially from the classic employer/employee format.[55] The industry operates almost entirely on the basis of contractors and subcontracting, in circumstances that cause the workers in question to fall outside the narrow definition of an employee.[56]

On major projects, large subcontracted packages are themselves subcontracted out, often multiple times, until those working on site are often nominally 'self-employed' or employed through employment agencies. The outcome is that even on a major project with several thousand workers engaged on site, it is entirely possible that the principal contractor may only directly employ 10 or 20 people. These will almost always be the senior office-based staff. Even

---

51 As in *Dooley v Balfour Beatty*, below, where the tribunal acknowledged that its decision was made having regard to the HRA.

52 Case No. 2203380/2009 (5 March 2010).

53 S. Griffith, 'Balfour Beatty wins blacklist tribunal', *building.co.uk*, 8 March 2010, available at: <http://m.building.co.uk/news/balfour-beatty-wins-blacklist-tribunal/3159499.article> (accessed 24 June 2011).

54 For a classic example of the problems this causes in cases of alleged anti-union activity, see *O'Kelly v Trusthouse Forte* [1983] ICR 728.

55 See M. Harvey, *Undermining Construction: The Corrosive Effects of False Self-Employment*, Institute of Employment Rights, 2001.

56 This is a problem familiar to students of labour law, and is examined powerfully by Harvey, ibid., who contends that there is evidence of mass false and illegal self-employment in the construction industry.

a large proportion of the technical and junior/mid-management team are often employed via employment agencies.

These are arrangements over which workers have no choice. They are the terms of engagement required by the companies, and it will be *very* rare that a major contractor would *ever* directly employ skilled trades such as brick-layers, carpenters, electricians, plumbers or engineers. Nevertheless, the major contractor still exercises control over all staff on their project, including those engaged by subcontractors. Quality control, inductions, discipline, access and egress, security and especially safety remain under the authority of the major contractor.

Steve Kelly

I appeared at Bury St Edmunds Employment Tribunal on 20 January 2010 for a one-day mediation. This was to avoid a costly, time-consuming three-day hearing, in the words of the chairman, which had been set for April. The case stemmed from a section of my 18-page blacklist file where I had been sacked from Colchester Barracks in 2007 for refusing to work from a mobile scaffold. **Sir Robert MacAlpine**, the main contractor had insisted in a safety induction that no worker should operate one of these towers unless they were trained and had a ticket to say they had passed the course. I was working for a subcontractor called **ECS Ltd**, from Norwich. Their supervisor said: 'It's easy to use – move this handle up, down, forward, back – simple!' Workers have been killed using these towers in the past. When I refused to use this tower I was sacked – reason given poor workmanship. This appeared on my file. **Sir Robert McAlpine** had contacted Ian Kerr at the **Consulting Association** and this, along with many other lies, has been placed on a secret blacklist file and used against me for the last 10 years and will be in the future, preventing me from working in construction, certainly on any large sites. A settlement was reached and I was awarded £2,400 – still blacklisted, still kept off sites, unable to organise workers.

The government's response

The government lifted the spirits of many people when it appeared willing to do the decent thing, announcing in 2009 that it would introduce laws to put an end to the blacklisting of trade unionists. Finally accepting its responsibilities in this area, it would be easy for the government to respond quickly, as the Employment Relations Act 1999 already gave it the power to introduce regulations to deal with blacklisting.[57] These powers had never been used because in the government's view there was no evidence that blacklisting continued to be a problem.

---

57 Employment Relations Act 1999, s 3.

The matter was considered again in 2004 during a review of the Act, and again it was thought that nothing needed to be done,[58] and there may well have been cause to believe that the Data Protection Act 1998 had done the trick with its treatment of trade union membership as sensitive personal data and subject to special protection as a result.[59] But having created great expectations that the law would be changed and the scourge addressed, the mood of trade unionists darkened when the small print of the government's proposals was carefully studied.

When the penny dropped, it became all too clear that nothing was going to change. There would be no right not to be blacklisted, no automatic compensation for being blacklisted, and no criminal penalties. Nor was it good enough to say that protection from blacklisting would apply only to 'trade union activities' and not 'trade union related activities'. This would leave it to the courts to decide whether an activity – say unofficial action – was in or out, and how far in or out.

Nor was it good enough to fudge the question of participation in industrial action. The government's strategy seemed to be based on the hope that the judges would say that official industrial action was protected, thereby permitting blacklisting to continue for those engaged in unofficial action, as well as those who had unwittingly got on the wrong side of the police on a picket line. These were by no means fanciful concerns, the tribunal in the *Dooley* case making clear that even if he had been an employee, they would still have decided against him because of the nature of his activities.

The tribunal in *Dooley* examined the applicant's blacklist file at some length, and drew particular attention to entries relating to his involvement with a body called the Joint Sites Committee, said to have been a loose group of activists operating outside the official trade union structures.[60] It also drew attention to his role as a shop steward and his involvement in industrial action. According to a majority of the employment tribunal, the activities of the JSC were not the activities of an independent trade union, albeit they were for the purposes of s 152.[61]

These and other points were put to the government forcefully by no fewer than 26 trade unions in the good faith belief that the government had engaged in a genuine consultation. But no significant change was made to the original proposals; the government now bending both knees in servile fealty to the construction companies, being told by the Heating and Ventilating Contractors' Association that the 'vetting of prospective employees was necessary to weed out troublemakers, criminal elements or other undesirable people'.[62]

---

58 DTI, *Review of the Employment Relations Act 1999*, 2003, para 3.20.
59 See Data Protection Act 1998, s 2(d) (though this applies only to membership of an independent trade union).
60 *Dooley*, above, note 52, para 7.2.
61 Ibid.
62 BIS, *The Blacklisting of Trade Unionists: Revised Draft Regulations*, above, note 19, p. 9.

So right on cue the government concluded that 'it does not wish to deter employers from vetting prospective employees'.[63] Even more alarming, the government was careful to ensure that the narrow focus of the new Blacklist Regulations 2010 will guarantee that 'virtually all vetting activity, which should *normally* have nothing to do with trade union matters, is left unaffected'.[64] What is this other than an open invitation to employers to continue to engage in blacklisting (even of trade unionists)?

We should thus not be surprised that allegations of blacklisting should surface before the ink on the regulations had even had an opportunity to dry, alleged to be alive and well on the most high-profile construction site in the world: the London 2012 Olympic Park. On 14 February 2011, Frank Morris was dismissed from the Olympic Park Media Centre by an electrical firm called Daletech Services who were contracted to Skanska, with Carillion being main contractor.[65]

For what they are worth, the regulations prohibit the compilation, use, sale or supply of a prohibited list,[66] a term defined to mean a list that 'contains details of persons who are or have been members of trade unions or persons who are taking part or have taken part in the activities of trade unions', and that is compiled 'with a view to being used by employers or employment agencies for the purposes of discrimination in relation to recruitment or in relation to the treatment of workers'.[67]

Under the regulations, it is unlawful to refuse to employ someone for a reason related to a prohibited list,[68] unlawful to subject someone to a detriment,[69] and unfair to dismiss an employee for the same reason.[70] An action may also be brought for a breach of statutory duty by someone who claims to have suffered loss as a result of the breach of the prohibition about the compilation, use, sale or supply of a prohibited list.[71] In all cases however, the only remedy is financial compensation, and there is no obligation on any court or tribunal (and in some cases no power) to order the confiscation and destruction of any blacklist.[72]

---

63 BIS, *The Blacklisting of Trade Unionists: Revised Draft Regulations*, p. 11.

64 Ibid., p. 9, emphasis added.

65 'Anti-blacklist demo targets Olympic site', *Blacklist blog*, above, note 50. The dismissal took place after Mr Morris blew the whistle on the continued use of the blacklist after a number of union activists were removed from the project, and a supervisor later admitted that they were dismissed because their name came up on a list of union troublemakers. Frank Morris's dismissal has resulted in numerous protests and an Employment Tribunal application supported by his trade union, RMT.

66 SI 2010 No 493, reg. 3(1).

67 Ibid., reg. 3(2).

68 Ibid., reg. 5.

69 Ibid., reg. 9.

70 Ibid., reg. 12.

71 Ibid., reg. 13.

72 On the powers of the civil courts (but not the employment tribunals, see ibid., reg. 13(2).

But apart from the failure to use the criminal law as a sanction and as a sign of public displeasure at particularly nasty practice, despite the failure properly to address questions of scope, and despite questions about remedies, the treatment of Ian Kerr's victims also left much to be desired, their treatment being compared very unfavourably with the treatment of people sacked in the 1970s for non-membership of a union where a closed shop had operated. Then, the incoming Tory government introduced a retroactive compensation scheme for the so-called victims.[73]

If a Tory government could compensate those sacked for not being union members, surely a Labour (a *Labour*) government could have done the same for people sacked because they were trade unionists? A scheme of this kind would provide a guaranteed minimum amount of compensation for people who appeared on the Consulting Association database, with the compensation to be increased for those who had suffered loss as a result. For good measure, some unions proposed that any compensation scheme should be paid for by the companies that had trafficked in human misery and had violated human rights.

Conclusion

The problems being encountered in the tribunal system and the refusal on the part of the government even to contemplate a retroactive compensation scheme means that the last port of call for the blacklisted may have to the Strasbourg court (though at the time of writing there is also the possibility of legal proceedings under the Data Protection Act 1998 eventually getting off the ground).[74] As has been the case with so many issues since the enactment of the HRA, it is the court in Strasbourg that continues to do the heavy lifting on human rights abuses.[75]

While in Strasbourg, there are a number of questions which the victims of blacklisting will no doubt wish the European Court of Human Rights to investigate. There is of course the obvious and important question of whether there has been a breach of their Convention rights (Art. 8 (privacy) along with Art. 11 (freedom of association)) which the government has failed to address, despite the much-vaunted human rights culture it claims to have introduced. This, however, is not the only question that needs answers.

---

73 Employment Act 1982, Sch. 1. See K.D. Ewing and W.M. Rees, 'Closed Shop Dismissals 1974–80: A Study of the Retroactive Compensation Scheme', (1983) 12 ILJ 148.
74 It is to be pointed out that the retroactive compensation scheme introduced by the Employment Act 1982 appears to have been stimulated at least in part by an adverse ruling of the European Court of Human Rights in *Young, James and Webster v United Kingdom* (1982) 4 EHRR 38.
75 See also *Gillan and Quinton v United Kingdom* [2010] EHRR 28.

Thus, why was the Department for Business, Innovation and Skills given access to the unredacted files of blacklisted workers, without the consent of the workers in question? Just as pertinent, what – if any – are the links between those who operate blacklists on behalf of construction companies and the State? Does (or has) the Metropolitan Police Special Branch,[76] and/or the security and intelligence services receive (or received) information from private sector blacklisters, and do these agencies provide information to blacklisters?

As has already been suggested, the failure of the domestic human rights culture to deal with the privacy and freedom of association rights of construction workers stands in sharp contrast to the willingness of the courts to fashion a private remedy based on privacy from the provisions of the ECHR for the super-rich, and their fawning desire to protect celebrities – such as Fred Goodwin, Andrew Marr and Ryan Giggs as well as countless others – from the unwanted attentions of the press.[77] Super-injunctions have been granted, and hundreds of thousands of pounds have been paid in settlements after journalists hacked into messages left on mobile phones.[78]

Beneficiaries include Sir Fred Goodwin, reported to have been protected by injunction to prevent details of an affair with a senior RBS colleague from being made public.[79] According to *The Independent*, Goodwin claimed that disclosure

> would have a very substantial impact on the way in which friends, colleagues and business contacts relate to me and therefore a serious nega- tive impact on my personal life and career.[80]

This just about says all that needs to be said about British human rights law. Already hijacked by those with money and power. And already more concerned to protect a failed millionaire banker and his mistress from embarrassment, than to protect low-paid construction workers and their families from a covert and sustained abuse of power that ruined hundreds of lives.

---

76 Now Counter-Terrorism Command: see A.W. Bradley and K. D. Ewing, *Constitutional and Administrative Law*, 15th edn, Harlow: Longman, 2010, ch. 25.

77 What is interesting is that in these cases the conduct protected from disclosure was the behaviour of the individuals themselves that was destructive of family life. In the case of the blacklisted construction workers it was the behaviour of others that was destructive of family life.

78 D. Sabbagh, 'News of the World phone hacking: 12 questions from the Guardian', *Guardian Organ Grinder Blog*, 24 January 2011. Available at <http://www.guardian.co.uk/ media/organgrinder/2011/jan/24/news-of-the-world-phone-hacking> (accessed 24 June 2011).

79 *Daily Telegraph*, 10 March 2011: 'Sir Fred Goodwin, the former chief executive of the Royal Bank of Scotland, has obtained a super-injunction banning the publication of infor- mation about him, it has been disclosed on the floor of the House of Commons.'

80 *The Independent*, 11 June 2011.

Brian Higgins

The Blacklist is an economic, social and political prison. I have served a life sentence and other workers continue to be imprisoned. In cases like my own, the Blacklist effectively takes the form of house arrest because of its effect on a person's social life. My wife was also deeply affected and badly scarred. More often than not, she was forced to financially support me, and our two children, on her low wage as a care worker. This has had a devastating effect on our standard of living. To her great credit my wife supported me and our family unstintingly. She held us together when things got really tough – which it did quite often. We kept our dignity intact and just managed to keep our heads above water by almost completely sacrificing our social life. My wife had to take out loans, which we could not afford, since my credit rating was zero due to very long spells of unemployment. All of this is the direct result of the building employers deliberately using the Blacklist, time and again, to deny me the right to work and to earn a living.

Part IV

The future? Confronting the Bill of Rights

15 Security, citizenship and responsibilities beyond the Human Rights Act

Towards a British Bill of Rights and Responsibilities in the UK

Derek McGhee

In this chapter, I will examine the political context associated with the debates on the Human Rights Act (HRA) and also the Labour Government's Bill of Rights and Responsibilities. Why? Because there are lessons to be learnt from our recent past as we move into this new period of transition under the Coalition Government, who have announced in their coalition agreement to establish a commission to investigate the creation of a Bill of Rights.[1]

It will be suggested here that these debates and proposals for a Bill of Rights in the UK are the site for the emergence of a clash between two types of politics: a 'politics of citizenship' and a 'politics of human rights' in which the 'dual commitments of liberal democracies', that is, to international human rights and collective self-determination[2] are in tension. This tension between the universal and the particular, with regards to civic rights and human rights is part of what Žižek refers to as 'the rebirth of the old distinction between human rights and the rights of citizens' which involves the process of narrowing the rights of citizens through repackaging the political rights of citizens as a mere 'secondary gesture'[3] for example, with regards to debates on the conditional relationship between rights and responsibilities; but also with regards to the processes of radical exclusion under the 'war on terrorism' where the treatment of foreign-born 'terrorist suspects' can be best described in Arendtian terms as a matter of deciding who has 'the right to have rights' in the name of public safety.[4] In this chapter, the tension between 'civic rights' and 'human rights' will be examined through examining what the recent

1 Cabinet Office, *The Coalition: Our Programme for Government*, HM Government, 2010, p.10. Available at: <http://www.cabinetoffice.gov.uk/news/coalition-documents> (accessed 17 June 2011).
2 S. Benhabib, 'Of Guests, Aliens, and Citizens: Re-reading Kant's Cosmopolitan Rights', in W. Rehg and J. Boham (eds), *Pluralism and the Pragmatic Turn*, Cambridge MA.: MIT Press, 2001, p. 363.
3 S. Žižek, *Welcome to the Desert of the Real*, London: Verso, 2002, p. 95.
4 D. McGhee, *The End of Multiculturalism? Terrorism, Integration and Human Rights*, Berkshire: Open University Press and McGraw-Hill, 2008, p. 25.

Labour Government and Conservative Opposition had to say about the potential Bill of Rights with regards to the relationship between: (1) human rights and 'public safety'; (2) rights and responsibilities; and (3) the need to bolster what is perceived to be a weak sense of citizenship in contemporary Britain. In many ways, this chapter is an examination of what Nancy Fraser, in her book *Scales of Justice*, calls 'the politics of framing', which involves debates on the setting of boundaries, associated with decisions on who is included and who is not included. For Fraser, the boundary-setting aspects of the political is among the most consequential of political decisions.[5]

The debates surrounding the potential Bill of Rights offer a rich vein of intersecting discourses and strategies, associated with what were thought to be our two main political parties in the UK in the run-up to the general election in 2010. For example, these debates are a site for us to recognize the tabloid collusive ambivalence of the Labour Government with regards to the HRA and their authoritarianism with regards to the British Bill of Rights and Responsibilities; but also to observe David Cameron's explicit hostility to the HRA. At the same time, when we step away from the party-political rhetoric, we can see that at least some aspects of our democratic institutions, such as the Joint (House of Lords and House of Commons) Committee on Human Rights (JCHR), have attempted to take a longer term view with regards to the development of a human rights culture in the UK. In many ways it fell to the JCHR, in the context of the Labour Government and Conservative Opposition's ambivalent, securitized and 'nationalistic' rhetoric on human rights and citizenship, to attempt to salvage the potential Bill of Rights from party political short-sightedness, illegality and jingoism.

The chapter will consist of two main parts. The first part will explore the relationship between the Human Rights Act and the potential Bill of Rights, and the second will examine the Labour Government's rationale for introducing a Bill of Rights. In this second part, I will examine how the Labour Government was attempting to use what they call a British Bill of Rights and Responsibilities as a vehicle for making responsibilities explicit, enhancing 'public safety' and for strengthening citizenship. Part two will also explore the JCHR's alternative UK Bill of Rights and Freedoms, which insists on the uncoupling of exclusive 'Britishness', citizenship criteria and contingent responsibilities from the Bill of Rights. It will conclude with an exploration of the initial signs that the potential Bill of Rights in the UK could be developed alongside Lord Goldsmith's recommendations in his Citizenship Review for the development of a statement of rights and responsibilities for citizens, not unlike the Dutch Charter of Responsible Citizenship. The conclusion will include analysis of the Green Paper *Rights and Responsibilities: Developing a Constitutional Framework*, published by the Ministry of Justice in 2009, and of

---

5 N. Fraser, *Scales of Justice; Re-imagining Political Space in a Globalizing World*, Cambridge: Polity, 2008, p. 22.

particular note here will be the shift in emphasis from the Bill of Rights and Responsibilities to a non-legalistic Declaration of Rights and Responsibilities. It will be suggested below that the later shift from a legal Bill of Rights to a non-legal charter or declaration (of responsible citizenship) is an attempt to resolve some of the opposition that the Ministry of Justice under Jack Straw has faced in its attempt to use the Bill of rights to address three 'deficits': the security deficit; the citizenship deficit and especially the responsibilities deficit.

The Human Rights Act: a (precarious) stepping stone to the Bill of Rights?

The Human Rights Act of 1998 has been described variously by former Home Secretary Jack Straw as 'not having an easy childhood' and as being 'an Aunt Sally; unfairly blamed for a host of other issues', especially through misreporting on the part of the media and sometimes through the misapplication of the Act by public authorities.[6] Ultimately the Human Rights Act was 'a victim of circumstance'[7] given that the 9/11 attacks in the USA happened when the Act had been implemented for barely a year. As a result of 9/11 and the ensuing 'war on terror' the same government that had introduced the Human Rights Acts pre–9/11 'came to see the Act as an obstacle in the so-called "war on terror" '[8] in the post–9/11 context. When we realize how closely connected the Human Rights Act and the potential British Bill of Rights are in, for example, the Labour Party's recent history, then the Labour Government's orientation to human rights and the Human Rights Act have a particular bearing on the questions 'What is the new Bill of Rights for?' and 'What is it supposed to do for Britain?' I shall deal with these questions in the next part of the chapter. In this part, I want to spend a little time exploring the relationship between the Human Rights Act and a potential British Bill of Rights.

Francesca Klug, in numerous speeches and articles delivered and published between 2007 and 2009, has traced the relationship between the Act and the potential Bill. Klug is extremely skilful in heading off the Eurosceptic backlash against the Human Rights Act (mostly spearheaded by the Conservatives under David Cameron) as being a foreign (European) imposition, when she reminds us, as did the *Governance of Britain* Green Paper, that British lawyers drafted the European Convention on Human Rights (ECHR).[9]

6 J. Straw, 'Changing the face of human rights', Ministry of Justice, 2009, p. 3. Available at: <http://www.justice.gov.uk/news/sp280109.htm> (accessed 17 June 2011).

7 Ibid.

8 F. Klug, 'A Bill of Rights: What for?', The Smith Institute, 2007, p. 4. Available at: <http://www.lse.ac.uk/collections/humanRights/articlesAndTranscripts/FK_SmithInstitute_07.pdf> (accessed 17 June 2011).

9 F. Klug, ' "Solidity or wind?" What's on the menu in the Bill of Rights debate?' *Open Democracy*, 2009, p. 8. Available at: <http://www.opendemocracy.net/article/solidity-or-wind-what-s-on-the-menu-in-the-bill-of-rights-debate> (accessed 17 June 2011). See also Klug's Chapter 2 in this volume.

According to Klug, the late Labour leader, John Smith, committed the Labour Party to a British Bill of Rights as early as 1993. Smith suggested a two-stage approach to this process. He suggested that 'the quickest and simplest way' of introducing 'a substantial package of human rights' would be first to pass a Human Rights Act, which would incorporate into British law many aspects of the ECHR, completing the processes that began under Attlee with the ratification of the ECHR in 1951, followed by Wilson in 1966 granting individuals the right to directly petition the European Court of Human Rights in Strasbourg.[10] The second stage, the stage we in Britain are currently in (or potentially entering), is to introduce a British Bill of Rights. The introduction of a British Bill of Rights was first suggested at the Labour Conference in 1993 by the then Home Affairs Spokesperson, Tony Blair, who, in support of an all-party Commission, called for the drafting 'of our own Bill of Rights', following the incorporation of the ECHR into UK law.[11] The 1997 Labour Manifesto reflected the first part of this process and the Human Rights Act was introduced the following year.[12]

As noted above, a year after the implementation of the Human Rights Act (implemented in 2000) the 9/11 attacks occurred in North American cities. One has to wonder how the Human Rights Act would be perceived in the UK if it were not for 9/11 and the subsequent 7/7 terrorist bombings in London. The Human Rights Act has suffered from a poor childhood indeed: not only has the Act suffered from post–9/11 ambivalence and lack of sustained support on the part of the Labour Government, the Act has also been the focus of a hostile media (especially sections of the tabloid press), who have taken every opportunity to perpetuate damaging myths about the Human Rights Act and the misapplication of rights to the undeserving – criminals and terrorists – in what Liberty has described as 'a concerted media campaign'.[13] Klug has suggested a degree of collusion, post–9/11 and especially post–7/7, between senior members of the Cabinet and this hostile media reporting, by suggesting that at times the former Prime Minister Tony Blair sounded 'like a cheerleader for the tabloids' negative spin' on the Human Rights Act.[14] The Department for Constitutional Affairs suggests that with regard to the media's reporting on the Human Rights Act, 'too much attention has been paid to individual rights at the expense of the interests of the wider

---

10 Klug, 'A Bill of Rights: What for?', p. 3.

11 Ibid.

12 Ibid.

13 J. Russell, 'Liberty's response to the Joint Committee on Human Rights: "A British Bill of Rights" ', 2007, p. 3. Available at: <http://www.liberty-human-rights.org.uk/pdfs/policy07/response-to-jchr-re-british-bill-of-rights.pdf> (accessed 17 June 2011).

14 F. Klug, 'A Bill of Rights: Do we need one or do we already have one?' Irvine Human Rights Lecture 2007, University of Durham, 2007, p. 14. Available at: <http://www.lse.ac.uk/collections/humanRights/articlesAndTranscripts/Durham07_Klug.pdf> (accessed 17 June 2011).

community'.[15] As well as what Klug describes as 'the tabloid onslaught against the Human Rights Act', which Labour Ministers compounded by showing little or no appetite to rebut these impressions,[16] there is also evidence that the Human Rights Act was bedevilled by poor public consultation and a general lack of preparation prior to implementation. For example, according to the Audit Commission's report *Human Rights: Improving Public Service Delivery*, published in 2003, 58 per cent of public bodies surveyed had no clear corporate approach to human rights.[17]

It is the ambivalent relationship between the Labour Government, the then Conservative Opposition and the Human Rights Act that I want to briefly focus on here. I want to first turn to the new Prime Minister David Cameron's views (when Leader of the Opposition) on what he calls a Modern British Bill of Rights, before returning to the Labour Government's agendas (in the next part). Ken Clarke has famously described David Cameron's ideas for the Bill of Rights as being xenophobic and based on legal nonsense, if he intends the Bill of Rights to be used as 'a get-out clause' from the ECHR.[18] It was during his speech on 'Balancing Freedoms and Security – a Modern British Bill of Rights', at the Centre for Policy Studies in June 2006, that David Cameron announced his party's intention to scrap the Human Rights Act and introduce what he calls 'a Modern Bill of Rights to define the core values which give us our identity as a free nation'. Cameron's intention in this speech was to attempt to outdo the Labour Government's increasingly tough stance on terrorism, and to court public opinion in the context of the confusion with regards to the alleged misapplication of the rights included in the Human Rights Act (as reported in some parts of the media). It was the *Chahal* ruling issued by the European Court of Human Rights in 1996 that, for Cameron, epitomized the failure of ECHR case law (compounded in the UK by the Human Rights Act). According to Cameron, the European Court and the Human Rights Act prevent governments from making judgments in the public interest if these judgments impact adversely on the rights of individuals, such as terrorist suspects. That is:

> A Home Secretary must have more flexibility in making a judgment and the public interest balance the rights of terror suspects against the rights of British citizens. At present the jurisprudence from cases such as *Chahal*

---

15 Department for Constitutional Affairs, *Review of the Implementation of the Human Rights Act*, 2006, p.1. Available at: <http://www.dca.gov.uk/peoples-rights/human-rights/pdf/full_review.pdf> (accessed 17 June 2011).

16 Klug, 'A Bill of Rights: What for?', p. 5.

17 Audit Commission, *Human Rights: Improving public service delivery*, 2003, p.7. Available at: <http://www.justice.gov.uk/guidance/docs/acrep03.pdf> (accessed 28 October 2011).

18 F. Klug, 'The Future: A constitutional settlement for modern Britain?', Smith Institute/Harvard Society Seminar, RUSI, 2007, p.2. Available at: <http://www.lse.ac.uk/collections/humanRights/articlesAndTranscripts/FK_SmithHansardJuly07.pdf> (accessed 17 June 2011).

prevent this happening. And the Human Rights Act compounds the problem. I believe it is wrong to undermine public safety – by allowing highly dangerous criminals and terrorists to trump the rights of the people Britain to live in security and peace.[19]

It should be noted that Cameron's solution to what he perceives to be the miscarriages of justice as a result of the inappropriate application of the Human Rights in British courts is different to the suggestions for rebalancing rights made by Jack Straw and former Home Secretary Jacqui Smith. Whereas Straw and Smith advocate the prioritization of 'public safety' through emphasizing ECHR Art. 2, the right to life, above other rights – which follows the previous Lord Chancellor, Lord Falconer's recommendations – David Cameron's solution is to abolish the Human Rights Act and replace it with a Modern British Bill of Rights and Responsibilities.[20] For Cameron:

A modern British Bill of Rights needs to define the core values which give us our identity as a free nation. It should spell out the fundamental duties and responsibilities of people living in this country both as citizens and foreign nationals. And it should guide the judiciary and the government in applying human rights law where the lack of responsibility of some individuals threatens the rights of others. It should enshrine and protect fundamental liberties such as jury trial, equality under the law and civil rights. And it should protect fundamental rights set out in the European Convention on Human Rights in clear and more precise terms.[21]

Cameron's initial ideas for his modern British Bill of Rights have many of the hallmarks of the Labour Government's own Bill of Rights and Responsibilities, especially the relationship between security, shared values, citizenship and responsibilities (which will be examined in the next part of this chapter). The major difference is that the Labour Government's intention, from John Smith in 1993 to the publication of the *Governance of Britain* Green Paper in 2007, was to build on the Human Rights Act. They perceived the Human Rights Act as a stepping stone to what Michael Wills (former Justice Minister under Labour) refers to as 'the next stage' of the UK's human rights story.

Although there is cross-party support for a British Bill of Rights, it should be noted that this potential document has become the repository for both the hopes and the fears of the nation. The Bill of Rights was seen by the previous Labour administration and also by the current Coalition Government as a

19 D. Cameron, *Balancing Freedoms and Security – A modern British Bill of Rights*, speech at the Centre for Policy Studies, 26 June 2006, p. 11. Available at: <http://www.guardian.co.uk/politics/2006/jun/26/conservatives.constitution> (accessed 17 June 2011).
20 Ibid., p. 14.
21 Ibid., p. 16.

major component of 'our' British national security strategy and citizenship strategy and as providing the opportunity for making British values and the responsibilities and duties that come with rights explicit.

Making responsibilities explicit and strengthening citizenship: the Labour Government and the Bill of Rights

The Labour Government, unlike David Cameron, had no plans for scrapping the Human Rights Act, but there have been a great many statements with regards to amending the Human Rights Act in respect of the interpretation of the ECHR.[22] Despite this, the Bill of Rights and Responsibilities is seen as an opportunity for addressing Britain's alleged (1) responsibilities deficit; (2) citizenship deficit; and (3) public safety deficit. It will be argued here that priorities 1 and 2 are potentially problematic because they create tensions between a domestic or territorially bounded 'politics of citizenship' and a universal 'politics of human rights'.

The determination to enhance 'public safety' in the Bill of Rights

It was in the *Governance of Britain* Green Paper (which was introduced a few months after Gordon Brown replaced Tony Blair as Labour Prime Minister) that the relationship between the potential Bill Of Rights and Duties and 'public safety' was introduced:

> The government itself recognized in its review last year of the implementation of the Human Rights Act, the importance which must attach to public safety and ensuring that government agencies accord appropriate priority to protection of the public when balancing rights. A Bill of Rights and Duties might provide a means of giving greater clarity and legislative force to this commitment.[23]

To add to this, Jack Straw stipulated a few months later in his Mackenzie-Stuart Lecture that 'Britain faces a new set of challenges, both internationally and at home, which requires us to look again at our mechanisms of rights'.[24] From the statement in the Green Paper, we can see that the Bill of Rights and Responsibilities is a component in Straw's wider project of rebalancing of

---

22 Klug, 'A Bill of Rights: Do we need one?', p.14.
23 Ministry of Justice, *The Governance of Britain*, CM 7170, 2007, p. 61. Available at: <http://www.official-documents.gov.uk/document/cm71/7170/7170.pdf> (accessed 17 June 2011).
24 J. Straw, Mackenzie-Stuart Lecture, University of Cambridge, Faculty of Law, 25 October, 2007, p. 2. Available at <http://www.justice.gov.uk/news/sp251007a.htm> (accessed 17 June 2011).

rights in favour of public security. According to Liberty, statements such as these undermine the Human Rights Act of 1998 by suggesting, as David Cameron has above, that in the Act insufficient regard is being paid to public safety and national security.[25] Liberty does not accept these criticisms of the Human Rights Act, suggesting rather that:

> public protection is at the core of the human rights framework. Not only do rights instruments like the 1998 Act play a vital role in protecting individuals against abuses by the state; they also require the state to take positive steps to protect the rights of those within their jurisdiction, including from the actions of other private individuals. The Human Rights Act requires criminal laws to be put in place to protect people from committing serious offences like murder, terrorism and rape.[26]

Liberty also reminds us that most of the rights in the Human Rights Act are not absolute and that 'one of the legitimate reasons for placing proportionate legal restrictions on the rights protected is public safety'.[27] The JCHR have been opposed to the government's ambitions for rebalancing the Human Rights Act in favour of 'public safety'. In their 2006 report *The Human Rights Act: the DCA and Home Office Reviews*, the JCHR demonstrated 'that there was no evidence that such an amendment to the human rights framework was necessary'.[28] In their *Bill of Rights for the UK?* Report of 2008, the JCHR stated that 'a surprising number of witnesses in our inquiry were opposed to a Bill Of Rights on this ground alone: they were concerned that the real motivation behind the proposal was to dilute the protections for human rights already contained in the Human Rights Act'.[29] The JCHR, in an attempt to reassure these witnesses and to send a clear message, placed the following in bold in their report:

> In our view it is imperative that the Human Rights Act not be diluted in any way in the process of adopting a Bill of Rights. Not only must there be no attempt to redefine the rights themselves, for example, by attempting to make public safety or security the foundational value which trumps all others, but there must be no question of weakening the existing machinery and the Human Rights Act for the protection of convention rights.[30]

25 Russell, op. cit., p. 9.
26 Ibid., p. 10.
27 Ibid., p. 10.
28 Joint Committee on Human Rights, *The Human Rights Act: The DCA and Home Office Reviews*, Thirty-second Report, 2006, pp. 35–9. Available at: <http://www.publications. parliament.uk/pa/jt200506/jtselect/jtrights/278/27802.htm> (accessed 17 June 2011).
29 Joint Committee on Human Rights (2008) *A Bill of Rights for the UK?* Twenty-ninth Report of Session 2007–08, p. 19. Available at: <http://www.publications.parliament.uk/ pa/jt200708/jtselect/jtrights/165/16502.htm> (accessed 17 June 2011).
30 Ibid., p. 20.

The JCHR's recommendations, in the 2008 and 2006 reports, were that the Labour Government must start acting consistently with regards to the HRA, if they were to successfully build on 'its achievements'. The Ministry of Justice cannot, on the one hand, talk about building upon the achievements of the HRA whilst also pandering to a hostile media's characterization of the HRA 'as some sort of terrorists' charter'.[31] Straw admitted to the JCHR that addressing this characterization of the Human Rights Act and the public's misperceptions 'is part of the framework for the current debate' on the Bill of Rights and Responsibilities.[32] The JCHR's consistent position, on the government's attempts to correct public misperceptions about the current regime of human rights protections under the HRA, is that 'the government should seek proactively to counter public misperceptions about human rights rather than encourage them by treating them as if they were true'.[33] The discourse on the necessity of rebalancing human rights in the name of public safety provides the overarching context for the examination of the unfolding tension to be explored below, with regards to debates on responsibilities and citizenship and the politics of human rights. The lesson of the 'war on terrorism' is that the distinction between citizens and foreign nationals (especially foreign national terror suspects) is that the former are considered to be 'rights-bearing' (although increasingly this is conditional on discharging the responsibilities of citizenship) and the latter, in many ways, are not.

The explicit articulation of responsibilities in the Bill of Rights

The presentation of the potential Bill of Rights as a 'next stage' in the evolution of Britain's human rights culture, as Michael Wills has suggested, is all about responsibilities, or more accurately the better articulation of 'the balance between rights to which we are entitled and obligations we owe each other'.[34] The better articulation of rights and responsibilities is not new; the alleged responsibilities deficit in Britain was a feature of New Labour's moral communitarianism as far back as 1995. For example, Tony Blair's lecture 'The rights we enjoy reflect the duties we owe' of 1995 depicted what Driver and Martell refer to as the New Labour perception that in the post-war years Britain was to eager to extend the scope of individual rights without any corresponding concern with the responsibilities attached to rights in the duties individuals owe as members of families and communities.[35] To overcome the responsibilities deficit, Labour's

---

31 J. Straw, ibid., p. 20.
32 Ibid.
33 Joint Committee on Human Rights, 2008, op. cit., p. 14.
34 M. Wills, 'The Constitutional Reform Programme', Leslie Scarman Lecture, 2008, p. 2. Available at: <http://webarchive.nationalarchives.gov.uk/+/http://www.justice.gov.uk/news/sp120208a.htm> (accessed 17 June 2011).
35 S. Driver and L. Martell, *New Labour: Politics after Thatcher*, Cambridge: Polity Press, 1998, p. 130.

communitarianism was, according to Driver and Martell, strongly laced with ideas of reciprocity and strong values.[36] Blair wrote: 'The only way to rebuild social order and stability is through strong values, socially shared, inculcated through individuals, family, government and institutions of civil society.'[37] For Driver and Martell, New Labour's communitarianism is about there being shared values to which we all adhere in the form of a 'new social morality'.[38] In an article written in 1997, Driver and Martell portray New Labour as being torn between what they describe as conformist and pluralist versions of communitarianism.[39] I think this is an accurate description of 'early' New Labour. However, if we fast-forward from the early days of New Labour to Tony Blair's last year in office as Prime Minister, in the post–7/7 context, we see that rather than being 'torn' between conformist and pluralist versions of communitarianism, the government had shifted into an explicitly conformist and morally prescriptive (integration) discourse. Citizenship, responsibilities and duties became intermingled in Blair's 'you are either with us or with the terrorists' conditional approach to integration. When it comes to the Labour Government's promotion of the Bill of Rights and Responsibilities, the communitarian concerns with regards to the alleged responsibilities deficit and the attempt to make the acceptance and sharing of particular values a condition of citizenship are a central feature. There are problems with this ambition (coming from both David Cameron's opposition party, and from Jack Straw and the Ministry of Justice) to better articulate the responsibilities that come with rights, and attempting to use the Bill of Rights and Responsibilities to reverse the alleged responsibilities deficit in contemporary Britain. For example, David Cameron, as noted above, suggests we need 'a modern Bill of Rights that . . . balances rights with responsibilities' and which 'spells out the fundamental duties and responsibilities of people living in this country';[40] whilst in the *Governance of Britain* Green Paper it was stated that a 'Bill of Rights and Duties could provide explicit recognition that human rights come with responsibilities and must be exercised in a way that respects the human rights of others'.[41] Liberty challenged this portrayal of a culture of rights without responsibilities in contemporary Britain. As with their criticism of the government's pandering to the misperception that individuals' rights are being prioritized over 'public safety', Liberty has already reminded us that, with few exceptions, the rights in the HRA are not absolute. It means that individuals' rights can be restricted for a number of legitimate reasons, the result being that it is permissible to make laws which restrict a person's rights in order to ensure compliance with individuals'

---

36 Driver and Martell, op. cit., p. 118.
37 Ibid., pp. 118–19.
38 Ibid., p. 119.
39 S. Driver and L. Martell, 'New Labour's Communitarianisms', *Critical Social Policy*, 17 (3), 1997, p. 27.
40 Cameron, 2006, op. cit., p. 2.
41 Ministry of Justice, 2007, op. cit., p. 61.

responsibilities to society.[42] At the same time, Liberty reminds us that there is a mass of criminal and civil laws that have existed for centuries that ensure that people act in accordance with their responsibilities to the state and other individuals.[43] These laws already operate to punish those who breach the criminal law and provide redress where a person has violated civil law responsibilities to others, that is, by acting negligently.[44] The problem, according to Liberty, is that David Cameron and Jack Straw's ambitions of trying to make these implicit and embedded responsibilities, obligations and duties explicit and 'easily understood',[45] by the public and new citizens alike, could be perceived as making individual rights 'in some way contingent upon compliance with one's responsibilities'.[46] The JCHR have similar concerns to Liberty; it is the potential for undermining the principle of universality through the overemphasis of the conditionality of rights (on the contingency that duties or responsibilities are performed) that resulted in the JCHR stating that 'rights cannot be contingent on performing duties or responsibilities'.[47] According to the JCHR, a number of the witnesses called to their inquiry expressed concerns that the 'inclusion of responsibilities in the Bill of Rights might mean that only the "deserving" would have full rights entitlement'.[48] Jack Straw told the JCHR that the longstanding desire to ensure that people realize that with rights come responsibilities was 'the first reason why the government is interested in moving beyond the Human Rights Act to a Bill of Rights'.[49] Straw informed the JCHR that he wanted to be able to confront people, who, in his view, have asserted their rights 'selfishly', that is, without regard to the rights of others, with a text which says, 'Yes, you have rights, but you also have responsibilities.' Straw stipulated to the JCHR that he was 'really keen on getting that out specifically'.[50] The JCHR recognized the importance of responsibilities to the debates on the new Bill of Rights, but suggested that the Labour Government's thinking about the relationship between rights and responsibilities was 'extremely muddled'.[51] More than that, the Labour Government had failed to reconcile their desire to increase a sense of responsibility in British citizens with the principles of universality in human rights conventions. The JCHR's position, as noted above, is unequivocal on the matter of the relationship between responsibilities and rights: 'human rights are rights that people enjoy by virtue of being human: they cannot be made contingent on the prior fulfilment of responsibilities'.[52]

42 Russell, op. cit., p. 8.
43 Ibid.
44 Russell, op. cit., p. 9.
45 Ministry of Justice, 2007, op. cit., p. 61.
46 Russell, op. cit., p. 8.
47 Joint Committee on Human Rights, 2008, op. cit., p. 6.
48 Ibid., p. 69.
49 Ibid., p. 68.
50 J. Straw, ibid., p.68.
51 Ibid., p. 71.
52 Ibid.

A Bill of Rights for British citizens?

The JCHR have particular problems with the term 'Britishness' and the use of 'British' as a prefix in the title for the proposed Bill of Rights. The JCHR anticipated difficulties associated with establishing a Bill of Rights on the basis of a statement of 'British' values. The main reason was that this label 'may or may not be accepted' by those people 'who consider themselves to be, for example, "English", "Scottish", "Irish" or "Welsh", but not "British"'.[53] Jack Straw's justification for applying the adjective 'British' to the potential 'statement of values' and the Bill of Rights, in his witness statement to the JCHR, can be described as yet another strategy to head off (yet also collude with) hostile media reporting and public attitudes with regards to human rights:

> The 'British' adjective in my view is important because there is the implication in the air that these human rights which equal in some people's minds, not mine or yours, a terrorists' and criminals' charter, are a European imposition and by Europe it is meant 'the Other', that somehow we are not part of Europe. I think it is important that we break that down.[54]

The JCHR take an alternative view: as noted above, they see the adjective 'British' as being counterproductive in that it could be detrimental to social cohesion and could be a source of division.[55] They also view the adjective 'British' as suggesting a link with British citizenship, which, for many of the rights within the Bill of Rights, would be inappropriate. The JCHR remind us that some legal rights are explicitly linked with citizenship; for example, the right to vote, the right to a passport and the right to consular access abroad. There are also certain rights in any Bill of Rights which may apply to all citizens, for example the so-called 'democratic rights' such as the aforementioned right to vote and also the right to stand for election. However, according to the JCHR the place occupied by the category of rights related to citizenship in any Bill of Rights would be relatively small.[56]

The connection between British citizenship, British values and the potential British Bill of Rights and Responsibilities was made by Michael Wills, the former Justice Minister, who suggested that the stepping stone between the Human Rights Act and the British Bill of Rights and Responsibilities was the formulation of a British Statement of Values, which would explicitly articulate previously implicit responsibilities and would also explicitly express 'our national identity':

> Our national identity matters . . . It was only in the years after the Second World War that we went through a period of introspection, lacking in

---

53 Joint Committee on Human Rights, 2008, op. cit, p. 29.
54 J. Straw, ibid., p. 29.
55 Ibid., p. 29.
56 Ibid., p. 26.

self-confidence when such discussions were often regarded with embarrassment. We are now far more successful and self-confident as a country and the government believes the time is right to find a way to express who we believe ourselves to be in a way that is inclusive and commands broad support.[57]

For Wills this was a pre-emptive strategy, in terms of the Labour Government getting in there first, facilitating a national debate before this process could be overtaken by 'others':

> If we don't do this, others will. National identity matters to people. If there isn't a national process to discuss it, in ways that are inclusive of everyone on these islands, then there is a risk that this territory will be colonized by sectarian and sometimes even poisonous views.[58]

For Liberty, this emphasis on 'Britishness' and the addition of the prefix 'British' to the statement of values and the Bill of Rights sends the wrong messages, and once again flies in the face of universality.[59] Liberty views the emphasis on Britishness as suggesting that the 'British' Bill of Rights would only protect the rights of British people.[60] Once again the tension between citizenship and human rights, and in particular the distinction between those who should and should not enjoy human rights protections, or more accurately whose human rights should be considered first and foremost, emerges here. These debates lead to a particular frame-setting discourse that could have profound effects on 'non-citizens', who seem to be 'wrongly excluded from consideration'.[61] This amounts to what Nancy Fraser would call 'misframing', which can result 'in a kind of "political death" '[62] for individuals and groups who find themselves outside the frame. In response to misframing, Liberty reminds us once again of the universality principle, that 'people have basic rights by virtue of being human'.[63] Liberty attempted to block any move that would prioritize the rights of the citizenry over the rights of others (for example third country, non-EU foreign nationals) who are resident in the UK, in the name of preventing further human rights abuses from occurring in the UK. They cite the results of recent misframing practices to support their opposition: 'as the Belmarsh internment policy and treatment of asylum seekers have demonstrated, it is indeed non-citizens that are most often in need of human rights protections.'[64] The

57 M. Wills, op. cit., p. 3.
58 Ibid.
59 Russell, op. cit., p. 5.
60 Ibid.
61 N. Fraser, op. cit., p. 6.
62 Ibid., p. 20.
63 Russell, op. cit., p. 5.
64 Ibid.

suggestion here is that a Bill of Rights and a Statement of Values cannot be used to shore up a sense of 'Britishness', if the result of this is that such a process is perceived as a means to prioritize the rights of British citizens first.

The JCHR is also opposed to the 'British' prefix with regards to the Statement of Values and Bill of Rights. The JCHR recognizes that the formulation of a Bill of Rights is a significant event of 'national definition'.[65] According to the JCHR, a national Bill of Rights is an expression of national identity and in the process of drawing up a Bill of Rights 'invites reflection about what it is that "Binds us together as a nation" '.[66] However, the JCHR was not persuaded that the term 'British' Bill of Rights was a helpful description of the Labour Government's proposal. The JCHR's primary concern was that giving the Bill of Rights the prefix 'British' could encourage an inward-looking view that human rights are linked to nationality or citizenship rather than being universal in their application.[67] The JCHR suggests instead that the term 'UK' Bill of Rights would be more accurate and appropriate and would also serve to demonstrate that the rights it contained are 'owned' by all of the people (Scottish, English, Welsh and Northern Irish) of the UK.[68] At the same time they suggest the removal of 'Responsibilities' and the addition of 'Freedoms' to the title of the Bill to represent the location of the UK Bill of Rights and Freedoms within established human rights convention, which, following Klug, would signify that the Bill of Rights would provide a unifying force, but not at the expense of recognizing 'the contribution of many countries, and most religions and cultures, to the human rights values recognized throughout the world today'.[69]

In many ways, the JCHR report *A Bill of Rights for the UK?* has taken on the role of filtering out the prioritization of the rights of some over the rights of others, and the discourses of responsibilities, Britishness and citizenship from the government's proposed British Bill of Rights and Responsibilities. The JCHR has performed the task of removing the contingency, exclusivity, restrictiveness and non-universality of the proposed Bill of Rights to propose their own UK Bill of Rights and Freedoms which is universal, inclusive and outward-looking (through referencing existing human rights conventions and standards). Moreover, the JCHR's recommendations contributed to the process whereby the Labour Government began to disentangle their strategies for increasing a sense of obligations, duties and responsibilities through the process of strengthening British citizenship from the processes associated with introducing the Bill of Rights.

There is one other development that I would like to mention, and that is the relationship between the debates above on the Bill of Rights and the

65 Joint Committee on Human Rights, 2008, op. cit., p. 28.
66 Ibid., p. 28.
67 Ibid., p. 30.
68 Ibid., p. 28.
69 F. Klug, 'A Bill of Rights: What for?', p. 13.

recommendations made by Lord Goldsmith in his wide-ranging citizenship review (2007–8). Lord Goldsmith's review and recommendations also focus on the wider challenges of strengthening a sense of citizenship and commonality for all in the UK. However, in my opinion, Lord Goldsmith's recommendations do not lead to the strengthening of 'our common bond of citizenship' through a Bill of Rights. Rather, in my view, many of Goldsmith's recommendations lead us down the paths to something like a British (or UK) Charter of Responsible Citizenship (similar to the Charter being developed in the Netherlands) which could potentially take the place of the proposed Bill of Rights and Responsibilities.

There were some signs that Jack Straw was beginning to take note of the developments with regards to the proposals for the creation of a Dutch Charter of Responsible Citizenship, in the context of the stiff opposition he and the Ministry of Justice faced from the JCHR and organizations like Liberty, which I have described above as a seemingly unreconcilable tension between the Labour Government's ambitions for the Bill of Rights with regards to public safety, responsibilities and citizenship, grouped here under the term the 'politics of citizenship', and their commitments to universal human rights. Jack Straw has stated that the proposed Dutch Charter of Responsible Citizenship 'is not intended to be a formal document with direct legal or even normative effect. The aim is to stimulate social change through increasing individuals' understandings of their responsibilities to one another, and their responsibilities to society as a whole'.[70] In my opinion, there are strong parallels between the proposed Dutch Charter of Responsible Citizenship, (or more accurately, Jack Straw's understanding of the latter) and Lord Goldsmith's recommendations for developing 'a narrative, non-legalistic statement of the rights and responsibilities of citizenship' in Britain.[71] Similarly to the proposed Dutch Charter of Responsible Citizenship, Lord Goldsmith advocated a narrative statement of British citizenship that both simplified and clarified 'the package of rights and responsibilities which demonstrate the tie between a person and a country'.[72] At the same time, Lord Goldsmith was adamant that Britain needs better emphasis on the relationship between those who already enjoy formal citizenship and the State[73] through the development of his ideas for a statement of citizenship rights and responsibilities. For Lord Goldsmith:

> One can imagine a number of circumstances in which such a statement could be of benefit, for example, as part of citizenship education or the

70 J. Straw, 2009, op. cit., p. 7.
71 Lord Goldsmith, *Citizenship: Our Common Bond*, Citizenship Review, Ministry of Justice, Executive Summary, 2008. Available at: <http://webarchive.nationalarchives.gov.uk/+/http://www.justice.gov.uk/docs/citizenship-report-full.pdf> (accessed 17 June 2011).
72 Ibid., p. 6.
73 Ibid., p. 98.

coming of age ceremonies . . . It could moreover make a much clearer statement of what we expect of citizens and what they can expect of their country.[74]

There is no way of knowing how these processes would have developed under the Labour Government with regards to the development of a Bill of Rights and/or a Charter of Responsible Citizenship. It will be very interesting to see how relevant these 'deficit discourses' and the shift of emphasis from the Bill of Rights to the Charter of Responsible Citizenship under Labour will be to the 'investigations' of the Coalition Government's commission on the creation of the Bill of Rights.

Conclusion: towards a British Declaration of Rights and Responsibilities?

The future of the British Bill of Rights and Responsibilities was already uncertain in the last year the Labour Government was in power. According to an article in *Monitor* (the Constitution Unit's Newsletter) it was reported that 'amidst the gathering economic gloom the government's constitutional reform plans are being quietly shelved'.[75] This slippage, according to *Monitor*, had impacted on plans for the Bill of Rights, which was to have taken centre stage in Gordon Brown's planned constitutional reform programme as introduced in the *Governance of Britain* Green Paper. It was reported that, despite all three main political parties being committed to introducing a Bill of Rights (in the case of the Conservatives, as a replacement for the Human Rights Act), the promised publication of the Green Paper on the Bill of Rights had been repeatedly postponed, even after the JCHR published their own detailed proposals and draft Bill in 2008.[76] According to *Monitor*, the main problem with the Bill of Rights was the lack of enthusiasm amongst Cabinet colleagues, and the proposed link between the Bill of Rights and the British Statement of Values.[77] According to Patrick Wintour, writing in *The Guardian*, the Labour Cabinet revolt on the Bill of Rights can be summed up in the following way: 'Some Cabinet ministers believe there is no demand for such a complex constitutional development and it will be regarded as irrelevant in times of economic stress or, at worst, be highly unpopular.'[78] Wintour highlighted the clash between

---

74 Lord Goldsmith, *Citizenship: our Common Bond*, p. 92.
75 'Constitutional Reform put on hold', *Monitor, The Constitution Unit Newsletter*, Issue 41, 2009, p. 1. Available at < http://www.ucl.ac.uk/constitution-unit/publications/tabs/monitor-newsletter/monitor-41> (accessed 17 June 2011).
76 Ibid.
77 Ibid.
78 P. Wintour, 'Cabinet revolt over Straw's rights and responsibilities plan', *The Guardian*, 4 November, 2008, p. 1. Available at <http://www.guardian.co.uk/politics/2008/nov/04/rights-bill-jack-straw> (accessed 17 June 2011).

the Ministry of Justice and the Home Office around the proposed Bill of Rights. Former Home Secretary Jacqui Smith has been described by Wintour as a leading opponent of the Bill of Rights. From Smith's perspective, the Bill of Rights 'will strengthen the hand of the judiciary over parliament', which would lead to 'further public alienation from the concept of human rights'.[79] Wintour reports that Smith's opposition to the Bill of Rights was backed by Home Office lawyers, 'who feel that they have a hard enough time trying to protect their decisions from the impact of the Human Rights Act'. Straw (see also Wills' response to such criticisms, as noted above), according to Wintour, was to make 'the unpopular Human Rights Act' more palatable by balancing the existing emphasis on rights with a new emphasis on duties and responsibilities in the Bill of Rights.[80] However, as noted above, this strategy of rebalancing rights and responsibilities, and the links between particularly 'British' values and the prefix 'British' in the proposed title of the Bill of Rights, have all been called into question and exposed as exclusionary, counter-productive and feeding the very myths and misconceptions they are setting out to challenge. More than that, in my opinion, the proposed Bill has become the repository for the clash of the domestic politics of citizenship and the politics of universal human rights. According to Melissa Kite, writing in the *Telegraph*, senior ministers were said to be unhappy with Straw's plans for the Bill of Rights as they feared they would 'be deeply unpopular with the public' and become 'a charter for expensive lawsuits', especially if the proposed ECHR+ aspects of the proposed Bill of Rights and Responsibilities, which also feature in the JCHR's UK Bill of Rights and Freedoms, such as social and economic rights, were included.[81]

I will end this chapter with one final development. The much-delayed *Rights and Responsibilities: Developing our Constitutional Framework* Green Paper was published in March 2009.[82] Despite, the JCHR's recommendations, Straw and Wills were still fixated on 'Britishness', 'responsibilities' and 'citizenship' in this Green Paper. However, one significant difference was the shift in emphasis in security discourse; that is, there is a relative lack of reference to the threat from terrorism in the Green Paper, with emphasis in its place on the 'crisis in the world's financial system'.[83] A further development was the stipulation in the Green Paper of the Labour Government's position on the

79 P. Wintour, *The Guardian*, 4 November 2008, p. 2.
80 Ibid.
81 M. Kite, 'Gordon Brown's Advisors Denounce Bill of Rights as "unworkable" ', *The Telegraph*, 9 November, 2008, p. 2. Available at: <http://www.telegraph.co.uk/news/politics/labour/3405947/Gordon-Browns-advisor-denounces-Bill-of-Rights-as-unworkable.html> (accessed 17 June 2011).
82 Ministry of Justice, *Rights and Responsibilities: Developing our constitutional framework*, 2009. Available at: <http://www.official-documents.gov.uk/document/cm75/7577/7577.pdf> (accessed 28 October 2011)
83 Ibid., p. 3.

relationship between rights and responsibilities. For example, with regards to the contingency of rights on responsibilities, it was stipulated in the Green Paper that:

> The government does not consider a general model of directly legally enforceable rights or responsibilities to be the most appropriate for a future Bill of Rights and Responsibilities... the imposition of new penalties is unlikely to be the best way to foster a sense of civic responsibility and encourage respect and tolerance for others and participation in the democratic process.[84]

The result of these constraints is that the Green Paper, as predicted above, has become less of a discussion paper on a Bill of Rights and Responsibilities and more a discussion paper on what Straw and Wills describe as 'the constitutional question of the relationship between the citizen and the state', which focuses on 'how this relationship can best be defined to protect fundamental freedoms and foster mutual responsibility as the country is going through profound changes'.[85] Thus this Green Paper, in my opinion, becomes a discussion paper for providing a 'clearer and more explicit understanding' of the relationship between rights and responsibilities in order to 'articulate what we owe, as much as what we expect' in order to 'foster a stronger sense of shared citizenship among all those who live in the UK'.[86] The Green Paper was peppered with statements such as these, all of which evidence the shift from the emphasis on the Bill of Rights and Responsibilities to replace this emphasis with something more akin to a British Statement of Responsible Citizenship. This shift in emphasis from the Bill of Rights and Responsibilities to something more akin to a non-legalistic declaration of responsible citizenship was evident in the Green Paper. For example, the creation of an 'accessible document' is mentioned on page 19. By page 26 other examples of 'national instruments' are listed, including the plans in the Netherlands to draw up a Charter for Responsible Citizenship, and by the end of the Green Paper they are referring to 'a charter or declaration' of rights and responsibilities,[87] before plumping for a non-legalistic declaration of rights and responsibilities in the final pages, which is described as having 'the advantage over other options for legal effect' by including 'broad aspirations' and focus on 'cultural change'.[88] Such a declaration, as noted above, in the discussion on Lord Goldsmith's recommendations for 'a narrative, non-legalistic statement of the rights and responsibilities of citizenship', according to the Green Paper,

---

84 Ministry of Justice, *Rights and Responsibilities: Developing our constitutional framework*, p. 10.
85 Ibid., p. 3.
86 Ibid., p. 17.
87 Ibid., p. 52.
88 Ibid., p. 53.

'would provide an opportunity to express rights and responsibilities in inspiring and motivating language, without the constraints placed by the careful drafting needed in legislative provision'.[89]

What we can deduce from this shift in emphasis, from a Bill of Rights to a Declaration of Responsible Citizenship, was that Jack Straw was attempting to better articulate rights and responsibilities and bolster British citizenship outside of the legalistic constraints of human rights frameworks. By so doing, it suggests that the intentions of Labour's 'domestic', 'civic politics' in and through the Bill of Rights with regards to public safety, responsibilities and citizenship could not, in the end, be reconciled with their 'dual' commitments to international human rights.

89 Ministry of Justice, *Rights and Responsibilities: Developing our constitutional framework.*

16 Replacing the Human Rights Act with a British Bill of Rights

Creating greater Parliamentary autonomy on human rights matters?

Helen Fenwick

Introduction

In response to the riots in August 2011, David Cameron was quick to attack the Human Rights Act on the basis that 'phoney human rights concerns' must not get in the way of dealing with rioters.[1] Some days later, in his analysis of the causes of the riots, he fleshed out his view that the Human Rights Act (HRA) was linked to the riots, and gave his solution – a British Bill of Rights:[2]

> As we consider these questions of attitude and behaviour, the signals that government sends, and the incentives it creates . . . we inevitably come to the question of the Human Rights Act and the culture associated with it. Let me be clear: in this country we are proud to stand up for human rights, at home and abroad. It is part of the British tradition. But what is alien to our tradition – and now exerting such a corrosive influence on behaviour and morality . . . is the twisting and misrepresenting of human rights in a way that has undermined personal responsibility. We are attacking this problem from both sides. We're working to develop a way through the morass by looking at creating our own British Bill of Rights. And we will be using our current chairmanship of the Council of Europe to seek agreement to important operational changes to the European Convention on Human Rights. But this is all frustratingly slow. The truth is, the interpretation of human rights legislation has exerted a chilling effect on public sector organisations, leading them to act in ways that fly in the face of common sense, offend our sense of right and wrong, and undermine responsibility . . . And as we urgently review the work we're doing on the broken society . . . I want to make it clear that there will be no holds barred . . . and that most definitely includes the human rights . . . culture.

---

1 Speech to House of Commons, 11 August 2011.
2 In a speech to his constituency, 15 August 2011.

Deep dissatisfaction with the HRA and a determination to repeal it was reflected in Conservative pronouncements in the run-up to the 2010 general election, and in the Conservative manifesto.[3] But when the Coalition Government was formed, for obvious political reasons, this became a much more difficult issue, given the differing stances taken on it by the Conservatives and Liberal Democrats prior to the general election.[4] The notion that a rapid repeal of the HRA might be undertaken, based on David Cameron's pledge to that effect to *The Sun* in 2006,[5] had to be put to rest. A partial and temporary solution – obviously unsatisfactory from a Conservative viewpoint – was found by consigning this issue to a Commission to examine the possibility of creating a British Bill of Rights (BoR). This allowed the uneasy compromise adopted by the two parties to subsist, for a time.

In the Programme for the Coalition Government, we were told that a Commission was being established to investigate the creation of a 'British Bill of Rights that incorporates and builds on all our obligations under the European Convention on Human Rights'. After May 2010, there was an uneasy silence on the issue of the Human Rights Act or a Bill of Rights for a period. Almost a year later, nothing more was known about the Commission; it was eventually set up in March 2011 and will report before the end of 2012.[6] Its full remit is:

> To investigate the creation of a UK Bill of Rights that incorporates and builds on all our obligations under the European Convention on Human Rights, ensures that these rights continue to be enshrined in UK law, and protects and extends our liberties. To examine the operation and implementation of these obligations, and consider ways to promote a better understanding of the true scope of these obligations and liberties. To provide advice to the Government on the ongoing Interlaken process to reform the Strasbourg court ahead of and following the UK's Chairmanship of the Council of Europe. To consult, including with the public, judiciary and devolved administrations and legislatures.

---

3 The Conservative Party manifesto promised to 'Replace the Human Rights Act with a UK Bill of Rights'.
4 The Liberal Democrats' manifesto promised to 'Ensure that everyone has the same protections under the law by protecting the Human Rights Act'.
5 He told *The Sun* that it was wrong to allow 'the human rights of dangerous criminals to fly in the face of common sense', 12 May 2006.
6 The Commission is headed by former Permanent Secretary, Sir Leigh Lewis. The eight members are: Martin Howe QC, Anthony Lester QC, Jonathan Fisher QC, Helena Kennedy QC, Anthony Speaight QC, Philippe Sands QC, Michael Pinto-Duschinsky and Sir David Edward.

So far it has produced one discussion paper, of a brief, descriptive and markedly bland nature, entitled *Do we need a UK Bill of Rights?*[7] No indication as to the possible form any Bill of Rights might take have emerged from the Commission as a whole.

It is arguable that the setting up of the Commission kept matters in stasis, perhaps in anticipation of the possibility that unfolding events and the political reaction to them might affect the public mood, and possibly create a build-up of feeling in which the repeal of the HRA became unavoidable. Cameron's reaction to the riots suggests that that is the case. In other words, political capital can be made in terms of allowing the Conservatives' stance towards the HRA to dominate. The Liberal Democrats are obviously placed in a difficult position, politically, since if they defend the HRA they could appear to be lacking in resolve to address the (apparent) causes of the riots. The background to the appointment of the BoR Commission, and the stances taken towards the HRA of its members, reveal the contradictions inherent, this chapter will argue, in its remit, especially when compared to the stance taken by Cameron on this issue over the last five years. The remit has nothing to say about complete withdrawal from the European Convention on Human Rights (ECHR) and, according to the remit, the BoR should incorporate ECHR obligations. But at the same time senior Conservatives and the Conservative nominees on the Commission appear to consider that the attempt should be made under the BoR to weaken the ties to Strasbourg created by the HRA – as Cameron indicated in the speech quoted above. The idea, it will be argued, appears to seek to utilise the BoR to increase the autonomy of the UK Parliament in human rights' matters. The extent to which that is the case and to which the BoR could be used, if at all, to achieve that aim forms a key theme of this chapter.

The pronouncements made by senior Conservatives prior to the election showed quite a striking lack of clarity as to the respects in which the BoR might differ from the HRA. As a result, Erdos asserted that any changes might be largely cosmetic.[8] However, this chapter contends that the changes mooted so far might lack clarity and appear to accord with the ECHR, but have the potential to be far-reaching. It will be argued that the BoR may – if Conservative aims eventually dominate – be used to try to create a move away from the balance the HRA creates between Parliamentary and judicial power, since a theme recurring in the speeches of Conservative HRA-sceptics relates to weakening the

---

7 Published August 2011, available on the Commission's website. It states: The four questions on which we seek your views are: (1) do you think we need a UK Bill of Rights? If so, (2) what do you think a UK Bill of Rights should contain? (3) how do you think it should apply to the UK as a whole, including its four component countries of England, Northern Ireland, Scotland and Wales? (4) having regard to our terms of reference, are there any other views which you would like to put forward at this stage?

8 See D. Erdos on the similarities in the approach of the different parties to this issue: 'Smoke but No Fire? The Politics of a "British" Bill of Rights', *The Political Quarterly*, 2010, 81(2), pp. 188–98.

influence of both the Strasbourg Court and domestic judges. Taking the pronouncements made reflecting such aims into account, this chapter speculates about the ways in which a Bill of Rights, if it ever comes into being, might differ from the Human Rights Act. This chapter considers what a Bill of Rights under the Coalition Government (or a future Conservative Government) might look like, taking account of ideas expressed by Conservative spokespersons prior to and after the 2010 general election,[9] and of answers given by members of the Bill of Rights Commission to the Political and Constitutional Reform Committee in June 2011.[10] In a chapter of this length it is not possible to cover all the possible implications of introducing a new British Bill of Rights. The chapter considers a selected range of issues that have been highlighted in pronouncements on this issue, which relate in particular to the key themes of breaking away from Strasbourg and enhancing Parliamentary autonomy.

This chapter only touches on the second aspect of the Commission's remit, its advisory role on the reform of the European Court of Human Rights, but comments from the Conservative-nominated Commission members[11] indicate that they view such a role as related to the enterprise of handing autonomy back to the UK Parliament by creating a more circumscribed role for the Court. Assuming that such a change could be brought about, greater freedom to tailor the BoR to the perceived needs of the UK with minimal interference from Strasbourg might appear to arise.

Repeal of the Human Rights Act

Repealing the HRA would obviously be a major, highly controversial and politically very difficult step. The terms of reference of the Commission make no mention of repeal of the HRA. The Commission has only been asked to consider the creation of a Bill of Rights. But the HRA is inevitably the elephant in the room: the Commission can hardly decide on the issue of the creation of a BoR without considering the fate of the HRA. It is understandable that some resiling from the position taken by Cameron in 2006 – whereby creation of a BoR was inevitably accompanied by repeal of the HRA – occurred when the Coalition Government came to power. As mentioned, the Liberal Democrats made a manifesto pledge in 2010 to retain the HRA, as did

---

9 David Cameron in a speech to the Centre for Policy Studies, London 26 June 2006, 'Balancing freedom and security – A modern British Bill of Rights' stated that the HRA should be repealed. See also in particular the Rt Hon Dominic Grieve QC March 23 2010 in a speech to the Human Rights Lawyers Association (which has not been published); he also posted a speech on the same topic in November 2009 on his blog.

10 See Commons Select Committee on Political and Constitutional Reform: UK Bill of Rights Commission – oral and written evidence – 9 and 16 June 2011, published 19 July 2011. Below this evidence is referred to in relation to the question number to which the answer relates. Available at: <http://www.publications.parliament.uk/pa/cm201012/cmselect/cmpolcon/1049/1049contents.htm> (accessed 15 August 2011).

11 E.g. Martin Howe QC in relation to Q82, ibid.

Labour.[12] Clearly, Cameron would (depending on the timetable that eventually emerges) want to get the repealing legislation through Parliament without damaging the Coalition, and without facing combined Labour and Liberal Democrat opposition. The position of the SNP, Ulster Unionists and Plaid Cymru would presumably depend on the stance taken as regards the devolution arrangements affecting the Northern Ireland Assembly, the Welsh Assembly and the Scottish Parliament – which add a range of further complications (this issue is briefly touched on below).

The members of the Commission appear to take diverging views on the question of repeal of the HRA, and it can probably be assumed that Helena Kennedy, Philippe Sands and Anthony Lester QC, at the least, would have to be convinced that the BoR would deliver the same degree of rights protection as the HRA, before they would recommend repeal. In giving evidence to the Constitutional Reform Committee, one of the Conservative members of the Commission[13] was asked about the differing Liberal Democrat and Conservative stances:

> Some people think that the purpose of this Commission is basically to give the two Coalition parties options at the end of 2012 whereby each of them will be able to come to a different conclusion as to what they want to put in their manifestos for the next election, based on the expert advice from their own party members on this Commission.[14]

Anthony Speaight replied: 'No, I don't see it as part of our mission. . . . I think the differences between different political parties are nothing like as great as is commonly supposed.' As to the question of accompanying creation of the BoR with repeal of the HRA, he said: 'My favoured option would be that, that in place of the Human Rights Act there would be a new statute – let's call it a UK Bill of Rights for want of a better label.'

Martin Howe QC, a further Conservative nominee, also appeared to favour repeal of the HRA, stating,

> There is a perception at the moment, I believe, among a section of the country, that the Human Rights Act is an alien import that comes in from abroad . . . The Human Rights Act, obviously in a sense it can be said to constrain or conflict with parliamentary sovereignty.[15]

---

12 The Labour Party manifesto stated: 'We are proud to have brought in the Human Rights Act, enabling British citizens to take action in British courts rather than having to wait years to seek redress in Strasbourg. We will not repeal or resile from it.'

13 Anthony Speaight, one of the Conservative nominees. It may be noted that Speaight had produced a pamphlet *The Human Rights Act – Legal Pathways* (2007), considering the implications of replacing it with a UK Bill of Rights.

14 Mr Chope, Q 37, Commons Select Committee on Political and Constitutional Reform, op. cit., n. 10.

15 In answer to Q77 and Q80, ibid.

On this point, Lord Lester in contrast said:

> [One] approach would be to keep the Human Rights Act as it is but perhaps have a political declaration with it. Another approach would be to amend or replace the Human Rights Act. That would be fraught with some difficulty. . .[16]

Clearly, the collective view of the Commission – if one emerges – is not yet known, but, bearing in mind the stance Cameron has taken on this issue, it would be surprising if as leader of the Coalition Government, he was prepared to take action to implement proposals that did *not* include the replacement of the HRA by the BoR. The terms of reference of the Commission could be interpreted as impliedly including the possibility of merely retaining the HRA, possibly with some modifications, but it is reasonably clear that such an outcome would not have the support of the Conservative Party.

Reconciling Parliamentary sovereignty with rights protection

A seminal constitutional decision involving a choice between judicial and Parliamentary checks on executive power, and therefore as to the allocation of power, had to be taken regarding the choice of model for the enforcement of the Convention when the Human Rights Bill was being considered. The choice made was to afford the HRA no special constitutional protection and to leave the ultimate task of curbing executive power to Parliament; so judicial rulings remain (at least as a matter of constitutional theory) subject to primary legislation. The HRA therefore sought to reconcile rights protection placed to a significant extent in the hands of the courts with parliamentary sovereignty. Although the Convention contains the familiar list of rights usually found in a number of Bills or Charters of Rights, the HRA was not intended to be a Bill of Rights, in the way that the US Amendments to the Constitution or the Canadian Charter are Bills of Rights, namely that those rights have a higher status than other laws: laws that conflict with the rights can be struck down. Further, unlike the German Basic Law or the US Amendments, the HRA can simply be repealed or amended like any ordinary statute and it is, therefore, in a far more precarious position.

So although there was a significant transfer of power to the judiciary, the HRA apparently imposed limitations on its use. On a face-value reading of the HRA, legislation incompatible with the Convention can be passed and is binding on public authorities (s 6(2)), unless s 3 can be relied upon to read the provision in question compatibly with the ECHR. Legislation declared incompatible with the ECHR remains valid (s 6(2), s 4(6)) and the executive

---

16 In answer to Q58, ibid.

may, but need not, bring amending legislation before Parliament, if a declaration of incompatibility is made (s 10). Legislation can be presented to Parliament which may be incompatible with the ECHR (s 19). It is readily apparent, then, that there was a contradiction between the liberal aim of affording the Convention rights efficacy in domestic law in order to aid in reversing the effects of the over-centralisation of power, and the aim of preserving the key feature of the constitution – Parliamentary sovereignty combined with the dominance of Parliament by the executive – which gave rein to that power. The factors underlying this contradiction form one of the central themes apparent in the human rights field over the last 11 years – the search for a means of giving efficacy to the rights in the face of hostile legislation, including post-HRA Labour legislation, such as the Terrorism Act 2000, as amended, and the Anti-Terrorism, Crime and Security Act 2001 (ACTSA).

Open defiance of the ECHR in the HRA-era?

But this chapter argues that, while there have been serious tensions between the ECHR and government criminal justice or counter-terrorist policy in the years 2000 and 2011, the particular resolution of the tension between rights-protection and Parliamentary sovereignty created by the HRA has *not* in general been utilised by the executive in the sense of seeking to defy the ECHR openly. The particular constitutional choices reflected in the HRA have on the whole *not* been exploited to allow the government, as dominant within Parliament, to disregard or limit the Convention rights to an extent that the Convention itself does not allow. As Keith Ewing wrote in 1999,

> we should be careful about distinguishing form from substance, principle from practice. As a matter of constitutional legality, Parliament may well be sovereign, but as a matter of constitutional practice, it has transferred significant power to the judiciary [under the HRA].[17]

The methods of recognising the doctrine of Parliamentary sovereignty utilised in the HRA – ss 3(2) and 6(2) – have *not* been the most significant factors in determining the balance between the exercise of governmental power and rights. Thus, a doctrinal analysis of the status of the Convention in domestic law is inadequate to explain its impact, since such an analysis has been superseded by the political stance taken by the previous government.

For example, after the derailing in 2004 of the Labour Government's counter-terror detention without trial measure in *A and others*,[18] it could, as a

---

17 K. Ewing, 'The HRA and Parliamentary Democracy', *Modern Law Review*, 1999, 62(1), p. 92.
18 (2004) UKHL 56.

matter of constitutional theory, have sought to rely on the Parliamentary sovereignty-preserving HRA provisions, ss 6(2) and 3(2)(b), allowing Parliament to pass legislation regardless of the Convention rights, which public authorities, including courts, must then apply. Had that occurred, the judiciary would, according to Lord Scott in the 2009 case of *AF*,[19] have loyally accepted Parliament's decision. Sections 6(2) and 3(2) have nothing to say about the necessity or proportionality of the measures needed to avert the crisis, as Art. 15 does,[20] and do not overtly demand that an emergency must be in being. (After the decision in *A and others*, the government appeared reluctant to risk seeking a derogation in 2005.) But the political reality would have been that the government would have doubted its ability to persuade Parliament to accept a scheme that openly failed to adhere to either Art. 6 or 5, unless it claimed that that was necessitated by the crisis. And clearly the question would have arisen as to why it did not seek a derogation, if it was so certain that the crisis demanded repudiation of Art. 5 or 6 standards. Further, open defiance of the ECHR, after receiving it into domestic law under the HRA, would have been politically difficult, and an eventual adverse decision at Strasbourg would have forced the government to revisit the issue. Obviously, the UK would have remained constrained by the ECHR at the international level, and probably would have found itself eventually in breach of its Treaty obligations.

So instead of relying on the HRA provisions allowing Parliament to pass legislation in breach of the ECHR, the government brought forward legislation – the Prevention of Terrorism Act 2005 – which was apparently ECHR-compliant but did not fully deal with the problem of being unable to prosecute or deport a certain group of persons suspected of terrorist activity.[21] It should be noted that s 6(2) *was* relied upon by the government as part of the response to the declaration of incompatibility in *A and others*: the declaration did not affect the validity of the offending legislation – Part 4 ACTSA – and therefore those detained under its provisions remained in detention. However, s 6(2) was relied upon only as a temporary expedient – to create a period of time (around three months) within which to prepare and bring forward the replacement legislation.

An important exception to the point above, as to the use of s 6(2) HRA, arises in respect of prisoners' voting rights. The Labour Government did not respond to the ruling at Strasbourg in *Hirst v UK*[22] to the effect that the failure

---

19 [2009] UKHL 28 [97].

20 They also place no restrictions on the Articles that could be violated. In contrast, under Art. 15, only certain rights are capable of derogation.

21 See further on this episode H. Fenwick, 'Recalibrating ECHR Rights, and The Role Of The Human Rights Act Post 9/11: Reasserting International Human Rights Norms In The "War On Terror"?' (2010) 63 *CLP* 153–234.

22 *Hirst v UK* (2004) 38 EHRR 825; *Hirst v UK (No 2)* (2004) 38 *EHRR* 40.

in the UK to allow such rights breached Art. 3 of the First Protocol. And in 2011, the UK Parliament voted to continue to disregard the decision at Strasbourg on such rights.[23] In *Greens and M.T. v United Kingdom*,[24] the Court ordered the UK to bring forward, within six months of the judgment becoming final in April 2011, appropriate legislative proposals to implement *Hirst*. Since the *Hirst* ruling, the offending provisions of s 3 of the Representation of the People Act 1983 have remained legally valid and applicable despite their incompatibility with the ECHR. Further, in *Tovey & Ors v Ministry of Justice*,[25] the High Court struck out a claim for compensation by a prisoner in respect of his disenfranchisement under the blanket ban. The ruling confirmed that as a matter of English law, taking account of the Human Rights Act 1998, a prisoner cannot succeed before a court in England and Wales in any claim for damages or a declaration. In April 2011, a panel of the Grand Chamber refused to hear the UK's appeal on the issue,[26] and ordered compliance with the *Hirst* ruling by 11 October 2011.

This is an unresolved matter that is bringing about a direct clash between Parliamentary autonomy and the authority of the European Court of Human Rights (ECtHR), and is likely to influence consideration of the BoR. But this is an exceptional situation, and the current government clearly does not view the HRA as providing an answer to it, merely on the basis that the HRA allows for departure from the ECHR, if consented to by Parliament. Similarly, the government has in general been reluctant to bring legislation before Parliament unaccompanied by a declaration of its compatibility with the ECHR. It has done so once – in the Communications Act 2003. But the provision in question, continuing the ban on political advertising, was not as controversial as are the matters of control orders or the issue of prisoners' voting rights. More importantly, its compatibility with Art. 10 was viewed as uncertain; the government did not accept that there was incompatibility, and its stance was vindicated by the House of Lords in *Animal Defenders*.[27]

Departing from the ECHR under a Bill of Rights?

So consideration of the potential relationship between a Bill of Rights and Parliamentary sovereignty is likely to take account of a political reality in which overt disregard of the ECHR has so far largely been avoided. An important driver for change, from the Conservative viewpoint, is to hand greater

---

23 The Tory backbencher David Davis and former Labour Home Secretary Jack Straw tabled the 10 February 2011 motion opposing reform, which was accepted by a majority of MPs (234 to 22).

24 Judgment of 23 November 2010.

25 [2011] EWHC 271 (QB) (18 February 2011).

26 On 12 April 2011.

27 *R. (on the application of AnimalDefenders International) v Secretary of State for Culture, Media and Sport* [2008] UKHL 15; [2008] 1 AC 1312.

power to Parliament to determine human rights issues. David Cameron has said that the HRA should be repealed and replaced by the BoR: 'so that Britain's laws can no longer be decided by unaccountable judges'.[28] The reference appeared to cover the Strasbourg Court as well as domestic judges, but it clearly does not indicate that the Conservatives favour handing greater power to judges. How far the 2012 Commission proposals might cover the possibility of creating greater autonomy for Parliament in the BoR is obviously unclear, but it appears highly unlikely that there would be Conservative support for weakening Parliamentary sovereignty.

Pronouncements from senior Conservatives prior to the election and preliminary statements from members of the BoR Commission indicate that it is highly unlikely that the BoR would be given a stronger constitutional status than the HRA has.[29] For example, Martin Howe QC, Commission member, said this in evidence to the Select Committee:

> Would a Bill of Rights for the United Kingdom represent a stronger constraint on Parliament than the existing mechanism, which I think some people call 'soft entrenchment', under the Human Rights Act 1998? I am not sure. That is certainly not something I favour.[30]

Michael Pinto-Duschinsky, a Commission member, has written on this (prior to being appointed to the Commission) that the HRA weakened Parliamentary sovereignty because it:

> obliged British judges to accept the interpretations of the very broad terms of the European Convention on Human Rights before their own interpretations. It obliged them to place these interpretations from Strasbourg before the meaning of the legislation passed at Westminster.[31]

Thus it seems highly probable that in a BoR put forward by a Conservative-dominated government, sovereignty would be preserved by equivalents to ss 3(2) and 6(2), and probably combined with a s 4 equivalent, rather than allowing judges a strike-down power. Obviously each of these possibilities offers opportunities to revisit the sections in the light of the experience of the HRA over the last 11 years, and the jurisprudence that has emerged. In particular, the Coalition Government might be tempted to remove or weaken

---

28 'Rebuilding trust in politics', speech, 8 February 2010.
29 Grieve has said that it will 'be possible to repeal or override part or all of a Bill of Rights in exactly the same way as the Government has routinely done to Habeas Corpus and Magna Carta', speech in *Liberty and Community in Britain*, 2006.
30 Answer to Q81, Commons Select Committee on Political and Constitutional Reform, op. cit., n. 10.
31 *Bringing Rights Back Home: Making human rights compatible with Parliamentary democracy in the UK*, Policy Exchange Paper, 2011.

s 4, which has come to be viewed as creating a de facto obligation upon the executive to act, even though technically a s 4 declaration can be disregarded. It is possible that the 'fast-track' procedure for amending incompatible legislation will be removed.[32] And it would be consistent with the aspiration of the Conservatives to weaken the link with Strasbourg not to include the provision in s 10(1)(b), to the effect that the power to take remedial action can be triggered by a finding of the Strasbourg Court. But creating greater Parliamentary autonomy in a radical and far-reaching sense clearly depends more on reform to the ECtHR, which is largely outside the scope of this chapter, rather than on any changes effected under the BoR.

But the Parliamentary sovereignty-preserving mechanisms in the HRA might in effect be bolstered when their equivalents are considered for the BoR as a concomitant to possible changes to the mechanisms affording the judges power to determine the interpretation and application of the rights. So it appears possible that the section of the HRA which, it is argued, handed a very significant measure of power to judges – s 3 – might appear in the BoR in a modified and weakened form.[33] Grieve has said in relation to the use of the interpretative obligation under s 3 that it is wrong that courts should 'have power to stand a statute on its head'.[34] The new s 3 would presumably refer to creating compatibility between the list of rights in the BoR, which would no doubt reflect all the ECHR obligations, without including the text of the ECHR itself. One possibility would be that the new s 3 could state that in the event of a conflict between decisions of the Strasbourg Court (as opposed to domestic decisions as to the interpretation of provisions of the BoR list of rights) and provisions in legislation, the latter must prevail, but a declaration of the incompatibility can be made. That in itself would not fully solve the problem – for Conservatives – of Strasbourg interventionism, at the Parliamentary level. But, combined with the possible changes to s 2 HRA that appear to be on the agenda as discussed below, it would prevent courts absorbing Strasbourg decisions into domestic law, allowing read-down of legislation via s 3 HRA, without affording the executive an opportunity to make a determination as to the favoured response. Such a change would not deal with the inroads made into Parliamentary sovereignty by the Strasbourg Court itself, again currently perceived as a serious problem by Conservative HRA-sceptics.

---

32 See D. Grieve: 'I am certainly intent on getting rid of the fast track procedure for primary legislation to be struck down in the event of declarations of incompatibility', speech at *Proposals for a British Bill of Rights*, British Academy/AHRC Forum, 8 March 2010.

33 E.g. the term 'reasonably' could be included on the lines of the equivalent provision in the Canadian Charter.

34 'It's the interpretation of the Human Rights Act that's the problem – not the ECHR itself', *Conservative Home blog*, 14 April 2009, available at: <http://conservativehome.blogs.com/platform/2009/04/dominic-grieve-.html> (accessed 15 August 2011).

Jowell has argued that under the HRA the courts were 'charged by Parliament with delineating "the boundaries of a rights-based democracy" '.[35] This view of the HRA, which can be referred to as reflecting an incorporationist stance, may be termed that of 'liberal constitutionalism' – it finds that the HRA created a shift of power from Parliament to the judges, removing human rights from the political realm. An opposing view[36] finds that courts, under the HRA, are able to engage in a constitutional dialogue between themselves, Parliament and the executive as to the interpretation of the ECHR.[37] The HRA asks courts to examine a legislative interference with a right, and, if it is deemed inappropriate to create compatibility between the interfering measure and the right under s 3 HRA, it asks them to inform Parliament via s 4 HRA that it has breached the Convention. The role the BoR may be intended to play from a Conservative perspective can be contrasted with that of the HRA, in terms of these opposing models, well established in public law literature, of dialogic constitutionalism or incorporationism.

As a number of commentators have pointed out, s 3 HRA has tended to be used to a greater extent than anticipated, a stance that obviously does not comport fully with furtherance of the dialogic model.[38] The BoR appears likely to resemble the HRA in creating an appearance of adhering to a constitutional dialogic model, while in actuality its Parliamentary sovereignty-preserving mechanisms are probably no more likely than those of the HRA to be utilised – in terms of *open* defiance of the ECHR. In other words, the government, whatever the nature of such mechanisms appearing in the BoR, is, as a matter of constitutional reality, still likely to be reluctant to announce that it intends to legislate in deliberate breach of its Treaty obligations. Thus, under a BoR, Parliament is likely to continue to tend to rely on the ECHR exceptions and derogation system, rather than on the equivalents of ss 3(2) and 6(2). However, although open defiance of the ECHR would be unlikely, and the BoR Commission's remit does not include leaving the ECHR system completely, the BoR could be used to limit and blunt the impact of decisions at Strasbourg, as far as the UK courts are concerned.

35 The quote is from J. Jowell, 'Judicial deference: servility, civility or institutional capacity', *Public Law*, 2003, p. 597.
36 See on this divergence of view, T. Hickman, *Public Law after the HRA*, Oxford: Hart, 2010, pp. 58–63.
37 See F. Klug, 'The HRA – a "third way" or a "third wave" Bill of Rights', *European Human Rights Law Review*, 2001, p. 361.
38 Section 4 appears to be used more than s 3. As of 2006: s 4 had been used 15 times, while s 3 had been used 13 times. Available from the Ministry of Justice at <http://www.justice.gov.uk/downloads/guidance/freedom-and-rights/human-rights/parts-one-to-six.pdf> (accessed 15 August 2011); the 2008 figure for use of s 4 declarations is now at 24, available at: <http://www.official-documents.gov.uk/document/cm75/7524/7524.pdf>. This point is referred to in A. Kavanagh, *Constitutional Review under the UK Human Rights Act*, Cambridge: Cambridge University Press, 2009, pp. 121–32.

Conservatives appear to consider, it is suggested, that departures from the ECHR could occur under a BoR in comparison with the HRA. But it follows from the discussion that such departures are unlikely to come about due to the creation of radically stronger measures to protect Parliamentary sovereignty. As discussed, such measures have not been extensively utilised under the HRA to allow for departures from the ECHR, except in the sense that s 6(2) applies to allow incompatible measures to continue to take effect for a time, as in the instance of prisoners' voting rights or in respect of the three months' gap between the declaration of incompatibility in *A and others* and the repeal of Part 4 ACTSA. But the previous and current governments have in general sought to stay within the ECHR, rather than openly repudiating it, as the HRA allows – with Parliament's consent. If strengthening the Parliamentary sovereignty-preserving measures of the HRA in the BoR is unlikely to hand determinations as to human rights matters to Parliament to a significantly greater degree, then the underlying purpose of the BoR, from the Conservative perspective – to set the UK largely free from the influence of Strasbourg – might appear to be unlikely to be realised, except in the sense that determinations as to acceptance of ECtHR decisions might be made more frequently by Parliament than by the courts. However, it is argued below that there is another possible method of undermining the rights recognised under the ECHR without necessarily appearing to do so, which is favoured by Conservative HRA-sceptics.

The relationship between Strasbourg and the domestic courts

There are signs that senior Conservatives prior to the 2010 election intended to use the BoR to seek to sever or weaken the connection with Strasbourg created by the HRA, s 2. Dominic Grieve has argued that the HRA had been 'interpreted as requiring a degree of deference to Strasbourg that I believe was and should be neither required nor intended'.[39] Instead, he said, a new Bill of Rights, which would replace the HRA, would make it clear that British courts could allow for UK common law to take precedence over decisions by the European Court of Human Rights in Strasbourg.[40] That could be achieved by requiring the domestic courts to take a different stance from Strasbourg, to depart from Strasbourg, possibly in specified circumstances. There are some signs that certain Commission members would have sympathy with such a

---

39 'Can the Bill of Rights do better than the Human Rights Act?', Dominic Grieve's Guest Lecture, Middle Temple Hall, 30 November 2009, available at: <http://www.middletemple.org.uk/Downloads/Grieve%20Bill%20of%20Rights%20lecture%2030%20 11%2009.pdf> (accessed 15 August 2011).
40 Ibid.

stance. Commission member Anthony Speaight said in evidence to the Select Committee:

> The European Convention on Human Rights is a noble venture with wonderful ideals, but if you look at where we are now, the court ... makes decisions that something or other is a human right that would not by the average Briton be regarded as a human right. . . . To be told – to take the current example that is uppermost in one's mind – that this country's penal policy, supported overwhelmingly by its legislators, is incompatible with human rights just strikes most Britons as nonsense.[41]

The replacement for s 2 HRA in the BoR could play a role in the hunt for 'greater subsidiarity'. From the point of view of the Conservatives on the Commission and the Conservative Party generally, this is clearly a key aspiration underlying this project.

Currently, in seeking to interpret the Convention rights under the Human Rights Act, the domestic judiciary 'must take into account' any relevant Strasbourg jurisprudence, under s 2. Those words appear to indicate that the jurisprudence is non-binding, but they do not reflect the position taken towards the Strasbourg jurisprudence in domestic courts. It was found in *Ullah*[42] in the House of Lords that the judges must follow any clear and constant jurisprudence of the Strasbourg court. In the counter-terrorism case of *AF*,[43] the stance taken by Lord Carswell, and accepted by the majority, was to the effect that a Strasbourg decision – *A v UK*[44] – upholding a higher due process standard than the previous House of Lords decision in *MB*[45] had done, had to be applied. It was considered by the majority that there was no leeway under s 2 HRA to do otherwise. Lord Carswell found (reluctantly) that the principle espoused by the Grand Chamber in *A v UK* differed from that adopted by the majority in *MB* but

> whatever 'latitude' might be permitted to the courts by the duty to take Strasbourg judgments into account under s 2(1) HRA, the authority of a considered statement of the Grand Chamber is such that our courts have no option but to accept and apply it.[46]

41 In reply to Q36, Commons Select Committee on Political and Constitutional Reform, op. cit., n. 10.
42 *R (on the application of Ullah) v Special Adjudicator* [2004] UKHL 26. See further J. Lewis, 'The European Ceiling on Human Rights', *Public Law*, 2007, (Win), p. 720.
43 See *Secretary of State for the Home Department v AF (No 3)* [2009] UKHL 28.
44 (2009) 49 EHRR 29.
45 [2008] AC 440.
46 'Views may differ as to which approach is preferable, and not all may be persuaded that the Grand Chamber's ruling is the preferable approach. But I am in agreement with your Lordships that we are obliged to accept and apply the Grand Chamber's principles in preference to those espoused by the majority in *MB*', at para 108.

The Strasbourg Court had upheld a higher standard of fair trial rights (demanding minimum disclosure of the evidence against him to the person to whom preventive measures had been applied, as discussed further below) than the House of Lords had upheld in *MB*. So despite the HRA, and the reliance on the Strasbourg jurisprudence demanded by s 2, the Lords had failed to interpret the Strasbourg jurisprudence in the way that Strasbourg would have concurred with.

In *R v Horncastle*,[47] also in the context of Art. 6, the Supreme Court considered that departure even from clear jurisprudence was exceptionally acceptable under s 2 HRA, as s 2 originally intended. The domestic provisions in question, the Court found, struck the right balance between the imperative that a trial must be fair and the interests of victims in particular and society in general. In other words, the Strasbourg test did not strike the right balance and therefore was not applied. The Supreme Court decided that the European Court's decision insufficiently accommodated aspects of the domestic process, and determined that, in those rare circumstances, it could decline to follow the decision, as it did. But the Supreme Court in *Cadder v HM Advocate (HM Advocate General for Scotland and another intervening)*[48] found that s 2 HRA required it to apply the decision of the ECtHR in *Salduz v Turkey*.[49] Thus, in effect, the Strasbourg jurisprudence, although not technically binding on domestic courts, may be viewed as coming close to having a binding impact via s 2 HRA. Clearly, the effect of s 2 HRA under its current interpretation from *Cadder* does not, in formal terms, limit Parliamentary sovereignty. But in terms of constitutional reality, it can do. If, as in *AF*, a court follows a Strasbourg ruling and accordingly 'reads down' legislation under s 3 HRA, then for a period of time (until and if amending or replacement legislation changes the position) the legislation assumes a form that differs from that which Parliament had determined upon. Thus, an area of law is interpreted and applied according to Strasbourg norms, rather than according to norms accepted by the Westminster Parliament.

Given that this position under s 2 HRA is not viewed as satisfactory from the point of view of the Conservative HRA-sceptics (i.e. probably the majority in the party), what options would be available in terms of re-framing the s 2 equivalent in the Bill of Rights? The idea, as expressed by Dominic Grieve, appeared to be to make provision in the BoR for an s 2 replacement, that would allow or require the judges, in effect, to apply the *Horncastle* principle in *most* circumstances, *not* as an exception. That could mean that domestic judges would tend to arrive at an interpretation of, for example, the equivalent to Art. 8 in the BoR, which broadly coincided with its more established interpretation at Strasbourg, and probably with domestic rulings under the

47 [2010] 2 WLR 47.
48 [2010] 1 WLR 2601. See in particular [33], [40], [41], [47], referring to [55] in *Salduz*.
49 (2008) 49 EHRR 421.

HRA in relation to Art. 8. But in certain circumstances their jurisprudence might diverge from that of Strasbourg. Possibly in order to achieve this, it would be necessary to include a list of circumstances under which departure from Strasbourg should occur. An obvious instance would be where there is a gap in the jurisprudence or where the instance in question was within states' margin of appreciation. More controversially, the list could include instances where Parliament had recently decided to strike a balance between competing rights or between rights and societal concerns differing from that struck at Strasbourg, reflecting the *Horncastle* stance.

One possible aspect of weakening the link to Strasbourg may be the inclusion of a provision expressly asking the judges to take account of decisions from other common-law jurisdictions rather than from Strasbourg. Anthony Speaight said on this to the Parliamentary Committee:

> One of the things that I hope will be very seriously considered in drafting any UK Bill of Rights is giving an express statement that English courts can and should take account of decisions on rights, expressed in the same or similar terms to our rights, by courts in other common law jurisdictions: Commonwealth countries and the United States of America.[50]

Obviously, however, none of this deals with the problem of a head-on clash between a legislative provision and a Strasbourg decision, although a changed s 2 equivalent might allow Parliament, not the courts, to deal with it.

The liberties and obligations to be protected/recognised under the BOR?

Including the text of the ECHR?

Under the terms of reference for the Commission, the British Bill of Rights is intended to incorporate and build on 'all the obligations under the European Convention on Human Rights, and protect and extend British liberties'. It is noticeable that the word 'obligations' is used; it presumably refers to the obligations that would be placed on public authorities under an equivalent of s 6 HRA. The terms of reference indicate that protection will be provided for the obligations of the European Convention on Human Rights, as opposed to introducing a completely new set of rights in a tailor-made UK Bill of Rights. That is the understanding of the Chair of the Commission, Sir Leigh Lewis, who said to the Select Committee:

---

50 Answer to Q49, Commons Select Committee on Political and Constitutional Reform, op. cit., n. 10.

I think the debate over a UK Bill of Rights has been seen as whether we should have a UK Bill of Rights in addition to our obligations under the European Convention on Human Rights.[51]

However, covering the same obligations as the ECHR does not necessarily involve using the *terminology* of the ECHR. For Anthony Speaight:

> . . . the Magna Carta is extremely important to the heritage of England and Wales, both because of its place in our history and because of the way in which its wording has been echoed in similar charters all over the world. . . . We had the Bill of Rights at the end of the 17th century. The Latin tag 'habeas corpus' has a value . . . if the debates about terrorist control, periods of detention and so on, instead of talking about rights under article so-and-so of the Convention, still used the tag 'habeas corpus' – it is nothing to do with the Human Rights Act that that went, as it was ditched a decade or two previously – is a resonance in that expression that echoes down the years . . .[52]

He appeared to indicate that different wording could be used, more redolent of English heritage.

A more comprehensive list of rights?

It would be tempting to see the introduction of a BoR as an opportunity to adopt a more comprehensive list of rights, relevant in the twenty-first century. From today's perspective, the 60-year-old Convention looks very much like a creature of its period,[53] with its provision against slavery[54] and its long lists of exceptions to certain fundamental rights. Its out-of-date feel has led a number of commentators to echo the plea put forward some years ago by Tomkins and Rix for 'a document of principle for the 1990s and not a document of

51 Answer to Q8, Commons Select Committee on Political and Constitutional Reform, op. cit., n. 10.
52 Political and Constitutional Reform Committee Minutes of Evidence UK Bill of Rights Commission (9 June 2011) Q39: available at: <http://www.publications.parliament.uk/pa/cm201012/cmselect/cmpolcon/1049/11060903.htm> (accessed 15 August 2011).
53 The Convention was drafted in 1949 and based on the United Nations Declaration of Human Rights. The Declaration was adopted on 10 December 1948 by the General Assembly of the UN.
54 Although slavery in the sense of human trafficking is still a live issue in Europe. See 26th Report of the JCHR on human trafficking 2005–6, HL Paper 245–1, HC Paper 1127–1, published 13 September 2006. See also *The Guardian*, 23 March 2007.

exceptions from the 1950s'.[55] Feldman has made a similar point: the Convention rights are 'by no means a comprehensive basis for a modern system of protection for [individualistic and public] values'.[56] The far more thorough South African Bill of Rights, which covers certain social, economic and environmental rights, provides an example of such a system. Liberty's *Manifesto for Human Rights*, put forward in 1997, proposed that a domestic Bill of Rights could be drawn up, based on the Convention, but using more up-to-date language and addressing certain of the inadequacies of the ECHR.[57] In particular, Liberty criticised the lack of minimum conditions for detention outside Art. 5, and the lack of a right to jury trial. It has also often been pointed out that the Convention contains no specific rights for children.[58] The Equality and Human Rights Commission (EHRC) found on the question of a more comprehensive instrument in 2010: 'The government should incorporate in any Bill of Rights a fully enforceable free-standing right to equality.' The Commission also advocated inclusion of a right to dignity and 'measures to increase participation and representation of particular groups such as women, ethnic minorities, disabled persons and older persons as provided for in relevant international conventions and principles'.[59]

When listed rights have been referred to by senior Conservatives prior to the 2010 general election and recently by Commission members, the references have been, it appears, to the list of ECHR rights in Schedule 1 HRA, with some additions, most obviously a right to jury trial,[60] and possibly with the creation of limits on the power of the state to impose administrative sanctions without due process of law – such as fines for speeding. None of the speeches of Conservative spokespersons prior to the Election made mention of the possibility of protecting the further rights under the later Protocols. Anthony Speaight said on this to the Select Committee:

> . . . my favoured option would be that, in place of the Human Rights Act there would be a new statute – let's call it a UK Bill of Rights for want of a better label – which would set out as the rights every single word that

---

55 'Unconventional use of the Convention', *Modern Law Review*, 1992, 55(5), p. 725. See also A. Ashworth, 'The European Convention on Human Rights and English criminal justice: ships which pass in the night?', in M. Andenas (ed.), *English Public Law and the Common Law of Europe*, London: Key Haven, 1998, p. 215.

56 See, e.g., D. Feldman, 'The Human Rights Act 1998 and constitutional principles', *Legal Studies*, 1999, 19(2), p. 170.

57 National Council for Civil Liberties 1997 (now Liberty). See also the Bill drawn up by the Institute for Public Policy Research: Constitution Paper No 1, 'A British Bill of Rights', 1990.

58 J. Fortin, 'Rights brought home for children', *Modern Law Review*, 1999, 62, p. 350.

59 *HRA Plus: Human Rights for 21st-century Britain*, EHRC, Spring 2010.

60 See D. Grieve, *Proposals for a British Bill of Rights*, op. cit, n. 32.

is in the European Convention but also some extra things, jury trial being one of my candidates for addition.[61]

The Human Rights Act has also been criticised for losing the opportunity to include certain social and economic rights, including some of those protected under the International Covenant on Social, Economic and Cultural Rights.[62] Obviously, if the opportunity arises various groups are likely to put forward arguments for specific additions to the current Schedule 1 rights, such as the inclusion of certain socio-economic rights.[63] On socio-economic rights the EHRC said in 2010:

> The government [the previous Labour Government] should consult on the full range of possibilities regarding the possible incorporation of socio-economic rights; which could have immediate effect; and whether some or all could be justiciable in some way. It should consult in this manner in relation to all the key socio-economic rights: the right to an adequate standard of living including housing; the right to physical and mental health; the right to education; the right to work, and the right to social security.[64]

But it is readily apparent that under a Conservative-dominated Coalition Government the addition of such rights is highly unlikely. Anthony Speaight said on this in 2011: 'I personally am more inclined towards a more minimalist statement of rights than one that goes in the direction of environmental rights and socioeconomic rights . . .'[65] It appears likely that the list of rights would echo those of the ECHR with few additions. Thus, any movement away from Strasbourg would not be likely to be effected by the list of rights covered.

Balancing rights with responsibilities?

In 2006 David Cameron said:

> The Conservative Party, under my leadership, is determined to provide a hard-nosed defence of security and freedom. . . . the right way to do that is through a modern British Bill of Rights that also balances rights with responsibilities.[66]

---

61 Answer to Q47, Commons Select Committee on Political and Constitutional Reform, op. cit., n. 10.
62 See K.D. Ewing and C.A. Gearty, 'Rocky foundations for Labour's new rights' (1997) 2 *EHRLR* 149.
63 The inclusion of children's rights is also likely to be argued for; see Children's Rights Alliance press release, 20 May 2010: *Bill of Rights could strengthen the rights of children*.
64 *HRA Plus: Human Rights for 21st-century Britain*, op. cit., n. 59.
65 Answer to Q49, Commons Select Committee on Political and Constitutional Reform, op. cit., n. 10.
66 'Balancing freedom and security – A modern British Bill of Rights' 2006, op. cit., n. 9.

Jonathan Fisher QC,[67] one of the Conservative nominees on the BoR Commission, wrote in 2006 on this:

> The inexorable reality is that the European Convention on Human Rights (ECHR) is a fundamentally flawed and lop-sided document, produced as a specific response to the horrors of Nazi Germany, with an entrenched bias in favour of individual rights. The document is hopelessly unbalanced by its omission to incorporate any notion of civil obligation into the text.

He noted that Art. 29 UDHR, '(1) Everyone has duties to the community in which alone the free and full development of his personality is possible', was omitted from the text of the ECHR; he continued to the effect that inclusion of civil obligations in a British Bill of Rights would:

> unambiguously declare to each and every British citizen the importance of individual responsibility and promote societal cohesion. It would place before them the notion of exactly what it means to live in a democracy, and it would create a milieu in which notions of good citizenship, social and environmental responsibility, civil engagement and community involvement could properly thrive . . . Today's children are tomorrow's responsible citizens, but there needs to be a framework [provided by a BoR incorporating civic responsibilities] in which the core values of human rights and individual obligations can be transmitted.[68]

The connections between these ideas and those expressed by David Cameron in 2011 in the context of the riots are readily apparent. Such ideas might also appear attractive from a Conservative perspective in relation to the prisoners' voting issue.

The possibility of referring to both rights and responsibilities in the BoR was raised in the Constitutional Reform Select Committee, in terms of referring to the obligations citizens could be expected to fulfil in order to access the rights. Mr Chope said:

> The biggest political problem seems to arise when people seek justice under the European Convention where they themselves have contributed to their own problems, perhaps, for example . . . somebody who has committed as an asylum seeker a crime but then is told under the interpretation of the Convention that, although he has committed a crime in the country to which he doesn't belong, he can't be sent back to the

---

67 Director of Research, Society of Conservative Lawyers.
68 A British Bill of Rights and Obligations Essay for the Conservative Liberty Forum (2006).

country from which he emanates because he might then be subject to the laws of that country and maltreated. One of the principles of British law has always been that if you want to get help from the courts you must come with clean hands. Do you see that that is one of the difficulties that there is at the moment and perhaps the concept of equity could be written into a Bill of Rights so that people would only be able to get justice if they themselves had acted fairly and reasonably . . .?[69]

Anthony Speaight agreed that that was one of the issues for consideration.

If the BoR was to impose both rights and responsibilities, it could imply that citizens would be placed under an obligation to *qualify* for rights protection by discharging such responsibilities. For example, prisoners could be excluded in certain circumstances from seeking to claim a right to vote, or other democratic rights (under Arts 10 and 11 ECHR) due to their failure to abide by civic responsibilities by committing criminal offences. Obviously that would be controversial and would depart from the notion that rights inhere automatically in humans. The EHRC's position on this issue is that

> . . . human rights can never be made contingent on the exercise of responsibilities. This position reflects requirements under international human rights treaties to which the UK government is a party. However, there may be merit in recognising in any Bill of Rights the responsibilities we have to protect each others' human rights. This could help to promote mutual respect, tolerance and a more cohesive society.[70]

This issue is returned to below.

Promoting a better understanding of the rights – but rejecting the European aspect of the HRA?

Part of the remit of the Commission refers to promoting a better understanding of rights. Sir Leigh Lewis, Commission Chair, was asked about this by the Chair of the Parliamentary Committee: 'Do you see it as part of your mission to help get a broader understanding in the UK of rights in general, and do you think your discussions will help that along the way?'[71] He replied that 'at the very least we may be able to give people more widely a better understanding of the facts, the position and the issues so that any future and further debate, and there is bound to be such, beyond the life of the Commission might be better informed'. However, one of the themes

---

69 Answer to Q49, Commons Select Committee on Political and Constitutional Reform, op. cit., n. 10.
70 *HRA Plus: Human Rights for 21st-century Britain*, op. cit., n. 59.
71 Answer to Q27, Commons Select Committee on Political and Constitutional Reform, op. cit., n. 10.

mentioned a number of times by Conservatives has referred less to creating a more accurate understanding of the HRA, or human rights in general, but to rejecting a European human rights culture as an alien import to the UK.

Negative perceptions of the HRA as protecting alien European human rights

The perception of the ECHR in the popular consciousness has posed a continuing problem for human rights advocates in the UK post-HRA. The inception of the HRA was not accompanied by the kind of popular debate that preceded the US Bill of Rights in 1789, or that accompanied the adoption of the Canadian Charter of Fundamental Rights and Freedoms as part of the patriation of the Canadian constitution in 1982. Although in 1998 the New Labour Government commanded widespread popular support, and the HRA was passed during its honeymoon period, it did not seek to make the case for the HRA to the British people. That proved eventually to create problems, post 9/11, when the HRA came under pressure in relation to counter-terrorist strategy, and the war in Iraq led to a rapid diminution of the Labour Government's popularity. As Francesca Klug put it: 'If the world hadn't shifted on its axis after 11 September 2001, the HRA may well have bedded down to become an accepted part of the legal and constitutional landscape of the UK.'[72]

Clearly, the hostility of parts of the media has been fuelled by the use of the HRA to aid in creating a tort of misuse of personal information. Lord Lester said on this issue to the Select Committee in 2011:

> . . . some sections of the media – self-interested, God bless them – have campaigned vigorously against the Human Rights Act, totally unscrupulously, completely unfairly, mischaracterising everything as being a result of the Human Rights Act. That I expect to continue and I have already seen that they seek to rubbish the Human Rights Commission as part of their campaign.[73]

He indicated that the hostility might spring from restrictions 'on their right to invade personal privacy' created by the HRA.[74]

It was possible in the post-HRA years for popular ignorance of and lack of adherence to the HRA to be exploited and manipulated by the Conservative Party and a hostile media.[75] The Labour Government after 9/11 also appeared

---

72 F. Klug, 'A Bill of Rights: what for?', in *Towards a New Constitutional Settlement*, The Smith Institute, 2007, p. 130.
73 Q59, Commons Select Committee on Political and Constitutional Reform, op. cit, n. 10.
74 Q65, Commons Select Committee on Political and Constitutional Reform, op. cit, n. 10.
75 See *Review of the Implementation of the Human Rights Act*, Department of Constitutional Affairs, July 2006.

remarkably reluctant to defend its own instrument. As Klug puts it: 'After the 2005 London bombings in particular, the Prime Minister sometimes sounded like a cheer-leader for this negative spin, threatening to "amend the Human Rights Act in respect of the interpretation of the ECHR".'[76] The appeal to fear of terrorism was effective in creating a misleading image of the HRA. A false dilemma was, it is argued, created by parts of the media, suggesting that the only alternatives are rights protection under the HRA or security. So such repeal would destroy the main barrier to introducing effective counter-terrorist measures. Further, various media myths were promulgated, such as that police had to supply fried chicken to a suspected car thief under the HRA[77] and that 'Serial killer, Dennis Nilsen, 60, received hardcore gay porn in jail thanks to human rights laws.'[78]

A British instrument reflective of traditional liberties rather than European human rights?

As a result, in discussions of the BoR, a number of references have possibly been made to British values rather than European ones, and to a shared cultural understanding of principles.

In 2006, Cameron spoke of 'a new solution that protects liberties in this country that is home-grown and sensitive to Britain's legal inheritance, that enables people to feel they have ownership of their rights'.[79] A Conservative member of the Parliamentary Committee questioning members of the BoR Commission in 2011 spoke of 'one of the biggest conflicts [as being] between what might be described as Continental jurisprudence and British jurisprudence'.[80] Creating a break under the BoR with the 'European' aspect of the HRA is seen from the Conservatives' perspective as important in terms of 'selling' the new instrument to the British people. Anthony Speaight said on this:

> . . . it is a great pity that the Human Rights Act is necessarily perceived to have based our rights on a charter of rights that comes from elsewhere. It may historically be the case that in the 1950s it was drafted by an Englishman, Maxwell-Fyfe, but that is an academic piece of information. The reality, particularly as it is interpreted as a living instrument by the courts, is that it is widely perceived as being from elsewhere. It is not

76 Klug, 'A Bill of Rights: what for?', op. cit, n. 72, p. 6. She was quoting the Prime Minister's statement on anti-terror measures, Press Conference, 5 August 2005.
77 *The Sun*, June 2006.
78 *The Sun*, May 2006.
79 'Balancing freedom and security – A modern British Bill of Rights', 2006, op. cit., n 9.
80 Mr Chope.

perceived as being part of Britain's heritage . . . it would be very attractive if we could have some sort of Bill of Rights.. . which much more directly reflects our own heritage.[81]

In contrast, Helena Kennedy said: '. . . it has to be told to the public: the people who were at the heart of creating the European Convention on Human Rights were British lawyers, and they drew on common law values.'[82]

If the Conservative view prevails it might mean that changes to the wording used to express the ECHR rights could be employed to create a distinctively 'British' feel to the instrument. For example, the free speech clause might not be labelled 'Article 10' or use the exact wording of Art. 10. The effects of any such change would not be radical, but might be viewed as necessary to generate popular support for the BoR and to persuade the judges to adopt interpretations of the rights differing from those of the Strasbourg Court.

Determining the *'true scope* of these obligations and liberties'

The remit of the BoR Commission does not, at face value, cover complete withdrawal from the ECHR. Sir Leigh Lewis, Chair of the Commission, was asked, in giving evidence to the Constitutional Reform Committee, whether the group's options were too limited by its terms of reference, which prevent the group arguing for such withdrawal. He did not completely rule out consideration of the possibility: '. . . if some members take a different view of what the terms of reference might cover . . . we will need to look at that.'[83] That issue is clearly distinct from that of the question of the content of the BoR. However, other ways of creating a distance between the impact of the BoR and that of the ECHR have been mentioned a number of times by David Cameron, Dominic Grieve and Jonathan Fisher QC prior to the general election and recently by Anthony Speaight.

Re-balancing or interpretation clauses in the BOR?

Dominic Grieve has mentioned the possibility of including 'interpretation clauses' in the BoR a number of times.[84] Cameron has spoken of the BoR solution as 'one which at the same time enables a British Home Secretary to strike

---

81 In answer to Q36, Commons Select Committee on Political and Constitutional Reform, op. cit, n. 10.
82 In answer to Q109, ibid.
83 In answer to Q7, ibid.
84 See *Proposals for a British Bill of Rights*, op. cit., n. 32 Such interpretation clauses were also referred to in 2009, Guest Lecture, Middle Temple Hall, op. cit. n. 39.

a common-sense balance between civil liberties and the protection of public security'.[85] Dominic Grieve has said on this: 'There is certainly a degree of interpretation where there would be greater flexibility in the Bill of Rights than there is currently in the ECHR.'[86] Jonathan Fisher QC, BoR Commission member, said in 2006 that a new BoR:

> would assist the Legislature and the Courts in balancing human rights in the public interest, by allowing the recognition of individual rights to be viewed contextually, through a prism of individual obligations owed to society. In this way, for example, a British Home Secretary would be afforded more flexibility in making a judgment in the public interest as to whether a foreign national should be deported to his country of origin in cases of terrorist or criminal activity.[87]

Lord Hoffmann said in his Judicial Studies Board lecture in 2009 that:

> . . . the fact that the 10 original Member States of the Council of Europe subscribed to a statement of human rights in the same terms did not mean that they had agreed to uniformity of the *application* of those abstract rights in each of their countries.[88]

He went on to say that the Strasbourg Court has '. . . been unable to resist the temptation to aggrandise its jurisdiction and to impose uniform rules on member states'.[89] Dominic Grieve in 2009 welcomed this criticism of the Court and said:

> The Conservative approach, which David Cameron set out in his speech in June 2006, is to replace the HRA with our own home-grown Bill of Rights. A Bill of Rights would be compatible with the ECHR. In areas where ECHR rights are absolute, such as the Article 3 prohibition of torture, those protections will not be removed. But there is no reason why

---

85 'Balancing freedom and security – A modern British Bill of Rights', op. cit., n. 9.
86 He continued: 'That I think is feasible. It would be quite wrong to suggest that it would completely transform the situation [in relation to the deportation of suspected terrorists at risk of torture in the receiving country]' (D. Grieve, BBC Radio 4: *Westminster Hour*, 25 June, 2006). See further: Justice, 'A British Bill of Rights: Informing the debate', Constitution committee, final report, 19 November 2007, available at: <http://www.justice.org. uk/data/files/resources/11/A-British-Bill-of-Rights.pdf> (accessed 31 October 2011).
87 *A British Bill of Rights and Obligations*, Essay for the Conservative Liberty Forum (2006).
88 *Judicial Studies Board lecture*, 19 March 2009, available at: <http://www.judiciary.gov.uk/ Resources/JCO/Documents/Speeches/Hoffmann_2009_JSB_Annual_Lecture_Universality_ of_Human_Rights.pdf> (accessed 19 July 2011).
89 Ibid.

our courts should be bound by Strasbourg Court jurisprudence, if their own interpretation is different, particularly where rights should be balanced by responsibilities.[90]

David Cameron as Prime Minister has indicated on a number of occasions that a BoR would allow the UK to escape from human rights constraints that he sees as offensive and as flying in the face of common sense. In other words, he has held out the BoR as the cure for non-commonsensical use of human rights laws. He made that point in the quote about the causes of the riots (above), in relation to the prisoners' voting rights issue, and in relation to the finding in 2010 of a breach of Art. 8, in respect of the requirement that certain sex offenders must be subject indefinitely to 'notification requirements', without a prospect of change if they had reformed.[91] In response to that decision, he made the point – which was echoed in the quote above from August 2011 about the BoR – that a Bill of Rights commission would be 'established imminently because I think it's about time we started making sure decisions are made in this Parliament rather than in the courts'.[92]

This issue has arisen in evidence to the Parliamentary Committee in 2011 from BoR Commission members, although in much less stark and melodramatic terms. Anthony Speaight has said:

> What could be done in a UK Bill of Rights is some tweaking of rights. In the Human Rights Act, there was one attempt by Parliament to tweak section 12, which in effect said where there is a conflict between privacy and free speech under articles 8 and 10, free speech is very, very important. That really was the message of section 12. It was saying if the seesaw is in any way like that, let the free speech end win. In my view the English judges have simply ignored that, so tweaking may not work very well. But that is a precedent showing that tweaking can be done, and it certainly is a possibility in a UK Bill of Rights that extra text can be added to a repeat of the wording of the Convention.[93]

The idea of interpretation clauses has, unsurprisingly, not been referred to by Baroness Kennedy, Lord Lester or Philippe Sands in evidence to the Committee.

---

90 *Conservative Home blog*, 14 April 2009, op. cit. n. 34.
91 The decision of the Supreme Court in *R (F) v Secretary of State for the Home Department* [2010] UKSC 17.
92 The comment was made at Prime Minister's Questions on 15 February 2011; Mr Cameron was responding to Tory MP Philip Davies who complained about the Supreme Court ruling that sex offenders could appeal against having to register with the police for life.
93 In answer to Q45, Commons Select Committee on Political and Constitutional Reform, op. cit, n. 10.

The references from Conservative HRA-sceptics (which includes the Conservative nominees on the Commission) appear to be to including a re-balancing provision (or an 'interpretation clause') in the Bill of Rights going beyond the exceptions and derogation system of the ECHR – which could, depending on its nature, shift the balance towards greater protection for certain societal interests. One possible model for such a re-balancing clause would be s 1 of the Canadian Charter of Rights and Freedoms, which 'guarantees the rights and freedoms set out in it subject only to such reasonable limits prescribed by law as can be demonstrably justified in a free and democratic society'. A re-balancing clause could also make reference to civic responsibility, as suggested by Jonathan Fisher QC in 2006 (above).

This idea has already attracted criticism: Jean-Paul Costa, President of the ECtHR said in 2010 of the BoR proposal:

> Introducing a British bill of rights could create a complex situation . . . it could mean that most rights [in the Convention] are protected to more or less the same extent, but not 100 per cent of them. This could create divergences between the case law [from Strasbourg] and the law in the UK.[94]

An 'interpretation clause' creating exceptions going beyond those expressly present does not appear in the HRA, except impliedly, in so far as it arises from Strasbourg jurisprudence,[95] and influences domestic law via s 2 HRA.

From an executive standpoint, this second possibility would have to be accompanied by the changes to the replacement for s 2 in a BoR discussed above, since otherwise the courts would merely tend to apply the Strasbourg jurisprudence, meaning that the balance struck between individual rights and societal interests, or between competing rights, would continue in general to echo that at Strasbourg.

Competing rights – in particular Arts 8 and 10

An interpretation clause could be employed to create a *new balance* between competing rights. The most obvious area that could be affected would be the current balance between Arts 8 and 10 in the context of privacy rights against the press, obviously a matter that sections of the press are extremely concerned about, arguably for the reason put forward by Lord Lester to the Select Committee:

> There is a commercial reason why some newspapers do not like the European Convention or the Human Rights Act. That is because they

---

94 Reported in *The Guardian*, 27 June 2010.
95 See on the possibility of departure from Art. 6 standards where absolutely necessary: *Rowe v United Kingdom* (2000) 30 EHRR 1, at [61]; *Botmeh and Alami v United Kingdom*, no 15187/03, (2007) at [37]; *Van Mechelen v The Netherlands* (1997) 25 EHRR 647, at [58].

don't like restrictions on their right to invade personal privacy and they rightly see the Human Rights Act, and the European Convention, as a restriction on that particular way of earning money.[96]

Dominic Grieve has said on this:

> Where rights are qualified and not absolute and a balance has to be struck between competing rights, as must happen in relation to many of the Articles of the ECHR, we should also consider if we wish through inter-pretation clauses to give a more detailed guide consonant with our own legal and political traditions than does the ECHR text itself as to the weight to be given to each of them.[97]

Specifically, Grieve has shown interest in creating a new balance between Arts 8 and 10, one which would be likely to give presumptive priority to Art. 10, departing from the balance created in *Van Hannover*.[98]

The Chair of the Select Committee clearly views this as an important issue for the BoR Commission: 'I am desperately hanging on to not asking you about the First Amendment right to tackle the questions about privacy.' Anthony Speaight has said on this that the role of the HRA 'has been benefi-cial. There is one significant area where I do not think that is the case, and that is privacy cases.' Lord Lester in contrast said on this issue: '. . . some sections of the media . . . like to take the benefit of Article 10 on free speech but not the burden of Article 8 on privacy'.[99]

Article 8 and deportation

A decision that has greatly exercised Grieve is that in *EM v Lebanon*,[100] in which a woman was not deported due to the violation of her Art. 8 right to respect for her family life she would suffer in Lebanon due to sharia law. Article 8 contains a second paragraph which allows for deportation if justified as necessary in a democratic society on grounds of national security and prevention of crime.[101] It would appear that Parliament would create a breach of Treaty obligations in overturning *EM v Lebanon* via changes in a BoR, since Strasbourg has accepted that deportation may be in breach of Art. 8, depending

---

96 Answer to Q65, Commons Select Committee on Political and Constitutional Reform, op. cit, n. 10.
97 See *Proposals for a British Bill of Rights*, op. cit., n. 32.
98 *Von Hannover v Germany* (2005) 40 EHRR 1.
99 Q59, Commons Select Committee on Political and Constitutional Reform, op. cit., n. 10.
100 [2008] UKHL 64.
101 See *Norris v Government of USA* [2010] UKSC 9.

on the question of the disproportionality of the impact on family life in relation to the aim pursued.[102]

This is a difficult issue for States because if a breach of Art. 8 is found to
arise due to deportation, no state action can remedy it, whereas diplomatic
assurances can, in the view of the UK government and House of Lords,[103]
remedy the situation where it is alleged that a breach of Arts 3 or 6 could arise
in the receiving country. In July 2011, the Home Secretary, Theresa May, told
the Commons Home Affairs Select Committee that she was concerned that
foreign criminals could use the 'right to a family life' under Art. 8 as a way of
successfully fighting deportation. She said that in the last three months of
2010, 99 foreign prisoners had successfully claimed that deporting them
would breach their right to a family life under Art. 8(1) in Britain. She went
on to say that Home Office officials are examining the definition to see if there
is scope to limit its use:

> This is one of the issues that we are looking at, to look at consideration of
> the definition, a better definition within Article 8 to see if that's a way in
> which we can provide greater ability for us to be able to ensure people are
> removed when it's appropriate to do so.[104]

Grieve views the decision in *EM* as one that has resulted from a judicial desire
to shadow Strasbourg in the HRA – and go beyond Strasbourg – and one
which could damage security in the UK if suspected terrorists could not be
deported in similar circumstances. He has already indicated that this is a
problem that he sees as one that could be remedied under a BoR.[105]

Non-materially qualified rights

Arguably, the non-materially qualified ECHR rights create even greater
problems from the Conservative viewpoint. Employment of an 'interpretation
clause' could have far-reaching effects since the intention appeared to be to
allow for the redefinition of non-materially qualified rights to suit the specific
situation in the UK. A re-balancing clause introduced in the BoR could
be used to introduce proportionality-based arguments into non-materially
qualified rights, limiting the scope and effect of the right. Assuming that
it was not intended to affect Arts 2 and 3, it would be likely to apply to

---

102 See *Boultif v Switzerland* (2001) 33 EHRR 1179; *Üner v The Netherlands* (2006) 45
     EHRR 421.
103 See *RB (Algeria) (FC) and another (Appellants) v Secretary of State for the Home Department
     OO (Jordan) (Original Respondent and Cross-appellant) v Secretary of State for the Home
     Department (Original Appellant and Cross-respondent)* [2009] UKHL 10.
104 See *Daily Telegraph* report, 6 July 2011.
105 *Conservative Home blog*, 14 April 2009, op. cit., n. 34. He also highlighted the case in
     2010: *Proposals for a British Bill of Rights*, op. cit., n. 32.

Arts 5 and 6 since Arts 8 to 11 already contain exceptions based on a broad range of societal interests if the interference is necessary and proportionate.

Articles 5 and 6, in contrast, make no provision for exceptions, apart from those already set out in the Articles (which are very limited in the case of Art. 6, applying only under Art. 6(1) to excluding the public and press from the hearing on national security grounds). Under the Strasbourg jurisprudence, the scope for placing limitations on the standards to be applied is limited – it can occur only on a 'strictly necessary' basis where national security demands it (or certain other pressing interests) so long as the hearing overall is fair.[106]

The British government in *A v UK*[107] put forward an argument for widening the exceptions to Art. 5 via introduction of a proportionality-type argument:

> The Government relied upon the principle of fair balance, which underlies the whole Convention, and reasoned that sub-para. (f) of Art. 5(1) had to be interpreted so as to strike a balance between the interests of the individual and the interests of the state in protecting its population from malevolent aliens. Detention struck that balance by advancing the legitimate aim of the state to secure the protection of the population.[108]

The idea of creating a balance – going beyond express exceptions – between the needs of society and individual rights in relation to Arts 5 and 6 has emerged in a number of instances.[109] In the public protest case of *Austin*,[110] the House of Lords unanimously concurred with Lord Hope's findings to the effect that in making a determination as to the ambit of Art. 5(1), the *purpose* of the interference with liberty could be viewed as relevant; if so, he

---

106 See *Rowe v United Kingdom* (2000) 30 EHRR 1, at [61]; *Botmeh and Alami v United Kingdom*, no. 15187/03, (2007) at [37]; *Van Mechelen v The Netherlands* (1997) 25 EHRR 647, at [58]. Thus, limited departures from certain aspects of a fair hearing, including full disclosure of the material on which suspicion is based or equality of arms, may be permissible, provided that these are strictly necessary to protect other vital interests, such as the safety of witnesses or national security. Article 5 does not allow people to be detained indefinitely even for the most pressing national security reasons, without a derogation.

107 (2009) 49 EHRR 29.

108 Ibid, at [148]. Sub-para (f) referred to provides that one of the permitted exceptions to the right to liberty is: 'the lawful arrest or detention of a person to prevent his effecting an unauthorised entry into the country or of a person against whom action is being taken with a view to deportation or extradition'.

109 See further, H. Fenwick, 'Recalibrating ECHR rights, and the role of the Human Rights Act post–9/11: reasserting international human rights norms in the "war on terror"?' *Current Legal Problems*, 63, 2010, pp. 153–234.

110 *Austin v Commissioner of Police for the Metropolis* [2009] UKHL 5.

found that it must be to enable a balance to be struck between what the restriction sought to achieve and the interests of the individual.[111] Lord Hope also found in *R v A*[112] (dissenting) that in the context of Art. 6 a fair balance must be struck 'between the demands of the general interest of the community and the requirements of the protection of the individual's fundamental rights: *Sporrong and Lönnroth v Sweden*'.[113]

If this idea were to emerge as an aspect of the BoR Commission proposals, or, eventually, as part of a Conservative proposal for a BoR, it would be of very doubtful compatibility with the remit of the Commission to protect all the ECHR rights. The *Sporrong and Lönnroth v Sweden* principle might be relied upon to seek to show that an interpretation clause was in accordance with the ECHR. But obviously this possibility would be highly controversial and likely to lead to successful applications to Strasbourg. The decision in *A v UK*[114] offered little encouragement to the idea that greater flexibility could be introduced into Arts 5 and 6; the Strasbourg Court expressly rejected the idea that exceptions could be read into Art. 5 going beyond those already accepted. Lord Hoffmann in *AF* said on *A v UK* that the decision

> was wrong and . . . may well destroy the system of control orders which is a significant part of this country's defences against terrorism [but the UK] is bound by the Convention, as a matter of international law, to accept the decisions of the ECtHR on its interpretation. To reject such a decision would almost certainly put this country in breach of the international obligation which it accepted when it acceded to the Convention.[115]

However, the idea of interpretation clauses – which the author has discussed in detail elsewhere[116] – clearly appears to be one which senior Conservatives are interested in pursuing and one that harmonises with the enterprise of distancing the UK from Strasbourg. Thus there is a clear contradiction between the remit of the Commission and the idea floated by some senior Conservatives, including David Cameron, that the BoR could give greater leeway to the courts to disregard Strasbourg, of especial significance in the criminal justice and counter-terror contexts. That latitude could only be granted by the Strasbourg court if it was prepared to assign a wider range of matters to States' margins of appreciation. However, it is possible that the twin remits of the BoR Commission – to advise on the nature of the BoR *and*

---

111 [2009] UKHL 5 at [27].
112 [2001] UKHL 25, at [91].
113 (1982) 5 EHRR 35, 52 [69].
114 (2009) 49 EHRR 29.
115 [2009] UKHL 28 [70].
116 See H. Fenwick, 'The Human Rights Act or a British Bill of Rights: creating a down-grading recalibration of rights against the counter-terror backdrop?', *Public Law*, 2012, Spring, forthcoming.

on reform of the Strasbourg Court – may hold out some hope to Conservatives of realising this objective. In other words, these plans might be given at least a colourable plausibility if reliance was placed on the idea of introducing a BoR containing a re-balancing clause and a s 2 HRA replacement, which was *combined* with a reform of the Strasbourg Court, that addressed the issue of its immense case-law burden by requiring it to devolve a wider range of matters to individual states. Leeway might then be created for adopting approaches in the UK of a more flexible nature than those tending to be adopted at Strasbourg (e.g. in *A v UK*, which took an absolutist stance to the issue of minimum disclosure under Art. 6(1)) which would not put the UK in breach of its Treaty obligations. Lord Hoffmann in his 2009 lecture said on this:

> Because, for example, there is a human right to a fair trial, it does not follow that all the countries of the Council of Europe must have the same trial procedure. Criminal procedures in different countries may differ widely without any of them being unfair. Likewise, the application of many human rights in a concrete case, the trade-offs which must be made between individual rights and effective government, or between the rights of one individual and another, will frequently vary from country to country, depending upon the local circumstances and legal tradition.[117]

Along with the remit of the BoR Commission to advise on reform of the ECtHR, in August 2011, in the aftermath of Cameron's speech on the riots quoted above, the Ministry of Justice stated that Justice Secretary Kenneth Clarke would be seeking 'important operational changes' to the Court when Britain takes over the Chairmanship of the Council of Europe in November. It was stated that Clarke would try to redraw the relationship with national courts to see if more issues could be handled nationally.[118]

Devolution issues

The exact relationship between a BoR and the devolved legislatures is clearly going to be a complex and problematic issue, one that at present has received little attention. This issue is one of those the BoR Commission has raised in its 2011 Discussion Paper.[119] Unlike the Westminster Parliament, the devolved legislatures are not free to disregard the ECHR. Under the Scotland Act 1998, actions by members of the Scottish government and legislation enacted by the Scottish Parliament must be compatible with the Convention. Under the terms of the Northern Ireland Act 1998, Ministers and Northern Ireland

---

117 *Judicial Studies Board lecture*, op. cit., n. 88.
118 See *The Guardian*, 17 August11, p. 8, article on the HRA by A. Travis.
119 Op. cit. n. 7. Question 3 relates to how a BoR 'should apply to the UK as a whole, including its four component countries'.

departments must act compatibly with the ECHR, and the Northern Ireland Assembly does not have competence to legislate in a manner incompatible with the Convention. The same is true of the Welsh Assembly under the Government of Wales Act 2006. As far as these legislatures are concerned, the ECHR is entrenched. Presumably the Commission will need to consider whether those requirements as to compatibility should be revisited under a BoR.

There is also the question of the relationship between a BoR and a Northern Ireland BoR. The Northern Ireland Human Rights Commission (NIHRC) was set up in 1999 and required to advise the Secretary of State for Northern Ireland on the scope for defining rights additional to the ECHR ones in a Bill of Rights for Northern Ireland. The Belfast (Good Friday) Agreement of 1998 states that the Bill should reflect the particular circumstances of Northern Ireland. In 2008, the NIHRC presented its Advice on a Bill of Rights for Northern Ireland to the government. The government published its paper 'A Bill of Rights for Northern Ireland: Next Steps' for consultation, and the NIHRC made a written response to that paper in 2010 in which it found that the response demonstrated a lack of understanding of the purpose and functions of a Bill of Rights; failed to take appropriate account of international human rights standards; and appeared to be suggesting the lowering of existing human rights standards in Northern Ireland.[120]

The government has announced an intention that the devolved legislatures should appoint members to an advisory panel, lawyers rather than politicians, to provide advice to the Commission on legal and technical aspects of devolution matters.[121] The question of the Northern Ireland BoR will obviously be one that the BoR Commission will have to seek to tackle, and the key issue will no doubt be whether Northern Ireland should have its own BoR and, if so, what should the relationship be between the Northern Ireland Assembly and the BoR? But in general, a key question will be whether the devolved legislatures should be subject to the rights listed in the BoR, as they are currently to the ECHR. If the agenda, which it is argued the Conservatives appear to be pursuing, eventually prevails, it would be in accordance with it for the devolved legislatures to be able to legislate contrary to such rights.

Conclusions

The BoR Commission appears to be divided between Liberal Democrat nominees who support the HRA (Kennedy, Lester, Sands, Edward) and Conservative nominees who want to see it repealed and replaced by an instrument that could appear to offer aid to the government in terms of escaping

---

120 *A Bill of Rights for Northern Ireland: Next steps*, Response to the Northern Ireland Office February 2010.

121 A. Speaight, in answer to Q50, Commons Select Committee on Political and Constitutional Reform, op. cit, n. 10.

from the demands of the Strasbourg Court and the ECHR (Speaight, Howe, Pinto-Duschinsky, Fisher). The Commission appears to be in the position of dealing with near-irreconcilable aims since the underlying concern, from the Conservative perspective, in relation to both express aspects of the BoR Commission's remit, clearly appears to be to enhance the autonomy of the UK Parliament at the expense of both Strasbourg's influence and the maintenance of ECHR standards, as interpreted at Strasbourg. That may amount partly to political posturing, to appease elements of the Conservative party, and the likely impact in practice, if the proposals were implemented eventually in a BoR, might well fall short of the aspirations expressed. However, such an aim is likely to influence both the outcome of the Commission's deliberations, bearing in mind the fact that Cameron nominated four of the members, and the reception of the proposals in 2012–13. It has been argued that 'the dead-locked membership of the Commission confirms the widespread expectation that it will spend most of its time producing rival dissenting papers that will be the basis of Conservative and Liberal Democrat manifesto commitments at the next election'.[122] Lord Lester, however, has said that the Commission was 'not going to split on party lines and argue like cats in a bag'.[123]

The timetable so far, set out at the beginning of this chapter, it is argued, lends credibility to the notion that the proposals are unlikely to be imple-mented before another general election: once the Bill of Rights Commission presents proposals at the end of 2012 they will need to be debated and it appears at present unlikely that agreement will be reached on them under Cameron's leadership, taking account of the general views of the Conservative party, given his interest in repealing the HRA and creating divergence from Strasbourg. If a general election occurs in 2014-15, the possibly divergent proposals may well form part of the different election manifestos, bearing in mind the likelihood that by that time the Conservative Party will no doubt have formed more radical proposals of its own. The proposals from Commission members opposed to the ECHR, involving cutting or weakening the anchor to the Strasbourg Court created by the HRA by the means described above, as part of a means of diminishing the general influence of the Strasbourg Court, might then appear in the Conservative manifesto. If the Conservatives were returned with an increased majority, then Britain would be viewed as having given the Conservatives a mandate to repeal the HRA and put those proposals into effect in the BoR. Thus it is very possible that the setting up of this Commission is merely a device to keep this issue out of the political arena for a time and to avoid confronting, for the time being, the different stances taken on it by the Liberal Democrats and Conservatives. The strong determination to create divergence from the Strasbourg Court and to seek to allow the UK

---

122   See *The Guardian*, 18 March 2011, article by A. Travis and P. Wintour.
123   Answer to Q58, Commons Select Committee on Political and Constitutional Reform, op. cit, n. 10.

Parliament greater autonomy to decide human rights matters is – unsurprisingly – coming from the Conservatives, including the Conservative members of the Commission.

This chapter concludes, then, on a depressing note. The appetite of a number of senior Conservatives for repeal of the HRA and diminution of Strasbourg influence appears undiminished, even enhanced, in the context of the Coalition. The Prime Minister has reiterated a number of times his view that the BoR can provide a remedy for the damage he views the human rights culture under the HRA as having done in Britain, and has referred approvingly to the setting up of the Commission, implying that it will produce proposals for an instrument fulfilling the aims he has set out for it. Yet the government has set up the Commission with a remit almost completely at odds with those aims. The contradiction between the role Cameron claims the Commission will play and the role it seems likely to play is becoming more apparent. Thus an air of unreality pervades the deliberations of the Commission; possibly its eventual proposals will prove merely irrelevant in the coming battle over the fate of the HRA.

Index